From Language Learner to Language Teacher

An Introduction to Teaching English as a Foreign Language

DON SNOW

 Teachers of English to Speakers of Other Languages, Inc.

Typeset in Avenir and ITC New Baskerville
by Capitol Communication Systems, Inc., Crofton, Maryland USA
Printed by McNaughton & Gunn, Inc., Saline, Michigan USA

Teachers of English to Speakers of Other Languages, Inc.
700 South Washington Street, Suite 200
Alexandria, Virginia 22314 USA
Tel 703-836-0774 • Fax 703-836-6447 • E-mail tesol@tesol.org • http://www.tesol.org/

Publishing Manager: Carol Edwards
Copy Editor: Ellen Garshick
Additional Reader: Marcella Weiner
Cover Design: Capitol Communication Systems, Inc.

ISBN 9781931185387
Library of Congress Control No. 2006910848

Table of Contents

Introduction

In the mid-1990s, I wrote an introductory book on English teaching entitled *More Than a Native Speaker: An Introduction to Teaching English Abroad* (TESOL 1996; revised 2006) for native speakers of English who were learning to teach English in nations such as China, Japan, Romania, and Saudi Arabia where English is mainly used and taught as a foreign language. To some degree, the issues addressed by the book were similar to those in any introduction to English teaching, but in other ways the content was somewhat distinctive because it specifically addressed the special challenges of teaching English in English as a foreign language (EFL) settings.

Over the past few years, I have continued to do training for English teachers working in EFL settings; however, I have spent more time training English teachers for whom English is a second (or even third or fourth) language rather than their native language. To some extent, the challenges faced by these teachers are similar to those faced by native English speakers who teach in EFL contexts. However, English teachers for whom English is a second language are in some ways a special group in that the challenges they face are somewhat different from those faced by native English teachers, and the strengths they bring to their teaching are also somewhat different.

This book is essentially a revision of *More Than a Native Speaker* that better addresses the needs and concerns of a special category of future English teachers, those who have learned English as a second language and who live and work in countries where English is generally not spoken as the first language. To be more specific, I make three assumptions:

1. I assume you learned English as a second language (or perhaps your third, fourth, or even fifth language) rather than your first. You probably learned English in school instead of at home and probably would not consider yourself a native speaker of English. This means that, while you may have an impressive command of English, your English may still not be as strong as you would like it to be, and you may be continuing to improve your English at the same time as you are preparing to teach it. However, this also means that you have extensive experience in language learning. You have certainly spent

much time studying English, and you may well have also studied other foreign languages, or languages and dialects in your own country that are different from your first language.

2. I assume that you live and teach in an EFL context, in other words, a setting where English is learned and spoken as a foreign language. This is quite different from teaching in English as a second language (ESL) contexts, where students are surrounded by English and often have a strong desire to learn it as quickly as possible in order to study, find a job, or simply interact with more of the people around them. In contrast, students in EFL settings have much less natural exposure to English and fewer opportunities to practice. This means that they often study English more to pass tests than to build communicative proficiency and that motivating students tends to be more of a challenge.[1]

3. I assume that you are a native of the culture in which you teach. This means that you have a native understanding of the students' cultural background and of the educational culture that surrounds you and the students. You also have the ability to speak to students in their first language, so you face fewer obstacles in communicating your ideas than a foreign teacher in your country would.

Here I note that English teachers like you are not a minor subcategory of the world's English teachers. As Braine (1999, xvii) points out, there are probably about four nonnative-speaking English teachers for every teacher who is a native speaker. Also, there are more English teachers in EFL settings (e.g., China, Japan, Pakistan, Russia) than in ESL settings like the United States and Britain. Finally, most of the world's English teachers are natives of the country where they teach rather than foreigners. So, in many ways, if you have the characteristics listed above, you represent the largest and most typical category of English teachers in the world.

The aim of this book is to provide new English teachers with an introduction to the concepts and methods of English language teaching. While the book provides an overall introduction to English teaching, four themes receive special emphasis: communicative language teaching (CLT), proficiency, language learning, and practicality.

Communicative Language Teaching

By and large, the theoretical perspective from which I write is that of CLT, an approach that assumes that the main goal of language learning is to improve the ability to use the language for

---

[1] Many scholars in recent years divide English teaching contexts into one of three categories: (1) Inner Circle nations, in which English is spoken as the first—and often only—language by the majority of the population (e.g., the United States, the United Kingdom, Australia); (2) Outer Circle nations, in which English is not the first language of most of the population but has some official role (e.g., in education) and is sometimes used for internal communication (e.g., India, Singapore; most of these are ex-colonies of the British Empire); and (3) Expanding Circle nations, where English is only taught and used as a foreign language and is generally only used for interaction with people from other countries (e.g., China, Japan). (See Kachru 1992 for further discussion.) My use of the term *EFL contexts* corresponds with the Expanding Circle category, and it is readers in this context that I have primarily in mind as I write this book.

I use the EFL/ESL categories in this book partly because these terms are familiar to many people; more importantly, I feel the phrase *English as a foreign language* better captures how teachers and students in Expanding Circle nations view English. For example, the concept of English as a foreign language translates directly and easily into many languages; the Chinese term *waiyu* and the Japanese term *gaigokugo* both literally mean *outsider* (i.e., foreign) language. I also wish to avoid any suggestion that English necessarily spreads like expanding circles on a pond, with Expanding Circle countries inevitably on the road to becoming Outer Circle countries. As noted, virtually all Outer Circle countries were once part of the British Empire, and, in that sense, their history is distinctly different from that of many Expanding Circle countries.

communication and that many or most activities in language classes will be genuinely communicative in nature. (Other basic assumptions of CLT are introduced in chapter 2.) I do not assume that CLT is the only "right" approach to language teaching or that its assumptions are always relevant or realistic in all settings. But I have chosen to draw heavily on CLT for several reasons.

First, as a Westerner who was trained in the CLT tradition, this is the one with which I am most familiar and can most effectively introduce. Second, I presume that teacher trainees who are willing to read a book on language teaching written in English by a Westerner are interested in views on language teaching that are currently popular in the West. Finally, I believe that even if a pure CLT approach to English teaching is not necessarily the best approach for English teachers in EFL settings to adopt, an understanding of its assumptions and methods is still valuable to you as a source of ideas, and introducing CLT ideas to you will help stimulate your own thinking about English teaching. Often the best way to see one's own ideas most clearly is to compare and contrast them with a different set of ideas, so even if the assumptions of CLT are not entirely appropriate to your context or teaching, looking at teaching issues from a CLT perspective may still help you sharpen your thinking.

Proficiency

If the goal of language learning is the ability to communicate, then it is very important to build students' proficiency—that is, their skills in using the language to express their own ideas, interact with others, and understand the ideas of others. As noted above, in many EFL settings, English study is focused to a large extent on passing examinations, and the assumption is that there is some correlation between good examination results and actual proficiency. To some extent this is true; students who do well on English language examinations often have a better functional command of English than those who do poorly. However, heavy focus on examination scores can also distort the goals of language learners, causing them to focus more on getting good test scores than on building actual English proficiency. Unfortunately, preparing for examinations is not always the same thing as building proficiency, and too often students invest a great deal of time in study efforts that do not help build proficiency. Therefore, as I consider the issue of language teaching, I give special attention to the question of how to teach students in ways that will both prepare them for examinations and help them build actual English skills.

Language Learning

An important goal of this book is to help teachers gain a better understanding of language learning, and to encourage and equip them for their own continued language learning. As I argue in chapter 1, it is of great benefit for English teachers—and, in fact, all foreign language teachers—to have as much as experience as possible as foreign language learners. As this book examines the various aspects of language teaching, it will at the same time examine the challenges that learners face with each of these aspects. My hope is that English teachers will not only gain a better understanding of these challenges, but also become more skilled themselves as language learners. This focus on language learning is an attempt to encourage and help nonnative-English-speaking teachers fully exploit one of their greatest assets—their rich experience as language learners.

Practicality

Finally, the emphasis in this book is on practicality. While important theories of language learning and teaching will be introduced throughout the book, they will be introduced and explained only as far as they have direct and practical value for language teachers. However, while theory (i.e., academic theory) is not emphasized in this book, theorizing is. English teaching is not a mechanical task in which you can follow a simple set of prescribed steps and expect good results. English teaching requires you to theorize a great deal: you need to be able to analyze a situation (e.g., the needs of students, the expectations of your school, the strengths and weaknesses of your textbook) and then make the best choices possible with regard to the goals you set, the methods you use, how you use in-class time, and so forth. In other words, from a practical perspective, what you need to develop is skill in analyzing and strategizing.

A Note on Terminology

In writing this book, one of the knottiest problems has been the question of terminology. There is a considerable and growing body of literature related to the special concerns of English teachers who are not native speakers of English, and in this literature these teachers are often referred to as *nonnative-English-speaking teachers* (NNESTs). This is in contrast to native-English-speaking teachers (NESTs). This terminology is somewhat controversial, and not all nonnative-English-speaking teachers are comfortable with it.[2] I must admit that I am not very happy with the term NNEST because it defines the majority of the world's English teachers by the one quality that they lack rather than by qualities that they possess in particular abundance.

Given that terms such as *native speaker* and *nonnative speaker,* and acronyms such as NNEST and NEST, are widely used and that even the TESOL caucus of teachers for whom English is a second language refers to itself as Nonnative English Speakers in TESOL Caucus, I sometimes use these terms and acronyms in the following chapters. However, more often I simply use the term *local teacher* to refer to teachers who are native to the country where they teach but not native speakers of English, and the term *foreign teacher* to refer to native-English-speaking (or near-native-speaking) teachers who have come from other countries. I have made this choice for two reasons. First, in many EFL settings the categories *local teachers* and *foreign teachers* are virtually the same as the categories *nonnative speaker* and *native speaker*; local teachers are virtually all NNESTs, and any NESTs present are foreign teachers.[3] Secondly, the audience of teachers for which this book is intended is not defined simply by whether or not they are native speakers of English. Instead, these teachers are defined just as much by the fact that they work in an EFL context to which they are native; in a sense, they are native speakers of the local culture and have an insider's understanding of the cultural context where they work as well as an insider's understanding of the students they teach. So, while the term is admittedly somewhat imprecise, I feel *local teacher* captures these diverse qualities better than a term that refers merely to whether or not English is a teacher's first language.

---

[2] See Braine (1999, xvii) for a discussion of the difficulties he faced when deciding on an appropriate name for the caucus within the TESOL organization that eventually took the name the Nonnative English Speakers in TESOL Caucus.

[3] Of course, some foreign teachers are NNESTs. However, in many cases such teachers have near-native command of English, so in the Expanding Circle setting they tend to function more or less like NESTs.

In writing this book, one limitation I face is that I am not a local English teacher myself and cannot write from that perspective. Writing as a local teacher to other local teachers is a task that I must leave to others. What I can claim is that I am an experienced language teacher who is familiar with the EFL setting and tries to the best of my ability to address the concerns of local teachers working in EFL settings. In short, while I cannot write *as* a local English teacher, at least I can try to write *to* local English teachers in a way that seriously takes their special characteristics and concerns into consideration. To the extent that I can identify with and empathize with local English teachers and their concerns, I have gained this ability through my long experience as a language learner and through my modest experience as a teacher of Chinese—my second language—and as a writer of curriculum and teaching materials for that language.

A second limitation I face is the reality that my teaching experience has predominantly been with students who are university-aged or older. While much of what is said in this book would apply reasonably well to teaching English to secondary school students, I feel that teaching English to children presents a rather different set of challenges with which I have little expertise. Therefore, I confine my focus to English teaching for adolescents and adults.

Acknowledgments

In my work on this book, I owe a special debt of gratitude to George Braine and Jose Lai for patiently hearing out my ideas about this project, encouraging me, and giving me copious quantities of good advice. I also wish to thank Huang Wanmei and Zhu Yeqiu for their insightful and enthusiastic feedback on the various drafts of this book.

Just as importantly, I wish to thank the students of the 2004, 2005, and 2006 English Teaching Methodology classes at Nanjing University for their feedback on drafts of this book. Their comments, suggestions, and insights have been very helpful in allowing me to see things from a local teacher perspective, so I wish to thank each of them: Bu Yanghui, Cao Liang, Chang Chen, Chen Bo, Chen Hairong, Chen Xiaojing, Chen Xiaojuan, Chen Xu, Chen Ying, Chu Weiyi, Cong Xiaoming, Feng Zhe, Gao Juan, Geng Hua, Guan Xiumei, Gui Tao, Hao Jue, Hao Yixia, He Fang, Huang Hao, Huang Niya, Huang Shuqiong, Huo Jianxia, Jia Guangmao, Ju Qiuhong, Li Jie, Li Jing, Li Xiaosa, Li Zhihui, Liu Dan, Liu Guangyuan, Liu Lu, Liu Ping, Liu Yuanyuan, Long Xiang, Lu Hongjuan, Lu Yun, Luo Shouyi, Ma Xiaohui, Miao Jianwei, Nie Yuefang, Pang Zhaohua, Pei Liping, Pu Xianwei, Qian Jingjing, Qian Jingyue, Qian Shanming, Qian Yanfeng, Ren Yuxin, Shan Guhua, Sun Xiaohong, Tong Guangyao, Wan Zhaoyuan, Wang Jing, Wang Ting, Wang Wei, Wang Xiaoyan, Wang Xin, Wang Xin, Wang Xueyu, Wang Ying, Wang Ying, Wang Yuanfei, Wang Zheng, Wen Xueqin, Wu Lingyun, Wu Xiaoqin, Xia Meng, Xu Fangfang, Xu Xiaoying, Yan Hua, Yang Fang, Yang Yihua, Yang Ling, Yang Yun, Yao Jing, Ye Zhengmao, Yu Mei, Yuan Jiali, Yuan Rong, Zha Xiaofen, Zhang Chunxia, Zhang Fangfang, Zhang Huali, Zhang Hui, Zhang Luo, Zhang Xiafei, Zhang Yan, Zhang Yanping, Zhao Hui, Zhu Jingyi, Zhu Xiaomin, and Zuo Wenjing. Last but certainly not least, I would like to give special thanks to Fang Mei, Ding Nan, and Cao Ning for their sharp editorial eyes and thoughtful suggestions.

PART I

Preparing to Teach

Chapter 1

Language Teachers as Language Learners

- A good language teacher should first and foremost be a good language learner.

- It is important for English teachers to be reasonably successful learners of English because this makes them better models of good English for their students, gives them greater confidence when using English in class, and makes them role models who can inspire students.

- It is also important for English teachers to have extensive experience as language learners because this gives them a better understanding of how to learn languages, helps them empathize with students, and makes them good role models for language learning habits and skills.

In this chapter—and throughout this book—I assume that a good language teacher should first and foremost be a good language learner. I feel this should be true for all teachers of English, including those who are native speakers of English. However, because my focus in this book is on local English teachers, I discuss this issue especially as it relates to teachers who learned English as a second language.

By the term *good learner,* I mean two rather different things. First, a good learner is someone who has succeeded in gaining the best command of English possible. Second, a good learner is someone who is a skilled and effective language learner, who knows how to learn a new language and how to teach this skill to students. I believe that this second quality may be even more important than having a good command of English, and in this chapter I make my case for why this would be true. I also discuss ways teachers can continue their own independent study of English by designing and carrying out language learning projects.

Why Should an English Teacher Be a *Successful* English Learner?

First and foremost, the English language skills of English teachers should be as good as possible. While this is not the only criterion for determining whether someone is a qualified or effective teacher of English, as I discuss below, it certainly is an important one. So, as Medgyes (2001) argues, "the most important professional duty that non-NESTs [nonnative-English-speaking teachers] have to perform is to make linguistic improvements in their English" (p. 440; see also Lee 2004, 244).

There are three main reasons why I feel it is important for local English teachers to gain a good command of English. The first and most obvious has to do with the model your English presents to the students. It is probably not overstating things to suggest that, at least while students are in your class, your English essentially becomes their English standard. Your English serves not only as the model that students will imitate, but also as a standard they will use in deciding what is right and what is wrong. In fact, one of your main roles is to set a standard for students and encourage them in their efforts to draw closer to that standard in their own mastery of English.

To set a good standard for students, local teachers do not need to have a native command of English, and such a command is perhaps not even very desirable. For the great majority of students in EFL settings, a nativelike command of English is simply not a realistic goal because they do not have adequate practice opportunities or exposure to native models to develop a full range of nativelike skills (Sridhar and Sridhar 1994, 46–47, cited in McKay 2002, 40). Instead, their goal is to develop a degree of competence in English that meets whatever communicative needs they have for English, and not every student needs native-level English skills; in fact, most do not. This being the case, a skilled nonnative speaker is often a more realistic model than a native speaker. Also, the growing use of English as an international language means that the students you teach are just as likely to interact with people who are not from English-speaking countries as they are to interact with native English speakers. This further reduces the need for students to strive to be just like native speakers in their use of English (see McKay 2002 for further discussion).

However, your English should certainly be as good as possible—well within the range that is generally understood and accepted internationally—because your English will affect the students' English in many ways. Perhaps the most obvious example of such influence is pronunciation: some students' pronunciation is inaccurate and hard to understand partly because the English teachers under which they studied when first learning English had poor pronunciation. The other side of the coin is that some students whose English is quite fluent and skilled were taught mainly or entirely by local English teachers whose English—although not native—was quite good. So the point is that one reason English teachers need to have a good command of English—accurate grammar, pronunciation, vocabulary usage, and so forth—is the impact their English will have in shaping students' English.

A second reason English teachers should have the best possible command of English is that it gives the teacher greater confidence when using and teaching the language. Even though many local English teachers are quite successful in learning English, many have not yet attained as high a level of competence in English as they would like (Liu 1999, 204). This leads Medgyes (2001)—a nonnative-speaking teacher of English himself—to note that nonnative-speaking teachers are "well aware of their linguistic deficiencies" (p. 434), and Medgyes (1999) concludes, "Indeed, most non-NESTs are all too aware that they are teachers and learners of the same subject" (p. 38).[1] This awareness naturally has the potential to negatively affect teachers' confidence when teaching English.

My own experience teaching Chinese when I was a graduate student at Indiana University may serve to illustrate the problem. Having learned and used Chinese for many years, I was reasonably confident of my Chinese skills and generally willing to speak Chinese in class. However, despite my years of learning the language, there was always a fear lurking in the back of my mind that I would make a mistake, pronouncing words with the wrong intonation or using a vocabulary item incorrectly. Worse yet was the fear that a student would notice my mistake and tell others. So a portion of my energy and attention was consumed by the effort to avoid making any mistakes—and to a degree this diverted my attention from the issue of how effectively I was teaching. (In contrast, while I make language mistakes when teaching English, I don't worry about it much because I am less vulnerable, and my credentials are less open to question.) Another concern I often faced was the possibility of a student asking a question I didn't know the answer to. Granted, when a student would ask something like "Is it OK to say . . . in Chinese?" I could sometimes answer confidently that the suggested sentence was either right or wrong. However, at times the sentence sounded questionable, but I couldn't be sure it was actually wrong, so I didn't know if the student had made a mistake or was just asking about something I hadn't learned yet. Sometimes the fear of such tricky questions would even cause me to shorten or omit an activity that might raise questions I wasn't sure I could handle.

Issues like the ones I faced when teaching Chinese are an inevitable part of teaching a language other than one's native tongue—in fact, such problems even crop up to annoy teachers who are teaching their native language—so teachers should not expect that they will ever go away entirely. However, the better your English is, the fewer such concerns you will have, not only because you are less likely to be caught in an embarrassing mistake, but also because your command of English will make it clear to everyone that you know your subject well, even if you do make an occasional mistake. Confidence in your language skills allows you to be less distracted by worry in class and makes you more willing to take risks—for example, being more open to class discussion and questions—because you are more confident that you can handle problems and challenges that may result. Also, confidence itself will benefit your teaching because students can sense a teacher's confidence and tend to respond positively to it.

A final reason it is good for local English teachers to have made significant progress in their mastery of English is that teachers who are role models of success in language learning can inspire and encourage students. Medgyes (1999, 51) tells the story of a Hungarian English

---

[1] In his research, Medgyes (1999, 2001) found that the areas in which non-NESTs claimed to have the most difficulty with English were (in order of importance) (1) vocabulary, especially usage; (2) oral fluency; and (3) pronunciation.

teacher who managed to achieve an almost native command of English despite the fact that he didn't start learning English until he was sixteen and didn't visit an English-speaking country until he was thirty. In many ways, this particular teacher was not ideal—he often did not prepare for class very carefully and tended to be impatient with slow students. However, he was still generally regarded as a good teacher because he provided a powerful, positive role model for students. As Medgyes concludes, "The fact that such a high level of proficiency is within a nonnative speaker's reach has an inspiring effect on his students" (p. 51).

One of the most important contributions that a local teacher can make to students is to show them that success in learning English—or other languages—is possible. The point here is not that a local teacher needs to have a perfect command of English; in fact, a local English teacher whose English is perfect may sometimes seem like an unrealistic role model for students, one that is far beyond their power to emulate. Students need a role model who can show them what they can achieve if they study and practice hard, and, to this end, the best role model is someone who has obviously faced the same challenges that students do but has made considerable progress in overcoming those challenges.

Why Should an English Teacher Be an *Experienced* English Learner?

By an experienced language learner, I mean someone who has spent considerable time studying and learning foreign languages and who knows a lot about language learning. While such people are often also successful language learners, it is still important to make a distinction between successful learners and experienced learners. Teachers who speak English well are not necessarily experienced and effective language learners; for example, they may speak English well more because they have had an unusual degree of exposure to the language (perhaps because they have studied English for many years or lived in an English-speaking country) than because they are skilled language learners who understand—and can explain—how to learn a language effectively and efficiently. Also, someone who is an experienced and knowledgeable language learner may not have the best command of English. For example, someone who has learned many languages but started learning English rather late in life may show flaws in pronunciation, vocabulary usage, and so forth, yet still be a skilled and knowledgeable language learner—and probably a good language teacher. So, in this section, my focus is on the reasons English teachers need to have as much experience as possible as language learners.

One of the most important reasons language teachers should be veteran language learners is that the more experienced teachers are as language learners, the more they can teach students about language learning methods and strategies. The field of language learning strategies has attracted increasing attention from scholars over the past decade or so within the international English teaching profession. There is now a substantial and growing list of books available on the subject of language learning strategies, and an English teacher can learn a great deal from these books about the various kinds of learning strategies and the role each plays in facilitating language learning.[2] Likewise, there is a large and growing literature devoted to the issue of second language acquisition—in other words, how people learn languages—and it is also of benefit to

---

[2] Probably the most important of these is Oxford's (1990) *Language Learning Strategies: What Every Teacher Should Know,* which not only introduces the categories and terms now widely used and accepted in the field of language learning strategies but also makes many suggestions for how these can be applied in foreign language classrooms.

a teacher to be familiar with the theories and findings in this field.[3] However, such theoretical knowledge in and of itself is not enough and should not be taken as a substitute for personal experience. For the classroom English teacher, it is probably more important to have a large database of practical ideas and stories about language learning that you can pass on to students. Academic references to theories and authorities generally don't impress students as much as an idea that is shared in the form of a personal story, so it is best if teachers have a substantial collection of such ideas and stories.

Of course, one good way to build a collection of language learning stories and ideas is by talking with other language learners and learning from their experience. However, it is equally important—if not more so—to draw on your own experience as a language learner. Keep in mind here that simply having experience as a language learner is not enough. Many language teachers have ample experience as language learners, but they have never thought much about what lessons they learned from that experience and don't have a conscious awareness of the strategies they used in their learning. (It is quite possible to succeed in learning a language even without thinking much about how you do it, but this generally only works if you are lucky enough to have a great deal of time for language learning, an especially good language program, or an environment where there are extensive opportunities to practice. On the whole, learners who reflect on the question of how to learn more effectively will tend to become more effective language learners and less dependent on luck or especially favorable circumstances.) To build a collection of strategies that you can pass on to students, you need to not only engage in language learning but also reflect on what lessons you learn from your experiences.

A second reason English teachers need to have substantial experience as language learners is that it helps them understand and empathize with students better. This is an area in which local teachers often have significant advantages over foreign teachers who are native speakers of English (Mahboob 2004, 137). As I argue in chapter 2, learning a foreign language is a battle of the heart as much as of the mind, and success and failure in language learning is determined to a large degree by affective factors (those dealing with emotions). Teachers who have spent considerable time trying to learn foreign languages know what the process feels like, so they are better able to empathize with their students. Keep in mind that empathy is not the same thing as sympathy; I am not talking about feeling sorry for students, hence trying to make their lives easier. There are times when a teacher needs to be strict and demanding, and to challenge students to work harder. Rather, the ability to empathize with students—to feel their joys and pains—helps teachers make many important teaching decisions more effectively. Teachers need to know how much they can and should demand of students, how much encouragement students need, what kinds of encouragement students need, what kinds of goals will effectively motivate them, and so forth, and the ability to make such decisions wisely depends heavily on the teacher's ability to sense how students are feeling. The ability to empathize with students is also important in establishing a bond with them. Students generally respond better to a teacher when they feel that the teacher understands them and can see things from their perspective than when the teacher is well intentioned but seems to have little idea what the language learning experience is like.

The final reason language teachers should engage in as much language learning as possible—and why they should continue studying languages throughout their careers—is that, by doing so, they provide students with a good role model of a language learner. You might think about the difference between this kind of role model and the successful learner role model

---

[3] Two reader-friendly but solid introductions to second language acquisition are Scovel's (2001) *Learning New Languages: A Guide to Second Language Acquisition* and Lightbown and Spada's (1999) *How Languages Are Learned.*

discussed above as the difference between the result and the process. Local teachers who have succeeded in learning English well inspire students to believe that success is possible. Local teachers who are personally enthusiastic about language learning and consider it valuable tend to inspire similar enthusiasm in their students (Dörnyei 2001a, 33; 2001b, 121). The role model of their ongoing study of English, or perhaps other languages, also helps students better understand what is necessary for success in language learning.

To the extent that students know you are still a language learner—of English or of other languages—they will have the sense that you still have much in common with them. A teacher who continues to engage in language study is like a guide who leads an expedition but is also a member of the expedition, sharing in its joys and difficulties. People are often more willing to follow this kind of leader than one who gives orders and directions from a comfortable office far away, someone who may have long ago forgotten what being on an expedition is really like.

If students know that you are still a language learner, and even occasionally see you working on improving your language skills, they may get the message that success in language learning results from sustained effort as much as—or more than—from some special gift for languages. If you only see athletes perform at the Olympic Games, it is easy to get the impression that they are top world athletes mainly because they were born with some special skill or talent. If, on the other hand, you see the athletes running on the track every day as they prepare for the Olympics, you get a more realistic idea of what lies behind their success. The same is true for language learners. Sometimes, the assumption about people who have learned to speak English or another foreign language very well is that they have a special gift for languages that allows them to learn effortlessly. The lesson you could easily derive from this is that for the lucky few who have such a language gift, excellent English is a present that drops from the sky—and that for everyone else there isn't much hope. However, just like athletes who see their coach running on the track every morning, students who see their English teachers working persistently to further improve their command of English or other languages are more likely to come to the conclusion that success in language learning results from sustained effort rather than from any special talent or gift and that any learner who is willing to work can be successful. This is precisely the message teachers want students to receive, and one of the best ways for you to teach this lesson is by modeling it in your own life.

In this book, I assume that the ideal English teacher is someone who not only knows English well but also knows how to learn English (and other languages) and can teach students how to learn English. This point is important to emphasize because many people assume that the most important criterion for determining who is or is not a good English teacher is how good the person's English is. Of course, if this is the only criterion used, the ideal English teacher is generally a native speaker. While native speakers of English generally have one of the qualities that make for a good English teacher—a good command of English—they do not necessarily have much understanding of how English is learned. Because they learned English at a very early age, they generally have little or no memory of how they learned it. Furthermore, they generally learned English in a setting where it was used constantly around them and where their English learning process was inseparable from their process of learning to communicate and interact with the people around them. Of course, the process by which native speakers learn English usually differs in many important ways from the process by which your students will learn English, so to the extent that native speakers understand the process of English learning, they have to learn this in indirect ways, such as through experience in learning other languages or observation of EFL learners. In contrast, local teachers who learned English as a foreign language not only have a command of English but also have experience with the process by which students will learn it. You therefore have some experience with all of the key elements for becoming an effective English teacher—if you exploit these experiences to the full.

Language Learning Projects

I have argued that the English skills of English teachers should be as good as possible and that English teachers should have as much language learning experience as possible. Both of these ideas suggest that it is important for you to continue learning English—as well as other languages—throughout your career. I now turn to the question of how to continue your study of English and other languages, in particular, how to keep studying on your own through independent study efforts that I will call *language learning projects* (LLPs).

A successful language learning effort needs to be designed according to the learner and the situation, so planning needs to begin with an analysis of the situation and the challenges and opportunities it provides. Obviously, there will be considerable variation in the situations and challenges faced by readers of this book, but I think there are three reasonable generalizations I can safely make about most of you, each of which has important implications for how you should design an English learning plan:

- **Generalization 1:** You are probably in an EFL context, so opportunities to contact and use English are limited. Despite the increasing use of English as an international language, in most countries where English is taught as a foreign language, it plays a limited role and is used only in certain kinds of settings. While learners of English generally can find opportunities to practice and use English, such opportunities are limited, and you often need to actively seek them out. This means that a study plan for English needs to consider how to maximize the opportunities available within the context.

- **Generalization 2:** You are probably not a full-time student of English, so you will only have limited time for your English study plan. Presumably, readers of this book are either teachers who have jobs, family concerns, and so forth that take up most of their time, or graduate students who need to balance English study with the demands of many other courses. Any English study plan therefore needs to be designed so that it is sustainable within the limited amount of time you have available. (In my own experience, after dealing with work and family responsibilities, people can often find only a few hours a week for language study.)

- **Generalization 3:** You probably need to study on your own rather than taking an organized formal English course. Often people cannot find time to take regular English courses that fit in with their schedules, and there may be no courses available that are appropriate to your level of skill and study needs and goals. In some ways, independent study is actually more efficient than taking an English class because it allows you to spend all of your time doing exactly what is most helpful and useful to you, whereas in an English class you spend lots of time doing things that are not appropriate to your needs or goals. However, the fact that you are not in a formal language course means that you are under less pressure to study—there is no test that you need to study for and no teacher who will hold you accountable. This means that you have to choose to study daily—despite the pressure of many other things that cry out for your time and energy—and it is very easy to put off English study or simply to give up entirely. A successful English study program therefore needs to be one that you can sustain even when there is little immediate pressure forcing you to study.

An effective independent English study effort needs to take these three important considerations into account. In particular, it needs to be sustainable—in other words, it needs to be something you will actually continue to do—over the long periods of time that language learning requires.

Here I discuss how to design and carry out what I call LLPs, independent language study plans that are designed to be sustainable in the kind of situation described above, in other words, in the kinds of situations many English learners the world over face. (In chapter 3, I also use the term LLP to refer to independent language study projects that you have students design and carry out as part of their work for regular language courses; these projects help build their ability to become more independent and autonomous as language learners.)

GETTING READY FOR LLPS

In the long run, the most important factor in determining whether or not you succeed in learning English is persistence; students who keep studying and practicing have a good chance at ultimate success, while those who give up do not. The key to language study, especially in situations where learners have the choice not to study, is therefore to study in a way that is sustainable—in other words, that minimizes discouragement and provides you with enough sense of progress and reward that you will keep studying. Before setting out to plan your own LLP, you can increase the likelihood that your project will be sustainable and ultimately successful by seriously thinking about the following questions.

How Much Time Do I Have Available for the LLP?

Time is a limited commodity, and you need to keep this reality firmly in mind when planning LLPs. When first planning an LLP, many people make big plans that would take massive investments of time to sustain. ("First I will review English grammar and memorize new vocabulary. Then I will listen to the BBC news on the radio each day. Then I will read Dickens for an hour . . . .") Obviously, a plan of this magnitude is unrealistic for anyone who cannot devote hours a day to English study, and the danger of such unrealistic plans is that they result in failure and discouragement, feelings that do not bode well for the survival of the plan.

What Opportunities Do I Have to Practice English?

EFL settings vary both in the amount of opportunity to use English skills and in the skills that you might have an opportunity to use. For example, in one setting, there may be relatively few printed materials in English but a constant flow of foreign backpackers coming through town. In contrast, in another setting, there may be few chances to speak or listen to English but a reliable supply of books, newspapers, or magazines in English. In the first setting, it would probably be easier for you to find or create opportunities to speak English, so an LLP geared toward that goal would be more exciting and easier to sustain; in the second setting, an LLP focused on reading skills would have a better chance of survival. When you have little chance to use what you learn, a study project tends to seem more pointless. In contrast, if you have a chance to use whatever knowledge and skills you gain through an LLP, the effort is more interesting and exciting, so it is easier to stay motivated and keep studying.

What Do I Like Doing in English?

Learners of English vary considerably in terms of what they enjoy and do not enjoy about using English. One person may hate the embarrassment of trying to speak English but find it reasonably comfortable and even enjoyable to read something written in English. Another may be bored to tears by reading books but get a kick out of trying to talk in a foreign language. A third may dislike English study in general but find listening to radio news in English somewhat tolerable because, even though it is hard work, it provides a way to find out something new and interesting about what is going on in the world.

The point here is that an LLP is more likely to be sustainable if the skill you choose to work on is one that you find reasonably interesting and even enjoyable. While this point is fairly obvious, it is worth emphasizing because all too often people ignore it, choosing goals and making plans based more on what they feel they ought to do rather than what they want to do (perhaps because, in their experience with English, enjoyment and interest have never been suggested as part of the equation). While such a spirit of self-denial is commendable, it is also dangerous when trying to keep an LLP alive; when people are faced with an unpleasant task, it is just too easy to decide, "I'll do this tomorrow," and tomorrow, and tomorrow. Such self-denial is also somewhat sad in that it ignores the real possibility that English study can be rewarding. Considering your own desires and interests when deciding what to pursue in an LLP is perfectly legitimate—in fact, it is desirable.

Of course, language study usually can't be driven by interest alone, and you often need to study in ways that are more useful than interesting. For example, someone who enjoys reading novels and wants to learn to read novels in English will inevitably also have to memorize a lot of vocabulary—whether this person enjoys doing so or not. However, the point I wish to make is that, as much as possible, learners should design LLPs that are as interesting as possible, especially when the LLP is an optional study effort that learners are free to abandon if they don't like it. It is better to spend time doing something you enjoy in English—such as reading English novels (with some vocabulary study thrown in)—than to become bored with a study plan and have it die.

As you prepare to design your own LLP, the bottom line is that your plan will have a greater chance of success if it is realistic in terms of its time demands, if it takes advantage of whatever opportunities naturally exist or can be created for using the skills learned, and if it plays to your interests as much as possible.

DESIGNING LLPS

Designing an LLP involves four main steps: (1) choosing a goal, (2) choosing study and practice methods, (3) making a concrete plan, and (4) setting criteria for evaluating progress. (See the end of this chapter for sample LLPs.)

Choosing a (Narrow) Goal

As I have suggested, in choosing a goal it is best for you to play to your interests and opportunities as much as possible. However, for the purposes of most LLPs, it is even more important that your goal be quite specific and narrow. The problem with broad goals such as *improve my reading* or *improve my speaking* (not to mention the even broader and vaguer *improve my English*) is that it is hard to tell whether you have actually achieved them or are even making progress toward them. Furthermore, with only a limited amount of time available to invest in the LLP, progress on a broad front is likely to be painfully slow. In contrast, given the same amount of time, progress toward a more specific goal like *improve my ability to read the news articles in an English language newspaper* or *get better at talking about my local community in English* is likely to be more readily evident as well as faster. Just as the flow of water in a river picks up speed when the riverbed becomes narrower, your progress toward a narrow, specific goal is faster than that toward a broader goal. The primary virtue of this speed is that when you can see and feel your progress, you are more likely to remain encouraged and motivated to continue the project.

Choosing Study and Practice Methods

Keep in mind that study and practice methods should be as similar as possible to the skill that you want to master. Students who spend a great deal of time reading English newspaper articles tend to get better at reading English newspaper articles, and so forth. Of course, as noted, things are not quite this simple. For example, if you are trying to improve your ability to read news items in the newspaper, you will also benefit from memorization of news-related vocabulary, such as names of places and people. However, overall this principle is a helpful one to follow.

Planning Where, When, and How Long to Study

Some people can make impressive progress in language study without having a very clear plan, just studying where and when the spirit strikes them. However, for most people the successful maintenance of an LLP involves planning for a place where they can study and practice effectively and finding reasonably regular times when they can study. On the whole, regular, sustained effort is more likely to produce noticeable progress toward the goal than more erratic efforts are and thus is more likely to generate adequate momentum to encourage you to continue.

Keep in mind here that the total amount of time per week you can give to an LLP may be quite limited, perhaps not much more than two or three hours. While this amount of time is hardly ideal—and a more significant time investment is more likely to generate encouraging results—it is often the reality for learners who are engaged in other full-time study or work. However, if the goal toward which you are working is narrow and specific enough, and the LLP is sustained over time, even this modest investment of time can produce adequate progress to sustain your motivation (whereas this amount of time would result in little apparent progress toward more broadly defined goals).

Setting Criteria for Measuring Progress

You will tend to have a stronger and clearer sense of achievement if you can see progress in your LLPs in quantifiable ways. To some degree, the goals of LLPs serve as indicators telling you whether or not you have made progress. However, goals are intended to set direction more than to measure progress, and even specific, narrow goals are often not concrete or quantifiable enough to show you your progress. Therefore, it is generally helpful to include criteria in your LLPs by which you can assess whether or not you have achieved your goals, indicators that tell you how much progress you have made toward the goals.

While these criteria do not all need to be scientifically precise, at least some of them should be concrete and quantifiable. For example, if the goal is *to improve my ability to read the news articles in an English language newspaper,* achievement criteria should include some criteria based directly on the goals, for example, *can read and understand the gist of English newspaper articles without using a dictionary.* However, it is best if there are also some very quantifiable criteria such as *have read fifty English newspaper articles and learned the vocabulary in them.*

THE BREAKTHROUGH CONCEPT

One obvious limitation of LLPs as described above is that you work only toward a limited set of language improvement goals rather than toward the enhancement of all your English skills. However, on the whole, I feel this trade-off is worthwhile because of all you gain in terms of sustainability. Furthermore, I assume that, eventually, for any given skill you work on, there is what I call a *breakthrough point,* that is, a point at which you can actually begin to use the skill for a useful or rewarding purpose. For example, in the development of conversation skills, you might reach the breakthrough point when you can strike up and sustain conversations with Western tourists without being so embarrassed that you beat a quick retreat. Or the breakthrough might occur when you can understand English novels well enough that you begin to find reading more fun than work. Or it could be the point at which your oral skills are good enough that your department begins asking you to translate when foreign guests come to the office.

Of course, the breakthrough point in all of these cases may not be a particular instant; it may be a longer process. Notice also that the breakthrough involves feelings as much as skill per se; it is often a point at which you become willing to apply the skill because rewards (e.g., access to new people and information, a sense of achievement) have begun to outweigh the costs (e.g., hard work, potential embarrassment).

But no matter how it is defined, a distinct and important change happens once you can begin to use your English language skills either for personal reward or for practical benefit, and, once you reach this point, your continued language learning takes on more momentum because you can use the language in contexts other than language study. In reference to the examples above, your conversation skills will continue to improve as you enjoy chatting with tourists, your reading skills will get better as you read for pleasure, and your listening skills will be further honed as you continue to translate. From this point on, the continued use and improvement of the new language skill takes on a life of its own. Once you reach a breakthrough point in one skill, you can then move to a different LLP building a different skill and targeted at a different breakthrough point. In my experience as a language learner and teacher, once you have reached a breakthrough in one area, the reinforcement and encouragement of that success is likely to motivate you to continue working toward other successes in English—and perhaps even toward study of other languages.

Looking Ahead

As should be clear by now, there are really two agendas in this book. In the following chapters, the focus shifts more to issues of language teaching. However, as you read those chapters, you should also be looking for what there is to learn about how to become a more effective language learner, both so that you can continue to improve your own English and so that you are better equipped to teach students how to be efficient and effective English learners. To this end, it is important that you

- learn all you can about the process of language learning, both by reading about the topic and by talking with your classmates and colleagues

- look carefully into your own past language learning experience for lessons about what does and does not facilitate effective language learning

- perhaps most importantly, continue your own study of English and other languages, honing your skill in using familiar methods and strategies while experimenting with an ever broader range of new methods and strategies

The more experience you have as a language learner, the better you can help students understand the process and challenges of language learning, and the broader the range of ideas, methods, and strategies you will have to teach them.

For Thought, Discussion, and Action

1. **a look back:** Think about your own foreign language learning experience to date, and list some lessons you have learned about what does and does not seem to work. Compare with classmates and discuss.

2. **language learning survey:** Ask several friends or classmates to talk with you about their foreign language learning experiences. In what ways do they feel their foreign language experience has been successful, and why? What has been hardest?

3. **my English progress so far:** Analyze your progress in English to date. Make lists of the following things:
   - What aspects of English do you feel you have made the most progress in?
   - What aspects of English do you feel least confident about?

4. **How good is our English?** Liu (1999) writes the following about nonnative English speakers who are training to become English teachers: "Although most of these students possess a considerable knowledge of English, particularly of grammar, not many of them have a good grasp of the use of the language" (p. 204). How well do you think this statement describes local English teachers in your country? How well does it describe you? If you think the statement is not entirely accurate, how would you modify it?

5. **What is hardest?** In a survey conducted by Medgyes (1999, 32–33), he found that the areas of English in which nonnative-English-speaking teachers (non-NESTs) had the most difficulty were, in order,
   - vocabulary (especially knowing whether any given usage of an English word is or is not appropriate)
   - oral fluency
   - pronunciation

   As you consider your own English, would you agree that these are the three most challenging areas? If not, what would the three most challenging areas be?

6. **inferiority complex?** Speaking of non-NESTs, Medgyes (1999) says, "Most of us suffer from an inferiority complex caused by glaring defects in our knowledge of English. We are in constant distress as we realize how little we know about the language we are supposed to teach. Indeed, most non-NESTs are all too aware that they are teachers and learners of the same subject" (p. 380). How well does Medgyes' statement describe your own feelings? If it does not describe your feelings very well, rewrite the statement so it better represents how you feel.

7. **confidence:** Have you ever felt lack of confidence in using English for teaching? In using it for other purposes? If so, describe the experience and how it felt.

8. **past language learning experiences:** Think of one successful English learning experience you have had (perhaps one particular course or study method you used), and prepare a detailed description involving everything you can remember that might be relevant. Then turn it into a story, and share it with a friend or classmate. Consider including answers to questions like these:

- What was your English level at the time?
- What was your goal?
- Why did you do what you did? What motivated you?
- What exactly did you do? (Describe what you did in detail.)
- What materials did you use?
- What role did a teacher play?
- What influence did classmates have?
- What was the environment in which you learned/studied like?
- Why did your approach work?

9. **improvement in English—goals:** List areas in which you would still like to improve your English. What kind of improvement would be most practically useful to you? What improvement would you find most personally satisfying? What would be most helpful in your teaching?

10. **improvement in English—challenges:** If you were to carry out a plan to further improve your English, what would the main challenges be? List them in order of importance. (Consider practical as well as methodological issues.)

11. **LLP task:** Design an LLP for improving some aspect of your English skills (or your skills in another language). (See Sample LLPs at the end of the chapter for plans that can serve as models.)
    - Start by considering yourself and your context:
      — How much time will you have? (Be realistic.)
      — What access to English and opportunities to use it do you have?
      — What do you like—and not like—about English study? How can you make your LLP as appealing as possible?
    - Then make a plan for your LLP:
      — Set yourself a narrow, specific goal, such as improving your speed for reading fiction in English, building your reading vocabulary, or improving your ability to listen to films in English.
      — Decide what breakthrough point you might work toward.
      — Decide what study and practice methods you will use.
      — Make a study plan, including when and where you will study, and so forth.

12. **LLP journal studies:** One way to learn more from an LLP about what does and doesn't work for you as a language learner—and about language learning in general—is to do a journal study as you conduct your LLP. An informal journal study would involve the following:
    - Before you begin the study, reflect on your previous language learning experiences and how they may affect your current LLP. It may also help to make a preliminary list of questions you hope to answer—things that you hope to learn about language learning through your LLP experience. Examples might include
      — Can I improve my reading speed enough that I won't become discouraged and give up on my LLP?
      — Can I work out an effective and efficient method for building my reading vocabulary?
      — Can I find an effective way to improve my listening by working with films?

- As you do your LLP, keep a log in which you record (1) what you do in the LLP, (2) what thoughts you have about it, and (3) what feelings you have as you go through the experience.
- Eventually, look back over the journal to see what patterns and discoveries await you.[4]

13. **native speakers as the standard?** McKay (2002, 40–41, citing Sridhar and Sridhar) points out that in EFL settings English teachers usually don't have enough exposure to English to allow them to achieve a nativelike command English, and she suggests that a native speaker standard is inappropriate as a goal in EFL settings. (She feels that a more reasonable standard would be some international form of English that is based on the English of all users worldwide, not just native speakers.) Do you think teachers in your country should try to achieve nativelike English (North American or British)? Should they try to teach their students to do the same?

Sample LLPs

VOCABULARY LLP

Goal: Build my vocabulary for reading.

Material: Magazines in English.

Plan: Read and study three times a week, one hour each session, in the morning before class.

Method:

1. Read articles from a magazine in English, marking unfamiliar vocabulary.

2. Look up new vocabulary in a dictionary, record it in a notebook, and study/review until I can recognize and understand the new words readily.

Criteria for measuring progress: I will have succeeded if I

1. create a thirty-page notebook of new vocabulary

2. can understand all the vocabulary in it when I see it either in the notebook or in a magazine article

FILM-LISTENING LLP

Goal: Build my listening comprehension of natural English conversation in films.

Material: Films in English on DVD.

Plan: Watch one film each week, in two or three sessions, at home in the evening.

Method:

1. Select DVD films with reasonably clear (modern) English.

2. The first time, watch the film all the way through with the subtitles turned off. Then write a summary of the story and any questions about parts I don't understand.

---

[4] For a more formal journal study procedure, see Bailey, Curtis, and Nunan (2001, 50).

3. Watch the whole film again—still without subtitles—and try to figure out the parts I didn't get the first time.

4. Go back to any unclear parts and watch them again with the subtitles (in English or my language) turned on.

Criteria for measuring progress: I will have succeeded if I

1. watch eight films using this approach

2. feel more comfortable watching films in English without subtitles

Chapter 2

Principles of Language Learning and the Role of the Teacher

- How well students learn a language ultimately depends more on their own efforts than on the teacher's. Thus, any attempt to understand effective language teaching must start with an understanding of language learning.

- Four basic realities of language learning are that a language is a tool for communication, that learning a language involves mastery of both knowledge and skill, that the struggle to learn a language is a battle of the heart as well as of the mind, and that learners differ from each other in ways that have significance for language learning.

- Language teachers are not simply transmitters of knowledge; like coaches, language teachers need to assist students in understanding the task before them, staying motivated, building discipline, and learning how to pursue the task on their own.

- Many of the assumptions in this chapter are based on the communicative language teaching (CLT) approach. While an understanding of these ideas should be valuable to you in your teaching, CLT is not the only legitimate approach to language teaching, and it is up to you to decide how to adapt elements of CLT to your own teaching situation.

Starting from the Language Learners

Even though this is a book about language teaching, any discussion of teaching needs to start with students. In recent years, more and more books on language teaching place students rather than teachers at center stage. This shift is due to a growing recognition that whether or not students succeed in learning a language depends more on their own efforts than on the teacher's and that a good program of instruction therefore needs to be student centered instead of teacher centered. This is not to say that the role of teachers and teaching is unimportant; far from it. However, effective language teaching needs to take the perspectives of students as its starting place—teachers need to understand as much as possible about what the language learning experience looks and feels like from the students' point of view.

WHY START WITH THE STUDENTS?

The first reason it is important to view language learning as student centered is that students are individuals who differ from each other in significant ways. For example, students differ in their language knowledge and skills; one student may read well and have a broad vocabulary but be almost incapable of speech, while another student may have exactly the opposite profile of skills. Students also differ greatly in their levels of motivation, their attitudes toward study in general, and their feelings toward English study in particular. One student may be quite diligent but resent Western cultural influence in her country; another thinks the West is appealing but has little love for study; a third doesn't care one way or another about English but would like to get a good grade on the final exam. Finally, students differ in their learning styles and strengths; a study method that is intolerably boring, confusing, or intimidating for one student may prove comfortable and effective for another. (More is said about this later in the chapter.) Consequently, the reasons for a student's successes or failures have to be sought at a variety of different levels and differ greatly from person to person; inevitably, no teacher-designed, one-size-fits-all lesson or program will meet the needs or suit the styles of all of the students in a class, and students need to find whatever path to success in English that suits them.

A second argument for student-centered approaches is that students will learn more effectively if they are active participants in the process than if they only passively follow the teacher's instructions. This is true even if for no other reason than much language study and practice take place when the teacher is not around to give instructions or to check up on students; students who view homework or small-group conversations as a welcome chance to develop their skills will make much better use of these opportunities than students who merely consider them a chore to be coped with as quickly as possible. To a large extent, students' success in English study depends less on how well the teacher presents lessons than on how well the students study.

The final reason that language learning needs to focus on students is that few programs of English study in EFL settings are long enough to guarantee that students will have mastered English by the time they leave the program. In many countries, English is offered in middle school and even primary school—often as a required subject—but students study English only a few hours a week and have little opportunity to practice what they learn. Even the few students who complete a university major in English still usually have gaps in their English skills when they graduate, and students who are not English majors or who study in a night school have even less English training and practice. Thus, if a high level of proficiency is the goal, students will probably have to continue study of English long after they leave the educational system. The students who are most likely to keep making progress toward mastery of English—and eventually succeed—are those who are already accustomed to designing and carrying out their own language study plans.

BASIC PRINCIPLES OF LANGUAGE LEARNING

Of the great many points one could make about the nature of language learning, I have chosen to focus on four basic assumptions of communicative language teaching (CLT) that students in EFL settings can easily lose sight of: (1) language is a tool for communication, (2) learning a language involves mastery of skills as well as knowledge, (3) learners need to give serious consideration to the impact of feelings on language study, and (4) learners differ in their learning styles.

Language as Communication

One of the most fundamental realities of language learning is that language is a tool for communication. As obvious as this point may seem, its implications are not always as clear to students as they should be. Remember that many students' experience of English learning does not encourage them to see English as a communication tool. The daily reality of English study for many students consists of memorizing words and rules in preparation for a test and rarely involves using English for communicative purposes. After years of this kind of study, it is only to be expected that students will come to see language learning as an exercise that is primarily geared toward formal accuracy, especially on tests. Such noncommunicative approaches to English study tend to focus students' attention on form instead of use and to undermine student interest; few students are excited by grammar and vocabulary study per se.

The study of English is potentially more appealing and even exciting if English is seen as a tool that makes communication with a new world possible, allowing students to talk face-to-face with someone from a foreign country, read books or articles from the world's vast library of material published in English, or even watch films and listen to songs in English. In all these cases, learning English means developing the ability to understand and interact with a universe that is largely inaccessible to those who don't know English. Here it is worth pointing out that although learning any language opens new doors, this is especially true of English particularly because of its growing role as an international language; English is now the language of publishing and speech for most international communication and is often used even by people from non-English-speaking countries when they need to interact with people from other nations.[1]

There are other reasons to emphasize the communicative nature of English, one being that such a focus may make language learning easier. Brown (1991, 36) notes that in learning their first language, children tend to focus on communication before accuracy and suggests that this order of priority should also apply to learners of a second language. Taylor (1987, 46) also suggests that a communicative approach to language learning helps students learn grammar more effectively because their desire to communicate ideas can make them more interested in learning grammar structures that help them get their meaning across.

If students are to view study of English as the learning of a tool for communication and to begin to taste the thrill of discovery that mastery of a new language can entail, they need to actually experience language as communication as early as possible in their learning. In an English class, this means using speaking or writing practice as an opportunity for students to share what they really think, feel, or believe.

---

[1] For example, Crystal (2003, 111, 115) points out that 70–90 percent of scientific journal articles and roughly 80 percent of the world's electronically stored information are in English.

Language as Both Knowledge and Skill

A second important truth of language learning is that it is mastery of a skill as much as acquisition of knowledge. In other words, it is not enough for students to know word meanings and structure rules; students need to be able to apply this knowledge quickly, even automatically, in order to express themselves smoothly in speech or writing, read at a reasonable rate, or comprehend spoken English rapidly enough to keep pace with the speaker. To build these skills, practice is necessary; study alone will not suffice.

Again, this point might seem obvious, but remember the unintended lessons that many approaches to language teaching leave students with. For many students, learning language has always been about learning grammar rules and memorizing vocabulary in order to be able to successfully figure out true/false, matching, and fill-in-the-blank puzzles on tests. Many students have had little training in speaking-listening skills that require speed and automaticity and can only be learned through repeated practice. Naturally, students' perceptions of what is and is not important in language learning are shaped by their experience in language classes, and it is not surprising if students do not fully appreciate the skill component in language use and are inclined to neglect practice in favor of study.

The fact that language use has a heavy skill component, which demands that the user perform complex operations accurately and quickly, has some important implications for the ways in which students must learn:

1. Language learners need a lot of practice. In order to learn to speak well, students need to spend a great deal of time speaking; in order to learn to read quickly and effectively, they need to spend a lot of time reading, and so forth. Almost all teachers would assent to this principle in theory, but in many English classrooms, the teacher still talks most of the time. Sometimes this is because teachers feel they need to dominate in order to maintain control in class; sometimes it is because teachers feel that if they aren't teaching (i.e., talking), they aren't really earning their pay. For whatever reasons, stepping off the podium and giving students a chance to speak (read, write, etc.) is more problematic than it may initially seem. Granted, listening to the teacher talk may help students gain knowledge and even improve their listening skills, but listening to the teacher is not of much use in helping students build speaking, reading, and writing skills unless it is also accompanied by significant practice opportunities.

2. Language learners need repeated practice. One important concept related to language learning is *automaticity*. The idea here is that many language skills require a student to do many different things at the same time; for example, speaking involves choosing words, applying grammar rules, and attending to pronunciation and intonation—all while trying to decide what to say. A speaker cannot consciously pay attention to all of these operations at the same time, so some of them must be practiced often enough that they can be performed automatically. The point is that it generally takes more than one practice opportunity to learn to perform any skill smoothly and automatically, and language learning is no exception. (For further discussion of automaticity, see Brown 2001, 55–56; Omaggio Hadley 2001, 65.)

   This point is important because students and teachers often unconsciously assume that what they are supposed to do in class is cover the material in the book; in other words, the teacher should explain the material, and the students should do any related exercises. Part of this unconscious assumption is that each point should only be covered one time and that, once the material is covered, students should know it. (Among students who have internalized this view of language learning, the protest that "We've done this already" is expected to effectively veto an activity whether or not they have really learned the target skill.) The problem, of course, is that covering material in a textbook is often not enough to allow learners to build necessary skills in using the material, and you may need to repeat activities several times before students can use the new material automatically.

Language Learning as a Battle of the Heart

A final fundamental reality of language learning is that feelings play a major role in language study and need to be taken seriously in planning a successful language learning campaign. As Oxford (1990) puts it, "The affective side of the learner is probably one of the very biggest influences on language learning success or failure" (p. 140). Learners who have a strong desire to learn and who feel good about their progress are far more likely to continue working hard over the long haul required in learning a language.

One reason emotions play such an important role in language learning is the long haul just mentioned. Learning a foreign language well involves a great deal of effort over a long period. The basic rules of English grammar and a survival vocabulary can be learned within a few months, but mastery of the language takes much longer. Students need considerable practice to develop effective skills in listening and speaking, not to mention reading and writing. It also takes a long time to amass a sufficient vocabulary for reading texts and listening to speech (e.g., radio, television) intended for native speakers. Finally, students can benefit from a good understanding of the cultures of English-speaking countries, not to mention the cultures of other countries whose people they might meet and speak to in English. All of this is particularly difficult for students in EFL settings to achieve because they have fewer opportunities for English practice and contact with Western culture than students in ESL settings have. The problem is especially severe for students of English in places such as Asia, the Middle East, and Africa, whose native languages, writing systems, and cultures have little in common with those of the English-speaking world and whose English study thus requires far more learning.

Some students are surprised by the amount of time and effort required to learn a language. Thinking back on my days as a beginning-level Russian student, I remember noticing in my college catalogue that the third-year Russian courses were literature courses. I therefore foolishly assumed that if I was going to read literature in the third year, the first two years of Russian class would be sufficient to teach me daily Russian.[2] Most language students are probably not quite this naïve, but unreasonable expectations are not rare. As Scarcella and Oxford (1992) point out, "Students are often unrealistic in what they believe they can and should accomplish in a given period of time, so their self-esteem suffers" (p. 58). Students who feel bad about their language learning are particularly vulnerable to discouragement and the temptation to quit.

Even if students realize that language study is emotionally demanding, they often fail to account for this problem in their study plans. Too many students assume that being a good student means toughing it out, slugging away at a language until they finally—and painfully—conquer it. Again drawing on my own experience, I remember fantasizing that if I could just read one big Russian novel—even if it meant digging my way through the book word by word with a dictionary—I would conquer the Russian reading problem forever. In theory, this strategy may

---

[2] Within a few months, I was disabused of the notion that one learned spoken Russian in two years of college courses, but the need to complete a language requirement kept me going. Sheer perversity pushed me into a third year, and I then learned that "reading" Russian in third-year courses meant slowly decoding texts with a dictionary.

well have worked if I had ever been able to sustain it, but the problem was that I never could.[3] This tendency to try and take a language by frontal assault, of course, often reflects the manner in which languages are taught, with inadequate attention to the emotional needs of learners.

Another problem arises from a peculiarity of the language learning process: the further students go, the more their rate of progress seems to slow. To some extent, this peculiarity is due to a phenomenon known as *plateaus,* which are often experienced by intermediate- and advanced-level learners. For reasons no one quite understands, many learners tend to make progress in spurts more than in a neat step-by-step progression, and between these spurts students often feel that they are making no progress; they have hit a plateau. These plateaus, however, are generally temporary and therefore do not pose a serious threat to students who know that plateaus are a common feature of language learning. (The best thing for a student to do is either just keep on studying or lighten up for a short break before plunging back in.)

A more serious problem arises from the fact that the more students learn of a language, the less visible impact each additional day of study makes on their skills, so progress becomes harder and harder to discern. The analogy of a river emerging from a mountain gorge onto a broad plain may help illustrate this phenomenon: as the river's channel widens, the river appears to slow down, although the same amount of water is moving over the same distance in the same time. Likewise, beginning-level language students can see their progress very clearly because they are making progress on a narrow front. Between lesson two and lesson four in a textbook, their knowledge of English doubles, and every new word they learn significantly increases their ability to communicate. However, as they reach more advanced skill levels, their progress becomes less apparent; successful completion of lesson seventy-four does not make as obvious an impact on a student's English skill level as completion of lesson six did, and learning low-frequency words like *manual* and *tome* doesn't enhance their ability to communicate as much as mastery of earlier words like *book* did. This means that students in the intermediate stages of language learning are especially vulnerable to discouragement because they often have relatively little sense that they are making progress. Intermediate-level students may have a hard time resisting the temptation to abandon English study—or to focus on just learning enough English to pass the test rather than really trying to develop any usable skills in the language. (In contrast, for advanced-level students who have achieved breakthrough in one or more English skills and can use their skills for rewarding or useful purposes such as watching films in English, a sense of daily English progress is less vital for sustaining their motivation.)

A final reason English study can be emotionally demanding is that the first years of English study in an EFL setting generally offer few rewards. In ESL settings, even beginning-level students of English have many opportunities to use the new knowledge and skills they learn, and each success they have in using English serves as a reward. The problem in EFL settings is not only that there are fewer opportunities to practice English but that there are fewer opportunities to experience the sense of success that comes from using English successfully for some kind of real-life communication. This is a problem especially for EFL students who are at beginning and intermediate levels because opportunities to use English tend to go to people whose English skills are relatively advanced. For example, if a English-speaking foreign visitor comes to a school, it is usually the most advanced-level English speakers in a class—or in the school—who get the opportunity to speak English with the guest. In short, students in EFL settings generally need to achieve higher English skill levels before they get a chance to use those skills in real-life situations (those

---

[3] This suggestion may sound a bit bizarre, but I assure you I am not the only language learner it has ever occurred to. For example, in chapter 6 of *How to Learn Any Language* (1991), Farber seriously suggests this approach for beginning readers, using newspapers instead of novels. To his credit, Farber makes it very clear that this approach is not for the fainthearted.

outside the English classroom), and this lengthens the period during which they need to wait for such opportunities. It is hard in such circumstances to sustain enthusiasm for language study.

Brown (1991) sums up the importance of affective factors in language learning: "The emotions are the foundation on which all your learning strategies, techniques, and gimmicks will stand or fall. . . . Without that emotional foundation, you are fighting an uphill battle at best" (p. 73). It thus makes sense to structure programs of language study in ways that give students a maximum sense of progress and reward, and encourage them not to give up.

Differences between the Learning Styles of Language Learners

The three points made previously are relevant to how individual students learn language; this final point has to do with how students as a group learn language. Learners vary considerably from one to the next in their learning styles, that is, the ways they go about learning. One contrasting set of learning styles that has received much attention has to do with learners' sensory preferences, and based on these learners are categorized into four groups:

1. **visual learners:** those who tend to learn best by seeing

2. **auditory learners:** those who tend to learn best by hearing

3. **kinesthetic learners:** those who tend to learn best by moving and doing things

4. **tactile learners:** those who learn tend to best through feel and touch

Another set of learning style categories has to do with the personality types of learners, and in this area some learning style contrasts that have been suggested include distinctions between

- **extroverted versus introverted learners:** This one is fairly self-explanatory.

- **thinking versus feeling learners:** This is a distinction between learners who are more cognitively oriented and those who are more affectively oriented. For example, in a discussion, thinking-oriented students would generally be more interested in the factual content of the discussion, while feeling-oriented learners would be more attentive to the feelings and emotional needs of others in the discussion.

- **closure-oriented and judging learners versus open and perceiving learners:** The former learners strive for clarity, results, and closure; the latter are more comfortable with ambiguity for longer periods and feel less internal pressure to resolve questions any time soon (for more categories, see Oxford 2001, 360–62).

Of course, no learner is a pure example of any of these categories, and most learners have elements of most or all of the above in their approaches to learning. However, a learner often leans in one direction or another, favoring some styles over others, and will presumably be more successful in a classroom where the teaching approaches used most often by the teacher match the learner's favored learning styles.

Obviously, it is not possible for each student to have a teacher and classroom situation tailored precisely to his or her preferred learning styles; this can't happen even in small classes, let alone the large classes that are common in EFL settings. However, teachers can do two important things to accommodate the varied learning styles of students. The first is to use a reasonably broad and rich variety of teaching techniques, so that each learner is more likely to experience a method that is relatively good match for his or her style for at least part of the class period. The second involves encouraging learners to explore different ways and approaches to language learning, so that they find study and practice methods that suit their style. This is one of the most important reasons any consideration of language teaching needs to start with a look at the learners.

The Role of the Language Teacher

When most people think of a language teacher, perhaps the first image that occurs to them is of a tidily dressed woman or man standing in front of an attentive class, explaining a grammar point or a new word. Then the teacher checks whether or not students understand the point by asking each one a question or two, patiently correcting any mistakes they make. Most people have been in language classes that were taught largely in this fashion. To my mind (influenced no doubt by many years in China), this teacher-centered approach calls up images of the great sage Confucius sitting amidst his disciples, explaining the Way and occasionally asking questions to check his disciples' comprehension; hence, I will refer to this approach as the Sage model of teaching. The Sage owes his exalted position to the fact that he knows more than his students do, and his primary task is to transfer his knowledge to his students. Once the students understand what the Sage is trying to explain, the teaching task has been successfully completed.

It is not surprising that the Sage model is influential in shaping ideas about the role of the language teacher. As noted above, this may be the model that you saw in your own secondary school or university language classes. It may well also be the predominant teaching model in your country, hence the role that students and colleagues expect you to play. However, there are also more subtle reasons behind the influence exerted by this model. One is that it is a natural role because it places a premium on expertise in knowledge of the subject. The primary qualification for Sage status is knowing more than the disciples; likewise, one of your primary qualifications as a language teacher is your superior knowledge of English. Another attraction of this model, as noted by Medgyes (2001, 434), is that it places the teacher in firm control of the classroom, with the power to steer away from uncertain or uncomfortable waters and to maintain the appearance of an orderly class.

A certain amount of the Sage is virtually inevitable in your teaching life, and I do not intend to suggest that the Sage model is bad per se. You do in fact know far more about English than students do, and one of your important roles as language teacher is to convey as much of that knowledge as possible to students. However, I would suggest that excessive reliance on this model has serious drawbacks. One of these is the teacher-centered nature of the Sage model. In this model, teachers are not only personally responsible for transmitting most of the knowledge students are to learn but also have the responsibility for deciding what is to be learned and how. One (usually unintended) side effect of this approach is that students learn to be passive, to do what they are told rather than actively finding ways to enhance their own learning. Another unfortunate side effect is that, as suggested earlier, the teacher's role may degenerate into one of covering material during class (i.e., explaining or simply mentioning it briefly), reducing class to a formalistic exercise in which the teacher skims over material primarily so that students can be held responsible for it on the final exam.

A second problem with the Sage model is that it tends to be classroom centered; in other words, it assumes that most learning takes place in the classroom and downplays the importance of work done by students on their own. Of course, even in the Sage model of teaching students are given homework, but it often seems that the homework is simply rehearsal for the main show. The subtle message of this assumption for students is that real learning requires the teacher; the temptation for teachers is to measure success by the polish of their classroom performances rather than by student progress.

A final problem with the Sage model is that it assumes that learning a language is essentially the accumulation of knowledge and that the battle is won once students understand what the teacher is trying to explain. Unfortunately, as I have tried to show, this assumption isn't true. Acquisition of knowledge plays an important part in language learning, but it is not enough—learning a language also involves mastering of a set of skills, and skills are not learned via explanation. Explanation is generally only the beginning of the learning process, and the teacher who plays the Sage role may put on an impressive show but leave students to face the real battle alone.

I would suggest that another helpful way of looking at the role of the language teachers is by considering the model of the athletic coach or piano teacher, a model that I will call the Coach.[4] The main advantage of this model is that it assumes that much—or even most—of the learning process takes place during practice away from the teacher's watchful eye and that success or failure in the learning process depends much more on what students do outside class than on what teachers do in class. A coach will certainly give useful tips on how a basketball player should make jump shots, but it is the player's hours of practice shots that teach the skill. Likewise, a piano teacher cannot teach students digital dexterity by explaining it; students must practice scales many times before they can play scales smoothly.

Of course, one duty of the Coach is to share knowledge of the subject (much like the Sage), but equally important parts of the Coach's role are (1) helping students better understand the learning process, (2) providing encouragement and cultivating students' motivation, (3) helping students build discipline through accountability, and (4) building students' initiative and responsibility for their own learning. These are not the only roles English teachers could adopt, but they are important because each has significant implications for how effective you are as an English teacher—not only in terms of how well you help students build their English proficiency but also in terms of how well you prepare them for standardized examinations. In the following sections of this chapter, I consider these four aspects of the Coach's role and the way they relate to basic principles of language learning and teaching.

HELPING STUDENTS UNDERSTAND LANGUAGE LEARNING

One of your first tasks as a language teacher is to help students understand the task of language learning. Keep in mind that the way students need to study English is quite different from the way they would study other subjects often taught in schools. Studying subjects like mathematics, history, or biology does involve some skill component, but the main task is to master knowledge of the subject. In contrast, as pointed out above, learning a foreign language involves a much heavier skill component than learning many other school subjects, so students should not approach English study with the same assumptions they have for learning other school subjects. This means that ideas like those introduced earlier in this chapter need to be explicitly discussed with students—preferably in the local language so that students understand clearly. The more you can help students understand about the process of language learning, the better prepared they will be to deal with the challenges it involves.

However, talking to students about language learning is not enough. If what you say about language learning is going to have much impact on the students, it must be backed up by the way you teach your courses. In other words, if you stress the idea that students should take responsibility for their own language learning, you need to find ways to structure room for student initiative into your courses. If you argue that language is a tool for communication, you must, as often as possible, allow students to use language for genuine communication in your

---

[4]I am hardly the first to suggest this analogy. See, for example, McKay (1987, xii) and Stevick (1988, 202).

courses. If you emphasize that mastery of English involves developing language skills through practice, you need to give the students ample opportunities to practice. Finally, if you urge students to attend to the affective side of language learning, you need to show similar concern for the issue in the way you structure class exercises and practice. Students will often learn more about the nature of language and language learning from what you do in your classes than from what you say.

A second way to help students become better language learners is to help them explore different methods and strategies for language learning. Such strategies fall into categories like the following:

- **strategies for learning language knowledge, such as vocabulary, grammar rules, sentences patterns, and cultural norms:** These would include strategies for discovering the knowledge (e.g., finding out what an unfamiliar word means), memorizing the knowledge, and reviewing it.

- **strategies for building skills, such as the ability to listen, speak, read, write, or translate:** These would include strategies for practicing skills, building fluency and automaticity, and finding and taking advantage of opportunities to use the second language for real purposes.

- **strategies for planning and directing one's language study:** These would include strategies for setting goals, choosing methods, choosing materials, planning study time, evaluating study results, and combining all this into an effective overall language learning campaign.

- **strategies for building and sustaining motivation in the process of language learning:** These would include strategies for making language study interesting, developing a positive attitude toward language study, and finding rewards in language study.[5]

In part, teaching such strategies involves sharing what you know about language learning from your own experiences, both positive and negative. (As noted previously, this is one reason your own engagement in language learning is so important.) However, it is equally important to encourage students to explore new methods on their own and talk with each other about what works and what does not. Often the mere fact that you raise this issue from time to time for class discussion expands students' horizons and serves as a useful stimulus, prodding them to get out of an old study routine that may have outlived its usefulness for them.

A final aspect of teaching language learning skills involves building students' ability to strategize—to analyze a situation, set language learning goals, and devise effective ways to achieve those goals. The ability to strategize is, of course, related to knowing many language learning strategies, but it is not quite the same thing. It is good for language learners to know about many language learning strategies because this gives them a richer menu of ideas to draw from. However, there is no such thing as a best strategy for learning any particular language skill—in other words, no single strategy is best for all situations, all learners, all skill levels, and so forth. An effective language learning strategy needs to be adapted to quite a range of factors, such as

- opportunities within the local setting to use the target language

- the demands of the school curriculum

---

[5] One widely used system divides strategies into the following six categories: (1) memory strategies, (2) cognitive strategies (applying reasons to specific tasks), (3) compensation strategies (coping with problems), (4) metacognitive strategies (awareness of one's own learning process), (5) affective strategies (managing one's feelings), and (6) social strategies (working with others). See Oxford (1990).

- the materials available

- the skill level of the learner

- the learning style of the learner

- the kind and level of the learner's motivation

- the goals of the learner

and many more. The point is that learners need the ability to choose and carry out strategies that are appropriate to all of the above—to strategize. This skill is developed not just by learning new strategies or study methods, but rather through practice analyzing one's situation and the challenges involved in learning the target language and in designing and trying out solutions.

ENCOURAGING AND MOTIVATING STUDENTS

In EFL settings where opportunities to use English are relatively rare, one of the main challenges faced by English teachers is how to motivate students in their English study. While many students are initially interested in learning English, it is not unusual for their enthusiasm to disappear over time, partly because learning a foreign language involves lots of hard work, partly because English doesn't seem immediately useful or relevant to their lives, and partly because they rarely get a chance to use the skills they learn. Indeed, as noted earlier, they generally need to persist in studying English for years before they reach a skill level that allows them to comfortably watch a film, read a book, or chat with a foreigner in English.

For many students, to the extent that they are motivated to study English at all, their primary motivation is what researchers call *extrinsic motivation* (see p. 30), in other words, motivation based on a reward that comes from outside the learner. Examples of extrinsic motivation would include the desire to get a good score on a test or get a good job. Such rewards can have significant power in motivating students to study and learn, but they are also problematic in some ways. For example, students who are motivated primarily by a desire to do well on tests may study only what they need to in order to pass the test, and once the test is over, they may lose interest in English study. Similarly, the motivating force of job opportunities may be weakened if the prospect of a job is years in the future; a reward that seems too distant may not have much power to motivate students to study today.

Rather than relying exclusively on extrinsic rewards to motivate students, many researchers who study language learning argue that English teachers should also try to build their students' *intrinsic motivation* (see p. 30) by encouraging them to consider rewards that come from within themselves, such as a sense of accomplishment, the love of learning new things, the love of creating, or the desire to pursue their own curiosity and interests. In fact, many researchers suggest that intrinsic motivation is a more powerful driving force than extrinsic motivation (Brown 2001, 76–77). One reason intrinsic rewards tend to be especially effective as motivators is that, coming from within the learner, they are always there to drive one's study—they are not years away, and they don't disappear when the test ends.

Motivating students is not solely a question of what potential rewards you encourage them to consider. For example, I have already touched on how student motivation can be affected by students' sense of progress, and I consider this issue in more detail in chapter 3. Another way to arouse and maintain student interest in English study is to make your courses as genuinely communicative as possible. Most people enjoy talking about themselves and learning about others, which provides a natural opportunity for speaking and even writing practice—and is certainly more interesting than rewriting sentences or parroting a memorized dialogue.

SOME EXTRINSIC REWARDS

- Good test scores

- Increased range of education opportunities

- Better job opportunities (wider range, better pay, more promotion opportunities, opportunity to travel)

- Ability to interact with people from other countries (for practical purposes)

- Access to professional information in English (e.g., in books, journals, Web sites, lectures)

- Access to wider range of information about the world and world events

- Easier travel

- Praise from teachers, parents, and others[6]

SOME INTRINSIC REWARDS

- Sense of accomplishment (pride, self-respect)

- Sense of confidence in one's ability to handle a wider range of situations

- Opportunity to pursue a wider range of interests (e.g., through reading books or watching films one likes in English)

- Sense of understanding the world better, being more in touch with the international scene, being a world citizen

- Opportunity to develop friendships with people from other countries (out of a personal desire to do so)

Here I wish to emphasize that the level of students' motivation is also significantly affected by the teacher—you. In fact, as Dörnyei (2001b) points out, some studies on motivation have concluded that the teacher is the "most important . . . motivational factor in the classroom" (p. 120). Dörnyei categorizes the influences a teacher has on student motivation as follows:

1. **personal characteristics:** Teachers can motivate students through characteristics such as being committed and personally warm.

2. **teacher immediacy:** Teachers can motivate students by coming physically closer (e.g., walking around the class instead of always staying at the front) and psychologically closer (e.g., knowing students' names and personalizing topics).

3. **active motivational socializing behavior:** Teachers can motivate students through behaviors such as presenting clear goals and tasks, giving good feedback, and encouraging students.

4. **classroom management:** Teachers can motivate students through such things as maintaining a sense of order in the classroom and ensuring that students maintain norms of appropriate (nondisruptive) behavior.

---

[6] This reward is something of an anomaly in that praise from people who one respects tends to have motivating power that is more like intrinsic motivation than extrinsic, even though it comes from outside the learner. See Brown (2001, 77).

In short, student motivation is something that you as a teacher can and should have a positive impact on. In fact, for some students this may be the most important contribution you make to their English study.[7]

BUILDING ACCOUNTABILITY AND DISCIPLINE

One of the greatest advantages of taking a language course (as opposed to studying a language on your own) is that it provides someone who holds you accountable for how much and how well you learn. In other words, when you take a course, you must study because tomorrow there might be a quiz, a test, a discussion covering tonight's reading assignment, or at least a teacher who will be disappointed if you don't do what you are supposed to. Thus, as long as human beings are naturally inclined toward procrastination and laziness, a third important role of the language teacher will be to ensure that students put in the many hard hours of work necessary for mastery of a language and to help them learn the discipline necessary to keep them working diligently when there is no longer a teacher around. Many of the ways in which teachers hold students accountable come under the heading of assessment and evaluation, discussed in chapter 4, but I note here that accountability is not only a matter of quizzes, tests, graded homework assignments, and other measures that students often view as more akin to the stick than the carrot. Accountability also includes praise, encouragement for work well done, and almost any other response that recognizes students' efforts. In fact, research in psychology indicates that rewards affect behavior more than punishment does (Brown 1991, 42; 2001, 76), and positive reinforcement often has more impact on students than negative reinforcement.[8]

The basic idea of accountability is that you consider students' efforts important and care whether or not they did their work. Some students will only work if threatened; others only need a gentle reminder. Most, however, are a little more likely to work if they know that they will be held responsible for doing so. As Littlewood (1984) notes, while excessive anxiety in a situation can hinder learning, "a certain amount of it can stimulate a learner to invest more energy in the task" (p. 59).

BUILDING LEARNER AUTONOMY

A final role of the language teacher is building learner autonomy, in other words, helping students learn to take charge of their own language learning by setting their own goals, making their own plans of study, and then carrying out their plans. As Brown (2001) notes,

> All too often, language teachers are so consumed with the "delivery" of language to their students that they neglect to spend some effort preparing learners to "receive" the language. And students, mostly unaware of the tricks of successful language learning, simply do whatever the teacher tells them to do, having no means to question the wisdom thereof. In an effort to fill class hours with fascinating material, teachers might overlook their mission of enabling learners to eventually become independent of classrooms—that is, to be autonomous learners. (p. 208)

When you plan your courses, then, you should think about ways to encourage students to take the initiative. There are an endless number of ways to do this: have students keep their own vocabulary lists, let them choose their own books for reading practice, have them choose topics for writing or discussions, ask them to tape their own listening material (e.g., from the radio), or

---

[7]For more ideas on how teachers can motivate language learners, see the teacher-as-motivator task in For Thought, Discussion, and Action at the end of this chapter. See also Dörnyei (2001a).

[8]A personal example: in high school I continued with Chinese lessons for four years—despite marginal grades—mainly because I liked the class and the teacher. (Thanks, Mr. Lee!)

even have them design and carry out study plans of their own as a component of your course. The important thing is for students to get into the habit of taking charge of their own study programs as much as possible.

I have suggested that you can and should help students learn to strategize in their English study. The way to teach this skill is not to tell students what to do; rather, you teach them to strategize by presenting them with problems or challenges they might face in their language learning, such as how to memorize new vocabulary most effectively or how to build their reading speed, and then encouraging them to think carefully about the problem and suggest strategies for dealing with it. As they suggest strategies, you then have the opportunity to help them by offering comments and suggestions or perhaps by pointing out problems they didn't think of and then asking them to think a little further. Here, you do not need to be able to offer the right answer to the challenge you present to students; as I argued earlier, there generally isn't only one right strategy for dealing with a language learning problem. However, as a result of your own experience as a learner and teacher, you should be able to guide students to better strategies than they might have found on their own. Furthermore, you make an important contribution to students' education simply by raising the question and encouraging students to think about it.

One specific technique for encouraging students to take control of their own language learning involves having students to undertake language learning projects (LLPs) of the kind introduced in chapter 1. In the framework of your course, an LLP is a separate, additional project in which students choose their own goals, methods, and study plans. While doing an LLP may be a required part of your course, students are expected to take as much responsibility as possible for all aspects of the project—including evaluation. The virtue of such projects is that, in addition to helping students learn a little more English, they help students become more independent and autonomous as language learners; the hope is that by helping students become accustomed to taking as much responsibility as possible for their own language learning, you are helping prepare them for the day when they will no longer have teachers and ready-made courses on which they can rely to drive their further language study. (See chapter 3 for further discussion of how to apply LLPs in English courses you teach.)

Getting students to take charge of their own language study is often more easily said than done. Many students have little real desire to learn English and only long for the day when they complete their requirement and can kiss the whole thing good-bye. However, there are other students whose whole attitude toward language study will change if you carefully but firmly hand the reins over to them.

Making Your Assumptions Explicit

The assumptions about language teaching I have presented are basic tenets of CLT and would not raise many eyebrows in the Western English teaching world. However, they would not all be taken for granted in many EFL settings, where different assumptions may influence the approaches of your colleagues and students. Here are a few examples:

- **focus on the student as learner:** In many societies, the teacher's social role is much closer to that of the Sage than that of the Coach; teachers are respected in the community primarily for their knowledge of their field, and their word is not to be challenged. In such a society, a teacher-centered approach to education may fit with the norms of the culture better than the student-centered approach I have suggested.

- **emphasis on the individuality of each student:** The emphasis on the student as a unique individual with a distinct learning style may seem rather foreign and Western in some societies. In comparison with the United States, for example, many societies are somewhat more culturally uniform, have a more standardized education system, and encourage individualism less.

- **language as communication skill:** In many countries, teachers do not emphasize the idea of language as communication, and it might be difficult for them to teach in a way that emphasized communicative skills heavily. In many countries, English teachers have had little opportunity to develop their English skills, particularly spoken fluency; in contrast, they may be very familiar with the formal features of English, especially grammar and vocabulary. They may also tend to give lectures that stick closely to the text because this allows them to prepare a limited body of material. This text-centered, grammar-analysis approach to teaching plays to their strengths; a highly communicative teaching approach that plays to the strengths of native-speaking English teachers might be not only unfamiliar but also very difficult to adopt.

Note that for many students who are in educational systems where test results determine their academic futures and careers, learning how to communicate often is not the primary goal; the primary goal is to score well on examinations. In such situations, while emphasizing language skills and proficiency is no doubt desirable, it would be irresponsible for the teacher to fail to prepare students for tests, and traditional methods may well be as effective in preparing students for examinations as communicative methods are—or more so.

My point is not to undermine all of the principles that I have argued for in this chapter; the principles of CLT are sound and provide one good foundation for language teaching. However, there is no single right way to teach English, and all teaching approaches have advantages and disadvantages, so it is important to carefully consider how appropriate these assumptions are to you, the students, and the setting in which you teach. In short, it is ultimately up to you to decide which of the recipes in the CLT cookbook will be of help to you in your work. What I suggest is that, even if the assumptions of CLT are not widely accepted in your country, considering them may still benefit your teaching, not least because borrowing judiciously from this particular cookbook may help you enrich the range of ingredients you have to draw on. Also, because all approaches to language teaching have weaknesses as well as strengths, adding some recipes from a different cookbook will help round out the diet of language learning approaches offered to the students.

If you adopt CLT approaches that are not familiar to the students, it is important to explain what you are doing and why in order to help students deal with any discrepancies between your language teaching approaches and their language learning expectations. To this end, I make two suggestions:

1. Communicate your assumptions explicitly to the students. Students should know what to expect in your class and how you perceive your role as teacher. You may sometimes also need to modify your assumptions so that you are more in tune with your class.[9]

---

[9] Nunan (1989) notes that this may even be necessary in classes in English-speaking countries: "It is not uncommon in adult ESL classes for the teacher to see herself as a guide and catalyst for classroom communication while the learners see her as someone who should be providing explicit instruction and modelling the target language" (p. 84). In such cases, Nunan recommends negotiation.

2. If you adopt some CLT approaches, do not explicitly or implicitly criticize other approaches to teaching. Instead, present your assumptions as just that—your assumptions—rather than as the only acceptable approach to language teaching. You might present CLT approaches as an alternative approach from which you are drawing because you think it will add something useful in your context. By approaching your teaching in this way, you are less likely to come into conflict with different approaches in your culture.

For Thought, Discussion, and Action

1. **the coach and the examination:** The chapter suggests that the roles described in the Coach model are important in preparing students for examinations as well as for building English language proficiency. Look back at each of the four roles and consider how relevant it would be to the task of preparing students for examinations in your country.

2. **choices in language learning:** One of the most important strategies for helping students become more independent and autonomous as language learners is to give them as much choice as possible about their own study. The more they make their own choices, the more they are likely to take responsibility for their own English study. Consider a typical English course in your country, and make a list of ways you could give students some choice in their English study (e.g., with regard to goals, homework, activities). Be as specific as possible.

3. **student motivation:** Survey several classmates who have already had experience teaching English, and ask them: How easy or hard has it been to motivate students? What strategies seem to work best? What strategies do not seem to work?

4. **intrinsic motivation:** Brown (2001, 80) argues that teachers should try to build students' intrinsic motivation as much as possible, and he provides the following checklist of criteria that can be applied to a language teaching technique (activity, etc.) in order to determine whether it promotes intrinsic motivation. (1) Analyze each of Brown's criteria, and explain how/why it would contribute to intrinsic motivation. (2) Decide which of these questions is most relevant in building the motivation of students in your setting.
   - Does the technique appeal to the genuine interests of the students? Is it relevant to their lives?
   - Do you present the technique in a positive, enthusiastic manner?
   - Are students clearly aware of the purpose of the technique?
   - Do students have some choice in (1) choosing some aspect of the technique and (2) determining how they go about fulfilling the goals of the technique?
   - Does the technique encourage students to discover for themselves certain principles or rules (rather than simply being told)?
   - Does it encourage students in some way to develop or use effective strategies of learning and communication?
   - Does it contribute—at least to some extent—to students' ultimate autonomy and independence (from you)?
   - Does it foster cooperative negotiation with other students in the class? Is it truly interactive?

- Does the technique present a reasonable challenge?
- Do students receive sufficient feedback on their performance (from each other or from you)?

5. **genuine communication:** This chapter suggests that one way to motivate students is to include as much genuine communication as possible in English courses. Make a checklist (like Brown's list in number 4) for assessing whether or not an activity is genuinely communicative.

6. **teacher as motivator:** Dörnyei (2001b, 138) suggests the following Ten Commandments for Motivating Language Learners. Consider these ten suggestions, and decide which would be more effective or relevant in your country and which less so.
   1. Set a personal example with your own behavior.
   2. Create a pleasant, relaxed atmosphere in the class.
   3. Present the tasks properly.
   4. Develop a good relationship with the learners.
   5. Increase the learners' linguistic self-confidence.
   6. Make the language classes interesting.
   7. Promote learner autonomy.
   8. Personalize the learning process.
   9. Increase the learners' goal-orientedness.
   10. Familiarize learners with the target language culture.

7. **feelings in language learning:** Think back to your experience learning a foreign language, and try to remember the role feelings played in the process. List ways in which feelings entered the experience and what impact they had.

8. **skill learning:** Think back on your experience learning some kind of skill (sport, craft, musical instrument, etc.). Describe the process, and compare it with your foreign language learning experiences. In what ways were the processes similar, and how did they differ?

9. **past language teachers:** Think back on positive and negative examples of language teachers you have had. Who would you like to be like, and why? Who would you not like to be like, and why?

10. **CLT:** Talk with a teacher in your country about CLT. Find out what he or she knows and thinks about it.

11. **LLPs in English courses:** This chapter suggests that one way to build autonomy in learners is to include some kind of LLP as a part of your courses. Choose a typical kind of English course in your country, one that you are familiar with, and try to adapt the LLP idea to that course.

Chapter 3

Course Planning: Knowing Where You Are Going

- The goals of a course should serve as the focus around which everything else is built, so it is important to have a clear idea of what the course goals are.

- Often the goals of a course are determined to some extent by a curriculum, textbook, or test. However, it is generally necessary—and always desirable—to also set your own goals for the course, not least so that covering material and passing a test do not become the only goals of the course.

- The textbooks and other materials used in a course should serve as tools to help you and the students achieve the goals of the course; they should not serve as a substitute for those goals.

- To some extent, the curriculum and materials of a course will determine the teaching methods you use in the course. However, you generally have at least some choice in what methods you will use and how often, and your choices should be based on the goals of the course.

- Students must learn to make and take responsibility for their own language learning plans. Hence, one goal of courses should be helping students learn to make and carry out language learning projects.

It would be fair to say that, during my first years of teaching, I really didn't have course plans per se. Rather, I generally had a course textbook of some kind, and the textbook essentially served as a substitute for the course plan, providing not only the material to be studied in the course but also the methods I used in class and even the goals for the course. For a beginning teacher, this was not entirely a bad thing. The textbooks were written by people who knew more about English teaching than I did at the time, and following them allowed me to teach better courses than I would have been able to generate had I been left entirely on my own to choose methods, materials, and goals. However, simply following the textbook was not always ideal. Even though the textbook writers knew more about English teaching than I did, they didn't know the students—their needs, desires, skill levels, personalities, and so forth. They also didn't know me—my strengths and weaknesses, my interests, and my personality. So, as long as I relied on course textbooks to provide the plans for my courses, they were like suits ordered sight unseen from some faraway clothing company—they fit adequately but never very well.

Ultimately, the direction of a course needs to be set primarily by its goals, and the methods and materials in a course should serve the goals rather than the other way around. In this chapter, I consider three of the basic elements of a course plan: (1) goals, (2) materials, and (3) methods. (A fourth important aspect of course planning—evaluation—is considered in chapter 4.) Of these three, however, I give the most attention to the first and most important—goals.

In this chapter, I also argue that one of your goals in any course should be to lead students toward taking responsibility for planning their own language study. By learning to actively consider their goals and methods, students are more likely to focus their study efforts in a way that will suit their styles, take advantage of their strengths, compensate for their weaknesses, and meet their personal needs. Students who study in this way will probably not only do better in their course work but also be better prepared to continue their study once their days in English classes end.

Goals

WHAT ARE GOALS?

Goals are essentially the results or outcomes you hope the students will achieve in their language learning. In the context of English study, they tend to fall into four basic categories:

1. Building language knowledge involves having students learn vocabulary, grammar, and cultural knowledge.

2. Building language skills involves building students' ability to use language to listen, speak, read, write, and translate.

3. Building language learning skills means helping students learn how to be more effective language learners.

4. Building motivation involves building students' interest in language learning and helping them develop and sustain motivation.

The first two kinds of goals, language knowledge and language skill goals, are the ones that both students and teachers tend to be most aware of when they think about language study, but the other two are equally important. If students have poor language learning skills, they are not likely to improve either their language knowledge or their skills very much; likewise, if students are not motivated to learn or have no interest, they will probably learn less and are more likely to cheerfully delete what they learn from their memories as soon as they have the opportunity.

When described in full detail, the process of setting goals for a course is actually rather complex and may be affected by many factors such as requests made by students, your own past learning experience, the demands of your department, the material in the textbook, and perhaps even reports in your local media about controversies in education. However, it is probably not too much of a generalization to say that for most EFL teachers, goals tend to come from two basic sources. The first of these would consist of outside authorities, such as the national education bureau, your own school authorities, or textbook writers, who give you goals that you must pursue in your English courses. These goals may be embodied in different ways, such as tests you must prepare students for, textbooks you must teach, or nationwide English standards you must help students meet. However, what these kinds of goals all have in common is that they are given to you, and you have relatively little choice about whether or not to pursue them.

The second kind of goal comes from your own understanding of what students need and what they would benefit most from. Ideally, of course, your understanding will take students' opinions into account; it should not be based on your opinions alone. However, many students do not have a very clear idea of what their goals are in language learning; some only know that they want to "improve their English," and others have no goal other than passing a test. Also, students are often unable to predict with any certainty what kinds of English skills or knowledge they will need in the future, which makes it hard for them to set goals. Finally, the students in any given class are not a monolithic group, and different students often have rather different goals, so even if individual students know what their goals are, the class as a whole may have no clear consensus. So, while you certainly want to be as aware as possible of the students' needs and goals and of the future situations in which they are likely to need English, you will often need to rely heavily on your own understanding of students' needs when you set goals for an English course.

For some kinds of courses, you have a relatively high degree of freedom to set your own goals, and consequently there is more need for you to consciously and explicitly set goals. Consider the following situation.

Case One

You are teaching a general English course in a college where all first-year students are required to take one year of English. There are fifty students in the course, and it meets twice a week, two hours each session. The required comprehensive English textbook for the course contains dialogues, reading passages, vocabulary lists, grammar explanations, and a variety of activities to build students' skills and knowledge. In your program, there are no standardized examinations, and the only tests students need to take are those you design.

In a course like this, you have a relatively high degree of freedom in goal setting. While your goals will probably be influenced by the material in the book and the expectations of your department, the absence of a standardized examination gives you considerable freedom to decide what goals you think should be set for the course. Furthermore, in this situation the need for you to set clear, specific goals is relatively obvious. The range of English skills and knowledge included in the textbook is very large, and you will have to make hard choices about what kinds of activities and material to devote your limited class time to. For example, you will need to decide how much emphasis to place on speaking and listening skills and whether or not to require much writing practice. If you try to give everything equal weight, students will probably not make much progress in any given area; in contrast, if you focus students' efforts to some degree, there is a greater chance that they will see and feel progress in at least one or two skill areas, and this may encourage them to continue studying English after the course ends.

Of course, in many EFL situations your freedom to set goals is more limited than in Case One because the goals of many courses are determined by a set curriculum, a required textbook, or a standardized test. However, even when teaching such courses, you will generally still need to make at least some choices about goals. Consider the following:

Case Two

You are teaching a general English course for middle school seniors who later in the year will face a nationwide standardized examination that determines whether they will have the opportunity for further education.

In this situation, you would have relatively little freedom in your choice of goals; obviously, your primary goal is to help students do as well as possible on the examination, so what you teach will be determined to a large degree by the demands of the examination. However, this does not mean that you don't need to set goals at all. First, the examination cannot tell you precisely how much priority you should attach to any particular kind of language skill or knowledge, much less how to achieve such goals. For example, you would need to decide how much time to spend on reading, how much time to spend explaining grammar, how much time to spend giving students practice with fill-in-the blank exercises, and so forth. You will need to choose how much emphasis to give to each kind of knowledge and skill, and this requires having a clearer sense of goal than just helping students pass the test. (Keep in mind that some goals—such as building students' reading skills or building their vocabularies—will both help prepare them for the examination and build their English proficiency; other goals—such as building guessing skills for multiple-choice test items—will be of little value for purposes other than taking the test. One of the main choices you will have to make is how much relative emphasis to give these two kinds of goals.) Second, the test will generally only suggest goals for language knowledge and skills; it will generally not give you much guidance in setting other kinds of goals, such as those related to how much time and attention to devote to activities that build students' interest in English study so that they continue to study English even after the examination is over. So, even for this kind of a course, you will need to make a number of your own decisions regarding goals.

These two cases suggest three important points. First, for virtually any kind of course you teach, you will need to consider the question of goals. Even when many course goals are determined for you, you will need to make some choices; furthermore, even when most goals are set for you, it is still a good thing to consciously go through the process of identifying goals so that you can clearly articulate and explain them to students. Second, goal setting can be seen as a process of strategizing that involves (1) listing the goals that are set for your course by outside authorities, (2) setting additional goals you feel are important as well as realistic within limits of time and energy, and (3) combining these into a coherent set of course goals for presentation to the students. This ability to analyze a situation and set good goals is one of the most important skills a language teacher needs to develop. Third, goals need to be set within a specific context, and different situations call for very different kinds of goals.

WHY IS GOAL SETTING SO IMPORTANT?

The most obvious benefit of having clear course goals, at least from the teacher's perspective, is that they set the direction for the course and guide other decisions you make about the course. Much as a destination determines the route of a journey, the kinds of equipment you need to take, and so forth, clear course goals help you make decisions about what kinds of materials you should adopt in a course, how to use those materials, what kinds of teaching activities to use in class, and what kinds of evaluation methods to use. Consider first what kinds of goals you might set for the following situation.

Case Three

You are teaching a course for middle-aged scholars who are preparing to go abroad to Western universities in order to participate in research projects, working in international teams for which English is expected to be the main working language. Most of the students have considerable experience reading and translating English but very marginal speaking and listening skills. No textbook has been assigned for the course, and there will be no examinations other than those you choose to set.

For this course, you have quite a bit of freedom to set your own goals because there is neither an examination nor even a required textbook to set goals for you. However, the upcoming challenges facing this group quite clearly suggest a number of goals.

1. First and foremost, you should build the students' listening comprehension. Lack of listening comprehension skills would not only hinder the professional work of these students but also socially isolate them from their teammates and from other people who live around them. Finally, poor listening skills would make daily life difficult.

2. Likewise, these students will clearly need to speak English in both their professional work and daily lives, so a second important goal would consist of helping these students develop at least survival-level skills in spoken English.

3. These students will need to take care of themselves socially in a Western cultural environment, so it would no doubt help if they learned something about the cultures of their host countries, at least basic daily-life information and norms of polite behavior.

Once your course goals are clarified, deciding how to use class time and what kinds of homework to assign becomes relatively straightforward. (For this course, you should clearly devote a significant portion of class time to speaking and listening practice, and for homework you should also assign as much listening practice as possible. It would also be a good idea to give some talks on Western culture.) The point here is that, once determined, the goals of the course in turn help you determine what kinds of teaching methods and activities you should use for the course and even help you decide what kinds of materials to choose.

An equally important, but perhaps less obvious, advantage of clear course goals is that they help students feel better about their language study, thereby improving the chances that they will learn willingly and be able to sustain that willingness over the long haul. Goals give direction to language study and serve as milestones that help learners see their progress. Without goals, language learning is a bit like rowing a boat in the middle of the ocean—even if you are moving forward, it is hard to tell if you are getting anywhere because there are no readily visible markers by which you can measure your progress. Likewise, unless learners have some way to mark their progress in English study, they may invest quite a bit of effort and still have little sense of progress.

One way you can help learners sustain a sense of forward motion is by breaking the massive task of learning English into smaller and more readily measurable units—stated as goals—that help them mark and feel their progress. To this end, it is helpful to have both general long-term goals and specific short-term goals.

General long-term goals enhance student morale by giving a sense of direction and vision; goals such as improved listening comprehension or increased reading speed offer the promise of a reward worth striving for. Without a sense of long-term goals, it is too easy for class exercises to seem to be an unrelated series of activities that are ends in themselves or that only serve to prepare students for the final test.

Of course, for goals to have a beneficial effect on student morale, students must be made aware of the goals—not only once at the beginning of the term, but on a regular basis. It is easy for teachers to overestimate the sense of vision and purpose that students have in language learning, particularly if the course students are taking is required, and it is also easy to overestimate how well students will remember a lecture on goals given on the first day of class. Even if you use the students' first language when introducing the goals of the course (as you probably should for most classes), the students will still probably forget at least some of what you say. So it is generally a good idea to continually remind students of why they are doing what they are doing. (My rule of thumb is that once students start chanting my little "We are doing this because . . ." speech along with me, they have probably internalized it.)

However, as Stevick (1988) suggests, long-term goals are not enough. They "are the hoped-for banquet at the end of a long hike. Your hikers also need snacks and water to sustain them along the path" (p. 128). Underneath the broad goals, you need to set goals that are specific and short term, goals toward which students can make observable progress during your course. For example, if the broad goal of a course is improvement of listening comprehension, more specific goals might include learning to understand the most common reduced forms of English words (e.g., *want to = wanna, don't you = dontcha*) or memorizing the names of the world's major countries and cities as an aid to understanding radio news in English. These latter goals are more finite than the broad goal of improving listening comprehension, and it is entirely possible that students can achieve them within a semester course, giving students the satisfaction of being able to point to a task successfully completed.

GENERAL PRINCIPLES FOR GOAL SETTING

The issue of what kinds of goals to set for the various aspects of English learning is addressed in more detail in chapters 6–12 (for specific discussion of goal setting, see appendix A). There are, however, several general principles—rules of thumb—that can help you as you think through the issue of goal setting for your courses.

Healthy Balance of Skills

In situations where your course is not intended to prepare students for a very specific challenge (e.g., the Test of English as a Foreign Language [TOEFL]), it is generally best to help students develop a balanced, general set of English skills and knowledge. In ideal situations, developing all of the language skills to a high level is no doubt desirable, but time limitations often demand that you choose what to stress in your classes and that students choose what skills to give the highest priority to. The following observations may be useful as you think through the problem of prioritizing goals:

1. **listening over speaking:** Usually it is best if students' listening skills are somewhat more advanced than their speaking skills. Even native speakers of a language can generally understand more than they can say, and many situations (e.g., watching TV, listening to the radio, listening to lectures) depend entirely on listening skills.[1]

2. **reading over writing:** Students are far more likely to need to read than write, if only because it is through reading that students gain so much of their vocabulary in EFL settings. Again, even native speakers generally read better and more often than they write.

---

[1] Scarcella and Oxford (1992, 139) claim, "Listening in almost any setting is the most frequently used language skill." This statement may be less true for English learners outside English-speaking countries—when learners may read more often than they listen—than for those in English-speaking countries, but the emphasis on the importance of listening skills is still well taken. See also Hedge (2000, 228–29) and Morley (2001, 70).

3. **communication over accuracy:** In most situations, communication is more important than accuracy. Although accuracy is very important in some situations (e.g., tests, formal writing), generally an English learner's primary need is to understand and be understood.

4. **vocabulary over grammar:** For listening and reading, an extensive vocabulary is more important than a thorough knowledge of English grammar (see Lewis, 1993, 33, for development of this argument).

Given these general features of a good balance, one way to decide where to focus your efforts is to assess the students' levels and then to emphasize those areas in which students need improvement to reach a good balance.

Basic Skills and Knowledge

A second general rule of thumb is that it is often best to emphasize fundamental knowledge and skills rather than highly situation-specific knowledge or skills. For example, stress general speaking and listening skills more than the fine points of job interviews, emphasize grammatical accuracy in writing more than the art of the memo, or build reading speed more than skills in literary criticism.

One obvious problem with situation-specific skills is that they are of limited value to students who never find themselves in the right situation. Another problem is that the speed of change in the modern world means that a situation for which you prepare students may no longer exist by the time they graduate. I am reminded of a class I taught for Chinese university students who were being prepared to work in trade companies. Because of their future job needs, the department wanted me to teach the class telex writing (a request that I ignored mainly because I didn't know how to write telexes). Despite the apparently uniform job needs of these students, when I interviewed them a year after graduation, I found that most never had any need to write telexes. Of course, since that time telexes have been replaced twice, first by the fax machine and then by e-mail.

Skill and Knowledge Goals

A third general rule of thumb is that in a course it is often best to have a mix of skill goals (listening, speaking, reading, and writing) and knowledge goals (vocabulary, grammar, and cultural information). As noted in chapter 2, students vary considerably in their learning styles; some students are better at memorizing, others at communication, and others at grammatical accuracy. By including both skill and content goals, you give students with different strengths an opportunity to demonstrate their ability, thereby increasing the chances that they can shine in some aspect of your course.

Building Students' Interest in English Study

Finally, enhancing students' interest in English study should in itself be a major goal. English teachers naturally tend to assume that students should be motivated to study English, so you may need to remind yourself that students often have no personal reason for being in your English class; they may be there purely because the course is a required part of a curriculum. In these cases, students are naturally interested only in what will get them past the test, and you cannot assume that their interest will go beyond such pragmatic concerns. If you want them to become genuinely interested in English study—as they must if they are to eventually master the language—you will need to make this a goal to work toward rather than an assumption to work from.

Materials: The Textbook

While teachers in EFL contexts are sometimes confronted with the problem of not having a textbook for a course, the increasing availability of English teaching materials worldwide means that this problem is increasingly rare, and more often than not EFL teachers are either assigned textbooks or at least have access to textbooks on which they can base their courses.[2] With regard to the issue of course planning, I suspect that the greater problem for most novice English teachers is the one mentioned in the introduction to this chapter, the temptation to short-circuit the goal-setting process by letting a textbook become a substitute for the course goals and plan. When this happens, course planning is reduced to a simple matter of covering the book.

As I have already suggested, covering the book is not a bad thing in and of itself. In fact, basing a course closely on a textbook can have many significant advantages:

- Basing a course on a textbook may save you lesson preparation time.

- The textbook provides continuity to the course and helps prevent it from degenerating into a series of unrelated activities.

- It facilitates students' study and review.

- Use of the textbook can help students feel better about their English study because it allows them to see progress in a very concrete way as they work through the book.

However, relying too heavily on a textbook to set the direction for your course can also result in a number of problems. The first is that, by design, textbooks generally include more material than you can reasonably teach. Textbook writers tend to assume that it is better to give you and the students too much material than too little, so they generally choose to provide more material than you could teach in the expected amount of time. For example, a single unit of a recent college English reading textbook written in China, *College English, Intensive Reading Book* (Shanghai Foreign Language Education Press 1997), contains all of the following: a two-page reading passage, notes on the passage, two vocabulary lists, fourteen exercises of various types, a two-page reading activity, a translation exercise, a writing exercise, and a paragraph-writing assignment. If you have a clear set of course goals that help you decide what parts of the textbook to emphasize, what parts to skim over quickly, and what parts to ignore, this wealth of material is not a problem. However, if you don't have such course goals to guide you, your choices may lack consistency and even become somewhat arbitrary.

A second problem that can occur when courses are based too closely on a textbook is a tendency to overemphasize the kinds of things a textbook conveys relatively well, especially knowledge of English grammar and vocabulary and perhaps reading skills. Heavy focus on a textbook can also encourage a corresponding neglect of language skills that are not so closely tied to textbooks, such as speaking and listening skills. While the increasing focus on oral English skills in many countries means that this has not been as much of a problem in recent years as it once was, the tendency to make covering the textbook the main goal of language courses is still one reason many students get an inadequate diet of speaking and listening practice.

However, the greatest problem is simply that when the goals of a course consist mainly of

---

[2] Of course, textbooks are not the only kinds of materials used in English courses; there are also a variety of audio or visual materials, and even computer software programs, that serve as the material for English courses. However, even when such materials are available, they are often accompanied by a textbook, and a great many English courses around the world are still based first and foremost on textbooks.

covering the material in textbooks, students gradually develop a sense that studying the textbook itself has become the goal. When this happens, English study becomes a formal exercise of moving page by page through a book. Such a goal has little power to engage or sustain students' interest in language study and may cause them to lose sight of the ultimate goals of English study.

The point here is not that textbooks are bad; in fact, when used properly to serve the goals of a course, a textbook can be a very useful tool that not only provides students with language input but also helps give direction and even a sense of progress to the course. However, a textbook should serve the goals of a course, and this means that teachers need to have a clear sense of what the goals of the course are so that these goals can be the basis for deciding when and how the textbook is used. When the textbook becomes a substitute for the goals of a course, all too often English study is reduced to page turning.

Methods

Teachers do not choose their teaching methods in a vacuum. Their choice of methods is significantly affected by the kinds of methods suggested in whatever course materials they teach and by the kinds of methods generally used by their colleagues. Also, as is often noted, choice of methods is influenced greatly by teachers' previous experience as learners, the "apprenticeship of observation" during which they spend thousands of hours watching their own teachers from primary school up through university (Bailey et al. 1996). So, to some extent, teachers' choices of teaching methods come to them ready-made.

To some extent, this is a good thing, especially for beginning teachers. A great deal of pedagogical wisdom can be found in textbooks and in the experience of other teachers you have ovbserved, and beginning teachers should take advantage of this rather than trying to reinvent the teaching profession from scratch through trial and error. However, you also need to be somewhat cautious as you draw on the methods that are suggested in textbooks or that you have seen other teachers use. While these methods may be good in and of themselves, you also need to consider how well they are suited to the goals you have set for your course. Borrowing methods from a textbook or from experience without due consideration can sometimes result in a mismatch between the method and the goal. To be effective for your courses, the methods you use must fit the goals you have set.

Consider the following example. I once took an oral skills course in Japanese in which the main method used for building oral skills consisted of having the students memorize dialogues in Japanese and then recite them from memory in class, as fluently as possible. This method had some real advantages to it, not the least of which was that it forced students to memorize quite a lot of Japanese sentences (many of which I remember even a decade later). However, as an approach to building oral communication skills, heavy reliance on this method also had some serious flaws, the main one being that it did relatively little to build our listening skills. Of course, there was a recording that contained the dialogues we were to memorize, so some listening practice was provided. However, every sentence we heard on the recordings we had already studied in the textbook, so we already knew what each one meant and didn't have to worry about comprehension. This left us ill-prepared for listening tests on which we were asked to make sense of Japanese sentences that we had not heard before—and ill-prepared to converse with real Japanese people. In short, heavy reliance on the dialogue memorization method did not match the stated goal of the course—building oral communication skills—very well.

Here I should emphasize that my intent is not to criticize dialogue memorization per se; in fact, it can be a very effective study method. Furthermore, if this method had been balanced with other activities that provided more listening practice, the results would probably have been much better. (Unfortunately, the time and effort involved in memorizing so many dialogues left the students with little time to find other Japanese practice opportunities.) The point is that while this particular method was a useful component in a program of Japanese study, overemphasis on it resulted in inadequate attention to other important aspects of oral communication skills. In short, when teachers—and students—choose methods and practice activities, they need to carefully consider what kinds of skills and knowledge the goals require, and then be sure that the methods used provide what is needed.

The question of what kinds of methods are appropriate to what kinds of goals will be addressed in more detail in chapters 6–12. A few general observations may be helpful here, however. The first is a rule of thumb: the best way to develop a language skill is to practice it, and the more the practice method resembles the actual application of the skill, the better. Simply put, the best way to learn to speak is to practice speaking, the best way to learn to read is to practice reading, and so on.[3] This rule might seem obvious, but not all methods suggested in textbooks or passed on to you by other teachers follow it, so both you and the students need to learn how to analyze what is involved in whatever skill students need to develop and how to design practice methods that replicate that skill as fully as possible.

A second observation is that while you should choose methods based on how well they fit your goals, you also need to consider what methods will be acceptable to the students. Some educationally sound methods may not work in your class because students find them too uncomfortable, too unfamiliar, too dubious, or simply too weird. In EFL settings, you need to pay particular attention to this problem because the students in a class will share a great number of common beliefs and customs concerning language study. You may run into united resistance if you adopt methods (perhaps based on ideas about communicative language teaching you learned in a university EFL teaching methods course) that conflict too much with the students' ideas. The question you need to ask yourself is, to what extent am I willing to invest time and effort in persuading students to reconfigure their approaches to language learning? It is impossible to predict how strongly a group of students will resist new and different methods for language learning—they may even be delighted to try a new approach. However, in general, the more your methods differ from those students are used to, the more time you will need to spend explaining and selling the methods. Failure to do adequate public relations work may result in increasing resistance and decreased cooperation from the class. So when you are planning your course, it is best to take a good look at your reserves of patience and take a radically innovative approach only if you are also willing—if necessary—to invest time and effort in selling your program.

Last but not least, when deciding what methods to use in a course, teachers need to have a very clear idea of what the goals of the course are. While your choice of methods is determined in part by your textbook and local teaching traditions, you generally have at least some freedom to decide what methods you will use in class and how often. Within that range of choice, as much as possible, choose methods and materials that lead to the goals you have set for the course.

---

[3] Obviously, I overstate the case a bit. As Nunan (1989, 40–45) points out, both real-world tasks (practice activities that resemble actual use) and pedagogic tasks (activities like grammar drills that isolate one specific aspect of a skill) can be useful. I emphasize real-world tasks in part because teachers tend to err on the side of using too many pedagogical tasks (often suggested by textbooks) instead of more realistic and communicative tasks.

THESIS WRITING—SYLLABUS (FALL 2005)

Dr. Don Snow

OVERALL GOALS OF THE COURSE

- Prepare you for writing your MA thesis.
- Prepare you for future research/academic writing.

SPECIFIC GOALS OF THE COURSE

Help you improve your

- research skills
- critical analysis skills
- paper planning (outlining) and organizing skills
- written English accuracy
- editing skills
- familiarity with proper citation and bibliographic format

MATERIALS: Handouts provided by the instructor.

OVERALL COURSE PLAN: The course will be organized around four projects:

1. an issue review paper in which you will choose an issue, read the relevant literature, and write a paper summarizing the discussion to date and ending with outstanding questions

2. a critical response paper in which you will read an article and write a critical response

3. a paper in which you will explain the issue you have chosen for your MA thesis and its significance

4. a preliminary outline of your MA thesis. This will involve writing a preliminary outline of your MA thesis, especially the first few chapters, focusing on the outstanding questions and research questions.

EVALUATION

Grades for this course will be based on your written assignments. (No tests.)

The Syllabus

One of the most effective ways to communicate the goals and overall design of your course to students is by giving them a syllabus, a handout written in either English or the local language in which you lay out the overall plan for your course.

As the sample syllabus in the box (for an EFL academic skills writing course) suggests, the basic parts of a typical syllabus are generally as follows:

1. the name of the course

2. your name and whatever contact information you wish to give students

3. the goals of the course (Dividing goals into the categories of overall and specific goals, as in the sample, can be useful but is not necessary unless you find it helpful.)

4. materials to be used in the course (This is especially helpful if students are expected to locate and buy their own textbooks.)

5. an overview of the course plan (Sometimes a syllabus includes a day-by-day agenda covering each class meeting, but generally it simply gives students a general outline of the flow of events in the course.)

6. an indication of how the course will be evaluated

One obvious advantage of making a syllabus for each course you teach is that it can help you plan and organize your courses; another is that giving students a syllabus is an effective way to communicate basic information about a course to them. But there is also a third important advantage: the impact that a syllabus has on students' motivation. Giving students a syllabus, and going over it with them on the first day of a course, helps give them a sense that the course has clear direction and purpose. (As with introducing the goals of a course, I would suggest that you generally discuss the syllabus in the local language rather than in English, especially if the syllabus is written in English.) Being able to see the overall plan of a course in this way helps them be more aware of the big picture—where they are going in the course and why—and this awareness tends to help build and sustain student motivation.

Language Learning Projects (LLPs): Working toward Breakthrough

As indicated at the beginning of the chapter, your ultimate goal is not only to teach students English language knowledge and skills; it is also to help them learn how to effectively plan and carry out their own language learning. Students who only obediently do what the teacher tells them to will not be very well prepared for the day when they are on their own. While still in formal language courses, they need to begin developing the habit of designing and carrying out their own language learning plans because this is what they will need to be able to do when they leave those courses. For this purpose, LLPs are useful in preparing students for autonomy—for the day when the apron strings are cut and they need to continue studying on their own without the benefit of a teacher and a ready-made course. Because LLPs have already been introduced in some detail (see chapter 1), here I address the question of how to integrate them into the English courses you teach. If you want to use LLPs to prepare students for life after your course ends, students need to begin doing LLPs and developing autonomous language study habits and skills long before graduation day.

As Nunan (1997, 193) argues, autonomy is a relative concept rather than an all-or-nothing proposition, and determining how much independence students are ready for and how much guidance they need at any given point is an art more than a science. My own approach is as follows:

*   If my sense is that students are not yet very accustomed to the idea of working on their own, I ask them to carry out limited-choice LLPs in which students only make some of the choices, often from a limited range of options. For example, for a course that involves a reading component, I might require that students do an LLP focused on building their reading skills but then have them choose specific goals (e.g., whether to focus more on building reading speed or on vocabulary) or the books they want to read. In this approach, in essence you fill out part of the LLP for students, provide a menu of choices

48

for other parts, and give them free choice in yet other parts. (When doing LLPs with students who are not yet accustomed to the idea of carrying out their own language learning plans and who may not have yet developed a high level of self-discipline, it is generally good to require a fairly high degree of accountability from students, perhaps in the form of journals, as suggested below.)

- If students seem to be ready for more autonomy, you can ask them to design and carry out full-choice LLPs in which they have a great deal of latitude in choosing their own goals, materials, and methods; demands for accountability would also be lighter.

For both limited-choice and full-choice LLP assignments, you would presumably ask students to make up an LLP plan that you would then provide feedback on. However, how much accountability you expect after that point depends on your sense of how willing students are to take responsibility for their own progress.

Keep in mind that students will not necessarily be able to design good LLP plans on their first try. Common problems are too many goals, vague goals, unrealistically high expectations, or mismatch between the goals and the methods. So, when you assign the LLPs, talk with students about how to design a good plan, and provide models to illustrate the concept. You will probably also need to help students during the first few weeks as they begin trying to carry out their plans, discover problems, and need to adjust or modify their plans.

One effective way to help students learn to carry out LLPs involves having them keep a journal in which they write about their LLP study. I normally suggest that the journal consist of two parts: (1) log entries in which students briefly record what they did during each LLP study session and (2) a reflections entry in which they comment on what does and does not seem to be working in their LLP. Students should make journal entries each time they study. You then collect the journals and respond with comments, suggestions, and encouragement. While keeping a journal adds to the time invested in the LLP, that additional time can be minimal. Also, keep in mind that the ultimate goal—building students' ability and willingness to engage in effective language learning on their own—is worth quite a bit of effort.

When introducing the idea of LLPs to students—and generally when teaching them about language learning—one of your greatest advantages as a local teacher is your ability to communicate with students in their first language. While talking with students in the local language about these things may deny students a little extra English listening practice, it dramatically enhances your ability to quickly and effectively help students learn very important skills. My personal feeling is that unless the students' English listening skills are quite advanced, you should normally take advantage of your native language competence in teaching about these issues. Furthermore, with regard to journals and LLPs, unless the students are at very advanced English levels, it is generally a good idea to allow students to keep journals in their first language rather than in English. While writing journal entries in English gives students a little additional English writing practice, it also dramatically increases the amount of time and effort that keeping a journal will involve. Students sometimes perceive LLPs as extra work, and when this extra burden is increased by the demand that they do a lot of writing in English, students are more likely to resent the assignment. (Keep in mind here that the whole idea is to increase students' willingness to do such projects.) Also, writing journal entries in English tends to distract students from the primary purpose of the journal, which is reflection on their English study rather than practice writing in English. If students find it difficult to express what they really think in English, often they will write down something else that is less authentic and interesting but easier to express in English, or simply omit much of what they would have said if allowed to use their first language. Your ability to read and respond to their journals in the first language makes it easier for you to oversee LLPs than it would be for

English teachers who don't know the local language. This is one of the areas in which your ability to communicate with students in their first language is a particularly valuable asset.

Toward the end of your course, a good way to increase the chances that students will follow through with their own study program after leaving your course is to talk with them about how to set up and carry out their own future study plans. Again, you might even have them write down a plan that you can then go over with them. Of course, there is no guarantee that students will follow through on the plans, but this is one last chance to encourage them and get them thinking about the issue. If your course has let students take the responsibility for at least some of their own language learning efforts, there is a good chance that their English study life will continue even after their formal English study program ends.

For Thought, Discussion, and Action

1. **setting goals (task A):** Pick one of the two courses described below, decide what goals you would set for that course, and discuss your choices with a friend or classmate. After you discuss your goal choice, look at Sample Courses One and Six in appendix B as a point of reference.

    • Beginning-Level General English: This secondary school English course is for a class of fifty students who have had little previous study of English. The students have already studied a few basic grammar structures and some vocabulary, and they can say a few common phrases, but they understand very little of what you say in class—including most classroom directions. This required course is part of the regular curriculum, so students expect to do some homework most evenings. The textbook for the course contains simple dialogues, short readings, vocabulary, and grammar notes. Your school expects you to teach the material in the book.

    • The English Club: This informal evening class, which is open to anyone, meets once a week for English conversation practice. The students who come have a wide range of skill levels. There is little consistency in who shows up or how large the group is. Some students are very interested in improving their English, and others are mainly interested in having fun and meeting new friends. There is no textbook, and no examination is expected. The sponsors' only stated goal is that participants improve their English, but an important implicit goal is that participants enjoy the class.

2. **setting goals (task B):** Using the models in number 1, write out a description of one typical course that you teach now or expect to teach in the future. Then do the following:

    • List any goals that are already set for the course (by the curriculum, textbook, or standardized test)—in other words, goals about which you would have no choice.

    • List additional goals you could set for the course, goals about which you do have some choice. Be sure to consider the possibility of setting goals for building language learning skill and motivation as well as goals for building English knowledge and skills.

    • Discuss your course and goals with a friend or classmate. Explain the situation, and explain why you set the (additional) goals you did.

3. **matching goals and methods:** Choose an English skill course you might teach (speaking, listening, reading, or writing) and the level at which you might teach it (beginning, intermediate, or advanced). Turn to the Goals Menu (appendix A), and find suggested goals

for your course and level. Based on the goals suggested there, list the teaching methods and practice activities you think would help students achieve those goals. (Keep in mind that a practice activity should be as much as possible like the actual skill it is intended to build.)

4. **analyzing a method:** In China, one practice method commonly used by students to develop their speaking skills is getting up early in the morning to spend half an hour or so reading lessons from their textbook aloud. Analyze this English study method, and list the goals this method would help students achieve. Be as specific as possible.

5. **analyzing a textbook:** Choose a textbook that you have taught or may have to teach in the future, analyze it, and list its strengths and weaknesses. Then consider these questions:
   - What is the best way to use this textbook in a course?
   - What parts of it would you emphasize and use the most?
   - What parts would you deemphasize or skip entirely?

6. **designing LLPs:** Imagine you will teach the following course:

   This general English course is for students who will finish a training program at the end of the semester and begin working as secondary school English teachers. A reading text is available for your course, but the school has given you considerable freedom to decide what you will teach and what materials you will use. The students have a fair command of basic grammar and vocabulary, can understand clear English, and can read newspaper and magazine articles—although only with difficulty and the help of a dictionary. After graduation, these students will work in places where there are few naturally occurring opportunities to use English outside their classrooms, and when they teach, they will only need to use very basic English. (Many of their English teaching colleagues will not use English in class at all.) Under these circumstances, it is not unusual for the skills of graduates to gradually deteriorate.

   Design one or more possible LLPs students could do as a part of this course to prepare them for continued English study after graduation. Be sure to realistically consider the kinds of possibilities these students might have to use English and the kinds of English language resources that might be available to them.

Chapter 4

Evaluation, Grading, and Backwash

- In-class evaluation is valuable not only for determining students' skill levels but also as a way of holding students accountable and encouraging them to keep working.

- *Backwash,* the impact that your evaluation methods have on what and how students study, is a very important factor to consider as you decide how to evaluate students.

- When designing tests for your courses, as much as possible you should use *direct measures,* in other words, testing measures that require students to perform in ways that are similar to real-life English use.

- When grading a group of students, you should try to strike a balance between improvement-based grading (measuring student progress against an objective scale) and class-curve grading (comparing students' performances with those of their peers). The former is fairer but can be more difficult to do well. The latter is more convenient and often more readily understood but is less fair.

In many countries around the world, English teaching is dominated to a large degree by nationwide, standardized examinations that students are required to take at various points in their academic lives. These tests often significantly shape the context in which students study English and have a great impact on how motivated they are to study English, what aspects of English study they focus on most, and what study methods they use. In many ways, these tests form the larger environment in which you will teach English.

However, for several reasons, these tests are not the main focus of this chapter. First, the precise kinds and roles of standardized tests vary considerably from one country to the next, and it would be impossible to discuss in detail the situation in each country. Second, if you learned English in the educational system of the country where you teach, you are no doubt already very familiar with the role that such standardized tests play in English teaching in your country. Finally, as a classroom teacher, you will probably have relatively little control over the system of standardized tests in your country, region, or perhaps even your own school.

The focus of this chapter is therefore on what you do have some degree of control over—the evaluation measures that you use in your own courses. These evaluation measures include tests and examinations, but they also include graded homework assignments, notes on classroom participation, and compositions written for portfolios. In short, evaluation consists of any way in which you measure and judge students' knowledge or skills. In particular, I focus on the general issue of how you use evaluation measures in your courses to encourage students to build actual English proficiency, as opposed to just good test-taking skills. (Specific measures for evaluating listening, speaking, vocabulary, and other areas are discussed in chapters 6–11.)

The Purposes and Effects of Evaluation

PURPOSES OF EVALUATION

Tests and other evaluative measures come in a variety of colors; tests alone can be broken down into four or more major categories.[1] However, the underlying purposes of almost all classroom evaluation fall into two major categories:

1. **diagnostic:** Evaluation is often a process through which teachers and school authorities assess how much progress students have made in their English study and what level of achievement they have reached. Such information can then be used for a variety of purposes, such as helping students know whether they are making progress and what areas of English study they need to work harder on, or helping the teacher determine how effectively a language course facilitates students' learning. Of course, teachers, school authorities, and even potential employers often use the resulting scores and grades to make judgments such as which students should be allowed to enter a school, what level of course they should be admitted to, which students should be given awards or scholarships, which should be eliminated from a program, or which should be given jobs.

2. **motivational:** The second main reason for evaluation lies in the impact it has on students' motivation. The most obvious motivational effect of evaluation on students is the incentive it gives them to study harder, but this is not the only reason evaluation can have a positive impact on student motivation. Madsen (1983, 4) points out that evaluation can

---

[1] See Madsen (1983, 8–9), Hughes (1989, 9), Bailey (1998, 37–39), and Harmer (2001, 321) for further discussion. For a theoretical introduction to language testing, see Bachman (1990) and Bachman and Palmer (1996).

also give students a sense of accomplishment by helping them see what they have learned, which can translate into more positive attitudes toward study.

No matter whether the intended purpose of evaluation is diagnostic or motivational, it has significant power to positively or negatively affect how students study. Of course, you often have only limited choice in how you evaluate and grade in your courses; many evaluation measures will already be set by the school system within which you teach. However, you will presumably have at least some choice about what evaluation measures you will use, and within the limits of what you can control, the issue to consider is how to use evaluation measures to motivate students to study in ways that will help them achieve the goals of the course. This leads to discussion of the phenomenon known as *backwash*.

WHAT IS *BACKWASH*?

A critically important issue to consider when planning evaluation methods is backwash (also known as *washback*), that is, the effect of your evaluation methods on students' study and practice methods. Put simply, students tend to do what they are rewarded for and not to do what they are not rewarded for. Thus, for example, if your tests and quizzes frequently include a listening comprehension section, students are likely to work on their listening. In contrast, if you rely entirely on written tests, students are not likely to invest much time in developing speaking skills, no matter how important you say oral practice is. Backwash is strongest when grades are very important to students, but even when grades aren't important, backwash can still occur because students, quite understandably, assume that the evaluation system reflects the teacher's sense of priorities.

Backwash can have either a positive or a negative impact on learning, depending on how closely the evaluation methods reflect the skill that students are supposed to develop. For example, if your goal is to build students' ability to express their ideas in English but you grade their exercises primarily on grammatical accuracy, the backwash will pull them away from the goal; in contrast, if you grade students' effectiveness in communicating their ideas, your evaluation measures will push them toward the goal. Well-designed evaluation methods ensure that the best scores go to those students who have studied and practiced in the desired manner and will encourage students to use good study methods.

Note that some kinds of evaluation measures encourage students to study or practice in ways that both prepare them for evaluation and help them build useful proficiency in English. For example, if you use interviews to test students' speaking skills, they are encouraged to prepare by speaking English to each other, perhaps practicing interview questions and answers in pairs. Such practice not only prepares students for the evaluation but is also very good for building spoken English proficiency. In contrast, use of other kinds of evaluation measures, such as fill-in-the-blank grammar test items, encourages students to study in ways that are of more limited use in building communicative language proficiency. Backwash becomes a problem mainly if you often use evaluation measures that encourage students to study in ways that help them get good grades but are not so useful in helping them build usable language skills.

ENSURING POSITIVE BACKWASH

Here are a number of suggestions for ensuring that the backwash from your evaluation measures is positive (see also Hughes 1989, 44–47):

1. Test the skills you want students to develop, even if it is not always easy. This advice might seem self-evident, but in practice this rule is often violated. As Hughes (1989) notes, "Too often the content of tests is determined by what is easy to test rather than what is

important to test" (p. 23). For example, the difficulty of interviewing large numbers of students means that interviews are not included in standardized tests such as the Test of English as a Foreign Language (TOEFL), and the result is that oral proficiency receives minimal attention from students preparing for such exams. The bottom line is that if you want students to practice a skill, you need to include it somehow in evaluation.

2. Ensure that students know in advance how they will be evaluated. Students who are surprised by the way a midterm or final examination is designed are not only likely to do less well but also have more reason to be resentful. In contrast, using in-class practice, homework, and quizzes to prepare students for an examination is not only fairer but also more likely to ensure that they study in productive and appropriate ways.

3. Use direct testing measures as much as possible. A *direct measure* is one that requires students to do more or less what they would need to do in real life. For example, an interview is a direct measure because it requires students to engage in real conversation. An *indirect measure,* in contrast, assesses only one discrete portion of a skill. A test in which students only pronounce words in isolation would be an indirect measure.[2] The distinction between indirect and direct measures is important because the more direct an evaluation measure is, the more likely it is to have positive backwash on students. Direct measures require students to practice skills in ways similar to how the skills would actually be used; indirect measures inevitably push students toward practicing discrete-point skills that are virtually never used in isolation in real life. (How often do people need to fill in blanks with correct verb tenses?) In other words, direct measures tend to encourage students to study and practice in ways that are more useful in building actual English proficiency.

This is not to say that all indirect testing is bad. Properly used, it provides a rapid way to check on and encourage important aspects of language learning such as pronunciation and vocabulary acquisition. However, evaluation for a course should not rely on indirect measures alone, and direct measures should generally carry more weight in determining grades. (For this reason, most of the evaluation measures suggested in this book are direct measures.)

Methods of Evaluation

TESTS

The backbone of evaluation in many educational systems consists of tests, especially midterm and final examinations. In fact, testing is so often the primary form of evaluation that some people tend to assume that testing and evaluation are virtually synonymous. Thus, I begin this discussion of testing by pointing out the many disadvantages of heavy reliance on tests.

Many problems with tests derive from the fact that they judge the work of several weeks or months based on a single, brief performance. One undesirable result is considerable pressure and anxiety for students, often more than is productive. Because of the unusual amount of pressure that tests generate, they are especially likely to produce negative backwash, including encouraging students to engage in short, intense periods of cramming rather than regular study and practice.

---

[2] This distinction is similar to that between integrative and discrete-point testing. See Bailey (1998, 75–77) for further discussion.

Another common problem with testing derives from the types of items often used on tests. While some common item types are direct measures, it is not uncommon for tests to include many indirect measures, such true/false, fill-in-the-blank, and multiple-choice items. The prevalence of this kind of testing is not surprising because there is a long tradition of testing language skills in this way, and these kinds of items are used heavily in standardized tests like the TOEFL. However, backwash from this kind of testing is generally negative because students are forced to become experts at guessing how to fill in blanks rather than learning how to really use language. Hughes (1989) also notes that "Good multiple choice items are notoriously difficult to write" and that most multiple-choice tests used by schools are "shot through with faults" (pp. 3, 61).

Despite the problems, it may be neither possible nor desirable to abandon testing entirely. Midterm and final examinations are deeply embedded in the educational systems of many countries, and you may have no choice in the matter. Another reality is that students may be confronted with other tests after leaving your course, and lack of experience in test taking would put them at a disadvantage. Finally, well-designed testing can motivate students to study and review productively. In short, the question is often not whether or not you should give tests but how to make sure that tests have the best possible backwash.

Test design and administration are topics normally addressed by a chapter or an entire book; here I suggest only a few of the most basic points to which you should attend when designing tests for use in your own courses.

1. As suggested above, use direct test items as much as possible. For example, to test listening, have students listen to a talk and then write a summary or write short answers to comprehension questions; to test writing, have students write a letter; and so forth. Direct testing tends to have better backwash than indirect testing, and a serviceable direct test is generally easier to design than a good indirect test because fewer tricks are involved.[3] (I should also explicitly point out that using direct test items for in-class tests does not mean that you are not preparing students for standardized examinations. Most standardized tests contain direct test items, so by using them in tests for your courses, you are preparing students for such items on standardized examinations. Furthermore, the proficiency that direct test items encourage students to develop generally stands them in good stead when they need to take standardized examinations.)

2. If you must use multiple-choice questions, true/false items, or the like, be sure to use an adequate number of these items. When tests only have a few items, each counts for a large percentage of the final score, and luck plays too large a role.

3. Check a test before administering it. It is not unusual for even a carefully crafted examination to have serious flaws that escape the eye of the test designer. One good way to minimize the possibility of problems is to have another teacher look over your test beforehand.

4. Use quizzes and practice tests to introduce students to your testing methods well before the midterm. This familiarizes students with the test format, gives you an opportunity to find and correct flaws in your approach, and maximizes the possibility of positive backwash by giving students a clear idea of how they should prepare.

---

[3] For further discussion of why multiple-choice items are so hard to design, see Bailey (1998, 130); see also Harmer (2001, 323).

5. Make your tests cumulative. There is little sense in requiring students to learn the material in unit eight for the midterm, only to rule it out of bounds for the final. By promising not to test students on material covered earlier in the term, you reduce language learning to a game and increase the chances that students will lose sight of the ultimate goal.

While abandoning testing entirely may not be either possible or wise, "it is advisable to evaluate students in a number of different ways rather than to rely almost exclusively on formal exams" (Bowen, Madsen, and Hilferty 1985, 356). Concentrating evaluation in a few major examinations increases pressure, test anxiety, and the temptation to cheat or cram rather than really learn material. It also maximizes the role of chance—one bad headache can seriously affect a student's grade if the grade is based mostly on one test. Tests are best used in conjunction with other evaluation methods.

QUIZZES

For several reasons, I advocate quizzes as a major part of any package of evaluation measures. First, quizzes are shorter than tests, so you can give them more frequently, thus spreading the evaluation process out over time rather than packing it into a few exams. This tends to both lower test anxiety and minimize the role of chance in determining grades. Frequent quizzes also help students get into the habit of studying regularly and discourage reliance on infrequent bouts of cramming as a learning strategy. Finally, quizzes "have even been known to help improve attendance, punctuality of arrival, and discipline at the outset of the class period" (Bowen, Madsen, and Hilferty 1985, 357). Here are a few suggestions on using quizzes:

- For maximum positive impact, give quizzes reasonably regularly, and make sure students know in advance what you expect of them. Pop quizzes—those that are unexpected and unannounced—may do more to alienate the class than to motivate study. Predictable, regular quizzes are fairer and more likely to promote study.

- Make the format of quiz items similar to the formats of the kinds of items you will use for tests. Otherwise, quizzes may mislead students as to how to prepare for tests.

- Keep quizzes short. It is only because of their brevity that you can find time to give and correct them regularly, and a short quiz is often all it takes to give students the extra push to do an assignment.

HOMEWORK AND IN-CLASS WORK

An obvious and important alternative to testing is evaluation based on homework assignments or in-class work. For example, writing can and should be evaluated based on many compositions rather than on one supreme, in-class effort at the end of the semester. Likewise, speaking can be judged in part based on performance in many small exercises during the whole semester rather than on one intense interview. Such an approach reduces fixation on examinations and shifts students' attention to the daily work of study and practice.

PORTFOLIOS

Another alternative to a final exam is having students make portfolios, that is, having students select the best pieces of work they did during the semester and then turn it in to you for a final grade. This approach works most naturally in writing courses, where you can have students choose, revise, and hand in a certain number of their best compositions. However, with a little creativity, you can adapt the basic principle underlying this approach—the idea that students get to choose their best work for evaluation—to other kinds of work as well. For example, you could include reading by having students read books, write reviews, and then turn in their best ones. In a speaking course, you might ask students to write dialogues or do role plays, tape their best work, and submit the tape. The main advantages of portfolios are that they draw on all the work a student does during the semester rather than reducing judgment to one all-important test and that they encourage students to assess, revise, and improve their own work.

SELF-ASSESSMENT

One final idea is to involve students in assessing their own work and perhaps even allow them to have a limited voice in determining their final grade. Consider the following self-assessment method for an oral English class, in which students fill out the three-item form in the box at the end of each class period.[4] The main advantage of using a form like this one is its positive back-wash—it encourages students to assess their own effort and serves as a regular reminder that their English progress depends largely on how hard they work, not on how well the teacher performs. It also allows students an opportunity to give the teacher feedback on a range of issues and helps the teacher stay in touch with students' responses to and feelings about the course.

SELF-EVALUATION FORM

1. I tried _____ % to use English in class today.

   90–100%   I tried my best to use English today. (I prepared well for this lesson before class, and I used only English with my partners.)

   80–89%   I tried hard to use English today. (I prepared for this lesson before class, and I used English with my partners almost the whole time.)

   70–79%   I tried to use English today. (I prepared a little for this lesson before class, and I used English with my partners most of the time.)

   60–69%   I tried a little to use English today. (I didn't prepare for this lesson before class, but I used English with my partners over half the time.)

   0–59%   I didn't really try to use English today. (I didn't prepare for this lesson, and I used English with my partners less than half the time.)

2. Today I think I learned:

   ☐   a lot of English

   ☐   some English

   ☐   a little English

   ☐   almost no English

3. Comments:

---

[4] This form was generously provided by Jay Lundelius from his courses in Kinjo Women's College in Nagoya, Japan.

Other forms of self-assessment might entail

- **having students check their own work:** For example, after a listening exercise, you might give a copy of the text to students and have them check their own answers or summaries.

- **requiring students to present a short critique of their work:** For example, at the end of a composition, students might be asked to state one or two of its strong and weak points. (This, incidentally, can make it easier for you to give feedback.)

- **having students submit a tentative grade for their work, along with a rationale:** The necessity of stating a rationale should help prevent students from taking this as a joke and provides a point from which you can give students a useful reality check. It may also be instructive for you to see what students think about the quality of their work.

While the idea of involving students in assessing their own work may at first sound somewhat idealistic, remember that, in the long run, this is one of the most important habits students need to develop. Students will not always be in formal English classes where they can rely on a teacher to assess their work and give them feedback; after graduation they will need to be able to do such things for themselves. By using even limited self-assessment measures in your classes, you can begin teaching students this very important lesson.

Grading

It is probably not too much of an oversimplification to say that there are two basic approaches to grading. The first and more common is to see a grade as indicating a student's level of ability at a given point in time, and this is often determined by comparing the student with his or her class-mates. The other approach is to see the grade as indicating how much improvement a student has made over a period of time, in which case the student is measured against himself or herself. Here I briefly examine the advantages and disadvantages of these two approaches to grading.

CLASS-CURVE GRADING

Many teachers and school systems grade using a class curve[5]—that is, comparing the performance of the student being graded with the performance of other students in the class. This approach to grading is very common and seems quite natural; however, it is also inherently somewhat unfair because students' grades are determined as much by the other students in the class as they are by the students' own ability. A young woman unfortunate enough to have unusually bright classmates—or classmates who have had more previous exposure to English—will probably be permanently condemned to lower grades than she would have had in a duller group (unless she can manage to wrest a higher class standing from some other member of the class and knock him or her down the ladder).

I would not want to exaggerate the potential of curve grading to create bad feelings in your classes. Despite the potential unfairness of such an approach, it is used so widely that most students accept it as an inevitable part of life, rather like colds or myopia. Grading on the curve also benefits many students—there are as many winners as losers—so it won't alienate an entire class. But you should not underestimate the potential of this approach to alienate some of the students in a class or to undermine their incentive to learn. When grades are based on comparison with

---

[5] The technical term for this is *norm-referenced grading*. See Bailey (1998, 35–37) for further discussion.

other students, students who learn more slowly—or those whose only sin was less English training before the course began—have to struggle simply to retain their current humble class ranking, and they may choose to give up rather than invest the extra effort needed to improve their class standing. They may also resent the overseer of such a system.

Despite the disadvantages of curve grading, I do not suggest doing away with it completely. First, eliminating class-curve grading simply isn't possible. Many if not most educational systems have it built into them, and you cannot change that fact single-handedly. Additionally, because curve grading is the norm in many school systems, students not only expect it but may even be confused by or uncomfortable with other approaches to grading.

Another reason that curve grading will not disappear soon is that it is too convenient. Grading on the curve is relatively easy, especially for a beginning teacher who is still in the process of figuring out the goals of a course. Comparing the performance of a group of students on a given task takes less preparation and planning because you can use a ready-made standard—the average performance of the students in that class. As you will see, other forms of grading require more preparation. Thus, what I suggest below is not that you abolish grading on the curve but rather that, in addition, you make a clear, genuine effort to award grades partly based on progress. This will go a long way toward restoring the motivation of weaker members of the class to keep plugging away.

IMPROVEMENT-BASED GRADING

If the goal of a course is to help students improve their English skills, it seems only reasonable to grade students based on how much they improve rather than on their level at any particular point in time. The motivational advantage of this approach for students who start out at a lower skill level is that they still have a relatively equal chance to get good grades; higher level students also see that, to get a good grade, they have to improve further rather than simply coasting along and doing the least work possible.

To measure improvement, you need to test students at the beginning of a course to determine their starting level of skill and then award final grades based on how much progress students make during the course. One way to measure this progress is by using a criteria system. Consider the sample scale on p. 62, designed for an oral skills course that stresses communicative effectiveness. With a form like this, you assess students' level at the beginning of the course, assess them again at the end, and base at least part of your grade on the amount of progress they make during the course.[6]

Given the advantages of improvement-based grading, why is it not used more often? One problem is that it can be difficult to see skill improvement over short periods of time, especially in broadly defined skill areas. Improvement in general skills such as reading and speaking takes place relatively slowly, and one or two months of study may not make enough difference for improvement to be noticeable. As Underhill (1987, 56) points out, this is particularly true at the advanced stages of English study, when progress becomes increasingly harder to detect. Considering the sample criteria system above, within a three-month course, students who started at level one might reach level two or even three, but a student who started at level four would probably still be in the four range at the end of the course. So, to be fair, any criteria system used for improvement-based grading needs to be designed in such a way that it does not unfairly penalize students who start at higher skill levels.

---

[6] For a more sophisticated speaking proficiency scale, see the American Council on the Teaching of Foreign Language's (1999) *ACTFL Proficiency Guidelines—Speaking.*

Beginning (1–2): For all topics, can express self only haltingly and with difficulty; is frequently unable to express ideas at all. Often fails to understand slow, clear, simple sentences, even after repetition or clarification. Mistakes (inaccurate pronunciation, intonation, or grammar) or limited vocabulary causes communication breakdowns.

Functional (3–4): Can discuss limited range of topics (self, immediate environment) with patient interviewer. However, on other topics communication is difficult and often breaks down; interviewer's patience is tried on almost all topics. Often misunderstands or fails to understand interviewer unless ideas are clarified or repeated. Mistakes sometimes interfere with communication, and lack of vocabulary seriously hinders communication.

Intermediate (5–6): Can discuss familiar topics easily and deeper or professional topics with difficulty. Can discuss own field much better than other topics of similar complexity. On unfamiliar topics, circumlocutions and breakdowns occur; patience of interviewer may be tried. Has trouble understanding rapid or informal speech but little trouble with clear, moderately slow speech. Range of vocabulary is adequate for familiar topics but still limits communication in some areas. Mistakes are still common but don't often interfere with communication.

Advanced (7–8): Can discuss wide range of topics; discusses own field with ease. Is occasionally forced to resort to circumlocutions or explanations by lack of vocabulary, but problem is generally resolved quickly; patience of interviewer is almost never tried. Communication virtually never breaks down on any but the most obscure topics. Can understand normal speech without difficulty and can follow some informal or rapid speech; interviewer doesn't need to pay any special attention to speech. Mistakes occur but rarely interfere with communication.

Nativelike (9–10): Easily discusses a broad range of topics and can understand even informal and rapid speech. Still has foreign accent, but this causes interviewer no difficulty. Mistakes are rare and almost never affect communication.

The second problem is that designing and using a good criteria system for a course takes time and effort, and requires you to think carefully about the skills and knowledge you expect students to gain. In order to design a criteria system, you need to do several things:

1. List the kinds of skills and knowledge you plan to assess. These items should be specifically tailored to the goals of the course.

2. For the low end of your scale, write a simple description of what you would expect the less advanced-level students in your course to know and be able to do in English at the beginning of your course.

3. For the high end of the scale, describe what you would expect the relatively advanced-level students to be able to do at the end of the course.

4. Then fill in the intermediate levels, basing this as closely as you can on the normal developmental pattern you expect of students in the course. (This is not always easy to do, and you may find that you need to gradually revise and refine your criteria system through trial and error.)

Obviously, creating and using such a criteria system requires more preparation than curve grading. In particular, it demands additional work from you at the early stages of the course, a time when you may still be focused more on getting through the next class period than on long-range plans. However, once designed and polished, a criteria system can be a very useful tool for adding an element of progress-based grading in your assessment.

RECOMMENDATIONS FOR COURSE GRADING

1. Base your grades on improvement as well as level of ability. Despite the problems involved in setting up an improvement-based grading system, in the long run the effort involved in setting goals and designing a criteria system works to your advantage because it forces you to prepare more carefully and ultimately makes your grading process simpler and fairer. Improvement-based grading also leads to more positive backwash than curve-based grading because the former focuses attention on skills rather than on classmates.

   However, as I have suggested, grading solely on improvement may be neither wise nor possible. It is difficult and problematic because the picture of student ability that such grades communicate may well be inaccurate. School authorities and others often take grades to indicate how good a student's English is, and your grades therefore need to represent ability as well as progress. It is therefore often wise to make the final grade a compromise between progress and ability. As for balancing ability and improvement (or effort) in grading, a good rule of thumb in borderline situations is to put a little extra weight on the side on which a student is stronger. One could argue that this is the fairest approach, and it is certainly the most politic.

2. Let students know how they will be graded. The most important way to ensure a sense of fairness in grading is to communicate clearly and regularly with students about what your goals and evaluation methods are and how you will grade. You can do this by explaining your grading system to students and by being consistent in the way you evaluate. Students who know what is expected of them are far less likely to become hostile over a bad grade than students who feel that they have been misled or caught by surprise.

For Thought, Discussion, and Action

1. **backwash:** Find a test paper that is or has been used in your country, and analyze it to see what kind of backwash you think it would have on students. Discuss your analysis with other English teachers from your country to see if their analysis agrees with yours.

2. **direct test measures:** Imagine you will teach the following course. (1) List evaluation measures you might use for this course, as well as your rationale for each. Describe each measure specifically. (2) Discuss your choices with a classmate or another teacher. (3) Optional: for a point of reference, look at the evaluation measures suggested for Sample Course Four in appendix B.

   Preparing for Study Abroad: This special one-semester preparation course is for people who are going abroad to study for graduate degrees in an English-speaking Western country. The students can read a broad range of materials in English, although they tend to read slowly, carefully, and with much dictionary use. They can understand much of what you say on general topics as long as you speak slowly and clearly, but they have trouble with natural or quick speech, and there are many words they can read but don't understand when spoken. The students are well motivated, but most also have jobs and sometimes cannot come to class or do homework. The course textbook consists mainly of articles about life abroad, and there is an accompanying tape on which the articles are read aloud. Main goals of the course include improving students' ability to (1) cope with long academic reading assignments, (2) follow academic lectures, (3) discuss academic readings, and (4) write academic papers.

3. **opinion poll:** Survey several friends (classmates, etc.) to find out the following: (1) What evaluation measures did they like least and most when they were students, and why? (2) What advice would they give for making the less palatable measures more palatable?

4. **portfolios:** For one course you expect to teach (or the course described in number 2 above), think of one or more ways you could incorporate some kind of portfolio as an evaluation measure. Discuss this question with other teachers to see what they think about the idea of portfolios.

5. **self-assessment (task A):** This chapter suggests that it may be good to include at least some student self-assessment in your courses and even possibly allow it to influence the final grade. How realistic do you think this idea is in the context where you teach? Is there any way you can reasonably incorporate some self-assessment in the courses you teach? Discuss this question with other teachers to see what they think; also ask whether they have ever tried using self-assessment or heard of a teacher trying it.

6. **self-assessment (task B):** Design a self-assessment form you might use for one of your own courses, either to encourage students to think more about how much effort they are investing in language study (like the sample form in this chapter) or to encourage some other kind of reflection you think will be useful for them.

7. **fair evaluation:** Discuss how to evaluate and grade in a way that motivates and encourages the weaker students in a course (those who tend to get low grades) as much as possible, yet is still fair and motivating for students who tend to get good grades.

8. **improvement-based grading:** This chapter suggests that it is desirable to determine students' grades at least partially based on how much improvement they make in English (not just how they rank in comparison with their classmates). Design one or more ways to incorporate some improvement-based grading in a course you will teach. Then discuss your ideas with other teachers.

9. **proficiency criteria:** Using the proficiency scale presented in this chapter as a model, design your own scale for one or more other courses (e.g., listening, reading, writing) that you might teach. After you finish, for a point of reference, you could compare your proficiency scale with those established by ACTFL (http://www.actfl.org/). At the time of writing, the Web site included proficiency scales for speaking and writing. Versions of the ACTFL proficiency guidelines for listening and reading can be found on a number of Web sites and in Rubin and Thompson (1994, 15–21), Omaggio Hadley (2001, 469–76), and Marshall (1989, 41–47).

Chapter 5

Lesson Planning and Classroom Survival

- Having a carefully constructed lesson plan in hand allows you to enter the classroom with considerably more confidence.

- Effective lesson planning, especially during your early days of teaching, rests heavily in good habits such as setting aside quality time for planning and putting the plan in writing.

- In lesson planning, one of the most important questions you need to consider is this: What is the best use of (precious, limited) in-class time? While a course textbook may help you decide the answer to this question, it cannot answer the question completely for you.

- Creating a warm, friendly class atmosphere makes teaching and learning easier for all concerned.

For all but the most self-confident novice teachers, the overwhelming priority during the first few months of teaching is getting through as many class periods as possible without disasters such as exercises that take twice as long as planned, instructions that students completely misunderstand, and activities that students respond to with overwhelming apathy. Another form of catastrophe—possibly the worst—is running out of activities when the class period is only half over. During my first year of teaching, my response when caught short was to have the class play Hangman, a harmless little spelling game that could easily dispatch half an hour of class time before everyone began to get restless. It didn't teach much English, but it allowed me to survive a class period without running out of material. In many ways, Hangman serves as a symbol of my early teaching days because the primary object of my class planning was to prevent myself from winding up like the hanging man himself, dangling in front of a class to which my inexperience had been suddenly revealed. As long as my focus was primarily on my own lack of confidence and need to avoid embarrassing myself, it was difficult to see past my needs to those of the students.

Ultimately, of course, your goal in each day's English lesson should be to provide a good learning experience for the students. However, until you have confidence that you can get through a lesson with your dignity intact, it is difficult to focus on higher level issues such as how to use the class period as effectively as possible. This chapter addresses the issue of planning for the class period, with an eye to getting you as quickly as possible past the survival stage.

Lesson Planning: Basic Habits

Ideally, much of your planning should already be done even before you sit down to make up tomorrow's lesson plan. First, the overall goals of the course—and often a course textbook—will help determine what kinds of activities are needed and why, so that you don't need to start from scratch each day with the question *What will I do tomorrow?* Furthermore, having a clear sense of overall goals often helps you focus on a relatively limited and stable set of activities that you draw on more or less regularly for lessons, thus decreasing the amount of time you need to devote to generating new ideas for the next day's class. Of course, you will want to build in some variety and variation from day to day lest the course become overly monotonous, but you will not need to rely too much on novelty and variety to keep the course interesting because the overall sense of purpose and direction will provide much of the drive necessary to engage students' interest and participation. In fact, as Stevick (1988, 7–8) notes, this regularity even helps students relax in class because it gives them a sense that you know what you are doing. This sense of overall structure and direction also gives you confidence that helps you weather days when students aren't very responsive or when an activity doesn't quite go as planned.

This description, of course, is the ideal, and it is a goal worth working toward. However, the problem for beginning teachers is often precisely that the big picture is not yet entirely clear. While you probably have tentative goals for your courses, and perhaps even a set of methods you plan to use on a regular basis, you are also no doubt all too aware that quite a bit of trial and error lies ahead before you will be fully confident that your choices of goals and methods are good ones. At this point in your teaching life, the issue of overall course goals may be more a source of concern for you than a source of security, so for the moment your course goals have only limited value as a rock on which to anchor your sense of direction and confidence. Furthermore, your ability to predict how things will go in class—how students will respond to a given activity or how long it will take—is also probably still somewhat shaky. During the early phases of your teaching life, the confidence with which you enter the classroom is often based less in your sense of long-term goals than in the efficacy of your day's lesson plan. So it seems appropriate to begin this chapter on lesson planning and classroom survival with discussion of the most basic—and important—lesson-planning habits that can maximize the chances of a good day in class.

The most important of these habits is also the most obvious: you need to make a plan for each lesson. A few gifted individuals can regularly wing it in the classroom and get by reasonably well, but such people are the exception rather than the rule (and many of them are more skilled at entertaining than educating). Teaching well and establishing a good classroom atmosphere are hard enough even if you prepare properly; to skimp on preparation is to beg for a lousy day in class.

The second important habit is to block out quality time in your weekly schedule for making lesson plans. Preparation can seem a rather ephemeral and insubstantial activity, at least when compared with classroom teaching or composition correcting, and it is therefore sometimes consigned to scraps of time left over from other activities. However, during your early days as a teacher, effective lesson planning probably places more demands on your concentration and creativity than paper grading or other activities do, so you should plan when your mind is freshest. Reserving prime time specifically for preparation ensures better lesson plans.

A third basic habit consists of writing down your lesson plans—in some detail—rather than keeping them in your head. A written lesson plan not only gives you something you can refer to in class when you need to jog your memory but also leaves you a written record to draw on if you want to use a particular lesson plan again in the future. However, the most important advantage is that writing a plan down forces you to think it through more carefully. Class plans you dream up but do not write down have a tendency to seem more thorough than they in fact are, much in the way that a polluted river seen in dim moonlight may appear a lot nicer than it really is. Letting plans first see the light of day on paper is generally very helpful in ensuring that you have worked out the details.

The final habit is that of writing flexibility into your lesson plans. One of the hardest things for beginning teachers (and even for experienced ones) is accurately predicting how long an activity will take. Sometimes an activity you thought would only take a few minutes engages students for a whole class period; other times, an activity you thought would generate discussion for at least thirty minutes dies after only three. For this reason, it is wise to have contingency plans; in other words, when you plan lessons, you should decide what parts of the lesson you can omit if things start running overtime and what additional material you can supplement your lesson with if the original plan doesn't last as long as you thought. As you gain teaching experience, your ability to estimate how long activities will run (and how enthusiastically students will respond to them) will gradually improve. However, the more important difference between novice and veteran teachers is that veterans have learned from experience that unexpected things will happen and that lessons rarely go entirely as planned, so it is wise to be prepared to make quick changes to the plan.

Aspects of a Lesson Plan

A BASIC LESSON PLAN FORMULA

There are as many ways to structure a lesson plan as there are different teaching situations, and no single plan can serve as a model for all situations. However, for planning many kinds of English classes, a basic initial formula would consist of the following parts:

1. **preview:** Giving students an overview of the day's lesson conveys a sense that there is a definite purpose and plan behind the day's activities. (This step may be done either before or after any warm-up activities.)

2. **warm-up:** Just as a concert often starts with a short lively piece to warm the audience up, a lesson often starts with a brief activity that is relatively lively. Its main function is to generate a good class atmosphere, but it can also be used for reviewing material from previous lessons or introducing new material in the day's lesson. Incidentally, the warm-up tends to set the tone for the lesson, and if it involves real communication, it will tend to reinforce the importance of genuine communication right from the beginning of the class period.

3. **main activities:** These are the main course of the day's menu, the more demanding activities to which most of the lesson will be devoted.

4. **optional activity:** This is an activity that you hope to use but are ready to omit if you are running out of time. (Normally, I simply designate one of my main activities as optional by marking it *If time allows* in my lesson plan.)

5. **reserve (or *spare-tire*) activity:** This activity is not a key part of your lesson plan but is available in case the other parts of the lesson go more quickly than planned, leaving you with unexpected time to fill.

6. **closing:** End the lesson by quickly reviewing/reemphasizing one or more main points of the lesson, and assigning homework.

How might this formula be applied to a specific lesson? The sample lesson plan on page 69 is designed for a fifty-minute class period in a first-year college English course. Because students will take a standardized English test covering the textbook, one goal of the course is mastery of the grammar and vocabulary presented in the book. The school officials have also made it clear that they want as much speaking as possible included in the course. Regular activities in this course are question-and-answer between teacher and students, vocabulary quizzes, pair and small-group work for speaking practice as well as practice of vocabulary and grammar structures, and in-class reading. Today's lesson introduces vocabulary concerning minor health problems and also sentence patterns and grammar for giving advice.

COMMENTS ON THE LESSON PLAN

- **timing:** Note that for each activity in the lesson plan, there is a rough estimate of how long the activity will or should take. Initially, you may have trouble accurately estimating how much time any given activity will take. However, planning an approximate time for activities, and even writing the time into your lesson plan, is still a good idea. This allows you to quickly see how your progress through the lesson period is matching up with what you had planned, so that you are more quickly alerted to the need to begin taking remedial measures such as speeding up or slowing down activities.

- **the point of an activity:** In the pair-practice activity, notice that the lesson plan includes an explicit reminder for students about the point of this activity. You do not need to state the point of every activity explicitly, especially when the point is obvious. However, students should know why they are doing what they are doing, so it is helpful to state this explicitly if there is any possibility that the point is not clear—and occasionally reminding students of long-term goals generally doesn't do any harm if even when the immediate

Sample Lesson Plan

(PREVIEW) THE DAY'S AGENDA (1–2 MINUTES)

- Before class starts, write the following agenda on the board: (1) *Do vocabulary quiz,* (2) *Practice new grammar structure,* (3) *Preview tomorrow's reading assignment.*
- At the beginning of the lesson, quickly go over today's agenda.

(WARM-UP) SURVEY (5 MINUTES)

- Introduce the day's topic by having students quickly survey each other asking, *What is the best way to treat a cold?*
- Close by asking a few volunteers to share the most interesting remedy they heard.

(MAIN ACTIVITY) VOCABULARY QUIZ (10 MINUTES)

- Give students a short quiz on words they studied for today's lesson (*headache, cold, runny nose, medicine*).
- Conduct the quiz by saying the quiz words aloud, and then having students write each word down and write a sentence that correctly uses the word and demonstrates knowledge of its meaning.

(MAIN ACTIVITY) NEW STRUCTURE (15 MINUTES)

- Introduce the structure for today (*How about . . . + ing?*) by complaining to a few students about some minor problems I have (e.g., *I feel a little dizzy*) and asking them to give me advice using the *How about (going to a doctor)?* structure.
- Put the structure on the board.
- Have students look at the dialogue in the book, find the target structure, and say what it is used for.
- Note that *How about . . . + ing* can be used as a suggestion or an invitation.

(MAIN ACTIVITY) PAIR PRACTICE (10 MINUTES)

- Give students the following situation: *Your friend has nothing to do and is bored. Make some helpful suggestions.*
- Point: Remind students that the goal is to practice using the new structure.
- Then have them practice in pairs. Have them change partners several times.
- Close the activity on a light note by asking students about the best and worst suggestions they heard.

(OPTIONAL ACTIVITY) SKIMMING PRACTICE (10 MINUTES)

- Have students quickly skim the dialogue in tomorrow's lesson and then tell me the main point of the lesson.

(RESERVE ACTIVITY) TWENTY QUESTIONS

If there is extra time, play this game.

- Tell students *I'm thinking about something in the room.*
- Have students try to figure out what it is, using yes/no questions to get clues. Only answer questions if they are properly formed.
- Give hints using the structure *How about asking questions about . . .* (e.g., *where it is, what color it is*).

point of an activity should be clear. (In my lesson plans, I often label such reminders with the word Point, as I did in the lesson plan above.)

- **closure:** Note that most of the activities in the lesson plan include a specifically designated closing step. Students generally feel better about ending an activity if it is somehow wrapped up and concluded rather than simply stopped, so the closing should be part of the plan. The closure step need not be very long; for example, having students quickly report what happened during their practice is a quick, light way to give a sense of closure to the activity in the sample lesson plan. A teacher comment or suggestion could also provide closure.

- **level of detail:** The sample plan may seem to be very detailed—perhaps overly so. However, my feeling is that for beginning teachers it is more dangerous to plan too little than to plan too much and that at first it is good to make quite detailed plans. As you gain teaching experience—and as you begin repeating lessons you have taught before—it becomes less necessary to plan in so much detail. (You can then copy old plans and modify them instead of creating new plans from scratch.)

- **variety:** It is generally best to build some variety into the activity types you use during a class period. For example, while the sample lesson plan consists mainly of oral skills practice, the reading and skimming practice provides a break from the heavy diet of speaking and listening. Students generally stay more alert if there is some variety in a class period.

- **language of the lesson plan:** There is no particular reason to write out your lesson plans in English, and you may find it easier and more efficient to write your plans out mainly in your first language. (For example, when teaching Chinese, I normally write out most of my plan in my first language—English. I use Chinese only for parts of the lesson plan where I need to prepare the precise Chinese wording necessary for purposes such as giving instructions or providing examples.)

The Textbook and the Big Question: What Is the Best Use of In-Class Time?

Like course plans, your daily lesson plans are often shaped largely by the material in course textbooks. In fact, sometimes the material in the textbook affects your lesson plans so much that the textbook almost seems to be a lesson plan, and it seems that all you need to do is explain the material in the book and have students do the activities the textbook prescribes. Textbooks, however, can't completely substitute for lesson plans because teaching involves too many practical decisions that the textbook cannot make for you. Among the choices you need to make, for example, are what material you should explain and how much you should explain it, how long you should spend on any given activity, which activities you should skip, what kinds of tasks you should assign to students as homework, whether or not you should add extra material or activities that are not in the textbook, and many more. Your lesson plan needs to address these practical issues and others like them.

There is, however, an even more basic question that the textbook cannot answer for you. In lesson planning, the most important question is, What is the best use of in-class time? Remember that only part of students' language learning process takes place in class. In fact, if students are to succeed in learning the target language, the most important part of their study happens outside class. Think for a moment about all the things students need to do in order to master English—practice listening, practice speaking, practice reading, practice writing, practice oral and written translation, learn vocabulary, learn grammar rules and how to apply them, and learn cultural information. Obviously, in most situations, there is not enough class time available for students to do all of this, and if they are to have any hope of learning English, they must do some or most of it outside class. So, to a large extent, lesson planning involves deciding what to use precious, limited in-class time for and what to have students do on their own.

One problem with treating a textbook as if it were a lesson plan is that this approach subtly suggests that you should spend much of your in-class time covering the material in the textbook—in other words, explaining grammar rules, vocabulary, and so forth. Textbooks also specifically mandate certain kinds of language skill practice. There are, however, other important uses of in-class time that are often not mentioned—or at least not emphasized—in textbooks, such as

- helping students improve their language learning skills

- building students' motivation

- getting feedback on how the course is going

Such uses of class time are at least as important as explaining material and practicing skills, but they will not be considered unless you view lesson planning from a perspective that is broader than the textbook's.

Given these choices, what is the best use of in-class time? Obviously, there is no fixed answer to this question. The answer depends, for example, on how much out-of-class study time students have, how willing and able they are to learn on their own, and how motivated they are to learn English. In each situation, you need to find a balance that suits the situation, the students, and you. There are, however, some rules of thumb:

- When deciding how to use class time, give priority to skills students can't or won't practice on their own. There is much that students can learn by studying or practicing outside class, so as much as possible, assign these kinds of tasks as homework. In-class time should generally be reserved for the kinds of practice that can't as readily be handled as homework.

- Try to minimize the amount of time you spend explaining new material (e.g., vocabulary, sentence patterns, grammar rules) from the textbook. You certainly can and should use class time to help students understand points in the textbook that are not clear to them and more generally to master the knowledge and skills introduced in the book, but don't just cover material for the sake of covering it. Keep in mind that explanations of such material often only help a few students in any given class; many students have already learned the material from the textbook, and others still don't understand the material after you explain it. As much as possible, have students study and learn it outside class as homework; in fact, one of the most important advantages of having a textbook is that it allows students to study such material outside class. Use in-class time to manage students' study of material in the textbook, not to repeat or replace it.

- Use a portion of class time to build students' ability and willingness to learn on their own. Given the idea of teacher as Coach (see chapter 2), in-class lessons are partly an opportunity to guide and manage students' language learning, not just an opportunity to teach language knowledge and skills. The more you can teach students about how to learn English, the greater the range of things that they will be able to do on their own.

Managing the Classroom

All teachers have to find a classroom style that they are comfortable with, and experience is the only tried-and-true way to do this. Meanwhile, here are a few practical pointers that may make managing a classroom a little easier.

SEATING

There are two primary considerations in seating. First, you want students sitting fairly close to each other when they are engaged in pair or small-group work. Physical proximity tends to make students more willing to talk to each other because it helps create a sense of group affinity and closeness; having students relatively close to each other also has the practical advantage of helping keep the general noise level down. The second main consideration is that you want to be able to get as close as you can to as many groups as possible so that you can see and hear what they are doing and can interact with them easily and naturally.

In classes where desks are easily movable and space is ample, achieving the two goals above is not particularly difficult. For pair or small-group activities, students can simply move their seats closer together, and for all-class activities, you can have them move into a row or semicircle arrangement. (Some teachers take it for granted that the best seating pattern is a circle because this seating arrangement allows students to have more eye contact with each other and quite literally moves the focus of the class away from the teacher, at least to some degree. However, in classes with many students, circles often become so large that students are only close to the classmates sitting to their immediate right and left, and the empty space in the middle becomes a forbidding no man's land that actually tends to dampen the conversational atmosphere. In contrast, traditional row-seating arrangements have the advantage of placing more students close to each other. My personal solution to this dilemma is to use a semicircle or forum arrangement that allows for multiple rows, hence placing more students closer together.)

The greater challenge occurs in classrooms where the desks or chairs are lined up in rows and bolted to the floor, and problems are exacerbated if students scatter themselves as widely as possible throughout the classroom. However, while such a situation is challenging, it is by no means the end of the world. For lectures or other teacher-focused activities, this seating situation does not pose major problems, although you may want to gently but firmly require that students not all bunch toward the back of the room as far away as possible from you. (Suggestion: Officially designate a few rows toward the back of the classroom as off-limits.) For group work, the trick is to get students into groups of three or four, bunched in squares (two students in the first row working with the two students immediately behind them in the second row) or triangles (one student from the first row working with two students in the row immediately behind). While such an arrangement may seem obvious, it is actually not the one most students form if you simply say, "Get into groups." Instead of turning around, students often naturally form a group consisting of three or four people sitting in the same row, with the result that the group is seated in a long line and the people at the far ends often cannot hear what is going on in the center. It is better for each group to consist of students from two different rows, front and back, so that they are closer together. Ideally, as many groups as possible should be immediately adjacent to an aisle so that you can more readily interact with them.

EYE CONTACT

Good eye contact is one of the main ways to establish and maintain a sense of student involvement in the lesson, especially when you are speaking to the whole class. While you do not need to catch the eye of each student in the classroom, you should make a conscious effort not to always look at a few favored students or a favored spot in the middle of the classroom. Rather, make a conscious effort to look from time to time at the students toward the sides of the classroom and far to the back and the front.

YOUR SPEECH AND VOICE

One of the most helpful things you can do for students—and one of the most important ways to maintain a degree of control and order in the classroom—is simply to speak loudly and clearly enough for students to hear you easily. Conversely, one of the surest ways to lose the students' attention and control of the classroom is to force them to strain too often and too hard to hear what you are saying. Granted, some teachers can effectively use a firm, quiet voice that motivates students to quiet down precisely so that they can hear what the teacher is saying, but this is a dangerous strategy for beginning teachers to adopt because it tends to work only when the teacher has already established a clear sense of presence and control. For most beginning teachers, the wiser strategy is speaking in a clear, reasonably loud voice that students have little trouble hearing.

A related issue is how quickly you should speak in English. When attempting to put a point across in class (e.g., giving instructions), you want to make sure that it is understood. However, if your speech becomes too simplified, it loses some of its value as listening practice for students. Try to strike a balance, speaking slowly and clearly (though not unnaturally) when necessary and a little more normally at other times to challenge students' ears.

Finally, speak with the expectation that students will listen to you. If you ask questions and don't wait for answers, give instructions but don't insist that they be followed, or simply keep talking without seeming to care whether students are listening or not, you send the signal to students that it is OK for them to tune you out, at least much of the time. Through your manner, try to convey the message that you want students to listen and respond—and that you are willing to wait or follow up as necessary so that they do.

TEACHER TALK

There is some debate as to how much the teacher should talk in a language classroom; some practitioners feel that teacher talk should be kept to a bare minimum while others point out that listening to your English provides one of students' main opportunities for listening practice. My own feeling is that in an EFL setting, particularly one where students have few other opportunities to listen to English, you should not be overly concerned about talking often in class. However, listening to you speak in English may be quite demanding for students, so you need to give them opportunities to speak not only because they need the practice but also because they may need a break from the strain of trying to follow you.

USING THE LOCAL LANGUAGE

As a teacher who can speak the students' first language, one choice you will need to make is how much and when to use the local language in class. There are some advantages to using English all the time in class, the main one being that it helps create an "English atmosphere." However, I would encourage you not to assume that using English all the time is necessarily the best or right thing to do. In fact, one of your main advantages as a local teacher is your ability to communicate freely and easily with students in their first language, and you should take advantage of this skill for things like

- quickly and clearly explaining unfamiliar vocabulary words or grammar points

- giving instructions

- answering questions (especially when students would not likely understand the answer if you gave it in English)

- teaching language learning skills

- talking about your own language learning

There is little reason to sacrifice all the advantages of your native command of the local language just to provide a little more English listening practice in class. (My personal approach to the use of students' first language is as follows: When I am teaching advanced-level students whose target language listening skills are quite good, I use the target language almost all of the time. When teaching beginning- or intermediate-level students whose target language listening skills are not so strong, I use the target language consistently and exclusively during some parts of the lesson to gradually build students' endurance and tolerance for functioning in the target language. During other parts of the lesson, I use the students' first language when it seems helpful to do so.)

INSTRUCTIONS

One of the most common reasons discussion activities don't go well is that instructions are either too complicated or not presented clearly. Basic tips for ensuring that students understand instructions include the following:

- Keep instructions as short and clear as possible. Lower level students, especially those with poor listening comprehension, are easily confused by complicated instructions, especially if given in English.

- Make instructions as specific as possible. Vague instructions such as *Talk about . . .* don't give very clear direction. Discussion starts faster and moves with more purpose if you assign students a more specific task, such as making a list, making a decision, or designing a plan. (For more on tasks, see chapter 7.)

- Repeat instructions twice, using the same (or almost the same) wording.

- Write down your instructions in your lesson plans, even verbatim. This permits you to repeat instructions more than once using the same words.

- Speak more slowly and clearly than normal when giving instructions.

- If you give instructions in English, check students' comprehension by having them repeat the instructions back to you. (Asking "Do you understand?" is generally of little use because students' instinctive response to this question is to nod their heads yes whether they understand you or not.)

- Check to see if students are actually doing the activity as you instructed. Often students appear to have understood the instructions—and they may well have thought they did—but when they begin the activity, it becomes clear that they actually didn't fully understand.

MOVEMENT

One way to establish better rapport with students, as well as to maintain better control of the classroom, is to step out from behind the podium (or teacher's desk) and move closer to the students. Physical closeness tends to create a feeling of emotional closeness, and students will tend to feel closer to you emotionally if you are near them during at least some of the lesson. I would suggest four rules of thumb for where you should be:

1. When you need to write on the blackboard or use other things at the front of the class, stay near the front so that you don't have to constantly run back and forth.

2. When you are speaking to the whole class for extended periods, stay at the front of the classroom but as close as practicable to the front row of students. (When possible, a semicircle seating arrangement helps in this situation because you are then closer to more students.)

3. When students are working individually, in pairs, or in groups, move around the classroom to check on them or simply to be nearer to them.

4. When a student is speaking to you in front of the whole class and you want the other students to hear what is being said, it is often best to move away from the student who is speaking. This may seem counterintuitive: if you are having difficulty hearing the student, your natural tendency is often to move closer. However, if you want the rest of the class to listen, move further away so that the student is forced to speak up.

QUESTION AND ANSWER

You will greatly enhance the effectiveness of a question asked to the whole class if you pause before calling on someone to answer; this ensures that everyone has the time and the motivation to think through an answer.

USING THE BLACKBOARD

In many classrooms around the world, the blackboard (or whiteboard) is still the teacher's primary medium for sending visual messages to students, so I conclude with a few suggestions on how to make use of it.

- Make sure that your writing is large enough for people in the back to read.

- Try not to waste a lot of time writing on the board during class. If you need to write something relatively long, put it on the board before class. (In situations where students do not have access to textbooks, you may need to write the necessary material on the board so that students can copy it before or after class.)

- Try not to talk to the board. If you need to write something on the board, pause for a moment and allow students a moment of respite from the sound of your voice.

- Use the blackboard to entertain. The main attraction of many of my classes is the pathetic attempts at drawing with which I illustrate points. Students laugh at the drawings, I make my point, and the atmosphere in class is a little lighter. If you can draw well, so much the better.

- When they are available, using devices such as overhead projectors or computers equipped with projectors has considerable advantages. However, remember that such equipment is somewhat more vulnerable to technological mishaps than blackboards are, so have a backup plan in case a bulb burns out or a virus suddenly causes your computer to crash.

CLASS DISCIPLINE

Unfortunately, some students have no interest in learning, and others are simply difficult people. However, in my experience, most students are willing to give you a fair chance and are generally well disposed toward a teacher who is reasonably pleasant and works hard. The first step toward establishing class discipline is therefore earning students' respect—even affection.

Earlier in this book, I touched on a variety of factors involved in the process of earning respect, including diligence in teaching and fairness in evaluation. As Ur (1996, 265) points out, even such basic practices as planning lessons carefully and giving clear instructions can help prevent discipline problems in class. However, no matter how ideal a role model you become, you will almost inevitably come across students who do things that you perceive as problematic.

To a large degree, the question of how to deal with discipline problems in an English class is shaped by your local culture, so it is impossible for me to make specific suggestions that are appropriate for all settings. I will, however, offer a few commonsense suggestions that may be of use. First, before exploding at somebody, fire a warning shot. One possibility is to specifically state the consequences of continued unacceptable behavior—in other words, make a threat. The best threats are those which you can and will carry out; don't threaten to kick a student out of class if you are not prepared to do so or if it is not within your power to do so. It also helps if threats are very specific so that a student doesn't cross the line due to ignorance rather than intent. "If you copy again, you will regret it!" is not as helpful to a student as "I will make you do the entire paper over again if I find a single phrase in it that is the same as your girlfriend's."

Second, try not to delay too long before clarifying and dealing with a problem situation. Failure to respond may well allow the situation to become worse and may also lower the reservoir of respect and support that other students in the class have for you. While it is very natural to want to avoid unpleasant confrontations with students, remember that a student's disruptive behavior often influences other members in the class and that you have a responsibility to maintain an environment in which other students can learn. Another problem with long-delayed responses is that they tend to become more spectacular when they finally do appear, and there is a greater danger that you will have lost the objectivity and emotional control necessary to handle the situation in a sensitive and appropriate manner. An early warning disrupts relationships much less than a blowup a few weeks later.

Establishing a Good Class Atmosphere

The success or failure of an English class should not be measured primarily on its popularity—it is, after all, a class rather than a variety show—but how students respond to your lessons is a real and important question, for pedagogical as well as emotional reasons. One way you can help motivate students to engage actively in English study is simply to make your class as lively and interesting as possible; on the whole, students tend to learn more about something they like and find interesting than about something that holds no appeal for them (Scarcella and Oxford 1992, 33). A class that is lively and fun is—all other things being equal—usually better than one that is boring or tense. It is also helpful if students find you encouraging and friendly, and if the class environment is as nonthreatening as possible (Littlewood 1984, 58–59). Of course, student response to your class is not entirely within your power to control; some students no doubt disliked school or English class long before they ever met you, and you cannot always expect to see a complete reversal in their attitudes. However, by developing a good rapport with students and by keeping your class as interesting as possible, you can often make a significant difference in students' attitudes and response.

ESTABLISHING GOOD RAPPORT

One of the best ways to build good rapport with students is to learn their names. This can require a considerable investment of time and energy, especially if you have many students. However, the investment will pay significant dividends as the term goes on, and is it generally worth the effort (at least for those classes you see most often).

The most obvious way to learn students' names is by asking them to stand up one by one and introduce themselves. The problem with this method is that if students just go through it quickly, you are not likely to remember any of the names; if they do it more slowly, it takes a lot of class time. Gower and Walters (1983, 49) suggest a number of other ways to learn students' names, including the following:

- At the beginning of a course, try to memorize students' names using the Name Game as follows: Have student A say her name, have student B say his name and the name of student A, and continue until the last student has to recite the names of all the students in the class—just before you do the same. This game requires considerable concentration and takes a long time in classes with more than thirty students. However, it tends to be quite effective in helping you learn many new names in a relatively short time, and it does the same for students (if they don't know each other already). The Name Game is also an excellent object lesson in the importance of repetition and concentration in memorization of vocabulary.

- Have students make up name/biography cards. If possible, have students attach a small photograph.

- Take attendance each day; this forces you to review names.

- Especially during the first few lessons, consciously make a point of using students' names.

- While students are doing pair or small-group work, spend time mentally reviewing their names.

- Use the returning of homework assignments or papers as an opportunity to review names.[1]

One reason learning students' names is effective in developing rapport is that it is convincing evidence of your interest in getting to know students as individuals. Another effective way to show your interest in students is simply by responding to what students say in language classes as much as—or more than—you respond to whether or not they say it correctly. This shows not only that you consider language use to be genuinely communicative but that you consider students people whose ideas and feelings deserve to be treated with respect. A third important way to develop rapport with students is by showing interest in their English progress. Of course, in large classes it is often difficult to establish a personal relationship with each student, but any show of concern that goes beyond correcting mistakes and assigning grades is usually much appreciated.

---

[1] See appendix C, Daily Life Module, Getting to Know You, for other activities to help you and the students get to know each other more quickly.

KEEPING CLASS INTERESTING

In chapter 4, I mentioned several of the most important ways to keep class interesting, but a quick review here may still be helpful.

Ensuring that students have a clear sense of direction and progress will go a long way toward maintaining morale. As suggested earlier, setting specific, narrow course goals allows students to more readily perceive progress, and regularly reminding students of why they are doing what they are doing is also helpful.

Regular use of genuinely communicative activities also helps keep class more interesting. One of the perennial favorite pastimes of the human race is chatting; most people love to talk about themselves, their activities, other people, world events, and just about everything else, and there is no reason not to take advantage of this interest in the classroom. Language practice activities that allow students to say what they want to say are inherently more interesting than non-communicative drills. If activities are to be genuinely communicative, it helps if they involve some kind of information gap; in other words, if student A knows something that student B doesn't, ensuring that student A has something to communicate. (This is in contrast to situations in which both partners already know what the other is going to say, a common situation in dialogue practice.) Students will generally be more interested in what their classmates say (or write) to them if they know the message will contain something that is new—and preferably interesting—to them.

Another way to enhance interest levels is by giving language learning activities some of the appeal of games. You can do this with many kinds of activities by introducing an element of fun and lighthearted competition. Consider a few examples:

- Conversation activities often seem more enjoyable if some kind of choice needs be made. For example, a mock job interview becomes more interesting if you have the employers interview more than one prospective employee and then announce which candidate they decided to hire and why.

- Content lessons can be livened up by introducing them with a short contest. For example, instead of just giving a lecture on Western holidays, divide students into groups and give them a few minutes to list as many holidays and their dates as possible. Reward the group that compiles the best list with praise or whatever else you have an adequate supply of. You can do the same with vocabulary (e.g., lists of colors, animals, feelings) or even grammar (e.g., lists of mass nouns, ways to describe things in the future).

- Even subjects as drab as spelling or vocabulary can become more interesting if you turn them into contests (spelling bees being a case in point). I, for example, liven up my Chinese vocabulary memorization by competing against myself. Each day as I look at my vocabulary list, I check to see if I can quickly and accurately pronounce the Chinese characters and state their meaning. If I can't, I have to review the word but leave it on the list. When I get one right, I allow myself the satisfaction of crossing it off my list.

Finally, part of the art of being a good teacher is knowing when to lighten the pressure a little bit by scheduling what I call *candy:* a game, song, or film for class. All of these can have educational as well as recreational value, but teachers would be kidding themselves if they didn't admit that they often use such activities more because students like them than because they offer the most efficient road to language proficiency. However, remember that one of the most important goals of any language program is to help students become more interested in studying the language, and a song that makes up for weakness in grammar teaching efficacy by kindling a student's desire to learn may affect the student long after a grammar point would be forgotten.

For Thought, Discussion, and Action

1. **lesson plans (task A):** Imagine that you will teach the following dialogue from a textbook. Using the format in the Sample Lesson Plan in this chapter, make a lesson plan. Then discuss your lesson plan with another teacher or classmate, and explain why you have designed the lesson as you did.

   (Han, a teacher who is applying for a job as a translator, is being interviewed by Bob. Pay special attention to verb tenses.)

   Bob: Please tell me about your education, Mr. Han.

   Han: I graduated from Zhongshan Teachers College in 1965. I was an English major.

   Bob: How about your work experience?

   Han: I have been teaching in Hua Dong middle school for the past thirty years.

   Bob: Have you ever been a translator?

   Han: No. I have always been a teacher.

   Bob: Why are you applying for this job?

   Han: Because I don't like children very much.

2. **lesson plans (task B):** Choose a lesson or unit from a local English textbook and do the following:
   * In groups, make a lesson plan for a two-hour class period. (Use the format in the sample lesson in this chapter.)
   * (if you are doing this in a class) Have one or more groups write their plans on the board.
   * Comment on one strong point of each lesson plan, and make one suggestion for improving it.

3. **lesson plans (task C):** Using material from one of the units in appendix C, make a plan for a typical lesson for the following course. Then discuss your plan with another teacher or classmate. (You may also find it helpful to look at Sample Course Two in appendix B as a point of reference.)

   Intermediate Oral English: This intermediate-level conversation course is for a large class of university students (not English majors). The students have already studied English for several years (mostly vocabulary, grammar, and reading) but have weak speaking and listening skills. They come from a variety of different majors, so it is not clear how they might use English after graduation. They seem enthusiastic, but this is not a core course, so they will probably not have much time to do English homework. (The course was recently added to the curriculum to encourage the students to build strong oral English skills, but it is not integrated into the rest of the program and meets only once a week for two hours.) There is no textbook or tape for the course, and there is no readily available photocopy machine. You have a fairly free hand with the course because there is also no standardized test or follow-up course to consider.

4. **information gaps:** Imagine you are teaching the dialogue in number 1 above, and you want students to use the dialogue as a model for practice conversations in pairs. However, you also want to ensure that there is an information gap in the exercise. List three ways you could modify the activity to include an information gap. Also write out the exact instructions that you would give students before the activity.

5. **the local language:** Thinking back on your own language learning experience, how much do you think a teacher should use the local language in class? For what purposes? Compare your thoughts with those of classmates.

6. **What would you do?** List several classroom management problems you anticipate or are concerned about (such as students who persistently talk while you are talking, who never speak in class, or who repeatedly miss class without explanation). (1) List possible strategies for dealing with each. (2) Discuss your strategies with a friend, a classmate, or a teacher from your country.

7. **games (task A):** The Sample Lesson Plan in this chapter suggests a game called Twenty Questions. Analyze this game, and list what language skills or knowledge it could be used to teach.

8. **games (task B):** Choose a language-based game you know, and analyze its value for English teaching. List what language skills or knowledge it could be used to teach; also list the skills and knowledge that it would not teach.

9. **games (task C):** Imagine that in class you want students to memorize the dialogue in number 1 above, but you want to make this activity as much like a game as possible. List several ways you could turn this activity into a game. Then pick the one that seems most promising (i.e., fun or interesting), and write out the instructions you would give students for the activity.

10. **songs:** Pick an English song that you like, and consider how you might use it as a language teaching activity. First, list the language points you could use the song to teach. Then write out a plan for a teaching activity using the song to teach useful language knowledge or skills.

PART II

Aspects of English Teaching

Chapter 6

Listening: Putting the Horse before the Cart

- In many settings, listening is the language skill used most often and the channel through which students get much of their language input. Development of listening skills is thus even more important than development of speaking skills.

- Students need to learn to use both bottom-up and top-down strategies when listening.

- Even in places where there are few chances to speak English, there may be relatively more opportunities to listen to English, so listening skills are a good target for breakthrough-type plans.

One of my most frustrating language experiences occurred in 1978 during a summer in Russia. I had recently completed a college minor in Russian, and even though I knew my Russian was not fluent, I assumed that I would at least be able to cope with basic conversation. I was thus disheartened to discover that, when confronted with real Russians in conversational situations, I was virtually helpless. The problem was not my speaking skills; I could generally make myself understood, if only imperfectly. The real problem was that I could understand almost nothing that I heard—everything seemed to be a blur of sound that was less clear and much faster than the Russian my teacher had always used in class.

Consequently, my speaking skills were virtually useless because I had no idea what to say. Even activities as simple as buying books involved emotional trauma because, when I plucked up my courage and asked the price in Russian, I could never understand the response. After several futile attempts to communicate with me verbally, the clerks generally resorted to writing or holding up fingers. Naturally, this was quite humiliating for someone who had spent three years in Russian classes, and I was frequently tempted to preserve my pride by pretending I had never studied any Russian at all.

Unfortunately, my experience with Russian is typical of that of many English learners. Bowen, Madsen, and Hilferty (1985) comment, "Students with ten years of English instruction and even more find that when they arrive [in an English-speaking country] they have major difficulties trying to comprehend even simple sentences of spoken English" (p. 83). This happens in part because many language programs—intentionally or accidentally—do not devote enough attention to listening skills. Another reason is that even when listening practice is provided, it often consists of the teacher's slow, clear classroom speech or language tapes on which unrealistically clear and formal voices read aloud materials that students have already read in their textbook. If students want to be able to listen to native English speakers, news broadcasts, or films, a diet of listening to slow, clear English is inadequate.

Students with weak listening skills face several problems. The first, illustrated by my example above, is they cannot function well in most conversational settings no matter how well they can speak. In contrast, students whose listening skills are good but who do not speak well can generally at least keep a conversation going by being good listeners and occasionally responding with simple questions, short answers, or even grunts and nods. A second problem is that much of students' language input normally comes from what they hear, and if this channel is blocked, students will learn less new English. So an emphasis on speaking at the expense of listening puts the cart before the horse, resulting in a learning process that is both slower and more difficult.

A third problem arises from the frequency with which listening skills are used; as noted in chapter 3, in some settings listening is the most often used language skill. Hedge (2000) points out that "of the time an individual is engaged in communication, approximately 9 percent is devoted to writing, 16 percent to reading, 30 percent to speaking, and 45 percent to listening. It is also undoubtedly the case that contemporary society exhibits a shift away from printed media and towards sound, and its members therefore need to develop a high degree of proficiency in listening" (pp. 228–29). Even in EFL settings where native speakers of English are few and far between, students often have opportunity to listen to English radio programs, television, or films. However, students who have not had much listening training are ill prepared to take advantage of these opportunities. This is especially unfortunate in that, given the scarcity of other opportunities to use English in many EFL settings, listening represents one of the most realistic targets for a breakthrough of the type described in chapter 1.

Listening Skills: The Problem and the Goal

One helpful way to think about the challenges students face in listening to English is to think back on your own experience of building listening skills. Among the challenges you encountered were probably some or all of the following:

- hearing small differences between English sounds (e.g., the subtle differences between the vowel sounds in *fear, fair, fire, far,* and *fur*)

- comprehending reduced forms of pronunciation, which are very common in normal spoken English (e.g., *fer* for *for, ta* for *to, wanna* for *want to*)

- attending to intonation or emphasis cues (e.g., it is only intonation and emphasis that distinguish "You want *him* to go?" from "You want him to *go!*")

- adjusting to regional, class, or group accents

- understanding vocabulary by listening to it (This often presents serious problems for learners in EFL settings because they learn most vocabulary through reading.)

- understanding grammar structures

- understanding rapid speech (Even speech in which students know all the vocabulary and grammar may be impossible to understand if it comes faster than students can process it. As Ur [1981, 19] notes, this is especially true when students listen for longer times because, as fatigue from listening to an unfamiliar language sets in, comprehension drops.)

- developing a range of cultural background knowledge (Lack of background information can deprive listeners of vitally important clues for comprehending a message; it also reduces their ability to predict what they might hear; see chapter 12.)

When you consider all of the ways in which a spoken English sentence can trip up learners, you may find it miraculous that learners ever learn to understand English at all. Fortunately, learners do not need to be able to cope with every aspect of every utterance in order to comprehend it. As Omaggio Hadley (2001, 179) describes it, the process of comprehension is much like that of completing a puzzle. Learners don't need to have every piece of the picture in place in order to make sense of it; at some point, the puzzle pieces that learners do understand allow them to guess at the whole picture, and this hypothesis guides the process of completing the picture.

Listening comprehension involves two basic processes, one known as *bottom-up* processing and one known as *top-down*. To understand these, imagine that you are a student who sees your English teacher on a crowded sidewalk and hears her say a muffled sentence including the words "How . . . today." One way you make sense of the sentence is through bottom-up processing—using the smaller pieces of the picture to figure out the larger picture. In this case, you use the words you heard—*how* and *today*—as data to help you understand the sentence. The other way to make sense of what the teacher said is through top-down processing—using background knowledge to guess what goes in blank spots in the picture. As Ur (1984) points out, "a real-life listening situation is normally rich in environmental clues as to the content and implications of what was said" (p. 5), and in the example, the context makes it fairly likely that the teacher's murky utterance was some kind of greeting. This knowledge helps you fill in the missing words.[1]

---

[1] For a detailed and entertaining introduction to bottom-up and top-down processing, see Bailey (1998, 47–49).

The analogy of completing a puzzle is useful for understanding the comprehension process, but it is faulty at one point: it implies that the goal is to complete every last piece of the puzzle. This is a mistaken assumption commonly made by language learners. As Hedge (2000) notes,

> Many language learners fail to realize that when they listen to their first language they do not actually hear every word. They also fail to appreciate that we integrate linguistic knowledge with our existing experience and knowledge of such things as topic and culture, and do not need to hear every word. This means that learners often have unrealistic expectations and try to understand each word of a listening text. (p. 237)

Unfortunately, many learners set this goal for themselves because it was the one language teachers set for them in their early years of English study. Learners who have this expectation may have trouble with listening at higher levels because they tend to freeze when they come across words or phrases they don't understand.

The real goal in most listening is not to understand every word but to comprehend the information that the listener wants or needs from a message. In the example above, the key is for the student to realize that the "How . . . today" question was probably a greeting; whether it was "How are you today?" or "How're ya doing today?" makes little difference. In some cases, a listener needs a high degree of comprehension (and retention); more often, getting the gist of a message is sufficient, and the rest is ignored or quickly forgotten.

These points have several important implications for learning and teaching listening skills. The first is that, in listening practice exercises, you do not need to expect 100 percent comprehension in all cases. The expectations you set for listening exercises, like the goals of listening in real life, should be appropriate to the situation, and you should often ask only that students work to understand the main points of a message.

The second implication concerns teaching methods. In real life, even native speakers do not always understand or hear every word when they are talking with someone or watching television—people mumble, cars pass by, and so forth. In most cases, however, these gaps do not cause serious communication problems because native speakers are skilled at filling them in; using situational or linguistic clues, they can guess much of what they did not hear or understand. Likewise, as students practice listening skills, they need to practice using top-down as well as bottom-up strategies—using all the clues available to help them guess.

A third implication is that the main way to build listening skill is through extensive practice. Listening involves solving many little problems of the kinds mentioned above in order to make sense of the puzzle—and doing so rather quickly. The ability to do this is built mainly through extensive practice listening to material at an appropriate level of difficulty—easy enough that students have a chance to figure out much of the puzzle, but hard enough that the material challenges their skills.

Listening Tasks in Class

The basic listening comprehension activity consists of a few basic elements:

1. **text:** Here *text* simply means something to listen to—for example, a story told by the teacher, a dialogue on a tape, or a TV show.

2. **context:** As pointed out, in real life most listening takes place in a context that provides clues for listeners as they try to comprehend a text. (This is in contrast to many language tests, in which students are often asked to listen to language for which there is no context

at all.) For example, understanding a conversation is easier because listeners can see the expressions and gestures of the person they are talking to; understanding a radio news broadcast is easier if the listener knows that the text is a news broadcast, which follows certain rules and patterns. So you should generally set some kind of context for listening exercises by explaining the background, showing pictures, and so forth.

3. **purpose:** In real life, listeners often have some idea of why they are listening to something, so it is entirely appropriate—and generally a good idea—to tell students what they are listening for before they hear something. While the most basic purpose of a listening task should be general comprehension, often the purpose should be more focused.

4. **task:** Most kinds of listening exercises work better if they are made into tasks, that is, if students are expected to respond in some way to the material instead of just listening to it. The task keeps students alert and helps focus their listening.

The types of listening practice activities suggested below are arranged roughly according to the level at which they are most likely to be appropriate, starting with those for beginning-level students. (Assigning a precise level of difficulty to these tasks is hard because you can make them easier or more difficult by adjusting the vocabulary, speed of delivery, clarity of speech, depth of content, and so forth.) While the activities here focus on listening practice, many also involve practice of other language skills.

SHOW AND TELL

This informal but engaging activity consists of bringing pictures or other objects to class, showing them to students, and talking about them. Looking at the pictures or objects helps students use top-down strategies to make sense of what you are saying. Show and tell provides listening practice and arouses interest in a topic; it also serves as a good informal warm-up or as a break from the rest of the lesson.

TOTAL PHYSICAL RESPONSE (TPR)

TPR is an activity in which you give students instructions, and they respond by doing what you ask rather than by speaking (similar to the game Simon Says). Because students respond with action rather than speech, they can focus more fully on listening to what you say rather than having to worry about generating an oral response at the same time.

This activity builds listening skills, especially for students at lower levels, and can be used to introduce or review vocabulary and even grammar structures. The physical activity makes for a good warm-up activity at the beginning of class or a break in the middle. TPR can be especially useful for teaching basic classroom instructions to students with very low listening skills, but it can also be used for more advanced levels; for example, I have walked students through weddings and baseball games TPR-style in lessons on Western culture.

1. Before the activity, make a list of the instructions you wish to use (e.g., *Open your books. Turn to page six. Touch your nose with your friend's pen.*).

2. Conduct the activity in a gamelike manner, repeating instructions and building up speed for faster student responses.

3. To make the activity more like a game, add the Simon Says element; that is, tell students they should only carry out the instruction if you preface it by saying, "Simon says."

TRUE/FALSE LISTENING

This activity involves reading short statements to students, some true and some not true; students then respond by telling you whether the statements are true or false. This activity can be used for reviewing vocabulary and culture content from previous lessons while providing listening practice. The more this seems like a game, the better—try to fool your classes with absurd statements and deadpan delivery.

1. Write a set of statements, drawing material (e.g., vocabulary, cultural information) from previous lessons. Some statements should be obviously true, others obviously not or perhaps even ridiculous (e.g., *Today is Tuesday. Students love tests.*). The activity is more enjoyable if the statements are a little tricky without being mean.

2. Ask students to listen to each statement, decide if it is true or false, and write down T or F on a numbered sheet. After the exercise, have students check their answers as a group, or ask everyone to shout out the answer (based on Ur 1984, 77–78).

DICTATION

In dictation, you read a short passage to students, and they write it down word for word. This activity is useful for practicing basic listening skills as well as basic writing skills such as capitalization, spelling, and punctuation. Dictation is recommended mainly for lower level students.[2]

1. Choose a short passage or dialogue.

2. Before dictating the passage, introduce any words you think will be new to students. Also, briefly set the scene by providing appropriate background information. This helps students bring top-down strategies into play and gives you a way to increase or decrease the difficulty of the exercise, depending on how much information you give.

3. Tell students to just listen. Read the entire passage aloud.

4. Read the passage again, breaking it into lines (corresponding to phrases or clauses), and have students write it down word for word. Lines should be relatively short—no more than seven or eight words. (Longer lines overload students' short-term memory.) If necessary, repeat each line two or three times.

5. Read the dialogue straight through one final time so that students can check their work.

6. Have volunteers or the class as a whole read the dialogue back to you as you write it on the board. Students can then check their work by looking at the board. Alternatively, have volunteers write different lines on the board, give the students a handout with the text and have them check their own work, or collect the dictations and check them individually.

TIPS

- While dictating, wander the aisles to see how much difficulty students are having. If necessary, slow down and speak more clearly. If the dictation is too easy, speak more quickly and naturally.

- One problem with dictation is that it trains students to listen for every word more than for meaning. One way to minimize this problem and focus students' attention more on meaning is to dictate questions and then ask students to answer them.

---

[2] There are a variety of possible procedures for dictation. This one is based on Bailey (1998, 13).

DICTOCOMP

In dictocomp, you read a short passage to students and have them write down what you say. Unlike dictation, however, in dictocomp you read the whole passage to students several times at a fairly natural pace rather than stopping after each sentence. This forces students to listen for and remember ideas, not just words. Dictocomp is more challenging than dictation, involves more listening for ideas and speaking practice, and requires students to draw more on their knowledge of grammar.[3]

1. Choose a short passage or dialogue. The passage might only be five to ten sentences long.

2. Set the scene of the passage for the students.

3. Instruct students to listen and try to remember. Then read the passage twice at fairly normal speed, without pauses between sentences.

4. Tell students they may jot down key words and phrases (not every word) as you read. Then read the passage a third time, slightly more slowly.

5. Either individually or in groups, have students try to reconstruct and write down the passage as they remember it. (Individually takes less time; groups provide opportunity for speaking practice and mutual assistance.) Tell students they need not use exactly the same words as the original passage but that the meaning should not be changed and the English should be grammatically correct.

6. Write the original passage on the board (or give it to the students as a handout), and have students check their work. As they check, circulate and answer questions, particularly on the grammatical accuracy of what they wrote. If it seems helpful, hold a general question-and-answer time. Alternatively, have groups write their passages on the board (but this can be slow).

TIPS

- To make a dictocomp activity more or less difficult, alter the length and difficulty of the passage, read the passage fewer or more times, read more quickly or slowly, or add or eliminate pauses between sentences. The right level of difficulty is the one at which most students are able to write down the gist of the passage after the third hearing. If they get most of it after the first or second reading, the dictocomp is too easy.

- If the passage is a dialogue, let students know who is speaking when—otherwise, they will be confused as to who is saying which sentence. One way to do this is to act out each character by changing your voice and body position. Another is to put a minimal outline on the board that tells students what turns the speakers are taking and how many sentences there are in each turn (e.g., *(1) Jim: _____. (2) Judy: _____. _____. (3) Jim: _____.)*

DICTATION FOR REDUCED FORMS

One listening problem you might want to address in class involves the reduced forms that are very commonly used in most dialects of natural spoken English, such as *doncha* (*don't you*), *gonna* (*going to*), and *wanna* (*want to*). It will be hard for students to follow movie dialogues, conversation between native speakers, and so forth if they cannot understand reduced forms.

---

[3] I have drawn my approach to dictocomp (also called *dictogloss*) from Bowen, Madsen, and Hilferty (1985, 272–73). See Bailey (1998, 47–49) for a slightly different approach.

1. Design a dialogue for dictation that includes a number of reduced forms like those mentioned above. Use either a dialogue you will read to students or a dialogue recorded on a tape that you will play for students. Many local English teachers do not use reduced forms much in their own English speech (and there is no reason you necessarily should), so you might use commercially produced tapes that record informal English speech or get a native speaker to record material for you. (Reduced forms occur mainly in informal spoken English, so for this kind of dictation, it is better to use dialogues rather than passages of written English.)

2. Conduct the dictation following the procedure suggested above, but be sure to read the lines naturally and fairly quickly and to use the reduced forms of the target items.

3. To check students' work, have students listen to the reduced sentences again and repeat them in their complete form.

STORIES

Stories are a relatively enjoyable way to give students practice listening to extended discourse, albeit of a fairly easy and interesting kind. In my experience, students especially like informal personal stories about you and your experiences; in particular, stories about your experiences as a learner of English would be valuable.

1. Choose a story you want to tell, and prepare as necessary.

2. Tell the story. My assumption is that this is best done as informally and naturally as possible; ideally, you want students to perceive this as a break from class rather than another exercise. However, you might at least ask students to try to remember as much of the story as possible, thereby hinting that this is not free time in which they can doze off.

3. As for checking comprehension, the inherent appeal of stories makes them one kind of listening practice for which accountability may not be necessary; many students will strive to understand just because they are interested. If, however, you wish to treat a story as a listening task, you can have students respond in one of the following ways:
   • Have students take notes and then write a summary or retell the story to a classmate.
   • Require students to be ready to ask a question or two—a comprehension question or one that pursues issues raised by the content of the story—after you finish.
   • Have students discuss what they did and did not like about the story or what they found interesting or surprising.
   • Have students revise the story to improve it.
   • Leave off the end of the story, and have students devise an ending of their own.

FOCUSED LISTENING

In focused listening activities, you help students anticipate what they will hear by giving them clues in the form of questions to answer or outlines, forms, or graphs to fill in. These clues help students focus their listening and make listening practice easier, especially for lower level students. They also encourage students to listen for important information rather than for every word.

1. Prepare a short talk of some kind, for example, a story or a lecture.

2. Decide what kind of clues you will provide. These can consist of anything that gives some signal as to what you will say and focuses students' listening, such as a set of questions to answer, a form to fill out, a graph to fill in, or a partial outline to fill in.

3. Write the clues on the board, or give students a handout. Ask students to look the clues over so that they know what they should listen for. To enhance motivation and encourage active listening, you might ask students to predict what your talk will be about.

4. Tell students to listen to your talk and take notes, writing down information that will help them complete the task. (If you want them to write out full answers to your questions, tell them you will give them time to write after the talk.)

5. Give your talk.

6. Check comprehension (see Talks and Lectures below).

An additional—and potentially light-hearted—form of focused listening involves altering a passage or dialogue, introducing contradictions or absurdities. Students then either shout out or take notes when they hear something suspicious (for more ideas along these lines, see Ur 1984, especially 75, 81, and 116–17).

PROBLEM-SOLVING SITUATIONS

In problem-solving activities, you orally describe a problem situation to students, have them take note of relevant information, and then ask them to deal with the issue. A classic in this genre is Sophie's Choice, an exercise in which students hear about a young woman who has to choose one of three appealing but flawed men as a marriage partner or ignore them all in favor of a career opportunity (Byrd and Clemente-Cabetas 2001). In another well-known activity, Spaceship, the world is about to be destroyed by a meteor, and a spaceship can take a limited number of people off to a new planet to restart the human race. Students are presented with candidates and their qualifications, and have to choose who should be on the spaceship.

Problem-solving activities obviously involve speaking as well as listening practice, but I list them here because the amount of information students need to take in through their ears weights the activity significantly toward listening. (See chapter 7 for further discussion of small-group discussion activities.)

1. Locate or design a situation that gives students a problem to solve. For example, if you were doing Sophie's Choice, you would prepare to explain Sophie's situation and the qualifications of each of her suitors. If the main focus of the activity is on listening practice, make sure the situation involves a fair amount of information that students have to listen to.

2. Present the situation and relevant information to students orally, having them take notes. (You might also allow them to ask questions.)

3. Have them discuss the problem situation in English in small groups, and prepare to offer a solution and their rationale.

4. Have each group present their solution and rationale.

5. Close the exercise one of these ways:
   - Have the class debate the merit of the solutions offered, perhaps following up with a vote.
   - Comment on the solutions offered, pointing out their weak and strong points.
   - Offer your own solution (preferably one that is ingenious and entertaining).
   - Review new vocabulary (or sentence structures) that emerged during the discussion.

TIPS

- Either look for problem situations in commercially available texts (see Ur 1981, 74–79, for a variety of such problem situations), or custom design them to fit the students' needs and interests.

- Make a problem-solving activity into a focused listening task by giving students a graph or form to fill out. For example, for an activity like Sophie's Choice, you could give students a simple table like the following before you give information about each of the eager suitors:

	Age	Occupation	Income	Interests	Bad Habits
Tom					
Dick					
Harry					

TALKS AND LECTURES

Talks and lectures help students improve their listening and note-taking skills, especially their ability to guess when listening to longer stretches of discourse in which they cannot possibly catch every word.

1. Locate information and prepare a talk.

2. Tell students what you are going to talk about, and ask them to take notes. (Taking notes forces them to listen more carefully.)

3. Give the talk. If students' listening skills are not strong, you may lose your audience, so keep an eye out for the glazed-over look that says your audience has been left behind.

4. After the talk, check comprehension by
   - asking questions
   - having students write a summary of your talk
   - giving a short quiz
   - having students write (and ask) follow-up questions based on what you talked about

TIPS

- Begin looking for topics in a natural place—your own experiences and areas of expertise. However, it is also good to consider students' needs, and if you can give a talk on a subject that is pertinent or useful to the students, so much the better. Talks on language learning and related areas (e.g., study skills) obviously help students in two ways at once. (You might use some of the information in this book as material for talks on language study and learning.) Talks on cultural topics are also especially useful.

- As in focused listening, make your talk easier to follow by first giving students a list of questions to listen for the answers to or by writing a simple outline of the talk on the blackboard. Also write down key new vocabulary words that you use. Visual aids of any kind are very helpful.

- For maximum benefit, choose the level of difficulty at which students can follow much of what you are saying but still have to guess some of the time. Students may need some instruction on how to take notes.

- When checking comprehension for talks on culture topics, have students talk or write about corresponding aspects of their culture, or have students work in groups to list similarities and differences between their culture and the one you talked about.

- In addition to giving talks yourself, use recordings of talks, lectures, or speeches given by others. However, if a recording is available, you should consider having students work with these individually as homework.

PRESS CONFERENCES

A more active alternative to talks and lectures involves having students prepare questions on a given topic and then interview you press-conference style. This activity is good for encouraging student initiative.

1. Choose a topic for the activity, and be sure you are prepared for any questions students might ask about the topic.

2. Tell students that they are reporters interviewing you so that they can write a story for the local paper. Give them the topic and some time to prepare questions related to the topic. Students can write questions individually, but it is often better for speaking practice to have students work in groups.

3. Have students conduct the interview like a press conference. To ensure that a few zealous students don't dominate the process, you might allow each group to ask one question in turn. That way, shyer students get their questions asked by the group representative. If there is less need to protect shy students, simply require that everyone ask at least one question.

4. If you plan to have students write reports, have them take notes. You may also want to put new vocabulary on the board.

5. To close, ask comprehension questions, or ask a few volunteers to tell you what they found most interesting or surprising about what they learned from the interview. Alternatively, ask each student to write a short report based on the interview.

Listening outside Class: Recorded Audio Material

It takes a long time and considerable practice to develop listening skills to a high level, and generally the practice that a student gets listening to the teacher in class is not sufficient. An important part of a good listening program therefore involves giving students listening comprehension homework and getting them accustomed to making good use of other listening practice opportunities available in many EFL settings.

In many nations, an increasing range of recorded listening options is available, including commercial English language recordings (e.g., tapes, CDs, and MP3 files specifically designed for English listening practice) and radio broadcasts in English. There are also ever more audio materials available on the Internet, such as news programs like those of the British Broadcasting Corporation (BBC), Voice of America (VOA), podcasts of programs from sources like National Public Radio (United States) and others, and material specifically designed to give students listening practice. (A number of the Web sites listed in appendix E offer listening practice opportunities.) Such materials can be made available to students as recordings spanning a wide range of both topics and levels of listening difficulty, and the methods for using these materials for listening tasks are essentially the same as discussed above. In this section, I focus primarily on the advantages and disadvantages of recorded materials in general (e.g., tapes, CDs, MP3 files) and suggestions for their use.

As a vehicle for listening practice, sound recordings offer three major advantages. The first and most obvious is that they allow students to practice listening to spoken English outside class. The second is that when listening to recorded materials on their own machines (as opposed to in a group in a language laboratory), students have a high degree of control: they can stop the tape or CD and review when they need to. The third is that a recording will not slow itself down the way a softhearted teacher will, so students must try to follow along at the speaker's rate of speed. This fact, combined with students' ability to control the number of times they listen, makes recordings a good way to expose students to more rapid, natural speech.

The great drawback of this format is that listening to recordings can be boring. Students have no visual stimulus other than a slowly rotating tape or rapidly spinning CD, and from personal experience I can assure you that both tapes and CDs keep right on rotating without protest if a student nods off to sleep. The problem is often exacerbated by the content of the recording, which may not have been intended to entertain. Unfortunately, finding new and more stimulating material is not always an option, so if students are to use recorded material effectively, they need to learn to stay alert.

STUDYING WITH RECORDINGS

Staying alert while listening to a recorded dialogue, story, or lecture is easier if students treat it as a puzzle to be unraveled. I suggest teaching students to use an approach something like the following:

1. Students should first listen to the whole recorded passage once, trying to get the general outline. If a script is available, students should not use it at this time—if they do, they will probably read more than listen. Taking notes or making an outline helps students stay on task; this also gives visible form to the puzzle.

2. Students should listen again to fill in the gaps in their notes or outlines. They should stop the tape and go back over sections as necessary.

3. Once students can squeeze nothing more from the recording, they should look for clues. At this point, it is especially helpful if they have a glossary of new vocabulary items that can provide helpful clues without giving away the whole puzzle. Armed with new hints, students can then return to the tape or CD for a third assault.

4. Finally, if a script is available, students should use it as the answer key to check their comprehension and solve any remaining mysteries. Afterward, it doesn't hurt to review the recording one or two more times for new vocabulary items. (Incidentally, students

who listen again after a good night's sleep will often be surprised to discover that they can understand things that fatigue caused them to miss the night before.)

If you assign recorded listening homework, you should cover it in class to give a sense of closure to the activity and to ensure that students actually did the work. If students do not have a script of the recording, you should go over the main points so that students can determine how well they solved the puzzle. If they have a script, you might provide closure by discussing the content of the tape or CD or simply by asking students what parts they found difficult and why.

CHOOSING APPROPRIATE RECORDED MATERIAL

In choosing recorded material for homework assignments, the material's level of difficulty deserves careful attention. In my experience, teachers and students both frequently err on the side of choosing listening material that is too difficult. I have alluded to the belief that a good, stiff dose of hard work, even if painful, will do wonders for language progress. The listening skills version of this hypothesis is that if you listen to an unintelligible news broadcast long enough, it will eventually become clear. While this theory may appeal to beliefs in the value of hard work, it is not a very effective way to develop listening skills. Listening to overly difficult material is very frustrating, and repeated listenings can improve students' comprehension only to a certain point. If material is too hard, students are frequently forced to give up on their ears and try to find another way to decipher the message (often by reading scripts, if available). Material that is too difficult also forces students and teachers to invest large amounts of time in working with small amounts of material, reducing the amount of both listening practice and vocabulary reviewed.

If you cannot find material at exactly the right level of difficulty for students, I feel that it is generally better to err on the side of using material that is rather easy. Relatively easy recordings tend to reduce learner anxiety, and you can assign larger amounts of material. Such material also allows students to guess the meaning of new words from context more easily and increases the chance that they will be able to understand words and phrases that they have previously learned by reading. Students thus get practice in rapidly recalling the meanings of semifamiliar words and improving the speed at which they process and comprehend what they hear.

When choosing recorded material, you need to be sure that the material provides genuine listening comprehension practice. While this point might seem obvious, it is still worth making because many kinds of commercially produced listening material involve relatively little comprehension practice. For example, some tapes and CDs that accompany textbooks consist entirely of a voice reading aloud the material found in the text. Of course, if the student has read the text before listening to the recording or reads it while listening to the recording, little actual listening comprehension practice occurs. Other tapes and CDs consist of pattern drills that require students to manipulate sentences or fill in blanks; these also require little comprehension once the student has figured out the pattern of the drill. To develop listening comprehension skills, students must listen to material that is new to them and that demands comprehension rather than a mechanical response.

PRODUCING YOUR OWN RECORDED MATERIAL

If you will frequently teach courses involving listening skills, it is a good idea to build a collection of recorded material that you can assign students, including perhaps even recordings you have made yourself. While making your own material requires an extra investment of time, producing materials tailored to the needs of your classes is often well worth the effort. It allows you to control the level of difficulty, choose content that you think students will find interesting, and personalize recordings by bringing in local topics or people. It also allows you to give students listening material for which they have no script.

There are several kinds of material you might collect or create:

1. **recorded interviews:** One of the best kinds of listening material consists of recorded interviews you conduct in English with other teachers, friends, visitors to your school, or even any experts you can locate. For example, I sometimes choose a topic or issue based on students' reading material, interview a speaker of the target language about the topic, record the interview, and then use it as listening material for students. Because these interviews are relatively unplanned and informal, they have the features of natural language (e.g., false starts, fillers, reduced forms) that are too often absent in commercial recordings. The fact that they are based on material that students have read means that students already have some background knowledge and vocabulary for the topic, so students can employ top-down strategies, but the spontaneity of the interview means that students cannot fully predict its contents.

2. **lectures:** You can record talks, given either by others or yourself, on topics of interest. Recordings of talks given in English by visiting speakers expose students to a wider range of voices and views; recording talks you give is a way for you to share ideas from fields you are interested in.

3. **stories:** People tend to enjoy listening to stories, so you can create interesting listening material by asking foreign visitors, guest speakers, and others to tell and record stories about their experiences in the local country or anything else that might be of interest to students. Of course this could be done through interviews (as above), but if you have contact with potential storytellers who are farther away, you could also ask them to record stories by themselves and send the recordings to you. Recordings of stories not only expose students to different voices and accents but also often expose students to more natural and informal styles of speech than are found in lectures.

Recordings need not be professional; in fact, it may be better if they are not. Normal speech is not flawless, and there is no reason recordings should be. The main result of insisting that recordings have no mistakes in them is that they become more burdensome for you to produce.

SOUND QUALITY

Obviously, when making your own recordings there are many advantages to working with digital formats such as CDs or MP3 files rather than tapes, including clearer sound (no tape hiss) and greater durability. However, tapes and tape recorders are still widely used and no doubt will be for some time to come.

When making tapes—and in working with recordings in general—it is important to pay attention to sound quality. Students already face many obstacles in efforts to understand recorded material, and there is no reason to exacerbate the problem with poor sound quality. Here are several words of advice:

- Always check tapes for sound quality. The sound quality on tapes deteriorates as they are used, so do not assume that a tape that was good last semester is still good now. Also, each time a tape is copied, there is some loss in sound quality, so copies of a tape made for students won't sound quite as clear as the original.

- If you plan to use a tape repeatedly over more than one semester, make a copy of the master right away, and use the second-generation copy to make further copies for students. The sound on the copies will not be as good as that of the master, but the master will deteriorate if it is often used for making copies, and eventually you will have to make the tape all over again.

- Learn a little about tape and tape recorder maintenance, and pass that knowledge on to the students. Poorly made tapes will quickly foul the tape recorder heads as they rub against the tape during recording and playback, so use the best tapes possible, and clean the heads on tape recorders frequently. Dirty tape recorder heads not only result in poor sound quality but also damage tapes. A bit of cleaning will often make the difference between a tape that is almost unintelligible and one that is reasonably clear.

LANGUAGE LABORATORIES

Language laboratories can be divided into two basic categories. The more useful kind consists of individual machines that students can use for doing homework. Such labs provide a place where students can work at their own pace on recordings of their own (or their teacher's) choosing. The more problematic (but thankfully increasingly rare) kind of language laboratory is essentially a master console hooked up to sets of headphones, which allows a teacher to play a tape or CD for a class. Such a setup allows a teacher to let an entire class hear the same recording under favorable listening conditions but also forces all students to listen to the same material at the same pace.

If you have to teach a language lab course using taped material, the main battle is generally against boredom, so remember to turn off the master tape or CD from time to time and wake students up with interaction or variety. TPR activities are helpful in labs; having students raise hands in response to questions helps keep them awake and lets you check whether or not they are paying attention. Language labs are also good settings for letting students listen to songs; music breaks the boredom, and students are much more likely to be able to hear the words to a song over headphones than through a small speaker in a big classroom.

Radio Programs

In many parts of the world, radio broadcasts provide one of the few opportunities to hear English regularly—and hence one of the best opportunities for the kind of breakthrough described in chapter 1. VOA and BBC World Service radio broadcasts are audible in many countries and can also be accessed on the Internet. Furthermore, many non-English-speaking nations (including China, Japan, and Russia) have English language broadcasts, usually news programs. Because of their fresh and timely content, news programs tend to be inherently interesting, and the absence of a script forces students to rely on their listening skills. A course of study that involves news broadcasts also has an unusually high degree of validity for students because the ability to understand news broadcasts is a useful skill in and of itself. More recently, in many countries the number of news programs in English—and other kinds of English language programming as well—found on television has been increasing.

The problem with most news broadcasts is that, for a number of reasons, they are quite difficult for learners to follow. First, while the speech of radio announcers is usually both clear and relatively standard, it may be somewhat rapid (especially when compared with that of the average English teacher). A second and larger problem is that news contains much low-frequency vocabulary and many names of places and people. Third, frequent and sudden jumps between topics make news programs difficult to follow; often, just as the listener has figured out what the announcer is talking about, the announcer switches to a new topic. Finally, news items are usually short, so they often include little background explanation or redundancy.

Because the availability of English news broadcasts makes them one of the best chances for students to develop an English skill that they can continue to use over the years, a particularly valuable course for advanced-level students is one designed to prepare them for news programs. Elements of such a course would include

- studying names of places and prominent people in current affairs. Place names are especially important because they often occur at the beginning of an item to establish the context.

- practicing by listening to lots of news items, using both bottom-up and top-down comprehension strategies. Students will need to be able to rapidly decode words as they hear them as well as guess effectively to fill in the many holes left by words or points of information they lack.

- regularly keeping up with the news using any means possible—including newspapers and news reports in the students' native language. The more students know about current news, the more background information they will bring with them to the task of understanding an English news broadcast.

At the early stages of a course, it is helpful to record or download news broadcasts so that students can listen to each more than once. This also allows you to provide students with a vocabulary list, and perhaps even a script if you can locate or make one. In the beginning of such a course, you might focus on a few ongoing news stories (e.g., the Middle East peace process, AIDS research) rather than exposing students to a broad range. Choosing a focus not only simplifies students' task but also demonstrates an effective strategy—building up background knowledge of a story—for making news broadcasts easier to follow.

As students improve to the point where they can get the gist of a story even when they listen to it only once, you can assign them to listen to radio or television broadcasts as homework and then come to class with notes or summaries for class discussion. Alternatively, you can give each student a beat, having him or her be responsible for stories on a given topic or news from a particular part of the world. Using this approach, students still need to listen to the whole news broadcast to find out if there is any news about topic or area they were assigned, but they will have a stronger sense that some part of that broadcast is their responsibility.

The goal of a radio or television news course is that ultimately students will become comfortable enough listening to news broadcasts that they will continue to listen long after your class ends. For students who have limited opportunities to use English once they leave school, news broadcasts might be one of the best channels through which they can maintain and develop their English skills.

Films and Videotapes

English language films are viewed widely throughout the world, either in theaters or on videotape or DVD. English language television programs—both imported and locally produced—are also available in some countries, but films are probably the most widely available and the most challenging, so I focus on films here.

Films have a number of important virtues as an opportunity for English practice. The picture helps students maintain interest, transmits cultural information, and gives students a valuable set of clues to work with as they try to decipher what they are hearing. Films are also designed to be entertaining, so the content is more compelling than that of textbook dialogues. A final benefit for advanced-level students is that films often have very natural English and provide a good opportunity to practice listening to material that has a range of accents and styles.

The great curse of movies flows from the final advantage; the natural conversational language in many films tends to make them difficult to understand. A student watching most modern films will encounter rapid, fragmented, or unclear speech; unfamiliar vocabulary (especially very informal vocabulary); regional or class accents; and problems arising from gaps in background knowledge. Additionally, the sound in many films is less than crystal clear; some actors talk over the sound of screeching brakes or gunshots, and others habitually mumble. As a result, unprepared students sometimes get lost somewhere early in a film and then sit in bewilderment through the next hour and a half.

In recent years, the increased availability of first videotape machines and then DVD players has made teaching film courses a much more realistic option. As with news-listening courses, one of the best arguments for offering film courses for advanced-level students is that such courses can pave the way for students to feel comfortable watching English language films after they graduate. Students who learn to sit back and enjoy a film, satisfied with comprehending as much of the language as possible and guessing the rest from the picture, can often tolerate enormous quantities of film watching.

In one common approach to teaching English with films, you show a film in small segments, allowing students to see each segment several times and supplying all the necessary vocabulary. Chopping the film up in this way lessens its appeal but has the virtue of making the film easier to understand, and this approach may be viable for classes of intermediate-level students who would have difficulty following films in their entirety. In a second approach, you provide students with an introduction (often a plot summary), a vocabulary list, and a list of comprehension questions, and then show the film in its entirety (preferably twice). (Films in DVD format generally have English language captions that can help students follow the dialogue—not to mention giving them a little extra speed-reading practice.) This approach maintains the integrity of the film but is generally not very effective in helping students understand unfamiliar language in the film; a written list of words does little to prepare students to recognize these words aurally when they come darting out of a cloud of barely understood dialogue. This approach is most suitable for students who are already very advanced in their listening skills.

If you have the opportunity to teach a course to advanced-level students using films, I recommend an alternative method that prepares students for a film by giving them an overview (hence enhancing their ability to employ top-down strategies), exposes their ears to some of the voices and vocabulary of the film (hence enhancing their ability to employ bottom-up strategies), yet leaves the film—and its appeal—intact. This method requires quite a bit of preparation on your part, but if you use it in a sustained way in a film course, the results are worth the effort.

1. Choose an interesting film that has as much clear dialogue as possible. Finding such a film is easier said than done; in my experience, you will often need to sample several films to find one that is suitable.

2. Watch the film and take notes on each segment of dialogue, noting where the dialogue occurs so that you can locate it later.

3. Select five to ten key segments of dialogue (hereafter called *scenes*). Include some but not all of the main turning points of the plot, scenes that contain key vocabulary, and scenes that are especially hard to follow. For a normal feature film, the total time of the selected scenes should be about ten minutes.

4. Record these scenes onto an audiocassette, CD, or digital file, leaving a few seconds of silence between each scene. If you want to be really professional, use a microphone to record scene numbers at the beginning of each scene, or even vocabulary items and explanations.

5. Prepare written material based on the scenes on the recording. I generally include a list of the film's characters, a brief introduction that provides the setting for each scene, and a list of vocabulary items for each scene. (If you encounter difficulties in this, you might call on the help of a foreign teacher.)[4]

6. Prepare a list of comprehension questions that students will answer later when they view the film. These may be based both on the scenes selected for the tape or CD and on other portions of the film.

When using this approach, I normally spend some time going over the tape or CD recording with students before they see the film—studying the recording is usually very hard work because the scenes appear without much context, so students may need both help and encouragement. Then I show the film at least twice. In my experience, both as a learner and as a teacher, the second showing of a film is very valuable because students will hear many things that they miss the first time.

When teaching with films, it is important to let students hear the sound as clearly as possible. The speakers on many TV sets are small, and in many classrooms there is a lot of echo; under these conditions, the soundtrack of a film is even harder to understand. If you can run the soundtrack of a film through a listening lab and have students listen to it on headphones, students will understand much more of the film. Another approach is to run the sound through a public address system or stereo.

Although the discussion here focuses on videotaped films, documentaries and TV shows make equally good—if not better—classroom material. Documentaries are usually narrated in nice, clear English, so they are easier to understand than many films. TV shows are more manageable than films because they are shorter, and the sound recording of studio-taped programs tends to be clearer. Commercially produced videotape series designed for English teaching, if available, can also provide an excellent initiation into film and TV viewing.

Evaluation

Most of the tasks listed in the section Listening Tasks in Class can readily be adapted for use as quiz and test items. For example, you can use true/false listening to check both listening skills and vocabulary knowledge. (Note, however, that this kind of test item makes it relatively easy for students to cheat.) Dictations or dictocomps can also be used as test items to check listening and even basic writing skills. (The main problem with dictation is that its backwash may focus students

---

[4]When preparing films for teaching Chinese, I often found that even though I could understand most of the film and do much of the material preparation work by myself, I still generally appreciated confirmation and suggestions from Chinese friends and colleagues. This not only saved me from making mistakes but also gave me more confidence in the accuracy of the materials I made.

too much on listening for words instead of meaning. As noted in the section on listening tasks, one way to ensure that students do not totally ignore meaning is to use questions as the dictation items and ask students to answer the questions.)

The most direct kind of item for testing listening skills—and the one with the best wash-back—consists of having students listen to a text (e.g., dialogue, talk, story) and then checking their comprehension in ways such as

- having students take notes and turn them in

- asking students to write an outline or summary

- asking a series of true/false questions based on the passage

- giving students short-answer questions

- having students fill in a grid, form, or outline

For these last three methods, decide whether or not to give students the task or questions before they hear the passage. If you do, it will help focus their listening and make the task easier. If not, you are testing memory or note-taking as well as listening comprehension.

For Thought, Discussion, and Action

1. **listening opportunities:** List opportunities students in your country have to listen to English. Try to include some less obvious opportunities that students might not think of.

2. **top-down and bottom-up listening practice:** Consider a previous language learning experience (or course) you had, and analyze the listening practice it provided. Did it mainly provide practice using top-down listening strategies, bottom-up listening strategies, or both? How effective overall was the course's approach in building your listening skills?

3. **listening activities:** For the following course, decide what listening goals you might set, and then choose kinds of listening activities from this chapter that you might use regularly in this course. Explain your choices to another teacher or classmate.

   Intermediate Oral English: This intermediate-level conversation course is for a large class of university students (not English majors). The students have already studied English for several years (mostly vocabulary, grammar, and reading) but have weak speaking and listening skills. They come from a variety of different majors, so it is not clear how they might use English after graduation. They seem enthusiastic, but this is not a core course, so they will probably not have much time to do English homework. (The course was recently added to the curriculum to encourage the students to build strong oral English skills, but it is not integrated into the rest of the program and meets only once a week for two hours.) There is no textbook or tape for the course, and there is no readily available photocopy machine. You have a fairly free hand with the course because there is also no standardized test or follow-up course to consider.

4. **dictocomp:** If you already teach an English course that involves listening skills, prepare and conduct a dictocomp exercise according to the instructions given in the chapter. Alternatively, try another kind of activity that you have not used before.

5. **problem-solving situations:** This chapter mentions Sophie's Choice and Spaceship as problem-solving situations that can be used for both listening and speaking practice.

Design a problem-solving situation of your own for use in an oral skills class. Then share your situation with other teachers for their suggestions.

6. **recorded interviews:** Practice making your own listening material by recording an interview with an English speaker.
   - Choose a topic (ideally one related to a lesson you will teach in an English course), and prepare a list of interview questions related to the topic.
   - Locate an English speaker, and record an interview with that person.
   - Turn the recording into material for focused listening by preparing a list of comprehension questions to give to students that cover the main points of the interview. (Of course, your original interview questions already provide a good outline to work from.)
   - Prepare step-by-step instructions you would give to students on how to use the tape for listening practice. (Try to make the process as much like a game or a puzzle as possible.)

7. **radio news:** Design one or more sample language learning projects (LLPs) students could do that involve using English radio news broadcasts to build listening skills.

8. **film watching to improve listening:** Survey several people about their experiences with trying to build their listening comprehension in a foreign language by watching movies. Questions include these: (1) Did they have some kind of plan or method? If so, what was it? (2) How successful was the effort? (3) What problems did they encounter? (4) What did they like about using films for listening practice? (5) What would they do differently if they were to try it again?

9. **subtitles:** When using English language films for studying English, students often need to choose whether and how to use subtitles (especially if they are watching on DVD). Analyze and list the relative advantages and disadvantages of each of the following approaches to use of the film for English study, and decide what knowledge and skills each approach would build—and not build. (Assume the film will be viewed twice.)
   - Local language subtitles are visible for both viewings.
   - English subtitles are visible for both viewings.
   - No subtitles are visible for the first viewing; English subtitles are visible for the second viewing.
   - No subtitles are visible for either viewing.

Sample LLP for Advanced-Level Listening Skills

Goal: Build listening comprehension, especially top-down skills and ability to listen to natural conversation between native speakers of English.

Material: Western TV situation comedy series (on DVD).

Plan: Study one episode a week, two hours of study divided into two sessions.

Method:

Session 1

1. Watch an episode straight through one or two times with no subtitles showing. Make note of which parts of the episode I didn't understand; guess what they might have said.

2. Turn on the subtitles and re-view the parts in question. Check my guesses to see if I was right. Make notes of any new expressions I want to remember.

Session 2

1. Review new material I made note of.

2. Watch the episode again with subtitles off.

3. Watch the episode again with the subtitles on to check my comprehension.

Criteria for measuring progress: I will have succeeded if I

- watch a whole season of the series (approximately ten to fifteen episodes)

- can now generally follow the dialogue in each of the episodes I watched, even if the subtitles are not turned on

- feel more comfortable watching the series without the subtitles turned on

- can understand more of a new episode the first time I watch it, even without subtitles, than I could before starting the LLP

Speaking: A Linguistic Juggling Act

Chapter 7

- Speaking in a foreign language involves a variety of operations, and learning to perform all of them quickly requires extensive practice.

- During speaking practice in class, the more students who can talk at any given time, the better. Pair or small-group work allows more students to practice speaking than large-group discussions or teacher-centered activities do.

- Most adult learners will not achieve native pronunciation in a second language. Clear but accented pronunciation not only is a more realistic goal but also may be a more desirable one.

- Some correction of students' errors may be helpful, but there is little evidence that correction improves students' accuracy much. Overcorrection can make students self-conscious and discourage them from speaking.

Having spent two years in a Japanese language program that focused almost exclusively on speaking, I should have at least a fair command of spoken Japanese. However, I don't. Part of the fault is no doubt my own—I certainly could have been more persistent in seeking out the many Japanese on our campus for practice. But, as mentioned in chapter 3, part of the problem also lay within the program, which consisted mainly of memorizing dialogues and learning to perform them as fluently as possible in class. This approach was successful in teaching me quite a bit of Japanese vocabulary and even some grammar, but it gave me little practice in expressing my own ideas in Japanese. Thus, when I tried to talk with a Japanese friend in Japanese, I was generally trying to put my own ideas into Japanese sentences for the first time, much like a piano student who shows up for a recital having practiced only scales. The results were uneven at best—whenever I wanted to say something that fortuitously coincided with a sentence I had memorized, I could rattle it off fluently and flawlessly, but whenever I tried to say anything else, I had to struggle for a painfully long time to put even basic sentences together. Unsurprisingly, I found these forays into real conversation frustrating and eventually gave them up to go back to just memorizing the dialogues in order to pass the course.

Unfortunately, this kind of problem is common in EFL settings. In class, genuine speaking practice may be neglected in favor of choral drills, and other kinds of practice opportunities are hard to come by, so students' ability to speak may lag far behind their knowledge of grammar and vocabulary. Much of your success as a teacher of spoken skills depends on how effective you are in creating practice opportunities for students, so, in the discussion of the teaching of spoken skills here, the emphasis is on ways in which you can provide students with the kinds of practice they need to develop oral skills.

The Process of Speaking: The Problem and the Goal

When you consider the parts of the speaking process individually, no single one presents overwhelming difficulties. For example, neither pronouncing a word correctly nor deciding what verb tense to use is impossibly difficult if you focus all of your attention on that single problem. The difficulty arises from the fact that, like a juggler who is trying to keep ten balls in the air at the same time while tap-dancing and playing the harmonica, a speaker has to simultaneously perform a rather long list of operations. Consider, for example, the case of Kim, a student who has overslept and arrived late for English class for the third time this week. He is now standing in front of a stern-looking foreign English teacher who wants an explanation. A peek inside his head will give a good illustration of all the things he needs to consider in the process of producing a sentence in English:

1. **goals:** "Should I try to win mercy or sympathy?"

2. **strategy:** "How would the teacher react if I lied and she found out? Should I be honest and play the contrite sinner or lie and play the misunderstood victim?"

3. **listener's background knowledge:** "Does she know the local traffic situation? Maybe I can get away with an excuse about the traffic."

4. **word choice:** "Do I say *crowded traffic* or *busy traffic*?"

5. **grammar:** "Is it *Excuse me to be late*, *Excuse me being late*, or *Excuse my being late*?"

6. **pronunciation:** "Pay attention to that consonant cluster at the beginning of E*xc*use . . . ."

7. **intonation:** "Does *Excuse me for being late, but there are always many cars in the morning* end with falling or rising intonation?"

8. **gestures and facial expressions:** "Do I look her in the eye or avoid her eyes? Do I smile or look unhappy?"

Finally, poor Kim's problem is compounded by the fact that he doesn't have very much time in which to make all of these decisions—it won't be long before the patience of an annoyed teacher wears dangerously thin.

Of course, not all English language communication situations involve the kind of immediate pressure Kim faces, but speakers normally need to cope with all the problems illustrated above, and they normally need to do so quickly. The time element deserves special attention. Some people—mostly English teachers—will wait indefinitely as a student struggles to construct an utterance in English, but most people are not so saintly and will sooner or later give up on students who cannot communicate at a reasonable pace. A student who can communicate an idea even faultily without slowing the conversation down too much is more likely to be able to sustain conversation when the opportunity arises than is a more accurate but slower comrade. Quicker students, then, are likely to have more conversation and practice opportunities and therefore continue to improve. These students will almost certainly also find conversation easier and more enjoyable, so they are more likely to seek out any opportunities that exist.

Hence, if students are to reach a breakthrough point in spoken English, their primary goal is to learn to express their ideas in English with a fair degree of fluency. Accuracy is also desirable, and issues such as correct grammar and proper use of vocabulary should not be neglected. In fact, communicative effectiveness and accuracy cannot be entirely separated; if a student's grammar or vocabulary is too far wide of the mark, the listener may get the wrong message or no message at all. However, it is safe to say that in most actual speaking situations, communication is more important than formal accuracy, so a course intended to teach speaking skills should place special emphasis on communication.

Clearly, then, one of your most important roles in a speaking class is seeing that students get the maximum possible amount of practice speaking English, particularly kinds of practice that allow students to express their own ideas. This is especially true for students at intermediate and advanced levels of speaking skills, but even at beginning levels it is desirable to give students choice in what to say so that they have to communicate ideas as well as words.

Pairs, Small Groups, and Large Groups

If I asked you to describe a good conversation lesson, perhaps the first picture to pop into your head might be of a teacher briskly fielding questions from an enraptured student audience or perhaps of a lively class debate. On a little reflection, the problem with the first option is fairly evident—in this kind of exchange, the teacher does most of the talking. The second activity might initially seem to be an improvement because it is more student centered; presumably the teacher need not say very much. However, the large-group focus of the activity means that, at any given time, only one student has a chance to speak. So in a fifty-minute class with twenty-five students, even if the teacher never says a word, each student would only get two minutes of speaking practice, and students would spend most of the period listening to their classmates, an activity that is probably less useful than listening to the teacher speak.

So how should in-class speaking practice be organized? In general, students should work in pairs or small groups as often as possible because this arrangement allows more students to practice at the same time. Pairs are the most efficient grouping in that they allow the most students to talk at once, but as Harmer (2001, 117) notes, the effectiveness of any pair work is affected quite a bit by how the two students get along. Small groups (of three or four students) still give many students an opportunity to speak but provide a bit more space for personality differences. For example, in a small group, the presence of at least two other people means that a shy student can sit back and listen most of the time but still feel like a participant. As Ur (1981, 7) points out, the physical closeness in small groups also helps improve motivation, so they provide a good environment for encouraging reluctant students to make their first attempts at speaking.

Breaking students into pairs and small groups has its problems, and several of these are discussed in chapter 13. However, students can generally not get adequate speaking practice unless they work in pairs or small groups, so a good rule of thumb is to break students into the smallest groups in which most of them will speak English a significant percentage of the time.

In-Class Methods and Tasks

This section briefly discusses activities often used in speaking classes. As in chapter 6, the activities are presented roughly according to level of difficulty. (See also appendix C.)

MEMORIZATION OF MATERIAL

Having read my rather negative depiction of dialogue memorization at the beginning of this chapter, you may be surprised to see it suggested here. However, the problem described there resulted from excessive reliance on memorization—and an absence of other kinds of speaking practice—rather than from memorization itself. A good case can be made for memorization of sentences or short dialogues that contain a large percentage of high-frequency phrases and sentences like *How are you?, What is that?, My name is . . .* , and so forth. Memorizing typical sentences may also help students learn sentence patterns and grammar. Furthermore, Stevick (1988, 51) argues that the conceptual simplicity of memorization and the strong sense that they have mastered the content makes memorization an emotionally reassuring task for beginning-level students. Finally, it may provide a good way to ease reluctant classes into speaking.

When requiring students to memorize passages or dialogues, encourage them to keep as much focus on communication as possible. While fluent delivery is nice, it is also important that students know what they are saying. Here are steps (from Stevick 1988, 70–76) for guiding students to memorize a short dialogue in class.

1. Choose a short dialogue or passage that contains a high percentage of material that is valuable in exactly the form in which it is memorized—in other words, commonly used phrases and expressions such as *How are you?* and *What time is it?*

2. Have students listen to you say the whole dialogue once or twice.

3. Teach the pronunciation of any new words.

4. Begin the process of memorization. A good trick for helping students memorize is to build sentences, especially longer ones, up from the end, hence preserving natural sentence intonation. For example, you would say,

   had ever eaten? (Students repeat.)

   the best she had ever eaten? (Students repeat.)

   my cooking is the best she had ever eaten? (Students repeat.)

   Did she really say my cooking is the best she had ever eaten? (Students repeat.)

5. If you are working with dialogues, have students role-play the dialogue in pairs, perhaps even acting it out. To close, have a few pairs recite their dialogues in front of the class, accompanying the language with appropriate actions.

CHORAL DRILL

This is essentially the all-class, repeat-after-me exercise in which you say something and students repeat it. While choral drill is of limited value in building communicative language skills, it can be useful for practicing pronunciation and intonation, for reviewing material, and for getting beginning-level students more accustomed to opening their mouths and speaking.

1. Choose a dialogue from a textbook, read it aloud line by line, and have students repeat after each line. So as not to overload their short-term memory, break long sentences into shorter parts. Students will pay more attention to pronunciation and intonation if they repeat after listening to you rather than reading aloud from their textbook, so if the dialogue is from their textbooks, have them close the book.

2. Have students try to replicate your pronunciation and intonation.

3. As with memorized dialogues above, have students role-play the dialogue in pairs, and close with a few short performances.

TIPS

- If the goal is to build students' mastery of normal speech intonation, use dialogues and other texts that approximate spoken (rather than written) language. (Learning to read literary texts aloud is also of some value, but probably more for students at higher levels.)

- As with memorization, preserve normal intonation when repeating longer sentences by building them up from the end.

- Many textbook series are now accompanied by tapes or CDs, so as an alternative to reading the dialogue aloud yourself, play the tape and have students repeat after it.

CLASSROOM CHAT

Classroom chat is my term for informal conversation between you and the students. In some ways, classroom chat is actually more valuable as listening practice than speaking practice because of the limited amount of time each student spends speaking. However, teacher-student interaction can be a good model of genuine communication if you are really interested in what you ask students about, and conversation with you may have a motivational impact on students that goes beyond the practice it provides, especially if the interaction is fun and nonthreatening. Classroom chat is a good way to begin or end a lesson or to provide a break in the middle; it is also a good way to introduce a topic and warm up before moving into a more organized activity related to the topic.

1. From whatever texts the class has been working with, come up with questions that will generate real communication. For example, if today's lesson in the book is on travel and the present perfect verb tense, a natural way to start class is by asking students "Have you ever been to . . . ?"

2. Chat with students, keeping the interaction communicative by responding to what students say rather than just passing judgment ("Good!") or making grammar corrections.

Tips

- Try to avoid asking questions whose answers you aren't really interested in. If you are really interested in the students' answers, your enthusiasm will spread to the students. If you ask real questions and expect real answers, this activity is a good way to establish the idea that English use should be communicative.

- When you ask a question, first address it to the class as a whole, and give everyone a moment to think before calling on someone. This pause allows all the students in the class to practice formulating a response even if they don't always have a chance to verbalize it. Talking with students in a random order also helps; students who don't know whether they will be called on next are more likely to try to think of a response to every question.

- To minimize teacher talk, start a line of questioning or a chain of dialogue, and have the students continue it. For example, after asking student A, "What did you do yesterday?" (for practice with past tense verbs), have student A ask student B the same question rather than doing it yourself.

- Remember that students called on to respond in public may get nervous and freeze. One way to help students who panic is to ask a question that involves limited choices (e.g., "Do you prefer reading or watching TV?"), which helps students toward a response. Yes/no questions are also easier to answer than open-ended ones but generate less speech.

- To reduce tension in class, rely mostly on volunteers to answer questions, only occasionally calling on students who rarely volunteer.

- As useful new words or structures emerge in the course of conversation, write them on the board.

MODEL-BASED DIALOGUES

Model dialogues are a staple item in textbooks used for oral skills courses, so the question is how to use these dialogues.[1] As I have suggested, beginning-level students sometimes benefit from simply memorizing short, basic dialogues, but as the dialogues get longer, this approach is more and more time-consuming. If the dialogues are at all realistic—culturally and linguistically—another useful approach is to use them as models of interaction involving both language and behavior. What is important here is not the dialogue as a whole but the moves that it illustrates—the things people do with language. (These are often called *functions*.) Consider the following sample dialogue:

Kim: *Let's* go get some food.
Jan: I *would really like to, but* I have a test tomorrow.
Kim: *Can't you* study later?
Jan: Not *really*. This is a *pretty* important test, and I haven't prepared much yet.

Moves (functions) in the dialogue include the following:

- **suggestions:** *Let's* + simple present tense verb is one of the most common and generic ways to suggest doing something. *Can't you . . .* introduces another suggestion, but a

---

[1] Even the idea of learning speaking skills from a book is rather odd; the very nature of the format pulls students toward reading and away from conversation. Arguably, a set of tapes might be a better "textbook" for a speaking course.

rather pushy one. Apparently, Kim and Jan are close enough that Jan doesn't feel the need to be overly polite.

- **polite refusals:** Jan uses the pattern *I would like to, but* + *(specific reason)* to refuse Kim's invitation; note also that she uses the words *really* and *pretty* to make the refusal less abrupt. Here, students should learn both the language and the idea that, to be polite in a Western context, an excuse should be believable and specific.

Treating a dialogue as a model of both language and culture moves will teach students to pay attention to patterns of behavior as well as language, and practicing the moves allows students to rehearse and learn specific material. This kind of practice is good for classes of mixed levels because it allows students who are unsure of themselves to stay close to the model, while those who are more comfortable have freedom to improvise.

1. Choose a dialogue that is a reasonably realistic model of how people interact as well as a good model of English.

2. Analyze the dialogue, and note the moves in it.

3. Present the dialogue to students, and have them analyze it. First, have them tell you what the participants in the dialogue do with language (the moves); then have them tell you what language is used to carry out the move.

4. After the points have been introduced and explained, have students practice a dialogue that has the same kinds of moves but not necessarily the same content as the model dialogue. For example, after studying the dialogue above, you might give student pairs the following instructions: (1) Student A, make a suggestion to student B, and be persistent. (2) Student B, keep finding polite excuses for refusing. This kind of practice allows students to improvise but also helps make sure that they practice new material learned from the text.

5. To quickly give closure to the practice, select a few pairs (either at random or by asking for volunteers) to perform their dialogues. The most obvious option for closing is to have all the pairs perform their dialogues, but this consumes a lot of class time and is often boring. A more enjoyable way to achieve the same end is to ask pairs what happened in their little encounters (e.g., "What excuse did Kim give you for refusing your invitation?"). Closing the activity this way draws attention to the content of the conversations and helps keep the focus on communication.

TIPS

- Encourage students to personalize dialogues, using their real names and backgrounds or creating new identities and playing new roles.

- To make pair practice livelier, have students move from partner to partner cocktail-party-style (see below) rather than only practicing in seated pairs; rotating also allows them to practice the moves in the dialogue several times instead of just once.

- Being stuck with an uncooperative partner can make pair practice burdensome, so either let students change partners often or choose their own partners. In my experience, partners who choose each other eventually learn to work together reasonably well.

PRESENTATIONS

The main advantage of presentations is that they allow students to prepare and practice in advance so that they can polish both content and language (e.g., vocabulary, grammar, pronunciation, intonation) before having to speak in English in front of other people.

Of course, the ability to present in English is itself a useful skill to develop. The main problem is that because presentations tend to take up a lot of class time, with only one student getting to speak at a time, they are better suited to fairly small classes than to very large ones. For maximum benefit to the greatest number of students, it is generally best to put a strict time limit on the presentations, maximize the amount of time students spend preparing for the presentation outside class, and do everything possible to ensure that the presentations are genuinely interesting and informative for other students to listen to. One approach to incorporating presentations in oral skills courses is as follows:[2]

1. Early in the semester, assign students the task of preparing a brief (three- to five-minute) presentation on a topic chosen either by you or by them. Let students know how you expect them to prepare and how they will be graded. In particular, let students know whether the main focus of the practice is on accuracy, content, presentation skills, or some combination thereof.

2. Schedule the presentations. It is generally best to spread the presentations out over a period of weeks or even months rather than packing them all into a few class periods; presenters' classmates are more likely to be attentive listeners if they don't have to sit through an hour or two of presentations.

3. Before each presentation, have students submit an outline or script of what they will present so that you can make suggestions to guide their presentation.

4. When students present, encourage their classmates to listen by letting them know you will check their comprehension after the presentation, if only by asking a few questions. Also encourage good audience behavior, such as clapping before and after the presentation and asking interesting follow-up questions.

5. As students present, take notes.

6. After the presentation, publicly praise the good points of the presentation and give one or more brief suggestions that would be of benefit to the whole class. You can give more detailed feedback either by meeting with the student or in writing.

ROLE PLAYS

Role plays are a form of pair practice that allow students freedom to play, improvise, and create. As Ur (1981, 10) points out, many students feel freer behind the mask of a role, and the element of creative play involved in role playing can do much to make a lesson livelier. These are useful as a way to practice not only language but also culturally appropriate behavior.

1. Create situations and roles for students. You may want to base these on a dialogue or something else you have studied in class (see Model-Based Dialogues above). When the situations are based on material from the textbook, role plays give students a chance to practice using previously studied material in a less controlled activity.

---

[2] My thanks to Ding Nan for suggestions on this approach.

2. Pair students and give them their roles. Often you will want to write each role on a separate piece of paper so that each member of the pair knows something about the situation that the other doesn't—as often happens in real life. Consider the following example:

A: There is a very good movie in town tonight, and you want a friend to go see it with you. B often goes to films with you, so you have decided to persuade her to go.

B: You plan to go to a party tonight with some classmates. These classmates don't want to invite A, so they have asked you not to tell her about the party.

3. After giving the members of each pair their roles, you might want to give them a moment to think about how to handle their situation.

4. Have students carry out the role play. While students should practice material they have studied, also encourage them to be creative and improvise.

5. To close, one alternative is to have one or two pairs do their role play for the whole class. This serves primarily to give a sense of closure and need not go on long. (Having each pair perform takes too much time, and other students spend too long sitting and waiting. Listening to classmates stumble through dialogues is not very good listening practice.) Another way to close is by asking a few students what the outcome of their role play was (e.g., was the invitation accepted?). This is much quicker than having students perform but still provides a sense of closure.

TIPS

- Encourage creativity. If students make an effort to entertain, role plays are more fun to do and watch. Be realistic, however, about the fact that not all students are hams and not all will be great public performers.

- While public performances may run too long if you are not careful, they have the advantage of allowing you a chance to comment on language or the cultural appropriateness of how students handle the situation.

SURVEYS

Surveys involve asking the same few questions several times to different people, so they are a good way for students to repeatedly practice questions and answers in a format that encourages genuine communication. (For lower level students, the survey is one of the easiest formats for relatively free communicative interaction.) Also, it is fairly easy to come up with survey questions that involve a real information gap and are of genuine personal interest to a class.

1. Decide on a topic or list of questions. This activity works better when you and the students are genuinely curious about the results of the survey.

2. Tell students the purpose or topic of the survey. Either list the questions you want them to ask, or give them a general topic and allow time for them to write their own questions individually or in groups.

3. Tell students how many classmates they are expected to survey and approximately how long they have to do it in. Alternatively, assign a time limit for each short interview.

4. Have students survey each other. You may need to occasionally encourage them to move on to a new partner. You can either join in, or wander and eavesdrop.

5. Close the activity by having a few students report their findings.

Tips

- As students conduct their interviews, have them move around the class as they conduct their interviews to make things more lively and keep everyone awake.

- Variation: Before the survey, have students prepare questions in groups so that each member of the group asks the same questions. Later, group members can get back together to compare notes and report results.

INTERVIEWS

Interviews allow pairs of students to converse in greater depth. They are a good activity for intermediate- or advanced-level oral skills classes because they allow in-depth exploration of a topic and provide students with practice in explaining opinions.

1. Decide what topic(s) you want students to interview each other on.

2. Give directions for the interviews. Tell the students the suggested topic and approximately how much time they will have. If you want students to write up their own list of questions, allow a few minutes to do this.

3. Pair the students. Often it is good to pair students with someone other than the person sitting next to them (whom they probably already know fairly well).

4. Have students carry out interviews. Once student A finishes interviewing student B, you can ask them to switch roles or even partners. You may want to set a time limit and call out when partners should switch roles.

5. To close, ask a few students to report some of the more interesting things they learned from their partner during the interview.

Tips

- Topics that involve opinions or information not shared by everyone in the class are best because they make interviews more genuinely communicative.

- Role-playing and interviews mix nicely; for example, one person might be a reporter and the other a famous person.

COCKTAIL PARTIES

Cocktail parties are a free form of speaking practice in which students get out of their seats and converse with different partners in a style similar to that of a real cocktail party. The basic rules of a Western-style cocktail party are that (1) you should talk to more than one person rather than talking to the same person the whole time; (2) you should generally stand as you chat rather than sit down; and (3) after talking with someone for a while, you must close your conversation and move on to someone else.

For this activity, you can either specify a topic (presumably related to other material the students have been studying) or give the students greater freedom by providing a list of suggested (but optional) topics. Note that this activity works best in classrooms where chairs can be moved aside or where there is ample free space; it is also relatively noisy, so consider the impact this chaos will have on nearby classes.

1. Explain the basic rules of a cocktail party to students. Also teach them a few lines for striking up conversations (e.g., *It sure is hot today.*) and for closing them (e.g., *Well, it's been nice talking to you, but it's getting late and I need to get going.*).

2. Let students know whether or not you want them to practice specific material (e.g., from a model dialogue), how long the party will last, and how many people you expect them to talk to.

3. Turn students loose, and join in. When time is up or enthusiasm runs thin, call the students back to their seats.

4. Close by asking a few students about their conversations. This is generally more fun—and other students will pay more attention—if you ask a specific question appropriate to the activity (e.g., *Tell me a little about the most interesting conversation you had* or *What new things did you learn?*) rather than having students summarize all their conversations.

PAIR OR SMALL-GROUP TASKS

In pair or small-group activities, students work together in pairs or groups to deal with a task that will generate a visible result. Merely telling students to "Talk about . . ." is generally not enough; a well-defined task gives students a clear sense of direction and lets them know exactly what they are expected to produce. Here are some examples of tasks:

- Make a list (e.g., *List the most beautiful places in your country.*).

- List reasons (e.g., *List ten reasons why middle school children should—or shouldn't—study a foreign language.*).

- List advantages and disadvantages (e.g., *List the advantages and disadvantages of using standardized examinations to determine who should have the opportunity to enter university.*).

- Prepare directions (e.g., *Prepare a list of directions for how a foreign tourist should bargain at the local market.* Or: *Make a list of suggestions for choosing a good bicycle.*).

- Decide whether or not (e.g., *Decide whether or not middle school students should be allowed to date.*).

- Make a choice (e.g., *Your friend has been offered two jobs—a stable but boring job in a bank and a riskier but more rewarding job putting out oil-well fires. Which should your friend take?*).

- Decide whether you agree or disagree with (a statement): (e.g., *Decide whether or not you agree with the following: Not wearing seatbelts when riding in a car should be against the law.*).

- Rank or prioritize (e.g., *In order of importance, rank your country's ten greatest heroes.*).

- Make a plan (e.g., *Plan the ideal three-day local vacation trip for a foreign tourist.*).

- Solve a problem (e.g., *A foreign teacher at your school is interested in world news but can't understand TV news programs in your country. What suggestions do you have for how the teacher can find out about world news while in your country?*).

1. Place students in pairs or groups of three or four. (Larger groups give fewer people chances to speak.)

2. Give groups a task (not just a topic—see above), and tell them how long they have to complete it.

3. Have each group appoint one recorder to write down what the group decides.

4. While groups discuss, wander from group to group, listening in and looking at what they have written. As you look at their lists, help with language difficulties, or just comment on their ideas.

5. To close, have each group briefly report its conclusions as you take notes on the board, and then discuss them.

TIPS

• Have students form groups of three or four students. Such groups are small enough that each student feels a sense of ownership, so even students who say little tend to remain engaged by listening and mentally formulating language.

• Small groups often work best if there is a discussion leader, so have the students in each group appoint one.

• Have just one person in each group take notes for the group. This tends to bring the group together, as everyone tends to look at the same piece of paper. Being able to see one set of group notes also makes it easier for you to see how groups are doing—for example, whether they are on task—and makes it easier for you to join in by commenting on a good point they have made, making a suggestion, or offering a correction. (In a noisy room, looking at the notes is often the only way you can know what is going on in each small group.)

• When the time comes for groups to report, ask each group to report just one comment or idea at a time rather than having one group give a long report while others sit and wait. (If one group reports everything first, the others are often left with not much to say.) Make several rounds of the class if necessary.[3]

• Remember that culture-related situations and topics can provide a rich fund of material for small-group discussion. (See chapter 12 and appendix C.)

DEBATES

Debates are good for generating excitement and interest in a topic. Their most serious drawback is that only one person can speak at a time during the debate phase of the activity, so the format suggested here includes substantial small-group activity.

1. Introduce the issue to be debated either as a statement (e.g., *Adolescents should be encouraged to take jobs.*) or a question (e.g., *Should adolescents be encouraged to take jobs?*). You may wish to supply some background to the issue and some relevant vocabulary.

2. Put students into small groups (teams) of three or four students, and either assign or allow them to choose an affirmative or negative position on the topic.

3. Have each team prepare a case consisting of one or more reasons why they hold the opinion they do, explanations, and evidence (e.g., examples) that supports their view. (This is the phase of the activity that provides most of the speaking practice, so allow ample time.)

---

[3] The primary value of small-group discussion lies in the practice rather than in the final reports, so keep the time devoted to reports to a minimum. However, as Ur (1981) points out, "It is not fair to students to ask them to put a lot of effort into something, and then to disregard the result . . . . What groups have done must then be displayed and then related to in some way the teacher and class; assessed, criticized, admired, argued with, or even simply listened to with interest" (pp. 22–23).

4. For the debate phase, I recommend a Ping-Pong format that follows lines of argument one at a time. The procedure for each line of argument is as follows:

   • One affirmative team states one of its arguments (with explanation and support).

   • One negative team responds to the affirmative team's argument with either questions or a counterargument. The students must respond directly to the argument raised by the affirmative team—they cannot begin a new line of argument.

   • Either the original affirmative team or another affirmative team responds to the negative team, and so on, following the line of argument until development ceases and repetition sets in.

   • One negative team begins a new line of argument, and so on.

5. As the teams develop a line of argument, roughly keep track of the flow of the arguments in a flowchart on the board.

6. At the end, close the debate by praising especially good points made by various teams.

TIPS

   • A good topic for debate and discussion has the following characteristics:
      — Students have some knowledge about the topic and some interest in it. It is hard to start a discussion when students have little idea what they are talking about.
      — Opinion is divided. No matter how good a topic is, if students all agree, there won't be much debate.
      — The topic is not too politically or culturally sensitive.

   • One way to locate good topics is to keep an eye on what issues are being debated in the local press and media. You might also ask the students to suggest topics.

LARGE-GROUP DISCUSSIONS

Discussions can be a good way to arouse class interest in a topic you wish to lecture about or have students write about, and they can also provide a useful break from the normal class routine. However, large-group discussions give each student only a brief opportunity to speak, and this severely diminishes their value as a form of speaking practice. To ensure adequate conversation practice, it is generally good to have students first prepare in small groups. Regular use of large-group discussion is best limited to small classes of advanced-level students.

1. Introduce the topic and any necessary vocabulary. (See Debates for suggestions on the characteristics of good discussion topics.)

2. Have students prepare in small groups. (This is where the students get most of their speaking practice, so allow ample time.) Require each group to come to consensus on a position that they can present to the rest of the class.

3. Begin the discussion by having the groups present their ideas.

Speaking Practice outside Class

Getting students to practice speaking English outside class as homework is not always easy. They may be too busy with other homework, find it too awkward to talk to their peers in a foreign language, or simply not have enough interest in English to practice when the teacher isn't around to make them do it. However, the limited amount of class time available for speaking practice means that some practice outside class is virtually essential if students are ever to develop their spoken English very much. One goal of your courses should therefore be to teach students to take responsibility for their own practice. To reach this goal, over time you should try to move students toward less structured, more voluntary kinds of activities. The following menu of homework activities is arranged from those which provide the most accountability to those which provide the least. (Most of these activities are very similar to those discussed as in-class activities, so I confine my comments to their use as out-of-class assignments.)

MEMORIZATION AND RECITATION

The use of memorization assignments for homework has one great advantage: students can readily be held accountable because you can easily tell who did the homework and who didn't. Memorization assignments can therefore be useful in getting students into the habit of doing spoken work outside class, and assigning them is better than assigning no speaking homework at all. However, memorizing texts tends to be hard, boring work; also, memorizing texts for recitation in class is not the same thing as practicing expressing one's own ideas in English. So memorization assignments are well worth considering as an option, but they shouldn't be the only kind of oral practice you assign students.

DIALOGUES AND ROLE PLAYS PREPARED OUTSIDE CLASS

Having students create their own dialogues outside class provides a fair degree of accountability, yet still allows students to practice expressing their own ideas in English. The main problem is that once students have invested time in preparing a dialogue or role play, you need to give them a chance to perform. However, watching such performances—especially if they are not very interesting—may not be the best use of class time. One way around this problem is to spot-check by selecting a few pairs or groups to perform and then allowing other groups to volunteer. If you have each group perform, put a time limit on the performances, and do everything possible to encourage performances that are creative and interesting for other students to watch.

SMALL-GROUP DISCUSSIONS OUTSIDE CLASS

Out-of-class small-group discussions can be handled in the same way as in-class small-group discussions and have the same benefits. The absence of direct supervision makes accountability more of a problem, but you can hold students somewhat accountable by having them turn in notes, tell you what the conclusions of their discussion were, or even just report how long they talked. Another way to provide accountability is to use the out-of-class discussion as preparation for an in-class activity such as a debate. Some students may still take advantage of your absence to avoid speaking English, but as long as some groups speak English a significant amount of the time, the activity is probably worth continuing.

For advanced-level students, a useful variation on this activity is an ongoing discussion group focused on a particular kind of topic or material. Examples of this might include a group that gathers to listen to and discuss the news or a reader's club that meets to discuss books. Another possibility is a group in which members take turns preparing presentations that the group then discusses. For example, I once participated in a Chinese language study group in which the three members each regularly made a presentation in their academic areas. We thus rotated among discussions of Chinese history, literature, and linguistics.

Appointing group leaders—or having groups choose their own leaders—ensures that someone in each group is responsible for getting things started and simplifies the process of holding the group accountable. Also, as with in-class, small-group discussions, groups will find it much easier to start their discussion and keep it moving if you provide a specific question (task) and clear instructions as to how the group should report on their discussion.

FREE CONVERSATION ACTIVITIES

For motivated students at any level, the ideal way to practice is to begin bringing English into their daily lives and using it for real communicative purposes. Students can do this in a variety of ways:

- gathering at English tables in a cafeteria or English corners on campus where students socialize and discuss issues in English (or at least partially in English)

- chatting in English in the dormitory or while taking a walk

- talking aloud to themselves or thinking in English

By breaking away from the idea that English is only used when they are in class or doing homework, students greatly increase their opportunities for practice. Combining English practice with social activity, as the first two methods above do, also has the potential to make English practice more enjoyable. Heavy-handed attempts to hold students accountable tend to destroy the spontaneity and fun of such activities, turning them into another form of homework. However, indirect ways of providing accountability, such as casually asking students what they talked about at the English table, are often sufficient to show that you consider such activities important.

FISHING FOR ENGLISH SPEAKERS

If you are in an area where there are foreign English speakers, one assignment to consider is sending intermediate- or advanced-level students out to find and speak with them. Because of the enormous range of situations possible, generalizations are difficult; sending students off to make friends with foreign soldiers and sailors on leave in your country is not quite the same as having students strike up conversations with tourists. However, no matter what kind of English speakers the students talk to, even a small dose of such practice helps reinforce the idea that learning to speak English is mastering a skill that involves more than grammar and vocabulary. Also, if some students are lucky enough to establish relationships with English speakers, they may have the opportunity for a lot of excellent practice.

If you require students to try to make contact with English speakers outside class, it is important to teach them culturally appropriate ways of approaching and interacting with the foreigners they want to talk to. If they annoy the people they try to talk to, the value of any practice they get speaking English could be outweighed by bad feelings created by the negative experience, so students need to know how to start out on the right foot. For example, they need to be warned of the dangers of seeming too pushy or giving the impression that they are more interested in practicing *on* someone (rather like a cat sharpening its claws on a piece of wood) than talking *with* someone.

It also helps if students being sent out to start conversations with strangers have a clear and culturally appropriate mission. For example, you might have students interview foreign English speakers on their reasons for coming to your country or on their impressions of it. Having a clear rationale for the activity will help students know how to start the conversation and will make it more likely that the interviewees will cooperate.

Pronunciation

EXPECTATIONS AND GOALS

When studying English, many students assume that their goal should be to achieve native pronunciation, presumably British or North American. To be more specific, they tend to assume that this is a reachable goal, a desirable goal, and a reasonable goal. Such assumptions are not entirely a bad thing, at least to the extent that they motivate students to work seriously and diligently on the quality of their English pronunciation. Nonetheless, I think any discussion of pronunciation needs to begin by pointing out that the goal of achieving native pronunciation is generally not possible, is probably not desirable, and can even be dangerous.

First, consider the issue of possibility. While learners can always improve their pronunciation, changing the pronunciation habits of adult learners after these habits are set is often difficult. Furthermore, it is relatively rare for even the best adult learners—those who start learning a language after their early teens—to achieve accent-free pronunciation in a foreign language. Of course, this does not mean that improvement in pronunciation is undesirable or impossible. When pronunciation problems affect intelligibility, it is vitally important that students try to improve their pronunciation; moreover, most students can improve their pronunciation, at least to some extent. Some pronunciation problems occur because students have an incorrect idea of how a word should be pronounced. For example, accenting the wrong syllable in an English word often hinders communication, and this problem is relatively easy to correct with instruction. Most students can also make limited improvements in their ability to pronounce sounds. For example, while they may always say *dis* instead of *this,* they may be able to learn to distinguish between long and short vowels (e.g., the difference between *hear* and *her*) in such a way that listeners can hear a difference. Most students can achieve a level of accuracy that makes them easily intelligible, and many can do much better. However, most learners will always have a fairly distinct accent, and even the best learners will generally have at least some traces of a foreign accent in their English.

Next, consider the issue of desirability. While it is certainly good for learners to have good pronunciation—in other words, to have pronunciation that is reasonably close to the standard they are trying to approximate—it may not be desirable for them to speak completely without an accent. People often judge a person's origin based on their accent, and if students sound like native speakers of English, people will often assume they are from an English-speaking country. The problem is that unless the students actually are from an English-speaking country—or have spent years living there—they will probably not know all the cultural rules for polite and appropriate behavior. When a person who speaks with an accent does or says something that is not entirely appropriate or polite (according to the norms of the English-speaking listener), the foreign accent signals the fact that a speaker should not be held to the same level of linguistic and cultural expertise as a native and serves to protect the speaker from misunderstandings.

Finally, there is the issue of danger. If students believe that they can and should learn to speak English with the same accent a native speaker of English would have, they may invest an excessive amount of time and effort in trying to improve their pronunciation. Of course, as noted, this effort may still not allow students to achieve accent-free pronunciation, and the resulting failure can cause them to become discouraged, perhaps negatively affecting their desire to study English further.

So, on the whole, a wiser and more realistic pronunciation goal for most students is clear but accented pronunciation, not native accuracy (Brown 2001, 284; Carruthers 1987, 192; Scarcella and Oxford 1992, 165). This is a model that you as a local teacher can and should provide. While you will no doubt also provide students with native speaker models recorded on tapes, CDs, and so forth, your own pronunciation is generally the model that is most immediately real for students. While you should strive to make your own pronunciation as good as possible, you should also have confidence that you do not need to have a native accent in order for your pronunciation to be a valuable model for students.

ASPECTS OF PRONUNCIATION

Many students tend to think of pronunciation primarily as the accurate production of the sounds of English words, but this aspect of pronunciation is neither the only one nor the only important one. Consequently, one way in which you can help students improve is by ensuring that they are aware of all of the important issues.

1. **accurate pronunciation of sounds:** Accurate pronunciation really involves two aspects, ability and knowledge. Students first need to learn to pronounce as many of the sounds of English as possible accurately.[4] The particular sounds with which students will have difficulty depend largely on what students' first language is, but some sounds in English, such as the *th* sounds in *think* and *this* or the short vowels in *head, hit,* and *put,* are difficult for students from many language backgrounds. The second aspect is making sure that students know what sounds they should pronounce in a given word. Common pronunciation problems include omitting sounds, adding extra ones, or simply pronouncing the wrong sound.

2. **syllable stress:** Unlike many other languages, English requires that one syllable in each word be stressed more than the others. The importance of putting the stress on the right syllable in English cannot be underestimated; as Bowen, Madsen, and Hilferty (1985, 85) point out, putting the stress on the wrong syllable is more likely to make a word unintelligible than is mispronouncing one of its sounds. For many students who are especially hard to understand, misplaced syllable stress is the main problem.

3. **sentence word stress:** In English sentences, not all words are given equal emphasis. Key words (usually the words that contain new or important information) are stressed and pronounced more slowly and clearly than other words are. Take, for example, the question *Are you going to go to Boston?* If the focus of the question is on where the listener will go, the sentence will sound something like *Ya gonna go ta Boston*; the word *Boston* would be pronounced clearly and with more emphasis. If, in contrast, the emphasis is on who is going, the sentence would sound like *Are you gonna go ta Boston?* While students don't necessarily need to learn to use reduced forms of the unimportant words in sentence, they should learn to stress key ones.

4. **sentence intonation:** Intonation patterns in English sentences primarily indicate the degree of certainty of an utterance, that is, whether it is a statement, question, or suggestion. Statements rise to a plateau and end with falling intonation. Most questions and suggestions end in rising intonation; however, *wh-* questions (*who, what, where, when, why,* and *how*) end with falling intonation. It is important for students to learn these patterns not only to communicate meaning but also to avoid unwittingly sounding rude or indecisive.

---

[4]A detailed introduction to the sounds of English can be found in many EFL/ESL and introductory linguistics texts (e.g., Ur 1996, 48, for standard British English and Brown 2001, 297, or Goodwin 2001, 134–37, for North American) and on many Web sites.

5. **enunciation:** Some students lack confidence in speaking or are unsure of their pronunciation and therefore speak either very quietly or not very clearly. Obviously, this makes them more difficult to understand, and students should therefore be reminded that speaking audibly and clearly is an important aspect of pronunciation.

TEACHING PRONUNCIATION

The ideal approach to student pronunciation problems is for you to work individually with each student, listening for problems, explaining the proper pronunciation (or intonation, etc.), modeling correct pronunciation, and listening to the student practice. However, this is usually not possible because of time limitations and class size, so the discussion here focuses on approaches you use with a class. These approaches fall into two categories: teaching students what sounds they should produce and practicing pronunciation.

Listening and Pronunciation

Unless you are fortunate enough to have very small classes, it will be difficult to give much individual attention to students' pronunciation. Students must therefore learn to rely on their ears to tell them how closely their pronunciation approximates that of the models they are trying to imitate. However, many students are not in the habit of listening carefully before attempting to repeat. In fact, they have often been trained for years to immediately repeat whatever the teacher says, no matter how vague their impression of the jumble of sounds they are trying to reproduce. Another problem is that while students are listening to the teacher's spoken model, their attention is often focused more on preparing to repeat than on listening. The teacher's sentence consequently serves less as a model for pronunciation than as a starting signal announcing that students should try to speak.

The first approach to pronunciation is thus helping students develop the habit of listening carefully before they speak. To do this, the first time you say a word or sentence, ask students to listen—just listen. They should not murmur the utterance quietly after you; instead, they should concentrate on fixing the sound in their memories. Repeating the model utterance several times before asking students to repeat allows them more chances to listen and helps students break the habit of blurting out a response as soon as you finish.

Exercises that require listening but no oral response may also help sharpen students' listening skills. Minimal-pair drills are particularly good for helping students learn to hear the difference between similar sounds. Minimal pairs are words that are pronounced exactly the same with the exception of one sound (e.g., *pin-pen, bid-bit*). To help students learn to hear the difference between the short *i* and *e* sounds, for example, ask students to raise their pen when you say the word *pen* and a pin when you say *pin*.

Training students' ability to hear sound distinctions will not necessarily result in good pronunciation. However, students who have not clearly heard a sound obviously have less chance to produce it correctly than those who listen carefully.

Modeling Pronunciation

A second basic procedure in pronunciation teaching consists of having students repeat after you using a choral drill procedure. One approach to such drill is as follows:

1. Choose a text that represents normal spoken English (as opposed to more bookish language). A dialogue from your textbook would be a good choice.

2. Read sentences aloud, clearly but at a fairly normal speed. Have students listen to each sentence once or twice before attempting to repeat it. Remind them that they should

be listening to and trying to mimic the rhythm, stress, and intonation patterns of your speech as well as your pronunciation.

3. As suggested earlier, build longer sentences up from the end.

Tips

- If you want students to prepare choral drill of a dialogue before class, it is best if they have a taped model to work with. Without having heard a dialogue before they repeat it, they may wind up polishing an incorrect performance.

- Choral drill is best in small doses. It generally only takes a short period of drill for students to get the point you wish to make, and drill beyond that point rapidly turns into mindless parroting.

- One fun way to practice the rhythm of English sentences is by turning a dialogue from a book, preferably one with short sentences, into a jazz chant. In essence, you find the natural rhythm of each sentence and then chant it with emphasis on the key words, something like a group cheer at a sports match. Clapping or pounding desks adds to the festive nature of the activity. This exercise is particularly good for driving home the point that not all words in English sentences get equal stress.

Performance of a Text

Once students can repeat accurately after a spoken model, the next step is to have them practice speaking from a written text. Keeping pronunciation accurate while reading a text aloud is more difficult than repeating after a teacher, but it is still easier than maintaining correct pronunciation in free conversation because students can focus their attention on pronunciation rather than on grammar or word choice.

1. Choose a text, and copy it for students. If the goal is to teach daily conversational English, choose a text that represents normal spoken English, though an argument can be made for sometimes including texts of literary and cultural merit (e.g., famous speeches, poems) that were also intended to be read aloud or recited.

2. Go over the text with students in class, and have them take whatever notes they need on pronunciation, syllable stress, sentence intonation, and stressed words.

3. Have students practice reading the text aloud (either in class or at home). Students should become very familiar with the text, perhaps even memorizing it (although the time and effort devoted to memorizing the exact words distracts attention from the primary point of the exercise).

4. Either have students perform the text in class or—if the equipment is available—have them record a reading of the text. The advantages of the latter approach are that students don't all have to listen to each other read the same text and that you can listen at your leisure, but the disadvantage is that it takes more of your time.

Accuracy in Free Conversation

Students cannot depend on always having someone around who is willing and able to correct their errors in pronunciation and intonation, so the final task—learning to maintain accuracy in pronunciation and intonation as they engage in conversation—is largely up to students. Ultimately, students need to learn to hear serious discrepancies between their own pronunciation and that of the models to which they are exposed, and then correct their own speech.

Correction

As mentioned previously, research has shown that correcting students' grammar errors when they speak often does not result in any improvement in their grammatical accuracy, so you should not assume that correcting students frequently when they speak English is necessarily useful. Also, correction can disrupt communication and discourage learners. However, error correction probably helps learners at least a little, and, summarizing the research, Hendrickson (1987, 358) suggests that teachers should correct errors at least some of the time—not least because many learners want and expect it. The question thus becomes when and how to correct.

Correction is most called for when errors interfere with communication—when you can't understand what a student is trying to say. The disadvantages of interrupting here are minimal because communication has already broken down, and it is particularly important for the student to know that the message is not getting through. According to Hendrickson (1987, 358–61) and Omaggio Hadley (2001, 268), other kinds of errors that are good candidates for correction include:

- errors that are highly stigmatized, that is, errors that might result in a student seeming rude, offensive, or ignorant. (I am reminded of a young official at a bicycle registration station in Guangzhou who led me into his office, filled out a form for me, then turned around and with a smile said "Get out!" Sensing miscommunication, I suggested gently in Chinese that *get out* was not entirely polite. He took this news in, pondered a minute, brightened up and said, "Get out, please!")

- frequent or patterned errors. For example, correcting occasional confusion between countable and uncountable nouns is less important than correcting a consistent, patterned failure to use plural forms.

- errors that reflect misunderstanding of a point that you have recently taught. For example, the *-s* added to verbs used in conjunction with the third-person singular pronoun (*I go/you go/she goes*) deserves more attention if you taught the point this week than it might at other times.

Some students are put off less by correction and learn more from it than other students, so part of the art of knowing when to correct is being sensitive to how much intrusion the students can bear.

One form of correction you can use in class is the one used most often by native speakers in natural conversation: a corrected repetition of the learner's faulty utterance. (Student: "I like to listen radio." Teacher: "Ah, you like to listen to *the* radio.")[5] This kind of subtle correction disrupts communication less than directly pointing out errors does and may help train students to listen for this kind of correction; however, unless you explicitly point out this habit to students as a form of correction, many may miss these corrections. A more direct approach to correction is to pinpoint the error by interrupting and repeating the few words right before the mistake (e.g., Student: "And then I eated the food." Teacher: "And then I . . ."), giving the student a chance to self-correct. This approach is appropriate for errors that are easy to correct quickly.

For either of the approaches mentioned above to work, your feedback needs to come as soon as possible after the erroneous statement. If you restate an utterance or call attention to an error immediately after it has been made, students are more likely to be able to find the problem.

---

[5] The technical name for this kind of correction is *recasting*.

Delayed correction is often more obtrusive because you first need to remind students of what they said wrong, which students may mistake for the correction itself, thus creating confusion and necessitating further explanation. Here's an example:

Teacher: A minute ago you said, "I like to listen radio."
Student: I like to listen radio.
Teacher: No, no, you said "I like to listen to radio," but you should say "I like to listen to the radio."
Student: Pardon?

All too often in such cases, you can begin correcting the error only after the student has been publicly convicted of committing it, so it is usually better to let the error go or make a note of it for later.

A final note on error correction: many students have the mistaken impression that all native speakers of English should and will correct mistakes; in fact, I have heard students complain quite bitterly about native speakers who fail to live up to this assumed obligation. You should let students know that this is an unreasonable expectation for native speakers of any language. Most people are not language teachers and do not engage in conversation for the purpose of teaching language. Additionally, in most Western cultures, correcting other people's mistakes is considered rude. As I have noted, native speakers will sometimes repeat corrected versions of flawed utterances, but they generally only correct or teach overtly when asked or when communication breaks down completely.

Students need to understand this because many believe that the only real road to success in English lies in being surrounded by native speakers who will overtly correct mistakes, a view that subtly suggests that any other approach is hopeless. Of course, being immersed in an English language environment is very helpful to a learner, but not because of correction. The main advantage of having such an environment is that it provides more opportunities for practice and extensive English language input. However, whether students are in an English-speaking environment or not, they will only benefit from English input if they learn to attend to it and then correct their own mistakes.

Evaluation

When considering evaluation of spoken skills, you should keep two goals in mind. Obviously, one goal is to find out how well the students can speak. However, I would argue that in many situations an even more important goal is the backwash that oral testing generates: students are most likely to practice speaking if you test oral skills. Backwash is especially important to consider with regard to spoken skills because they are more difficult to test than other language skills, with the result that such testing is often neglected.

Interviewing is generally the best way to evaluate spoken skills, so I focus on interviews here. However, complete reliance on interviewing may be impractical in many situations, so other approaches to evaluation are also briefly discussed.

INTERVIEWS

Interviewing is the form of evaluation closest to actual conversation and therefore has excellent backwash on students. It also allows you a rare opportunity to focus on the speaking skills of individual students in a situation where you can determine their level of speaking skill relatively accurately. The main drawback of interviewing is that it is very time-consuming, sometimes prohibitively so for large classes. Interviews are often used as a pretest (and a chance to get to know the students at the beginning of a course) and as a final examination.

Preparing for the Interview

The first step in preparation is deciding what exactly you are looking for. Grammatical accuracy? Use of material taught in your course? Pronunciation? Overall communicative skill? Something else? Your choices should flow naturally from the goals you set for your course and the kinds of practice activities you have asked students to engage in. The backwash will be stronger if you let students know well in advance of the final examination how they will be evaluated and how they should prepare.

Secondly, draw up a list of topics or questions, giving yourself an adequate supply so that you need not use exactly the same ones with each student. Questions should reflect a range of difficulty so that you have easier ones for students at lower levels and more challenging questions for students with more advanced skills. Open-ended questions are best (e.g., *What do you think about . . . ? Tell me about . . . .*) because they don't result in dead-end, yes/no answers; they also allow you to see how much students can elaborate on a point, which is one indication of their level of speaking ability. Natural questions for a pretest interview with students you don't know would be questions about their backgrounds, families, interests, and professions. For a final interview, you might discuss issues raised during the course, other courses the student is taking, or future plans.

Many teachers draw up a marking chart to help them grade during the interview. A simple chart consists of a list of the items you are looking for with a point scale for each. Consider the following simple example for a course in which communicative effectiveness was stressed:

Ability to express ideas	1	2	3	4	5
Range of topics	1	2	3	4	5
Listening comprehension	1	2	3	4	5
Intelligibility	1	2	3	4	5

In designing such a scale, make sure it clearly reflects the goals of the course so that students are rewarded for doing what you have asked them to do. While this point may seem obvious, it is worth emphasizing because sometimes the skills you have emphasized in your course are difficult to assess—and you may be tempted to place more emphasis on other aspects of spoken skills that are easier to assess.[6]

Conducting the Interview

Normally, you should allow an average of at least five minutes for an interview, plus a little time between interviews so that you can take notes and give scores. For advanced-level students, you will need longer interviews to give you an idea of their range of competence. Interviewing students is a demanding task, and your ability to make good judgments will drop quickly as you become tired. It is therefore best not to plan to do several hours of interviews in one fell swoop.

---

[6] In designing a scoring chart for interviews, you might want to look at a proficiency scale such as the one in chapter 4. However, it is also important to adapt the ideas on such charts so that your assessment chart reflects the goals of your course.

Generally, a one-on-one interview should have three basic phases: warm-up, body, and wind-down. The following is one typical approach:

1. **warm-up:** Open with a few easy pleasantries to relax students. During this phase, you may also try to determine approximately how good their spoken skills are so you can choose appropriately challenging questions for the body of the interview.

2. **body:** In this part of the interview, try to challenge the students' speaking (and usually listening) skills by asking more challenging questions and maybe asking the students to perform tasks such as describing a picture, explaining how to do something, or entering into a role play with you. Be careful not to turn a pleasant chat into an overwhelming ordeal, but be sure to raise topics and ask questions that give students a chance to show what they can do. Hughes (1989, 105) suggests that you not dwell on a question if an interviewee gets into trouble; rather, switch to another topic to give the interviewee a fresh start.

3. **wind-down:** End with a few easy questions so that the students don't leave the interview feeling devastated.

Taping interviews allows you to focus on the conversation during the interview and listen again after the interview—but makes the process even more time-consuming. Taking notes during the interview and assigning a grade immediately is much more efficient but can distract both you and the student during the interview. Getting a second opinion from a colleague who either participates in the interviews or listens to them on tape does much to increase the reliability of your grading.

PAIR OR SMALL-GROUP ASSESSMENT

If you have large classes, interviews may be impossible even once during a semester. In such cases, a good alternative consists of assessing pairs or small groups of students. This approach is not only less time-consuming than one-on-one interviews but is also closer in nature to the pair and small-group activities often used in oral skills classes, so it tends to have very beneficial backwash on the seriousness with which students engage in those activities.

1. Design one or more testing tasks for pairs or small groups. These should be as similar as possible to the kinds of activities that you normally use in class. For example, if you often have students do pair work based on model dialogues, this would be a good test task. Or, if you have students do a lot of small-group tasks, base your test activity on one of these. Normally, you will choose one basic test format but have a list of different topics or questions from which the pairs or groups will draw.

2. Design a scoring system you can use as you listen to the pair or group. As with scoring systems for interviews (above), it should be designed to reinforce whatever you have emphasized in your course.

3. Let students know what the test format will be, preferably as early as possible. In fact, you might do a dry run in class so that students are very clear about what you expect from them (and so that you don't need to waste a lot of time during the test explaining the format to students).

4. Organize students into pairs or small groups, and schedule a time for their test.

5. When they arrive for the test, have them draw one or more test tasks from a hat. (You may want to have each group arrive a few minutes before the test, draw a topic, and prepare a bit while the previous group is taking the test.)

6. During the test, take notes, and assign a tentative grade. (You may want to wait until you have heard all the groups before assigning a final grade.)

LISTENING AND WRITING QUIZZES

For extremely large classes, you may find that any evaluation of oral skills is difficult and can only be done once or twice, thus resulting in fewer grades and less reinforcement than you would like. In these cases, you may supplement oral skills evaluation with quizzes that require students to listen to something and respond in writing. Obviously, written quizzes are not an ideal way to assess speaking skills, as no actual speaking is involved. However, listening is a vital part of oral communication, so testing listening tends to have the positive backwash of forcing students not to rely on text study alone. Writing does not involve as much time pressure as speaking, but, like speaking, it is a productive skill that requires students to learn to express their ideas in English. So, in situations where other oral assessment is impossible, this method provides at least some incentive for students to practice oral skills and build their productive command of English.

A simple form of this quiz involves orally asking students questions and having them write answers. A more complicated approach is to orally present students with a situation and require them to write dialogues based on your instructions. (Dialogues are more appropriate than essays because the language in dialogues is closer to the language of daily communication.)

1. Design a conversation framework that involves moves/functions you have taught in class, for example, *First, A and B meet on the bus and greet each other. A then asks why B didn't come to dinner last night. B apologizes and offers an excuse. A then invites B to dinner another time.*

2. Present the framework to students orally while they listen and take notes.

3. Ask the students to write a conversation consisting of six turns (A—B—A—B—A—B) that follows the framework and accomplishes the moves it requires. Encourage students to write the shortest dialogue that fulfills the instructions.

4. Grade the dialogues for linguistic accuracy and cultural appropriateness.

This type of quiz is not without problems. Students often need some time to get used to this format, so you should practice with the class a few times before the first real quiz. The format also puts students whose speaking skills exceed their listening skills at a real disadvantage; I have seen some flawless dialogues that had nothing to do with the instructions given. However, the stress on listening is also the greatest advantage of the quiz; the backwash will encourage students to focus on oral English rather than just studying the book.

For Thought, Discussion, and Action

1. **speaking practice:** Choose a textbook used in your country for English oral skills classes. First, list the types of speaking activities it includes. Then, for each activity, carefully analyze the kinds of skills/knowledge that the activity would help students build—and the kinds it would not help them build.

2. **small-group speaking practice:** This chapter suggests that, to build speaking skills, you should give students as much practice in pairs or small groups as possible, but also points out that students may not always cooperate with this approach. How effective is the use of small-group or pair practice in your country? How can you ensure that students use English as much as possible during such activities?

3. **speaking activities and course plans:** Choose a sample course from appendix B. Then, with that course in mind, go through the list of speaking activities in this chapter, and select several that you think would be suitable for use in that course. Be ready to explain the rationale for your choices.

4. **model-based dialogues:** Using either a dialogue from a local English textbook or the sample dialogue below, analyze the dialogue for the moves (functions) it contains. Then write a plan for an oral skills lesson making use of this dialogue.

   Anne and Mick are arguing—politely—over whether cats or dogs make better pets. (Listen especially for how they indicate disagreement.)
   Anne: I think that cats usually make better pets than dogs. For one thing, they are quieter.
   Mick: That may be true, but sometimes they make a lot of noise crying at night.
   Anne: For another thing, cats are more affectionate.
   Mick: Really? I don't think so.
   Anne: Of course they are. They always love to sit on your lap.
   Mick: That's just because they want something from you.
   Anne: Yes, but they are so sweet about it.

5. **cocktail parties:** If you are already teaching an English course that involves speaking skills, prepare and conduct a cocktail-party activity (or another activity that you haven't used before) according to the instructions given in the chapter.

6. **small-group tasks:** Choose one or more of the following topics, and turn it into a well-defined task for oral skills practice: *food, weather, pollution, local history, cultural values.*

7. **speaking practice outside class:** In your country, if you assigned speaking homework outside class, what problems do you think you might encounter? What kinds of out-of-class speaking assignments might work best?

8. **the local pronunciation standard:** This chapter suggests that it is not necessary for students—or even local teachers—to attempt to achieve nativelike pronunciation in their English. What do you think of this? What standard should teachers tell students to work toward? How strict or lenient do you think teachers should be with regard to students' pronunciation?

9. **pronunciation learning:** Reflect on your own experience learning the pronunciation of English or another language. How hard or easy was it? What kinds of instruction and practice were most helpful to you?

10. **correction:** Reflect on your previous English learning experience. Did any of your teachers correct you as you spoke English? How did you react to the corrections? What approaches to correction did you find most helpful?

11. **interviews:** This chapter suggests that interviews are the best way to assess students' speaking skills. How realistic is this for the situation in your country? Could you use individual or group interviews at all? If not, what other assessment measures could you use to ensure that students are encouraged to build their speaking skills?

12. **language learning project (LLP) for speaking skills:** Design an LLP you could suggest to students to build their speaking skills as part of an English course you may teach.

Sample LLP for Speaking Skills

Goal: Build spoken fluency, that is, my ability to express ideas in English reasonably quickly and smoothly; practice incorporating material (new words, phrases, grammar structures) learned from texts into my productive spoken skills.

Material: Texts in English from a textbook, magazine, or storybook.

Plan: Read and retell two texts a week, one text per study session, about one hour per session.

Method:

1. Read the story or passage, and make a rough outline of the content.

2. In the outline, include new words, phrases, and grammar structures I want to learn and incorporate into my spoken English.

3. Using my outline—but not the original text—retell the story or passage aloud in English to myself. Try to look at my outline as little as possible.

4. After I retell the story, look back at the original text, and check to see if I correctly incorporated the new material I wanted to learn.

5. If I have the time and energy, retell the passage again without looking at my outline.

6. At the beginning of my next study session, quickly retell the old passage for review before I look at the new one.

Criteria for measuring progress: I will have succeeded if I

- study twenty texts using this method

- can now more fluently and confidently go back and retell these stories or passages, incorporating some of the new words, phrases, and grammar structures

- can apply some of the new material I learned in other speaking situations

Chapter 8

Reading and Decoding

- Effective reading involves use of both bottom-up and top-down strategies.

- Many students of English learn to read in a slow, careful manner, relying almost entirely on bottom-up strategies (intensive reading). Overreliance on this reading approach makes reading slow and often painful, and tends to discourage students from doing any more reading than necessary.

- Students who also learn to read in a more rapid, active way (extensive reading) are more likely to reach a breakthrough point where reading becomes a useful and even enjoyable skill.

Like many students of Chinese (and other languages), I learned to read by slowly carving my way through short but difficult texts with a dictionary, trying to memorize every word and figure out the grammar of every sentence. Not surprisingly, this was not an activity I enjoyed. However, fate intervened in the person of a Chinese history professor who suggested that, since I had studied Chinese for three years, it was time for me to start using my Chinese in his class. He presented me with a collection of short stories—Chen Ruoxi's *Lao Ren* [Old People]—and told me I had a week to finish the book and write a critique. I was horrified. I had never tried to read anything longer than a short story before, at least not within a week, and knew that there was no way I could apply my look-up-every-unfamiliar-word strategy to a whole book and still finish on time. So I resigned myself to disaster, calculated how much material I had to cover per day, and scraped through the assignment as best I could.

To my great surprise, two things happened. First, despite the large number of words I didn't recognize, I was generally able to catch the drift of the story and, in the end, was able to write a critique of which I was even moderately proud. Equally important, for the first time in my foreign language reading life, I actually became interested in what I was reading.

Admittedly, this challenge came to me in the right form at the right time. Chen Ruoxi's clear, straightforward style made her work relatively easy to read, and I found the Cultural Revolution setting of the stories fascinating. I had also been studying Chinese long enough that my reading vocabulary was adequate for making some sense of what I was reading. But I still feel lucky that my history professor intervened when he did because I was well on the way to entrenching the habit of a painfully slow and careful approach to reading Chinese and had already started to believe that this was the only way an American could ever read Chinese—or any foreign language.

The intensive reading approach with which my study of Chinese reading began is natural for beginning-level students. When almost every word and structure is new, this slow approach makes sense as a way for students to learn new words and grammar. What often happens, however, is that heavy use of intensive reading as a strategy for learning vocabulary and grammar becomes confused with reading itself. For many students, the single greatest problem in learning to read a foreign language is that habits and skills intended for language learning become their only approach to reading, resulting in both poor reading strategies and a miserable experience. My discussion of reading skills in this chapter thus gives much attention to intensive reading and extensive reading, and to the importance of teaching students to read extensively as well as intensively.

Reading: The Problem and the Goal

Even when people learn to read their first language in elementary school, their attention is often focused primarily on the problem of decoding words, so it is not surprising that they instinctively tend to think of reading as a process of looking at words, one after another, and then adding them up to see what they mean. However, studies show that reading is in fact a combination of bottom-up and top-down processes. In reading, bottom-up strategies consist primarily of combining vocabulary and grammar clues to build meaning. Top-down strategies, however, are equally important. When good readers begin reading a text, they generally have some knowledge of the topic. This knowledge, combined with clues provided by the genre of the text, will enable readers to guess much of what they will read before they actually read it. For example, even before beginning a newspaper article with the headline "Plane Crashes in Alaska," good readers have a rough idea of what kind of material the article will contain and even the order in which it will appear.

As they read, they do not devote equal attention to every word or sentence. Material they already know will receive less attention than new material, and material they expect is skimmed over more quickly than material they don't expect. The best way to understand reading is therefore to see it as a process of active guessing in which readers use a variety of different kinds of clues to understand a text and to take what they need or want from it, generally as quickly as possible (for further discussion, see Carrell and Eisterhold 1987, 220–23; Scarcella and Oxford 1992, 95; Hedge 2000, chapter 6).

This reading process, of course, is quite different from the way most students of English—or any other language—are first trained to read. Instead of being encouraged to use extralinguistic knowledge, students are expected to carefully decode a text, slowly studying every word and sentence and constructing meaning almost entirely from the aggregate meaning of the words on the page. To ensure that they understand every word and every detail of the text, students are encouraged to make heavy use of reference works and devote large amounts of time to relatively short texts.

Intensive reading is not necessarily bad. It is necessary when material is very difficult or when a high degree of detail comprehension is necessary, and the slow, careful approach to each text also allows students to study vocabulary and grammar. However, if this is the only approach to reading that students learn, the following problems arise:

1. Readers who rely on bottom-up processes to the exclusion of top-down processes often have comprehension problems. Habitual focus on detail means that intensive readers often get the details but miss the general picture. As Bowen, Madsen, and Hilferty (1985, 230–31, 244) note, the time spent decoding also causes readers to lose the drift—hence the meaning—of a text and may even result in their making more mistakes in comprehension.

2. Intensive readers are slow and are consequently unable to read very much material. This reduced input from reading, in turn, slows other important parts of the language learning process. For example, the limited amount of text that is read means that readers review and consolidate less vocabulary (see chapter 10). The intake of cultural knowledge through reading is also limited. For students who go abroad to study, slow reading can even limit opportunity for social interaction; for example, on Western college campuses, international students who are intensive readers are often noted for their absence from any activity other than classes and meals—they need to spend most of their time at home or in the library struggling to cope with reading assignments.

3. The general unpleasantness of intensive reading—as both a language learning and a reading process—tends to discourage students from reading English. This unpleasantness is too often exacerbated when teachers assign short but very difficult texts packed with new words, a practice that further diminishes any interest students might have had in English reading.

It can be argued that intensive reading is necessary at the early stages of learning English when learning vocabulary and grammar is more important than learning reading skills per se. However, if students come to believe that this slow, word-by-word process is the only way to read in a foreign language, they will have little chance of ever reaching a breakthrough point where reading in English becomes so rewarding and interesting that it is self-sustaining. Students who eventually learn to read well enough to understand English novels, magazines, or newspapers without intolerable investments of time and effort will tend to maintain or even improve their skills after leaving formal English language programs; in contrast, those who only read slowly and painfully are more likely to regress. For this reason, students should be introduced to and encouraged to use extensive reading approaches as early as possible.

Methods for Teaching Intensive Reading

Intensive reading is the core of English programs in many countries, and the methods and assumptions used in intensive reading classes may have significant impact on the ideas and learning strategies that students bring into your class. Traditional approaches to intensive reading tend to focus more on building students' knowledge of English grammar and vocabulary than on teaching reading skills per se, and such approaches also implicitly teach students to rely mainly on bottom-up reading strategies. A typical unit is often taught as follows. First, students are expected to carefully read a passage at home, looking up all the new words and making sure they understand the grammar in each sentence. They may even be asked to memorize the passage or translate it. Then, in class, the teacher lectures on the text, explaining most of the grammar and words or questioning students on these points. Students are not encouraged to guess but are expected to work hard and make sure they know all the right answers.

Such an approach has the advantage of allowing teachers to devote a significant amount of time to vocabulary and grammar knowledge. However, by modifying the approach described above, you can place more emphasis on building reading skills and also help students develop a better balance between bottom-up and top-down reading strategies.

IN-CLASS METHODS FOR BEGINNING-LEVEL STUDENTS

If you need to teach students who have never read any English before, the first task is to help them see the correspondence between written symbols and spoken words and sentences. Here are a few basic methods:

- **teaching the alphabet:** English spelling is rich with irregularities, but there is enough correspondence between letters and sounds that knowing what sounds the letters of the alphabet commonly represent will benefit students.

- **reading aloud as students follow along:** This will focus students' attention on words rather than letters and will help them begin learning to pronounce words as units instead of as collections of discrete sounds. Bowen, Madsen, and Hilferty (1985, 224) also note that following along as someone reads is a good way for students to learn what punctuation is for.

- **having students read aloud:** You can have the class read a text aloud as a group (resulting in a fair amount of cacophony) or have them read semiaudibly to themselves. Sometimes you might ask individual volunteers to read a passage aloud, but be sensitive to the fact that what is easy for you is very difficult for students just learning to read. Practice should provide maximum support and expose students to minimum public embarrassment. At very low reading levels for English learners, texts should consist primarily of words that students already know in spoken form. This allows a little thrill of discovery when a new word is successfully decoded and helps reinforce the link between written and oral language.

INTENSIVE READING FOR INTERMEDIATE AND ADVANCED LEVELS

For students who can read simple texts (e.g., dialogues, stories, articles) in English, a good basic approach to intensive reading lessons consists of three parts:

1. prereading activity (in class) to build use of top-down skills

2. reading and studying the text (outside class) to build vocabulary and grammar knowledge as well as bottom-up reading skills

3. questions and comprehension check (in class) to focus on meaning

Here I focus on each of these in turn.

Prereading Activities

One way to encourage student use of top-down strategies is through the use of prereading activities that require students to actively make predictions about what they are about to read. Some basic prereading activities are described below.

PREDICTING

Even before starting to read a text, skilled readers can often make at least some educated guesses about its content based on the title of the text and other available clues (e.g., author, source, general kind of text). Even if the predictions are incorrect, having students guess will make them more alert when reading than if they are simply moving their eyes purposelessly over a string of words.

1. Give students a text. (If the text is from some source other than the course textbook, you might try to preserve its original setting. For example, photocopy an article from a magazine directly from its original location so students can see that it is from a magazine.)

2. Have them look at the text's title and setting, and ask them to make a guess as to what the text is about. (If the text is by an author the students might know, the name is another clue they might be directed to.)

3. Encourage all guesses, right or wrong, but especially those which seem to make good use of the evidence available.

4. Have students check their guesses when they reread the text more carefully later.

SCANNING

Scanning is an activity in which students look quickly through a text to find specific information, usually by looking for key words. The primary purpose of scanning is to find parts of a text that one needs to read rather than to get an overview of the text as a whole. Note that students may misunderstand the purpose of this activity, assuming that it is some form of fast reading, so it is particularly important to explain that scanning is a useful skill in its own right and to explain its purpose.

1. Prepare a reading text and a list of words in the text that you want students to scan for. (Scanning practice works best with longer texts, preferably several pages.)

2. Explain to students that their task is to locate the target word as quickly as possible. When they find the word, they should call out where it is (usually by telling you the page and paragraph number).

3. Give students the text and then the word you want them to find. Then have them start.

135

4. When a student locates the target word, congratulate him or her. Then move on to the next target word.

5. Close by praising the student who finds the most target words most quickly.

SKIMMING

This common prereading activity involves quickly looking over a text and reading a few select parts of it to get an idea of what it contains. Many students are resistant to the idea of skimming in a foreign language (largely because of well-developed intensive reading habits), so in-class skimming exercises play an important role in familiarizing students with this skill as well as convincing them of its legitimacy and value. The ultimate goal is for students to develop the habit of skimming a text on their own, so over time you should encourage students to first skim whenever they have occasion to read an English text, especially a long or difficult one.

1. Give students a reading text. (Skimming practice works best with texts that are more than one page in length.)

2. Tell students to skim through the text quickly, reading only the following parts:
   • titles and subheadings
   • a few sentences from the introduction
   • the first lines of some paragraphs
   • proper nouns (names) and numbers (These are easy to spot and generally helpful in quickly determining what is being discussed.)
   • a few sentences from the conclusion

3. Give students a time limit (one that makes slow careful reading of the text impossible), and have them start reading. While students are skimming, it may help if you call out the time, creating an atmosphere somewhat like that of a horse race. Hearing how much time they have not only reminds students to keep moving but adds a degree of fun and freedom that may help convince them that it is really OK not to be reading carefully.

4. When the time is up, ask students what they have discovered about the text and what guesses they have about the remainder of its contents. You might even list their guesses on the board and have the class go back to check them out later after they have read the passage more carefully.

FOCUSED READING

Like focused listening (described in chapter 6), for focused reading you first give students several questions and then have them quickly read through the text to find the answers. The questions not only help give focus and purpose to the students' reading but also make the task easier by providing valuable hints as to what might be coming in the text ahead. This activity can be used to preview a text that you have assigned as homework or as an independent in-class activity.

1. Look over the text you will assign, and write several comprehension questions that cover the main points of the content.

2. Write the questions on the board, and give students a time limit that is adequate for reading the text—but tight enough that they are pushed to read quickly.

3. Have students quickly read through the text to find the answers.

4. Check by asking students for the answers to the questions.

For lower level students, use simple comprehension questions. For advanced-level students reading more sophisticated texts, open-ended opinion questions are generally better (e.g., *Was the author of this story biased?*).

In a variation on this activity, you have students skim a text, write their own focused reading questions, and finally read the text to try to answer their own questions. Having students generate their own questions is one way to encourage them to think more actively about what they should be looking for as they read.

Reading and Studying the Text outside Class

There is nothing inherently wrong with having students read and study intensive reading passages in class, and it may be a good idea to do this from time to time so that you can see how students read a passage. However, class time limitations will mean that you often ask students to read and study passages at home. Intensive reading textbooks usually come equipped with a supply of reading passages, vocabulary lists, notes on grammar, and comprehension questions, so the question is what the students should do with all these resources as they study at home. One possibility is to require students to study using a procedure like the following:

1. Students read the entire passage straight through. During this first reading, they mark unfamiliar vocabulary and structures, but they do not stop to look these up in the glossary or a dictionary. (This first reading helps students build extensive reading skills.)

2. Students study unfamiliar grammar structures and vocabulary. Tell them to learn the meaning of new words and structures and also to learn how they are used in the passage.

3. Students read the passage again, more carefully. During this second reading, they stop to study any problematic points of the text.

4. Students prepare questions to ask you about any section of the passage they do not understand. While the emphasis is primarily on comprehension of the passage, they should also note questions on grammar and vocabulary.

Discussing the Text in Class

The traditional in-class intensive reading lesson consists largely of lecture on the passage. One problem with this approach is that, too often, the lecture is unnecessary and boring for students who did their homework well and over the heads of those who didn't prepare or whose listening skills are weak. Another problem is that a lecture approach encourages students to passively wait for the teacher to solve problems. Below are some alternative uses for class time.[1]

QUESTION AND ANSWER ABOUT THE TEXT

The goal of an intensive reading lesson is not just to explain what a particular text means but rather to teach students how to unravel the mystery of a text for themselves. Students should therefore play as active a role as possible in figuring out each reading passage and should be encouraged to take the initiative by asking you for whatever explanation they need. Consider the following typical paragraph from an intensive reading passage:

> Scientists at Sussex University appear to be on the way to discovering how the mosquito, carrier of diseases such as malaria and yellow fever, finds its target. They have found that the best way to avoid being bitten is: stop breathing, stop sweating, and keep down the temperature of your immediate

---

[1] Intensive reading lessons are often used for teaching vocabulary and grammar. However, to keep the focus here on reading, I have rather artificially segregated these aspects of teaching into their own chapters (see chapters 10 and 11 respectively).

surroundings. Unfortunately the first suggestion is impossible and the others very difficult. (Guang-dong Bureau of Higher Education 1991, 17)

A procedure for dealing with this passage through question and answer in class is as follows:

1. Have students ask you questions about whatever they don't understand. (If they have prepared the passage as homework in the manner suggested earlier, they should come to class ready with some written questions.)

2. When possible, respond to questions by giving clues so students figure out the answers to their own questions. Consider a few examples:
    *   The word *target* (sentence 1) might cause some confusion, particularly if students' dictionaries only list a basic meaning such as *something to shoot at*. You might respond by asking whose target is being discussed and then asking students to consider what a typical mosquito might be interested in. You could also encourage them to look at the following sentence (where the implication is that the target is *you*).
    *   Students preoccupied with knowing the exact meanings of words might ask about *Sussex University* (sentence 1). This question probably isn't worth the investment of much time, so you might just translate the name for them or reassure them that it is only important to know this is the name of a university.
    *   The insertion of the long clause "carrier of diseases such as malaria and yellow fever" in the first sentence might trip up some students, especially those who read slowly. A good tactic for dealing with complex sentences is to have students break them down into smaller simpler sentences. Here the result would be two sentences: (1) *Scientists at Sussex University appear to be on their way to discovering how the mosquito finds its target.* (2) *The mosquito is a carrier of diseases such as malaria and yellow fever.*
    *   The phrase "keep down the temperature of your immediate surroundings" (sentence 2) might cause confusion, especially because it seems to be an absurd suggestion. To respond to this, you probably first need to ask the class whether these suggestions are intended to be serious or not, and call their attention to sentence 3. Having established that the suggestions are not serious—indeed, they may be intended as a joke—then go back to the phrase in question, and piece the meaning together using the meanings of the words.

One problem with relying on student questions is that students are sometimes too shy to ask or may simply be accustomed to listening to the teacher lecture, so you may need to invest some time and nurturing before you can be reasonably sure that students will ask when they don't understand. You can minimize this problem by isolating a number of potential trouble spots in the text and asking specifically whether or not students understand them; it is easier to get students to nod yes or no than to get them to ask questions. Another alternative is to require students to each write one question about the reading passage and give it to you before class. A more punitive strategy is to give a comprehension quiz after your class explanation, perhaps even focusing on those points you suspect students should have asked about but didn't.

For classes that go to the opposite extreme by asking about everything, set limits on the kinds of questions that you will answer. One suggestion is to make a rule that you will only answer questions relevant to comprehension of the passage being discussed. For example, you might tell students that you are willing to explain what *target* means in this passage but refuse to be drawn into an exhaustive explanation of all of its other possible uses. Such a rule will make life easier for you because contextualized questions about vocabulary, grammar, and meaning are easier to deal with, and it will keep students focused on the primary goal: comprehension of the text.

Study of Word Usage

One advantage of intensive reading is that its slow pace allows students to take note of how words are used in a text, so they learn usage along with meaning. However, students often study only the meaning of words unless you remind them to attend to usage as well, so it is often good to devote some class time to examining word usage.

1. Choose several words or word groups from the text that are new to students.

2. Call students' attention to the first word, and have them note the words around it necessary for proper usage. For example, in the passage about the mosquito, if students underline *on the way* as a new item, they should also note that it is followed by *to* + a gerund ("to discovering"). This is in contrast to "the best way" in the following sentence, which is followed by an infinitive ("to avoid").

3. After students note the usage of a new lexical item, a time-honored practice method is to have them make a sentence using the new item—either right after you point out the usage of an item in class or as a homework assignment. Making sentences is a good way to help students remember the usage of a new item as well as explore variations. While this exercise can easily degenerate into copying if you ask students to create sentences for a long list of words, I would recommend it in limited doses for items that pose usage problems.

Listing of Main Points/Outlining

For intermediate- or advanced-level students who are reading expository passages, a useful exercise is to have them outline the flow of ideas in the passage. This can be done either as an individual reading/writing activity or in class as a small-group project. For an in-class activity,

1. Divide students into groups, and have each group list the main ideas of the reading passage. Ask that they write out each main idea in a brief clear sentence; encourage them to state ideas in their own words rather than copying directly from the text. For more advanced-level students, require a proper formal outline that both summarizes the main ideas and makes clear the relationship between them.

2. As groups report, list the main ideas on the board.

3. To close, ask the class to decide which of the ideas in the text is most important.

Interpretive Discussion of a Passage

To fully comprehend a passage, students, especially those in advanced-level classes, often need to understand more than the surface meaning of the text. The opportunity for careful scrutiny of a passage created by intensive reading can be profitably used to deal with deeper questions related to bias, tone, and purpose. Such questions are challenging—after all, even native speakers of English might debate an author's objectivity or purpose—so this kind of activity is best used only with relatively advanced-level students. Such issues, however, are important to consider because they are critical to comprehension of a text, and students who are thinking of these questions as they read are more likely to notice clues that throw light on the issue.

1. Have students work in groups to answer the following questions about the passage:
   - main idea: What is the author most concerned about communicating?
   - bias and stance: Is the author objective or biased? Does the author portray a character in a sympathetic or unfavorable light?

- tone: Is the author serious or joking?
- purpose: Why was this written? Is the author trying to entertain? Persuade? Explain? Some combination of these?

Also tell students to be ready to support their answers by pointing out evidence in the passage that supports their hypotheses.

2. Close by having each group present its theory and evidence for class discussion.

STUDYING GENRES

Some of the most interesting patterns of a culture are found in its genre conventions, the customary patterns into which a culture organizes various kinds of texts. Knowledge of such genre conventions helps students predict what they will encounter in texts and provides a helpful starting point for evaluating texts by writing critical reviews (see chapter 9). Intensive reading classes provide a good opportunity to introduce such conventions to students.

One approach is simply to point out the formulas underlying whatever texts students are studying in class, but a more interesting alternative in advanced-level classes is to have students try to discover for themselves the formulas of target-culture texts. Below is one possible procedure.

1. Choose a text that is fairly typical of some target-culture genre (e.g., a mystery story, a love story, a news story, or an academic article).

2. Prime the pump by having students describe the formula for a familiar genre within their own culture; for example, the typical conventions of a love story or perhaps a martial arts film.

3. Then have students study the target-culture text you chose and list what they think the conventions of the genre are, as they did for a genre familiar in their own culture.

4. Have students report their analyses. Then fill in with more information as necessary.

In-Class Methods for Teaching Extensive Reading

To a much greater extent than intensive reading skills, the development of extensive reading skills may mean that reading in English becomes rewarding and enjoyable enough to become an end in itself. If such a breakthrough occurs and students begin to regularly read English books, newspapers, and magazines, they will naturally continue to develop their reading skills, vocabulary, and cultural knowledge. Unfortunately, students reach this breakthrough point only after considerable study and practice. Two important preconditions for a reading breakthrough, the acquisition of a large recognition vocabulary and a fund of cultural background knowledge, are discussed in chapters 10 and 12. This section focuses on two aspects of building extensive reading skills: increasing reading speed and enhancing ability to guess unfamiliar vocabulary.

READING SPEED PRACTICE

One important aspect of building students' extensive reading skills is training them to read more quickly. This can be emotionally difficult for students accustomed to intensive reading because they are more comfortable reading at a slower pace. However, as I have noted, increased reading speed is important not only for enabling students to cover more material but also for enhancing their comprehension. Reading specialists suggest that the minimum effective reading speed is 200 words per minute, the average is 250, and the optimum is 400–500 (Bowen, Madsen, and Hilferty

1985, 244). For many students, reaching these speeds will require breaking some deep-rooted habits, and speed-reading practice in class is one good way to start.

Improvement in reading speeds tends to be very gradual, so students should not expect their speed to improve dramatically during a semester course. However, doing exercises like this in class helps students see the importance of working to increase their reading speed. The primary value of this type of exercise lies not in the actual rapid reading practice that it provides but rather in its power to break the habit of reading slowly and intensively. The fact that this activity goes on in class with the teacher's approval also helps convince students that it is really acceptable to read in this way.

1. Find passages that are short enough to be read within a class period and easy enough that students don't often need to resort to dictionaries. (Ideally, you should use readings that are somewhat longer than those often used for intensive reading. However, you may have to make do with whatever reading passages there are in the students' textbook, doing a quick extensive-style reading of a passage in class and then having students read it again more intensively for homework.)

2. Estimate the number of words in the selected passage.

3. Have students quickly read the text as you keep time. To remind them that they are working against the clock, use the blackboard to mark the time elapsed, or simply call out the time. When students finish reading, have them note how long it took them to read the text and then divide the number of words read by the time taken, arriving at a words-per-minute figure.

4. Have students record their scores and try to increase their speed over time.

5. After the exercise, do a quick comprehension check to remind students that speed is not the only goal. Ask general questions on main points so that the focus stays on getting the gist of the text quickly rather than on detail comprehension.

GUESSING VOCABULARY

In extensive reading, students should keep dictionary use to a minimum because frequent dictionary stops slow reading speed and tend to break the train of thought, thus hampering comprehension of the broader flow of ideas and making reading less enjoyable. If students are to learn to read extensively, they need to develop the habit of guessing the meanings of most unfamiliar words or simply skipping over them and forging ahead. The following useful exercise for helping students become more comfortable guessing could be combined with the exercises described above for building reading speed.

1. Have students quickly read a passage in class, underlining unfamiliar words but not stopping.

2. Have students report some of the words they underlined, and choose a few for class discussion. (Here you might remind students that they are to practice guessing; many at this point will naturally tend to start looking through their dictionaries.)

3. For each word, have students ask the question, *Can I quickly guess enough about the word to keep going?* In many cases, they need only a general idea of the meaning of an unfamiliar word, which they can often guess from context. For example, in the sentence *She picked the chrysanthemum and smelled it,* knowing that a chrysanthemum is some kind of flower

is probably sufficient, and a student who guesses this can continue reading without any serious loss of comprehension.

4. If the students cannot guess much about an unfamiliar word, the next question you should have them ask themselves is, *Do I need to understand this word?* Readers can often skip over unfamiliar words without serious loss of comprehension, and this is preferable to repeated stops. Of course, when skipping over a word causes students to lose the train of thought completely, they should stop and look the word up, but for extensive reading they also need to learn to become comfortable not knowing the exact meaning of every word they run across.

Extensive Reading outside Class

For students to achieve a breakthrough in reading, they will almost certainly need more extensive reading practice than is possible in class, so an important part of a reading program is having students read outside class. While English language reading material may not be easy to come by in some countries, often at least some books, newspapers, or magazines will be available in English. With the spread of Internet access, there are also many more opportunities to read texts online or to download and print out texts. When such reading material is available, extensive reading skills are often worth special attention because of the potential for breakthrough.

CHOOSING MATERIAL

In some places, there simply isn't much reading material of any kind available in English, but in most places the more common problem is finding enough material that is at an appropriate level of difficulty for the students. In China, for example, a wealth of textbooks are available, as are English newspapers and novels in English. The harder part is finding longer texts—interesting fiction, in particular—for students who are not quite ready for classic English novels.

Assuming that some choice is available, the best materials for extensive reading are those that are interesting and not overly difficult. To the extent that students have the choice of whether to read or not, you might think of the decision as a form of cost-benefit analysis: students will be willing to read when the benefits gained from reading outweigh the investment of time and effort. The break-even point will differ from student to student and will also depend greatly on the kind of material available, but it is safe to assume that students are more likely to voluntarily read interesting and easy materials than those which are neither.

Different rules of thumb have been suggested for determining what level of difficulty is appropriate for an extensive reading text. Scarcella and Oxford (1992, 108) believe that a text is too difficult if a student has to resort to the dictionary more than once or twice per page to look up unfamiliar words that can't be guessed and are important to comprehension. Bowen, Madsen, and Hilferty (1985, 231) suggest that if a student gets 85 percent of the words right when reading a text aloud, the text is not too hard. My more rough-hewn approach is to have students open a text they are considering and read a paragraph or so from the middle. If they can more or less follow what is going on, the book is probably easy enough for extensive reading.

ALL-CLASS READING ASSIGNMENTS

Sometimes you have enough copies of a book to have all of the students in your class do extensive reading practice with that same book. A suggested basic cycle of activities would go as follows:

1. Start with prereading activities in class. (See Prereading Activities above.)

2. Whether the reading material is a short story, an article, or part of a novel, assign a certain amount of out-of-class reading and suggest approximately how much time students should spend reading. This will remind students to work toward increasing their speed. As with intensive reading, providing students with comprehension questions or broader interpretive questions will help focus their reading.

3. To provide accountability and closure, combine extensive reading assignments with writing or discussion activities. Perhaps the best kind of activity is some kind of oral or written evaluation, recommendation, or review of the book. For lower level students, this might simply be a brief statement as to why they did or did not like what they read; you might ask more advanced-level students for a review or critique. (See chapter 9 for a discussion of review writing.)

INDIVIDUAL READING ASSIGNMENTS

When possible, it is good for a course to incorporate limited-choice language learning projects (LLPs; see chapter 3) in which students choose at least some of their own reading material. While LLPs may be somewhat more difficult to manage than having students all read the same thing, they are preferable for students at higher levels because individualized LLPs accustom students to choosing their own material. LLPs are also often a practical necessity when you can't find enough copies of any single book for everyone in the class. The extra trouble of setting up and managing such a system is generally well worth the effort because, when students can begin choosing their own material, they are likely to begin viewing reading in English as an activity that might become an ongoing part of their lives. For such situations, the following is a suggested cycle of activities:

1. Tell students roughly how much material you expect them to read, and then have them choose their own reading material. (I generally specify a general number of pages I expect students to read and then have them choose books with approximately that number of pages.) To make the system more flexible and enhance accountability, use contracts that specify how much reading students will do, in what books, and by what date. For example, if you have asked everyone to read at least 300 pages during the semester, one student might meet the obligation with one 70-page book and one of 230 pages; another student might have two 150-page books. (Quantifying assignments by number of pages tends to push students toward books with small pages and big print, a problem you may wish to account for in your calculating system.)

2. Encourage prereading activities. For example, ask for a very brief, preliminary report on the kind of book and possibly some guesses as to what it contains.

3. As discussed above, encourage students to time themselves as they read and try to build their speed over time.

4. The most natural way to provide accountability is to have students write reviews or present recommendations orally in class. You could also ask students to write summaries, responses, or cultural comparisons. Cheating is obviously easier if the students are

reading books you haven't read, but between your knowledge of what a text is likely to contain and the student's report, you can usually get a sufficiently clear idea of how well the student has done the reading.

Hedge (2000) suggests a "reading syndicate" variation of this procedure "in which members of a group read different books and share their experiences. The outcome is often a peer conference in which students can take on the roles of asking questions as well as answering them" (p. 219).

Evaluation

Evaluating reading by having students write reviews, give oral book reports, and so forth tends to have better backwash on students than examinations do because such measures place more emphasis on daily work and encourage students to think about what they read at a deeper level. However, for situations in which you need to give quizzes or tests, here are some suggested methods.

BEGINNING-LEVEL READING TESTS

For students at very low levels, testing their ability to comprehend sentences is appropriate. You can construct one such test by writing a series of statements and then asking students to mark them true or false. A variation involves making up a list of questions to which students have to answer yes or no. The statements and questions can be based either on general knowledge or on a picture drawn on the board.

SKIMMING QUIZZES

To construct a simple skimming quiz, give the students a passage, and then ask them to skim and find out as much as they can in a very limited amount of time. When time is up, take away the passage, and have students write down the main ideas. When grading such quizzes, be careful to give higher scores to students who provide a sketchy overview of the whole passage than to those who do a thorough job on the beginning of the passage but ignore the rest.

PASSAGE AND COMPREHENSION QUESTIONS

The traditional reading comprehension test consists of several short reading passages (each one no more than a few paragraphs long) and comprehension questions for each. The kinds of questions you ask will depend in part on what you have emphasized in your course. If you have stressed guessing vocabulary from context, you should include some items that test this skill. If your focus has been on content comprehension, questions should emphasize this aspect of the passage. If you have had students work with issues of author bias, tone, and other deeper aspects of comprehension, these are fair game as well. Intensive reading tests normally evaluate students' comprehension of both main points and details, so give students ample time to read the passage carefully. You may even allow students to use dictionaries.[2] Passages for extensive reading tests should be longer, time constraints should be tighter, less emphasis should be placed on detail comprehension, and dictionary use should almost certainly not be permitted.

---

[2] In real-life intensive reading, students use dictionaries, and their effective use is an important part of the skill being tested. However, if part of your goal is to prepare students for other reading tests, make sure that the rules of your test conform to those of tests students will take outside your class.

Here are some test items you might consider:

1. **true/false:** True/false (or yes/no, good/bad) items are easy to grade, but you need a great many to have a reasonable level of test validity.

2. **multiple choice:** Like true/false items, the various forms of multiple-choice items (including matching) are easy to grade. However, as noted in chapter 4, they are difficult to construct well. Their backwash is also questionable as they encourage students to hone skills in guessing between alternatives. My personal feeling is that you should avoid using multiple-choice items unless they are widely used in your country and students need to be prepared for them.

3. **short answers:** These items take various forms. The most obvious would be a simple question such as *What are the writer's two main arguments?* However, completing sentences (*The writer feels that smoking . . . .*) and filling in a form or grid are other useful forms of short-answer items. Short-answer items can be more difficult to grade than true/false or multiple-choice items; some answers will be partly correct, others may not be wrong but appear off the topic, and others may simply be hard to decipher. However, short-answer items can more easily go straight to the heart of a passage than can multiple-choice or true/false items (which tend to force you to test details), are easier to construct, and tend to have better backwash.

PASSAGE AND OUTLINE

Another way to check reading comprehension is to ask students to read a passage and then write an outline. This kind of test is more difficult than answering questions and should probably only be used with classes who have had practice with outlining. It also tends to work best for expository reading passages. However, it is a good task when you want students to extract the most important elements from a passage.

You can make passage-and-outline tests somewhat easier by the use of short-answer questions that are organized around an outline of a passage. In other words, your questions might look something like this:

1. What is the main thing the author is trying to persuade us to believe?

2. What is the first reason?

3. What evidence does the author mention to support this first reason?

4. What is the author's second reason?

5. [etc.]

Hughes (1989, 126–28) suggests an interesting variation of this kind of item in which students are given an article (in his example, one on migraine headaches) and several randomly ordered statements describing the contents of the passage. For example,

- "She gives some of the history of migraine."

- "She recommends specific drugs."

- "She recommends a herbal cure."

- [etc.]

Students then read the article and place the statements in the order used in the article.

PASSAGE AND SUMMARY

A simple form of reading test that is especially appropriate for testing extensive reading skills involves giving students a passage to read within a time limit and then taking the passage away and having students write a summary of its contents. This kind of test is easy to administer (though in large classes you may need help in collecting the reading passages from students promptly) and has good backwash, but it also places fairly heavy demands on students' writing skills. This type of test is best used with students who have practiced writing summaries of passages in class.

CRITIQUE

A very challenging kind of intensive reading examination consists of giving students a passage that presents an argument and then having them write a critique or rebuttal of the argument. Because this tests critical thinking skills and writing skills as well as reading comprehension, it is only appropriate for classes in which this kind of critical reviewing has been practiced.

TRANSLATION

The ultimate detail test is to have students translate a passage in English into their first language. This test, again, is recommended only for classes that have had practice in translation.

CLOZE TESTS

Cloze tests are sometimes used to evaluate reading skills, so I discuss them briefly here. Cloze tests contain a passage from which words have been deleted (every tenth word or so); students read the passage and fill in the blanks with appropriate words. Open-ended cloze tests allow students to fill in the blanks with any words they think would be appropriate; multiple-choice cloze tests give students options from which to pick. My rather lukewarm attitude toward cloze tests is due in part to the fact that it is not clear that they measure reading skill (Hughes 1989, 129). However, my main objection is that their backwash may be to encourage students to practice cloze exercises rather than to read.[3]

For Thought, Discussion, and Action

1. **What do you enjoy reading?** Survey one or more of your classmates (friends) by asking them what kinds of things they enjoy reading in their first language and in English.

2. **learning to read a foreign language:** Ask one or more classmates (friends, etc.) about their experiences learning to read in English. What were the challenges and rewards? What did they find helpful in their effort, and what was not helpful? Based on their experience, what advice would they give about teaching students to read in English?

3. **teaching intensive reading:** Choose a typical English textbook from your country, one that includes reading passages. Then prepare a lesson plan in which you teach the text intensive-reading style. Finally, discuss your lesson plan with other teachers.

---

[3] See Bailey (1998, 60–63) for discussion of potential pitfalls in the use of cloze tests and how to avoid them.

4. **teaching speed reading:** If you are already teaching a course that involves reading skills, try preparing and conducting a speed-reading exercise (or another activity of a kind that you have not used previously) according to the instructions in the chapter.

5. **getting students to ask questions:** In many countries, getting students to ask questions about a text is not always easy. List several strategies you think might help you get students to ask more questions in class, and then discuss the strategies with other teachers.

6. **choosing reading materials in English:** Make a list of the kinds of reading materials in English that are available in your country. Questions to consider about each kind of material include
    - How widely available is it?
    - How much does it cost? Can students afford it?
    - What is its level of reading difficulty?
    - Would it be interesting to students?
    - Would it be more appropriate for intensive reading or extensive reading?

7. **assigning extensive reading (task A):** This chapter suggests that it may be good to assign students extensive reading as part of their homework. If you tried to do this in your country, what would the challenges be? How could they be overcome? Could this idea be adapted for use in the kinds of courses you will teach?

8. **assigning extensive reading (task B):** Imagine you have been assigned to teach one of the sample courses described in appendix B. Design an extensive reading LLP you could suggest to students as part of one of these courses.

Sample LLP for Reading Skills

Goal: Build reading speed for reading novels in English.

Material: A novel that is interesting and not overly difficult.

Plan: Read for one hour a night, three nights a week.

Method:

1. At the beginning of each session, mark the time and the page number I start from.

2. Read as quickly as possible without completely losing the train of the story. As long as I have a rough idea of what is going on, keep reading.

3. Do not stop to look words up in a dictionary unless I become completely lost. (If this happens often, find an easier novel.)

4. At the end of the hour, mark how many pages I have read.

5. Over time, try to increase the number of pages I can read in an hour. (Remember that reading speed only improves gradually, so do not expect sudden leaps in my reading speed; look for gradual progress.)

Criteria for measuring progress: I will have succeeded if I

- finish reading two or three novels using this approach

- reduce my average reading time by several minutes per chapter (as measured by my pages-per-minute score)

Chapter 9

Writing: Keeping Your Head above Water

- By making writing a communicative activity, you increase students' interest in writing and your interest in what they write.

- Students need to learn to find and correct their own errors, so it is not necessary or even desirable for you to find and correct every error on each paper.

- The ability to write well entails learning to plan and edit as well as write.

- Large class sizes in EFL settings make it important for you to learn to respond to student writing quickly and efficiently and to find ways to reduce the paper-marking load.

Writing is probably the skill that local English teachers are most hesitant to teach. One problem is just the amount of work involved—going over papers is time-consuming, and responding to papers requires a lot of effort. This burden is made heavier when you have to read papers that students were not interested in writing and you aren't really interested in reading. The second problem is that as a teacher for whom English is your second language, there is always some concern that you won't be able to find and correctly edit all of the students' mistakes. Unlike teaching speaking, where you don't need to correct so much and where your corrections soon vanish into the air, teaching writing more often requires you to decide whether what a student wrote is right or wrong and then to put your judgments into (relatively permanent) written form. Often, of course, you can do this confidently, but sometimes you aren't sure yourself whether what a student wrote is acceptable or not. If you feel an obligation to find and correct every error, teaching writing can be very stressful.

The other side of the coin, however, is that teaching writing skills can also be very rewarding. It gives you an excellent opportunity to help students improve the accuracy of their English in a variety of areas such as grammar, usage, vocabulary, and even spelling. Perhaps even more rewarding is the opportunity to help them learn how to organize and express their thoughts more clearly in a foreign language. And, finally, the ideas that students share through their writing are themselves potentially very interesting, and teaching writing gives you a chance to get to know students better and explore new ideas with them.

This chapter discusses traditional concerns related to the teaching of writing, such as various tasks that can be assigned, the steps of the writing process, and the mechanics of paper marking. However, this chapter would not be complete—or even very helpful—if it ignored the practical problems that confront local teachers in the large writing classes that are typical of EFL settings; the grandest writing theories seem irrelevant if you are confronted with a pile of compositions you don't want to read. I offer no magic solution to these problems, but I discuss ways to minimize them, not the least of which is seeing that both you and the students have some interest in what is being written.

Writing as Communication

Many ESL/EFL textbooks approach the issue of writing by teaching students the proper forms of written English (how to write a sentence, a paragraph, and so on) and then suggesting topics that primarily give students an opportunity to practice using these forms. Other approaches begin with the message, encouraging students to find something they want to say and then moving to the question of what form will best help them communicate their message. There is no conclusive evidence that either of these approaches to teaching writing is the right one. However, I would suggest that a writing course that stresses the message is generally more interesting than one that stresses form and that, by stressing the message, you can use the inherent human desire to communicate as an engine to draw students into writing.

Be forewarned that even if you intend to focus on writing as a communicative activity, it is very easy to become overly concerned with issues of formal accuracy. One reason is that written language is generally expected to be more formally correct than spoken language, so flaws seem to cry out for correction. The relative permanence of written language also means that teachers can scrutinize compositions slowly and carefully, devoting far more time to finding grammar errors than would be possible with ephemeral spoken language. Finally, obsession with grammar and form is sometimes encouraged by a cult of martyrdom among writing teachers, who compete with each other to see who slaves for more hours over each batch of papers. In this competition, well-marked papers are concrete evidence of the teacher's merit.

The thrust of my argument here is not that you should ignore grammar and form; training in grammatical accuracy and the forms of composition should be an important part of any writing course. However, overemphasis on form can lead to neglect of the message itself. In turn, students may fabricate artificial messages in order to practice grammar or expository form. Students' tendency to ignore communication is compounded when compositions have no audience other than the teacher, and as Raimes (1983) notes, "Traditionally, the teacher has been not so much the reader as the judge of students' writing" (p. 17). Compositions that come back to students covered with grammar corrections and comments on form serve to confirm the students' belief that writing is a formal exercise. Unfortunately, most students aren't very interested in writing formal exercises, and most teachers aren't very interested in reading them.

Teachers would be kidding themselves if they thought that students wrote compositions primarily because they wanted to tell teachers something; students in writing courses are generally all too aware that the primary reason they are writing any given paper is that the teacher requires it. This, however, does not mean that students cannot become interested in conveying a message if they are given the chance. Below are several general principles that will help you ensure that a writing class is as communicative—and interesting—as possible:

1. Make an effort to generate interest in topics before asking students to write. One way to do this—and get in some good speaking practice—is to discuss a topic before writing about it. If students have not considered or discussed an idea, they are less likely to become deeply interested in it. An equally important reason for talking over ideas is to demonstrate that you are genuinely interested in the ideas themselves as well as the compositions that they lead to.

2. Use naturally existing information gaps and opportunities for communication. There is a great deal you don't know about the students—for example, their opinions and experiences—so compositions are a natural opportunity for students to share their ideas with you. What the students don't know about each other (e.g., stories from childhood) provides a second natural information gap. Take advantage of these.

3. Ask students to write their own ideas in their own words as much as possible. Many writing texts are filled with exercises that require students to rearrange sentences or correct flawed compositions. Such exercises can be useful for teaching specific writing skills, but they certainly do not provide students with an opportunity to communicate in writing. A steady diet of such exercises will drill home the impression that writing is simply making sure that words appear in the proper formal patterns.

4. See that writers have a real audience for their ideas. If you have asked students to write about their ideas, respond to what they say as well as to how they say it. If you are having them write about themselves, have them share what they write with other members of the class. Students need to experience the interest of others in what they have to say if they are to make an effort to communicate.

In-Class Writing Activities

Normally, a writing course is made up of a mix of writing activities, including both shorter writing activities done in class and longer assignments that involve writing at home. This section will introduce a number of in-class writing activities. (Some of these involve other language skills in addition to writing and are introduced elsewhere in the book, so they receive only brief treatment here.)

COPYING

Students at very beginning stages of writing need practice that allows them to focus on basic formal features of written English—spelling, capitalization, and punctuation—as well as on grammar and vocabulary. For students who are completely unfamiliar with the roman alphabet, copying sentences or even short texts from the textbook or blackboard is a way to learn English handwriting.

DICTATION

Dictation exercises provide an opportunity for students to focus on capitalization, punctuation, and spelling without needing to worry about grammar at the same time and can be used even at very elementary levels. (For procedure, see chapter 6.)

DICTOCOMP

As a writing exercise, dictocomp is somewhat more challenging than dictation and is a better way to practice basic grammar points. (For procedure, see chapter 6.)

NOTE-TAKING

Note-taking is a valuable skill in and of itself, and it is also a good way to develop listening and writing skills. The writing component can be strengthened if you ask students to use their notes as a basis for writing a summary or response to what they heard. (For procedure, see Talks and Lectures in chapter 6.)

SPEED WRITING

Helping students develop smoothness in their writing can be quite difficult if they see grammar and spelling errors as unforgivable crimes and always break their train of thought to look up words in a dictionary or check a grammar rule. Such students tend to write slowly and painfully, and it is not unusual for the progression of their ideas to seem choppy. One solution to this problem is an activity called speed writing, in which students put their ideas down on paper in as uninterrupted a manner as possible, leaving correction for later.

One goal of speed writing is for students to gradually increase the amount of text they generate in a given amount of time, so, to be effective, this activity needs to be repeated, and students need to keep track of their scores so that they can see their progress. Students may be concerned that, when writing so rapidly, they will make a much greater number of mistakes, so to put their minds at rest, tell them that they can go back over their compositions and check accuracy later. (They may actually discover that they are almost as accurate when writing quickly as when writing more slowly and carefully.)

1. Give students a topic, and tell them to write as much about it as they can within a limited amount of time, perhaps five to ten minutes.

2. Have the students count and record the number of words they have produced.

3. Award praise based on how much text is produced.

After the speed-writing exercise is completed, an additional option is to have students use the compositions they produced for proofreading practice by going back over what they have written to find and correct mistakes. This, however, should be kept distinct from the speed-writing activity itself so that students don't become overly focused on accuracy when they are doing the initial exercise.

IN-CLASS ESSAYS

Even if you prefer to have students do most of their writing at home, it is generally a good idea to occasionally have students write short compositions in class. One advantage is that you can actually see how quickly or slowly students produce text and how much they use reference tools. This will help you determine what problems students face in their writing and what kinds of practice they need.

1. Give students a topic or question on which to write, and set a time limit. (One common practice is to give students thirty minutes—five for planning and twenty-five for writing.)

2. As students write, observe their writing process, and see what you can discover. In most real-world writing tasks, it is normal to make use of reference tools such as dictionaries, so consider allowing dictionary use.

3. When time is up, collect the papers, and respond to them as you would other papers.

FILLING OUT FORMS

One special kind of writing you might address in class is filling out forms. The formal language of most forms (e.g., *marital status, occupation, length of intended stay*) is worthy of special attention.

Out-of-Class Writing Activities

In addition to in-class writing, writing courses generally include longer writing assignments for which much of the work of planning, writing, and revising is done outside class. Such assignments not only allow students to write longer and more carefully crafted compositions but also allow more time for planning, editing, and revising than is possible with in-class compositions.

Often, the types of writing you have students do will be determined in part by the materials you work with, by a school curriculum, or by the specific needs of the students. However, usually you will have some leeway in determining what kinds of compositions you will ask students to write. This section will discuss various types of out-of-class (homework) writing.

DIALOGUE WRITING

For beginning-level students, dialogue writing is a good way to allow some creative freedom in writing while still keeping the task conceptually simple. Dialogues can be based on models in student textbooks. (See Model-Based Dialogues in chapter 7.) The dialogues can be performed in class as well as handed in.

STORIES

Narrative writing is conceptually easy because chronological order provides a natural and simple organizational pattern, and most students have ready-made material in the form of their own experiences. A final bonus is that many people enjoy telling stories about themselves, and these stories are often fun to read. (Students can also practice narrative writing by retelling or summarizing a story that they have heard or read, though this tends to be less interesting for both the writer and the reader.) Story-writing assignments are a good opportunity to encourage writers to think how to structure what they write for maximum effectiveness with a given audience. A story writing activity can be conducted as follows:

1. Introduce a topic by sharing an experience you had (a remarkable coincidence, dangerous incident, or particularly stupid mistake). Either write the story out for your class, or present it orally.

2. Ask students to respond with a similar story from their own experience.

3. Once the stories are written, have the students share them with other class members, either by reading them aloud (in small classes) or by passing them around to be read by other students. Public sharing is probably best when stories have already been edited and polished, thus allowing students more confidence and pride in the quality of their work, but sharing of rough drafts for peer response can also be useful.

PERSONAL LETTERS

Letters are an easy genre but one in which students can write about a broad range of topics ranging from the very simple to the profound. As Raimes (1983) points out, "If a language student will ever need to write anything in the second language, it will probably be a letter" (p. 85). Letters thus have the advantage of high surface validity; students who assume they will never write an academic paper in English might well consider the possibility of writing a letter in English much more realistic and hence have more motivation to learn this skill. Many students also have experience writing letters in their own language, so this is not as abstract and foreign a genre as some other forms of writing.

1. Introduce basic conventions of personal letters such as the following:
    * typical ways to start a letter (e.g., *Dear . . .*)
    * formatting of letters (where to place the opening, closing, and date)
    * typical closings for a letter (e.g., *Sincerely, . . .*)

2. Assign a topic about which you want students to write, preferably one appropriate to the personal letter genre. Here are some possibilities:
    * Have students write an advice letter based on a problem situation (e.g., where to go for winter vacation, how to get the best price for a product).
    * Assign a topic that is generated by a situation—either serious or light: a letter of apology for some misdeed or a love letter to a famous movie star.
    * As Ur (1981) suggests, present students with a "provocative" letter that is "insulting, appealing, complaining, threatening" (pp. 98–105), and then ask them to produce a response. (Ur suggests combining the letter writing with class discussion.)

Now many people write e-mail messages instead of personal letters, so a variation on personal letter assignments involves teaching students to write e-mail messages. One of the advantages of e-mail is that, with the growing access to computers around the world, in many settings the students can get real writing practice through e-mail pen pals, chat rooms, and other online opportunities.

APPLICATION LETTERS AND RÉSUMÉS

In many countries, the kind of business letter students are most likely to write is a letter of application, accompanied by a résumé, so this assignment has high face validity. Application letters also provide a good opportunity to discuss cultural aspects of how one presents oneself. For example, a student writing a business letter to a Western reader needs to learn to get to the point quickly without indulging in a long flowery prelude that a Western reader might find superfluous and annoying. Also, students writing application letters need to learn the fine art of presenting their strong points in an objective, quantifiable way so that they do not seem subjective and overly boastful to a Westerner. It isn't as good to say, "I was the best student in my school" (subjective judgment) as it is to say, "I had the highest grade-point average" (objectively demonstrable fact).

1. Teach students the format you want them to use for their letters and résumés.

2. Introduce basic conventions for writing an application letter, such as those above.

3. Create one or more job advertisements to which students will respond with their application letters and résumés.

4. Have students outline their letters and résumés, carefully choosing points they wish to make and supporting the points with explanation and detail. You may want to go over these and provide feedback before students write.

5. Have students write the letters and résumés and turn them in. Alternatively, combine this activity with a simulated job fair in class in which some students take on employer roles and others take on job-seeker roles. The letters and résumés could then be read by the employers and serve as the basis for a job interview.

BUSINESS LETTERS

Another kind of writing skill that may be personally useful to students is the ability to write business letters. In many ways, business letters are short expository compositions, so the basic organizational patterns of expository writing can be taught in the context of business letters. Like any other form of expository writing, the business letter is composed primarily of paragraphs that consist of the following components: point(s), explanation, and specific details or evidence. The importance of accuracy in business letter writing also provides a natural context for the introduction of proofreading and editing skills. Students may see the importance of making a good impression in an application letter—hence not making too many grammar mistakes—more readily than in other kinds of writing assignments, so business letters may be an opportunity to motivate them to invest the time and effort necessary for developing editing skills.

1. Present students with a business-related situation in which they would need to write a letter. Such situations might include the need to renegotiate a price, plan a meeting or conference, clarify details of a shipment, or (politely but firmly) present a complaint.

2. In class, have students plan the strategy they will use in the letter—what approach they will take, what points they will make, how they will support their points, and so forth. This could be the focus of a small-group discussion activity.

3. Have students write their letters.

4. Collect the letters, return them (unread), and then have students edit or proofread them (either in class or as an additional out-of-class assignment). Then have the students turn the letters in again, this time for your response and feedback.

OPINION PAPERS (BASIC EXPOSITORY WRITING)

Perhaps the most basic expository writing assignment is a paragraph or short composition that presents an opinion and reasons for it. While writing an academic paper or a business report is obviously more complex than expressing an opinion in a paragraph, the basic point-explanation-detail organizational pattern is the same for all of these.

1. Start with an opinion question such as "What is the best place to visit in our country?" or "What do you find most difficult about learning English?"

2. In response to your question, have students write a paragraph or short paper that
   • first states their opinion
   • then explains anything in the opinion that needs to be explained (For example, if a student suggests that the national capital is the best place to visit, she should develop her answer by explaining why.)
   • supports the explanations with specific details and examples

EXPLANATORY PAPERS (EXPOSITORY WRITING)

The primary purpose of an explanatory (expository) paper is to convey an idea as clearly as possible, usually following a point-explanation-detail organizational pattern: an idea is usually presented at the beginning of a section of discourse (which may range in length from part of a paragraph to several pages), developed through explanation, and supported through the use of examples and concrete details that make the ideas clearer and more memorable.

When writing explanatory papers, writers obviously need to consider the background knowledge of the intended audience—an explanation is only effective if it is based on knowledge that the audience already has, and it is only interesting if it tells audience members more than they already know. So, when assigning students to write explanatory papers for which you will be the primary audience, encouraging students to think carefully about what you probably already know and don't know about the issue will not only improve their explanatory writing in general but also make it more interesting for you to read.

One of the most natural and interesting kinds of writing assignments involves asking students to state and explain an opinion (in a more formal and organized way than in Opinion Papers above). A suggested procedure is as follows:

1. Decide on an issue you would like to have students write about, or let them choose one.

2. Introduce the issue to students, and ask them to write a paper stating their position on it.

3. Use the papers as a starting point for an in-class discussion activity by requiring some or all of the students to present a brief (two- to three-sentence) summary of their opinion and explanation and then moving into discussion.

4. As you read and respond to the students' papers, be sure to respond to the ideas as well as the language.

ARGUMENT PAPERS

Argument papers require students to state a position on some issue; explain why they hold the position they do; and provide evidence to support the points they make, that is, convince the audience to believe these points. To some extent, the distinction between argument papers and explanatory papers is somewhat artificial; argument virtually always requires explanation, and most expository writing has at least some element of persuasion. Also, the basic structure of an argument paper (*position + argument/explanation + evidence*) is similar to that of explanation. However, the primary goal of an argument paper is to persuade rather than to explain, and in writing argument papers, the use of evidence is more important.

Of course, you can assign students to write argument papers that are independent of other work they are doing in your class, but often it is even more effective to integrate argument writing with reading and speaking skills by basing the writing task on an article that students read, discuss in class, and finally write about.

1. Locate an article that presents a controversial viewpoint or raises a controversial question. (See Debates in chapter 7 for ideas on choosing topics.)

2. Have students read the article in class or at home and make notes on their response to it.

3. To help students generate and clarify ideas, have students discuss the article in class, either as a pair or small-group task or as a debate activity.

4. Have students write the paper.

CRITIQUES

A critique or review is a special kind of opinion paper that evaluates a book, film, article, or even an idea. Most critiques contain the following parts: (1) summary, (2) discussion of the strong and weak points of the subject of the review, and (3) a final judgment and recommendation to the potential audience. The main difference between a critique and an argument is that the former purports to examine two sides of an issue fairly. The appearance of fairness is critical to the success of the critique, so it is particularly important to discuss both good and bad points. Critique writing thus provides good practice in the examining of an issue from a variety of viewpoints.

Critical reviews are among the most demanding forms of writing to teach, particularly if the text (or book, movie, or article) being reviewed is from another culture. Critique writing requires a high level of comprehension of the text being reviewed and places heavy demands on students' critical thinking skills. This is especially true if the text being reviewed has been produced by a competent professional; flaws are often not immediately obvious, and the student is thus at a loss as to how to do anything more than humbly praise. However, the greatest problem is often deciding on a standard by which to judge the book. A reviewer can certainly start with the question, *Did I like it?*, but ultimately needs to answer the more difficult question, *Was it a good book?* The former question is one of personal taste; the latter implies a standard that is more universal, and finding such a standard can be a real problem.[1]

---

[1] When having students write critiques, I ask that they first try and determine the intended purpose(s) of the text they are critiquing and then judge it on whether or not it achieves its purpose. One problem with this approach is that students from non-Western backgrounds sometimes find it difficult to determine the purposes underlying the various genres of Western texts. When such problems occur, I find it useful to devote some class time to discussing the genres of Western writing and media and what range of purposes is normally found within each genre.

However, critique writing also offers significant benefits. First, it can be a good way to get students interested in writing because it draws on one of the most natural of human instincts—the desire to evaluate. (After seeing a film or reading a book, the first topic of discussion is inevitably, *Was it good?*) Critique writing also helps students learn to think critically about what they read or see rather than taking the printed or recorded word as sacred. Finally, critique writing is a good way to respond to books, articles, tapes, or audiovisual material and is an effective way to combine writing with reading or listening.

1. Choose an article (or book, film, or other work) that you want students to critique. Articles that are somewhat controversial, unusual, extreme, or risky often work best; those which are highly polished and play very safe tend to be hard to critique. (Rule of thumb: if you can't find much interesting to say about a text, students will probably also have a hard time.)

2. Have students read the article and take note of its strong and weak points.

3. To help students generate ideas, have the students discuss the article in small groups. However, for this kind of writing assignment—where there are often only a limited number of good points a review might reasonably make—it is important that you not reveal too much of your own viewpoint.

4. Have students write the review.

RESEARCH PAPERS

Research paper assignments not only help students build useful research and writing skills but also give students an opportunity to learn more about the topic they research. In English language classes, one particularly appropriate kind of research paper involves having students research and write a report on some aspect of a culture that is foreign to them.

1. Either assign topics, or have students pick their own. (You might draw on the ideas in appendix C.) Topics that are fairly narrow and specific tend to result in better papers.

2. Have students research their topic using whatever resources are available (e.g., in the library, on the Internet). Then have them write the paper.

3. To give the project a stronger communicative aspect, have the students share what they learn—or at least the most interesting highlights—with their classmates. Brief classroom presentations are one option but tend to consume a large amount of class time. (If you choose to have students do presentations, you might cut down on the total number of projects by having students work and present in groups.) Alternatively, have students generate a one-page highlights handout to be duplicated for their classmates, or prepare a poster session during which students display their work.

4. Suggest that, when writing up their results, students compare and contrast their findings with their own culture.

A BRIEF DETOUR

Whether or not students in a given country really need training in expository or academic writing genres is a question that should be raised more often than it is. The common assumption that expository writing should be the focus of EFL writing courses may be based less on the actual needs of EFL students than on the fact that many English teachers are trained in academic environments where expository writing is stressed. However, there are a number of reasons why training in expository writing may benefit even students who are not preparing for careers in the academic world:

1. Familiarity with norms of Western expository and argument writing will help students in their English reading. Many kinds of texts—including journal articles, editorials, and even some magazine articles, newspaper articles, and books—follow these norms, so familiarity with how this kind of writing is put together will give students a clearer idea of what to expect as they read.

2. Knowledge of the norms of expository writing is also a window on the culture of the West. For example, the preference of most English-speaking Westerners for a simple, direct form of business communication rather than a more ornate or flowery style is a reflection of the way business is done in the West; the impatience of Westerners with communication that is indirect, unexplained, or unsupported by specific factual information carries over into spoken as well as written communication.

3. Expository writing skills require the ability to analyze issues and problems as well as to write about them, so teaching expository writing almost inevitably moves from the realm of language into the Western approach to critical thinking skills. In the process of learning expository writing, students have intense, sustained exposure to different modes of organizing and presenting ideas, and this provides a rare and precious opportunity to wrestle with an important aspect of another culture.

Planning and Editing Writing

Reaching a breakthrough point where students can write in English well enough to deal with education or work-related tasks—or even social correspondence—involves more than just the ability to produce text in English. Generally, people expect a higher degree of organization, clarity, accuracy, and polish in written language than in spoken, so in addition to generating texts, students need to learn to plan and edit them. To this end, much of the work in most writing courses involves students producing multiple drafts—working mainly outside class—that help them learn to write texts that are relatively well planned and carefully polished.

The writing process is often described as having three parts: planning, writing, and revising. You need not always insist that students follow this strict, three-step process in their writing because it is not entirely natural; normally, some planning and editing occurs during the writing phase, and new plans often emerge during the editing phase (see Richards 1990, 108, and Omaggio Hadley 2001, 312, for further discussion). However, especially as students move toward more advanced levels of writing skill, they should begin learning that good writing starts before the first sentence is written and doesn't end with the last word of the first draft.

PREWRITING AND PLANNING

The planning of a composition can be broken down into three parts: generating ideas, organizing them, and noting them down for later reference.

Generating Ideas

Essentially, generating ideas means finding something to say. Sometimes ideas come naturally, but students are often faced with the problem of being required to write about something they have never thought about or have no opinions on, and if they do not generate ideas before starting to generate text, their papers will be harder both to write and to read.

Many of the speaking skills activities discussed in chapter 7 (such as pair or small-group tasks, debates, and large-group discussions) are effective ways to help students generate ideas before starting a paper. Brainstorming, another useful prewriting activity, involves giving students a topic or question and having them think of as many ideas as they can as quickly as they can; all ideas, no matter how absurd or farfetched, are written down. After a large number of ideas are generated, students go back and choose those that seem worthy of further thought.

I also find it useful to talk with students in writing classes about when and how they think best. For example, I tend to think best when walking alone and talking to myself, jotting ideas down in a little notebook as they occur to me. Others may find that they think best sitting in a quiet room or talking ideas over with friends. Many students' natural tendency is not to think about what they will write at all until they actually sit down to start writing, so talking with students about where and how they do their best thinking will help underscore the importance of thinking as a part of the composition process.

Selecting and Organizing Ideas

This step is probably the most difficult one to isolate from the others; writers continue to add, subtract, or move ideas throughout the writing process. However, making an initial effort to select and organize material will give students a good head start.

The first—and sometimes most difficult—decision students have to make is exactly what aspects of a topic to focus on. Most topics are broad enough to allow more than a single approach, so students need to decide what points to emphasize. The second step is determined by the first. Having decided what to focus on, students need to look at their material and decide what ideas and details suit the focus. The problem most often encountered here is that students are reluctant to omit any of the precious material that they so painfully generated, and they often try to find ways to shoehorn almost all of it in. You will need to stress that part of becoming a good writer is learning to eliminate irrelevant material. Finally, students need to arrange the points in the most effective order and decide what to say about each.

Noting Ideas Down

Perhaps the most important aspect of teaching students to plan what they write is ensuring that they actually do it. Students are often tempted to cut corners in their work, and the preparation step for writing is one of the corners most often cut. Many students don't see it as important or simply don't do it because they are busy, and it is easier to get away with not preparing a composition than with not writing it. If you require that students produce a written plan before they write—anything from a scribbled list to a neat outline—it is not only easier to hold students accountable for the planning phase of writing but is also more likely that they will produce a good paper.

Before starting to write, students should at the very least list the main points of their paper. More advanced-level students can often benefit from learning how to write formal outlines because they require students to decide what points they will make in what order and to consider how points relate to each other (e.g., which are main points and which are supporting points). The ability to write a good outline is a skill that may take students some time to master, but it is very helpful in more advanced-level writing.

EDITING AND REVISING

In foreign language study, it is generally recognized that the hardest skill to master is writing, and no matter how good students are, it is unlikely that they will reach a level where they can turn out a polished, flawless first draft of a composition in English. (In fact, this is a trick that even most native speakers of English can't pull off with any regularity.) An essential part of learning to write is therefore learning how to edit and revise one's own work.

Editing can be divided into two processes: revising to improve its content and proofreading to catch and correct errors.

Revising

In theory, most students would agree that it is good to revise their papers. However, for a number of understandable reasons, in practice students' enthusiasm for actually doing such revision tends to be weak. One problem is that students may see little reason to invest further time polishing a presentation of ideas they never had any real interest in. A second problem is that, even when students do try to revise, they often do so the same night as they write, when they simply have neither the energy nor the freshness of perspective to see flaws of organization and logic that they might notice the next morning. The upshot is that many students never actually do any revision or make only feeble efforts that don't produce any markedly noticeable improvements. Granted, as Harmer (2001, 146–50) points out, with the growing availability of computers and word-processing software, it is now considerably easier for students to revise their work because they do not need to recopy papers in their entirety. However, human nature being what it is, getting student writers to revise will probably always be a challenge.

One of the best ways to convince students that revising really is worth the effort is to ensure that they actually do revise papers, and that they do so seriously enough that the effort generates results and allows them to see for themselves how much better a revised paper can be. One way to ensure that real revision happens is to use class time for revising, not least so that students attempt revising some time other than the same night the paper was written. Another approach is to occasionally have students hand in drafts that you then hold for a period of time before handing them back—unedited—for revision. This latter approach allows students a rare opportunity to look back on their own work with fresher minds and higher energy levels than they normally bring to the task. A final way to ensure that students actually write a second draft of a paper is to have them turn in both the old and the new draft to you. You then grade the new draft based partially on improvement.

Another approach, called *peer revising*, involves having students exchange papers to give each other feedback on content. Initially this may not work very well because students often go to the extremes of being either too polite to their classmates or too zealous in the role of critic. You may need to remind students that the role of the reader is to offer helpful suggestions rather than final judgments and that the role of the writer is to listen to and take note of the suggestions rather than defending him- or herself from them. Of course, the writer may ultimately choose to reject suggestions, but it is best to listen carefully first; even an unwise suggestion may alert the writer to a point that needs improvement.

You can enhance peer editing by giving students a checklist to guide their revision efforts. A simple list of such questions might include these:

- Is there anything that I don't understand?

- Is there anyplace where I want to know more?

- Is there anyplace where I wanted an example?

- Is there anything that seems out of place?

- Is there anything that seems unnecessary?

Ultimately, the most important thing you can do to help students develop editing skills is to make writing a communicative activity in which they take a genuine interest. The more interested students are in their message and the response of their audience, the more likely they are to master revision skills. Without that interest, no amount of theory will help.

Proofreading

Proofreading is a difficult skill for most students to master, not so much because they cannot correct mistakes as because they cannot find them. Sometimes both teachers and students assume that proofreading is a process of mechanically applying grammar rules to every sentence in a composition in order to find the bits that are wrong. However, it is more realistic—and help-ful—to view proofreading as a process of looking through a text to find things that students are not sure about, which they can then check in a reference book if they have the time and inclina-tion. In short, students are not looking for mistakes; they are looking for places where they are not sure. If students are able to write on computer word-processing software, the grammar-check-ing function can help students locate many probable errors and also provides feedback as they attempt to correct the offending sentence. However, ultimately it is best if students can build their own ability to find potential trouble spots, and this ability depends heavily on *language sense*, an instinctive knowledge of what is definitely correct and what is dubious. Students who have been exposed to a great deal of correct English will often be able to tell that something looks funny, whereas students who don't have this sense generally can't proofread very well. (This is one reason it is important for students to read and listen to as much English as possible.)

One exercise that helps students improve their proofreading skills involves handing out a composition into which errors have intentionally been inserted by an evil-hearted teacher and then asking the students to find and correct the errors. The advantage of this approach is that students can work together on the same composition in groups. As students become more skilled in spotting errors, the next level is to have students exchange compositions with each other for proofreading. While students' ability to spot errors in their classmates' compositions is often not dramatically better than their ability to see their own mistakes, generally they can call their partner's attention to at least a few points that need to be checked. Third, as suggested above, students can practice proofreading compositions of their own that they produced during speed-writing exercises or other in-class writing assignments. Finally, it is worthwhile occasionally to have students proofread their own papers in class. (This last exercise should be used sparingly, as once students get the idea that they can proofread in class, they aren't likely to do it at home. However, limited doses of in-class proofreading may drive home the point that if students proofread when their minds are fresh—instead of at midnight—they may find mistakes they would otherwise have missed.)

Ultimately, the ability of students to catch and correct their own errors depends in part on their becoming aware of their personal problem areas—patterns in the kinds of mistakes each student tends to make. By paying attention to compositions that you edit and then keeping a record of the kinds of errors that appear most often, students can learn what they personally need to pay special attention to so that they can narrow the field of their proofreading efforts.

Teaching students how to use reference tools is another important aspect of helping them develop proofreading skills. Bilingual or monolingual dictionaries that have plenty of examples are especially valuable tools for writing because the examples provide students with models of grammar and usage as well as word meaning.

THE WRITING AND FEEDBACK CYCLE

Going through all the steps suggested above for a paper results in a process that involves several rounds of drafts, feedback, and revision. A typical cycle might look something like this:

1. Students do prewriting activities in class, followed by planning of the composition (making notes or an outline) at home.

2. You give students feedback on their plan, either orally or in writing.

3. Students write the first draft.

4. You read the first draft and give feedback.

5. Students revise and make additional drafts.

6. You do final marking and grading.

This is obviously a lot of work to put into one paper, and you do not need to have students go through all of the steps above for each and every writing assignment; at times you may wish to have them do an exercise that only involves planning a paper, or you may practice the editing stage alone by having students edit a composition written by someone else. However, going through all of the steps for at least some of the writing tasks you assign is worth the effort so that students become used to the idea that all of these steps are an important part of writing.

Responding to Student Writing

RESPONDING TO CONTENT

You should not be the only audience students write for, but you will often be the audience they are most influenced by. Thus, if you want students to take writing seriously as communication, you must respond to the message of a paper as well as to its grammar. You may agree, disagree, ask questions, add information, or comment on what you find interesting or confusing; sometimes you need to tell students that you suspect they were just filling paper. The point is that your response should convince students that you are paying attention to what they have to say.

Comments in the margin are the best way to give feedback about specific aspects of a composition because the proximity of the comments to the portion of the text you are talking about makes them easier to understand. Questions in the margin are an especially effective way to help students know how to revise and improve their papers while still encouraging them to think for themselves. Unlike comments like *awkward* or *confusing*, questions don't seem like a slap on the wrist, and they also establish a sense of conversation rather than judgment. Students are generally more willing to look over and learn from the feedback you write if there is an occasional *good* or at least *OK* amidst your margin comments. (Of course, you may want to write your comments in the students' first language rather than in English. This is faster and easier for you as well as easier for the students.)

Comments at the end of the composition can provide a general summing up of the strengths and weaknesses of a composition and perhaps a few personal responses to the ideas. Here are a few suggestions:

- The longer comments are, the less likely they are to be absorbed and digested, so it is better to make one or two points clearly than to discuss every flaw in the paper. (Remember that deciphering your handwritten comments may take some effort, especially if they are scrunched in at the bottom with lines leading all over the page.)

- Students are more likely to read the comments if you include some good news with the bad. Generally, you can find at least one nice thing to say about a paper, and this takes some of the sting out of other comments. It also helps if you phrase bad news as suggestions for improvement rather than criticisms.

There is no reason to confine your responses to written comments. Assuming that you have students write about something you are genuinely interested in, there is no better way to convince students of your interest than to talk with them about the papers. If, for example, you had students write about their favorite kinds of music, you might spend a bit of class time asking follow-up questions.

RESPONDING TO FORM

There is no single, sure-fire approach to composition marking that will ensure rapid student progress in formal accuracy (Bowen, Madsen, and Hilferty 1985, 263; Omaggio Hadley 2001, 317). In fact, one of the most frustrating aspects of teaching writing is that no matter how carefully you mark papers, students' formal accuracy often improves only slowly. This is especially true in EFL settings where students are only able to devote a limited amount of time to English study and an even smaller portion of that time to writing. However, marking grammar, spelling, vocabulary, and cultural errors is still an important part of responding to student compositions. Feedback can help students improve accuracy, particularly if you ensure that students pay adequate attention to the feedback; they will not be able to correct every error pointed out to them, nor will they learn from every correction, but they will learn some of the time. Another important reason to provide feedback is that students expect it, and if you don't provide it, students may assume that you are derelict in your duty. The question is thus not whether to mark errors but how to mark effectively.

Raimes (1983, 149) points out that the goal of your marking strategy is to help students improve their own editing skills. This suggests that marking a paper well usually does not mean finding and correcting every mistake in it; it means giving students the fewest clues that still enable them to locate and correct a substantial number of their own errors. If all goes well in your class, over time you should be able to give fewer and vaguer clues, thus forcing students to rely more on their own correction skills.

For students who have little ability to find and correct their own errors, the best marking system is one that helps students locate errors and gives them clues as to what is wrong. You would normally do this by underlining errors and marking them with proofreading symbols that indicate what kind of error was made. A basic system might include the following symbols:

S	spelling mistake
T	verb tense error
WW	wrong word
N	problem with a countable noun (which should either be plural or preceded by a determiner like *the, a,* or *this*)
Awk	awkward
F	wrong form of word (e.g., verb form instead of noun)
^	insert word(s) here
Ø	omit

Using such a system takes a little additional effort in the beginning because you need to design it and then teach it to students. However, the advantage of such a system is that it dramatically simplifies the editing process but still requires students to correct their own mistakes, hence increasing the likelihood that students will learn from them.[2]

For problems that students should be able to diagnose and cure by themselves, you may choose to simply point out the problem by underlining it. Another method, appropriate for students with more advanced editing skills, is to mark lines or paragraphs in which there are errors, indicating only the number of mistakes, and having students both find and correct the problems on their own. This approach has the advantage of training students to locate errors by themselves, albeit with some help. As students become even more skilled proofreaders, you may choose not to mark errors in student compositions at all, instead making a comment at the end of the paper as to the kinds of problems students should look for as they edit. These last approaches assume considerable editing skills on the part of students and may initially prove impractical for many classes. However, the goal should be to move in this direction because these approaches reinforce the idea that students ultimately need to be able to find and correct their own errors.

When you notice problems that students probably can't correct on their own, you might occasionally just correct the error for them. However, such corrections often deal with points far enough above students' current skill level that they won't learn much from the correction and are also easily ignored by students, so they should be kept to a minimum.

In my comments on correction, I assume that you should correct errors selectively rather than attempting to point out or correct every problem in each student paper. I feel a selective approach is preferable for several reasons. The first and main reason is that it is often hard for students to learn from too many corrections at once. In fact, when students get back a paper that is covered with corrections, they often tend to feel overwhelmed and hopeless, so rather than trying to learn from all the corrections, they simply give up and ignore all of them. In contrast, if the corrections on the paper are limited in number and focused on a limited range of problems, it is easier for students to digest the feedback. (Of course, when you adopt a selective approach to correction, you need to let students know that you are doing this—and explain to them why this is better for them.) The second virtue of selective correction is that it is less stressful for you. If you feel an obligation to find and correct every mistake, you will not only have to invest more time working on each student paper but also feel much more pressure. In contrast, allowing yourself some freedom in choosing what problems you will and won't respond to reduces the pressure on you. This, in turn, increases the chances that you will be willing and able to include writing in the range of skills that you teach.

Having invested effort in marking a paper, you should ensure that students pay attention to the feedback. This may sound obvious, but after several hours correcting and grading, you will be tired of a certain batch of papers and more than happy just to hand them back to students and move onto something else. Likewise, students often look at the grade, glance at the errors, and file the paper away. Even with the best intentions in the world, busy students will generally not pore over their mistakes unless there is a good reason to do so. The tragedy of this situation is that maximum pain results in minimum learning.

One way to ensure that students learn from your feedback is to avoid letting overwork consistently drive you into omitting the editing stage of the composition process. Even if you do not feel that you have time to have students write a completely new draft of a paper you have marked, ask them to correct the errors you have marked and then turn the original draft back in so that you

---

[2] Many ESL, grammar, and writing books contain examples of marking systems, but you can easily design a system for yourself, and it may be best if your system reflects the grammar points you have emphasized in class.

can check the corrections. (If you mark the corrections in a color of ink that differs from your original marks, the new corrections will be easier for students to find.) Another way to encourage students to learn from their mistakes is by having them keep a personal grammar notebook in which they make note of their errors and corrections. Keeping such a notebook is one of those good intentions that students honor more in theory than in practice, so you might want to collect the notebook occasionally to show students that you are serious.

GRADING COMPOSITIONS

Skilled professionals are often able to grade compositions reliably and consistently by relying on overall impressions. However, the ability to grade reliably in this way takes considerable experience to develop and is often difficult to maintain as the grader becomes tired. Thus, I would not recommend this approach to new teachers who are grading large numbers of compositions.

A more consistently reliable approach involves establishing a set of criteria before beginning to grade compositions. You can draw on a ready-made scale like the American Council on the Teaching of Foreign Languages' (ACTFL's) *Proficiency Guidelines* (1999; see the footnote in chapter 4), but often it is best to design your own system based on the points that you have emphasized in your course. Designing a criteria scale forces you to carefully think through what you are looking for as you grade and will both speed the grading process and help you remain more consistent and fair, even as your eyelids droop and your mind begins to cloud. To avoid writing a new scale for each assignment, you may want to design a basic system based on the goals of the course and then modify it to handle the special features and emphases of specific assignments. The Goals Menu in appendix A may help you decide what to look for when setting up a criteria system for grading compositions.

One way to make grading a little more precise—and to give students clearer feedback—is to give two grades to a composition, one for form and one for content. Perhaps the greatest advantage of this is that it reminds you to respond to the content of papers as well as to their formal accuracy. It is easy for grammar errors to loom disproportionately large in the mind of a tired grader, and this can create problems if you tell students in class that content is most important but wind up letting grammar determine most of your grade.

Managing the Load

One of the unpleasant realities of teaching a writing course is that it often turns into a slugging match between you and piles of student compositions, a match that turns especially frustrating when you spend long hours trying to salvage poorly written papers only to find that the next round is little better. To a certain extent, this reality is inevitable. As Raimes (1983, 4–5) points out, even many adult native speakers of a language find writing difficult, and the consensus is that writing is the most difficult language skill for nonnatives to master (Bowen, Madsen, and Hilferty 1985, 253; Nunan 1989, 35). Also, no matter how well a writing teacher manages homework assignments, teaching writing generally requires more out-of-class effort per hour of class time than teaching other English skills, especially to the large classes that are common in EFL settings.

The analogy I use for writing classes is that they are like going hiking with a heavy backpack—no matter how you arrange the pack, carrying it will take some effort. However, the hike offers rewards as well as work, and by arranging the pack well, you can make the trip much more pleasant. As promised in the introduction to this chapter, I offer no ultimate remedy for the paper correction problem, but I suggest a few ways you can minimize your burden and maximize your effectiveness through your choice of writing assignments and through editing and marking strategies.

ASSIGNMENTS

The bane of the writing teacher's existence is the raw-sewage paper—the unplanned, unedited paper written by a student who believes it will get a decent grade if only it is long enough. There may well be a place for free writing in a program, but no teacher should be forced to read all of it any more than a piano teacher should be required to listen to hours of a student playing scales. Careful structuring of assignments can do much to prevent this situation.

1. Guarantee that students plan and edit a paper before you have to read it. As suggested in this chapter, you can ensure planning by giving students time in class to plan—under your watchful eye—and by asking to see written evidence of planning. Likewise, to increase the chances of a serious attempt at revision, have students write a draft of a paper and bring it to class. Once you check to see that a draft was written, either give students time in class to revise, or make revision a homework assignment. Alternatively, collect the papers and hold on to them for several days before giving them back for revision.

2. Make the goals of a writing assignment very clear and specific. This not only helps students know what they are supposed to focus on but also makes your work easier by giving a clearer focus to your response. Consequently, when you sit down to read student papers, you will already know what limited set of points you are looking for. A variation on this is to have students submit a list of points on which they want feedback, thus requiring students to focus your editing. This method has the added advantage of involving students more actively in the feedback process.

3. Put upper (not just lower) limits on the length of compositions. As long as students believe that long compositions will get higher grades than short ones, they will be tempted to skimp on planning and editing to save as much time as possible for generating text. Even students who have good intentions about editing their massive creations are often so exhausted by the process of writing them that in the end they just finish writing the paper and go to bed. Putting upper limits on length helps students take seriously your pleading assertions that long is not necessarily good and can help ensure that students reserve some time for planning and editing.

4. Choose topics you are genuinely interested in. Like most writing teachers, I am guilty of having asked students to write on topics of dubious appeal, such as *Describe a room* or *My summer vacation*, because these are examples of a particular form of writing (description and narration, respectively). But after years of suffering through stale piles of essays, I have finally learned not to ask students to write about things I don't want to read about. Having students write about things you want to read about not only helps student motivation by making writing more genuinely communicative but also makes reading the papers much less draining for you.

RESPONSE AND CORRECTION

For responding to the ideas in a paper, short comments or questions in the margins of a paper often take less time to write than comments at the end, and—as noted above—may be more effective.

When dealing with error marking, the keys to efficiency are focus and selectivity; marking a paper is much easier if you know exactly what you are looking for and if you are not looking for everything. This approach to marking is also generally better for students than marking every error in a paper because they are most likely to benefit from correction if there are only a limited number of lessons to be learned from it; a paper covered with corrections tends to overwhelm more than teach. Selective marking is also less likely to drive weaker writers into a state of despair every time they get a paper back.

One way to focus your marking is to look primarily for errors related to points you have taught in class and to let most other errors go. A second approach is to look for patterns in a student's mistakes. This tends to be more time-consuming, but such tailoring of feedback can be very helpful to students. Other criteria for deciding what errors to mark include the seriousness of the error (those which interfere with communication being most important) or the difficulty that students will have correcting the problem.

LOW-TEACHER-INVESTMENT WRITING ASSIGNMENTS

Generally, to get enough writing practice, students will need to write more than you can reasonably expect to read and respond to, so you will need to give some writing assignments that you can either process very quickly or not read at all. When giving any of these assignments, you should spend some time selling students on the idea that writing practice is still valuable even when there is no teacher to carefully mark every error. As with the development of any other language skill, writing practice is useful in and of itself, especially if students are using it actively as an opportunity to rehearse application of points learned in class or through reference materials. Kinds of assignments that do not necessitate lengthy teacher response include the following:

- **journals:** Journals give students an opportunity to write about daily events, past experiences, thoughts, or almost anything else. You only need to read over entries occasionally and comment briefly, generally responding to the ideas more than the language.

- **material to share with other students:** As suggested above, you might have students write for each other instead of you. Material written to be read by other students can include personal stories, position papers on issues (as a prelude to discussion or debate), or newsletters on personal or local events.

- **pen-pal writing:** For this type of writing, you find people who are willing to correspond with students by letter or by e-mail. Retirees or students might be good potential correspondents. The advantage of pen-pal programs, Internet chat rooms, and other writing exchanges is that they not only provide an opportunity for writing practice that you do not need to edit but also reinforce the idea that writing is a real communication skill rather than a lifeless class exercise.

Evaluation

I will say little about tests for writing because writing is a skill area where it is especially important to deemphasize testing in favor of grades on other writing assignments. Timed writing under testlike conditions is rare in real life, and it has the undesirable effect of discouraging planning, editing, and use of reference tools. In-class testing, however, ensures that you see student compositions that you know were not copied or written by someone else and for which you have a reliable idea of how much time students invested. Therefore, while the majority of a writing course grade should generally be based on the regular assignments, it may also be wise to include in-class writing tests.

An in-class writing test is essentially the same as an in-class composition. Give students a topic and a time limit within which to complete an essay. The topic(s) should be within students' range of knowledge and should include an indication of the type of writing expected (e.g., letter, argument). It is best if the topic presents a clearly defined task rather than only a general topic. *Explain why you do/don't* . . . is much better than *Write about* . . . because the former gives students a better idea of what is expected of them. If the topic is clear, thirty minutes is generally more than adequate time for the production of a writing sample. Students should be encouraged, perhaps even required, to spend some time taking notes and organizing before they begin to write; in fact, it may be desirable to ask students to hand in their preparation notes (in English or in their native language) along with the paper. Students should also be encouraged to save a few minutes at the end to check for mistakes, though they will probably only catch a few of the more obvious errors at best. There is no good reason not to allow students to use dictionaries unless your test is intended to prepare them for some kind of standardized test in which dictionaries are not allowed.

For Thought, Discussion, and Action

1. **learning to write:** Think back on your own experience of learning to write in English. What were the most significant challenges? What kinds of activities and practice helped you the most?

2. **enhancing your interest in student writing:** This chapter suggests that, as often as possible, you should ask students to write about topics you are interested in reading about, especially if you will be the main or only audience for the composition. (1) Think about and list interesting topics that students could write to you about. (2) Share your list with a classmate or colleague, and see if that person has some good ideas to offer to you.

3. **doing speed writing:** If you teach an English course that involves writing, have students do a speed-writing exercise according to the instructions given earlier in the chapter. (Teachers who have not had much experience with this activity may worry that students will make too many mistakes when writing quickly, so you may want to check students' work the first time they try this to see whether or not the number of errors goes up dramatically. It probably won't, but seeing is believing.)

4. **choosing writing activities:** Choose one of the sample courses described in appendix B. Then, with that course in mind, go through the list of writing activities in this chapter, and select several that you think would be suitable, both in class and out of class. Be ready to explain the rationale for your choices.

5. **generating ideas:** Ask several classmates or friends how they generate ideas when trying to write a paper and how they organize the ideas before writing. Make note of useful strategies that you could suggest to students.

6. **telling stories:** Make a list of good personal-experience stories you can tell that might effectively prime the pump for a story-writing assignment for the students. For fun, you might exchange one or more of your stories with classmates or friends.

7. **writing with e-mail and the Internet:** Explore the feasibility of having students write in English to people in other countries using an Internet chat room or e-mail.

8. **devising a marking system:** Devise a marking symbol system you could use when editing papers for a writing class (perhaps a modified version of the system suggested in this chapter).

9. **responding to (large numbers of) papers:** Find one or more teachers who have taught writing, and ask them about the strategies they use for effectively coping with the demands of paper editing.

Sample Language Learning Project for Writing Skills

Goals: Build note-taking skills; build listening skills; build ability to accurately write simple compositions (based on DVD documentaries).

Material: Television documentaries or feature programs in DVD format (e.g., National Geographic features).

Plan: Listen to one or two features a week, and write one or two compositions a week.

Method:

1. Watch the documentary (with the captions turned off) and take notes on the content. (Repeat if necessary or helpful.)

2. Write a composition that tells the story in the documentary.

3. Watch the documentary again with the English captions on. Check my composition against the text of the documentary. Make note of new vocabulary and phrases I want to learn.

Criteria for measuring progress: I will have succeeded if

1. I study ten documentaries using this approach

2. I create a notebook that is at least thirty pages long

3. The compositions toward the end of the notebook are longer and more detailed than those at the beginning

4. I feel more skilled and confident in note-taking

Chapter 10

Vocabulary: Students in Charge

- Mastery of a foreign language involves learning thousands of words, and it is difficult to teach more than a fraction of them in class. In vocabulary study, it is therefore especially important for students to learn to rely primarily on their own efforts.

- Students do not need to learn to use every new word to the same degree. For reading and listening, students need a large receptive vocabulary of words that they can understand though not necessarily use productively.

- The teacher's main role in vocabulary teaching is facilitating student study and providing accountability.

The very idea of teaching vocabulary strikes me as somewhat problematic. Not that vocabulary can't be taught—it can be, and teaching it is not terribly difficult. But when I look back on my own language learning experience, I note that not very many of the foreign language words I know were taught to me in a language class by a teacher, or by anyone at all. Most of them I learned by studying textbooks, using vocabulary lists and flash cards, guessing from context as I read or listened, or looking them up in my trusty old dictionary. In short, I did most of my vocabulary learning on my own. More to the point, I don't see how I could have developed an adequately large vocabulary had I learned only new words taught in class.

On a moment's reflection, it is not hard to see why students must be self-reliant in vocabulary acquisition. First, they need to learn thousands of words, more than even the most zealous teacher is likely to be able to explain in class. Second, learning any single word often involves much more than memorizing its basic meaning; it also involves learning how it is used, what other meanings it has, what connotations it has, what other words it is used with, how formal it is, and even how frequently it is used. Obviously, such a thorough introduction to a few words, let alone the huge number of words a student eventually needs to master, would take far too much class time.

This chapter examines what students need to achieve in vocabulary study and how they can pursue these goals. Throughout, I argue that vocabulary study provides an especially clear case for why it is so important for learners to take command of their own language learning.

Vocabulary Acquisition: The Goal

It is helpful to think of command of vocabulary as falling into two categories: productive and receptive (Nation 1990, 5). *Productive* command of a word involves being able to use it appropriately in speech or writing. As suggested above, productive command can require knowing quite a lot about a word. Take the everyday word *dog* as an example:

1. **basic meaning:** A *dog* is a four-legged creature that can be trained to chase sticks.

2. **other meanings:** *To dog* = to follow persistently. *Dog-tired* = very tired. *A dog* = something worthless or useless. *Dogs* = slang for *feet. You dog!* = You scoundrel!

3. **parts of speech:** *Dog* is usually a noun, but can also be a verb (*The scouts dogged his trail for hours.*). It can also modify nouns like an adjective (as in *dog tag* or *doghouse*).

4. **usage:** When it is a countable noun (*a dog, dogs*) it usually refers to an animal. When used as a mass noun (*I like dog.*), it refers to a controversial dinner option.

5. **connotation:** Even though people think of the dog as man's best friend, the word generally has bad or insulting connotations. However, *dogs* (feet) has a rural flavor. *You (swarthy) dog!* has a slightly antique sound to it, conjuring up visions of a swashbuckler in an old pirate movie.

6. **collocation:**[1] *Dog* is often paired with *cat* (*It's raining cats and dogs.*).

7. **level of formality:** When referring to the animal, *dog* is not markedly formal or informal. *Dog-tired* is somewhat informal, and *dogs* (= feet) is very informal.

8. **frequency of appearance:** The word *dog* is much more common than the synonym *canine*.

---

[1] *Collocation* refers to the degree to which words tend to appear together—to be good friends, so to speak.

Students do not need all of this information about the word *dog* to begin using it in speech or writing, but they need to know that these other aspects of vocabulary exist and that learning them is an important part of learning how to use words properly. A word needs to fit in its sentence and context in terms of meaning, usage, connotation, collocation, formality, and frequency and may be amusing, unintelligible, or even offensive if it does not.

Receptive command of a word involves being able to comprehend it, generally in context. The good news is that receptive command does not involve as thorough a knowledge of usage, collocation, and the other issues mentioned above as productive command does. In fact, even with only a weak grasp of a word's meaning, a student can often still understand it when it appears in context (as most words do). The bad news is that students need receptive command of a very large number of words if they are ever to be able to read or listen to native English. A productive vocabulary of between 1,000–2,000 words is generally adequate to allow people to express themselves in daily English interaction (Fox 1987, 308–09; DeCarrico 2001, 287). However, a vocabulary of 7,000–10,000 words is necessary to make most average texts accessible; in fact, an educated native speaker of English may have a receptive vocabulary of 45,000–60,000 words (Gairns and Redman 1986, 65).

These figures suggest that a good working vocabulary has a particular shape. To be functional, students need a relatively small fund of words that they know well and can use productively in speech and writing, and a much larger receptive vocabulary of words that they understand in context. This point is worth emphasizing because some courses of English study do not make a distinction between productive and receptive vocabulary; from the beginning, students are expected to be able to use all the words they learn. The problem this can create is that teachers or curriculum designers, realizing that it is impossible for students to gain full productive control over many words very quickly, may cut down on the amount of vocabulary.[2] This, quite predictably, lengthens the amount of time it takes students to reach a breakthrough point in reading or listening.

Learning and Teaching Vocabulary

Some English teachers feel that an important part of their job is to carefully select the words students should learn and then devote class time to teaching those words. However, this approach can be problematic because you aren't always in a position to carefully select what words students will learn. You may not know what words a student should and shouldn't learn, and even if you do, choices are often determined primarily by what words appear in textbooks. The larger problem, however, is practicality. Time in class devoted to vocabulary explanation is too often time taken away from other class activities, and as Lewis (1993, 122) notes, it would take literally hundreds of hours for a teacher to teach students an adequately large vocabulary. You should also ask yourself why students can't be expected to study vocabulary on their own. In my experience, I have made far more progress when I have structured and carried out my own vocabulary-learning programs than when I have relied more on a language class to determine my rate and method of vocabulary acquisition.

Given the importance of students' taking charge of their own vocabulary acquisition, the discussion in this chapter centers more on how students learn vocabulary than on how you teach it.

---

[2] Lewis (1993) points out that for many years an influential view in the language teaching field was that the vocabulary load should be minimized for students while grammar was stressed. In contrast, he argues persuasively that "the first thing students need to do is to learn to understand quite a lot of words" (pp. 9, 115).

You will no doubt teach some vocabulary in class, but your primary roles in the process of vocabulary teaching are helping students set appropriate goals for their vocabulary learning efforts, integrating the teaching of vocabulary into the practice of other language skills, and encouraging students' efforts and fortifying their resolve by checking up on them. How these roles work themselves out in the classroom will vary somewhat according to the level of the students more or less as follows.

BEGINNING LEVEL

At this level, you may not need to devote as much attention to helping students set vocabulary acquisition goals because the words they learn will be determined largely by their textbooks, and much of the vocabulary presented will be high-frequency vocabulary over which students need productive as well as receptive command. The smaller amounts of vocabulary introduced—and the relatively greater importance of each item—mean that at this level you can and should try to find ways to introduce and practice new words in class. On quizzes and tests, you should hold students accountable for both receptive and productive command of all or most of the vocabulary introduced in the materials.

INTERMEDIATE LEVEL

At this level, students' reading and listening skills should begin to move ahead of their writing and speaking, so your first task is talking with students about the difference between receptive and productive vocabulary; furthermore, you should encourage them—as they learn new words—to make a distinction between vocabulary they need for productive and receptive use (Bowen, Madsen, and Hilferty 1985, 325–26).

Secondly, you need to devote more attention to teaching students to become better independent vocabulary learners. At this level, text materials will probably be introducing larger amounts of new vocabulary, so you will not have time to introduce and practice every new word in class; your focus should thus turn toward helping students understand what they need to learn about new words. As new vocabulary appears during various kinds of English lessons, you should raise questions of formality, connotation, and so forth (see Strategies for Learning Vocabulary below) to increase students' attention to these issues.

Finally, you need to motivate students to devote more attention to vocabulary acquisition, stressing it as part of your evaluation program. Regular, short quizzes are an especially effective way to get students in the habit of studying vocabulary daily rather than relying on pretest cramming. (On quizzes and tests, you should begin making a distinction between vocabulary you expect students to have productive command over and vocabulary that you only expect them to understand in context.)

ADVANCED LEVEL

At this level, students need to move toward the ability to read and understand native English, hence the need for a large receptive vocabulary is pressing. They should also be doing more work with real English materials and less with textbooks, so they will naturally encounter a wide range of new words, many of them with relatively low frequency. Students need to make most of their own decisions about which words to add to their vocabularies, and while you might still hold students accountable for limited sets of new words encountered in your class materials, much vocabulary testing should occur indirectly through reading and listening comprehension tests.

Your task, then, especially when teaching intermediate- and advanced-level students, is less to teach vocabulary than to help students learn how to go about the task themselves. To this end, the following sections consider what students are up against as they build their vocabularies. I find it helpful to think of the problem of learning a new word as having three parts: (1) discovering what the word means; (2) memorizing the meaning(s) of the word; and (3) learning other features of the word (e.g., usage, connotation).

The discussion of these three problems assumes that learners in EFL settings acquire most of their new vocabulary from books. Of course, it is good if students can also learn new words through listening, and you should give students as many opportunities as you can to hear new words in class, on tape or CD, or in any other way possible. However, in EFL settings, books are usually more widely available and generally easier to use than any aural source of new vocabulary, so for the foreseeable future this is likely to be how EFL students learn most new words.

Strategies for Learning Vocabulary: The Discovery Phase

The first step in learning a new word is discovering what it means. As I have noted, this would not be a problem if a student only needed to learn a few words. However, to build a large receptive vocabulary, students need to discover the meanings of literally thousands of words, so efficiency becomes a primary concern in considering strategies for finding out the meanings of unfamiliar words.

DICTIONARIES

When a student encounters an unfamiliar word, the most obvious strategy for finding out what it means is looking it up in a dictionary. This strategy obviously has a number of significant advantages. Good dictionaries provide a wide range of information on connotation, usage, and other issues as well as on meaning, so they are very useful for students who want to gain productive control of a word. However, an equally great advantage of dictionary use is that dictionaries make students self-sufficient in their ability to discover meanings of new words. It is thus worthwhile to invest class time in teaching students what kinds of dictionaries to use and how to use them.

In some countries, students rely heavily on small, inexpensive, glossary-type dictionaries—either in either print or electronic form—that do little more than list words in English along with a translation into the local language. Such dictionaries often only list one or two possible translations of each English word, hence promoting the false belief that there is a neat, one-to-one correspondence between all English and local language words. The absence of examples or information on usage also subtly encourages students to ignore usage when memorizing words. On the other hand, these dictionaries are usually adequate for helping students discover meanings of new words they encounter when reading. Moreover, the availability and convenience of these dictionaries are advantages that should not be overlooked.

Dictionaries (printed or electronic) that have more information are better, especially if they have an ample supply of examples so that students can learn usage as well as meaning. Examples reinforce the notion that ideas are expressed differently in different languages and that a local language word that would be translated one way in one English sentence will often have to be translated differently in another context. There is nothing wrong with bilingual dictionaries (despite the prejudice of many English teachers against them) if they include adequate examples in English.

As students begin to use dictionaries for English study, one initial problem may be learning how to efficiently locate the desired word. This involves learning and practicing alphabetical order so that looking up a word does not take too long. The greater problem is teaching students what to look for in an entry. Many students view learning vocabulary as a simple process of finding out what the local language equivalent is, so they may be satisfied as soon as they locate it. You may need to explicitly teach students to pay attention to other important information. Of course, students cannot stop and engage in a major learning effort every time they look up a word, but once they have invested the time to locate the word, they can certainly invest a few extra seconds in glancing at the entry to learn a little more than the word's basic meaning. Questions you should teach students to ask themselves include these:

- **Does this word have a local language equivalent or not?** Some English words have close local language equivalents; others don't. In a good dictionary, this should be obvious from the entry; if a lot of explanation and examples are necessary for the word, it probably has no single equivalent, and the student should remember to pay special attention to it.

- **How is this word used?** Encourage students to examine at least one example of how the word is used and to remember the example as a model for usage.

- **Does the word have a strong connotation?** Are strong negative or positive feelings associated with it? Is it associated strongly with a certain context? The pattern of examples will provide important clues.

- **Is this word markedly formal or informal?** Again, look at the examples.

- **How is it spelled?** Unfortunately, English spelling is not as logical as that of many other languages, so this requires special attention.

- **How is it pronounced?** Saying the new word aloud a few times not only allows pronunciation to be learned but is also an aid to remembering the word.

The major disadvantage of heavy reliance on the strategy of looking up unfamiliar words in dictionaries is that it is slow. When students are first learning how to use dictionaries, time spent looking up words is time well spent in developing a useful skill. However, once students know how to use dictionaries, each minute spent looking for a word is essentially a minute wasted. When there are only a few words to look up, this is not a serious problem, but if you ask students to read a passage that is loaded with unfamiliar words, they may spend the lion's share of their study time simply thumbing through pages (a fact that you should consider before giving students assignments that will involve extensive dictionary use).

GUESSING WORDS FROM CONTEXT

Guessing from context, discussed in chapter 8 as a reading strategy, is also a strategy for learning the meanings of new words. For example, in the sentence *Harry paused in the garden to smell a petunia,* students have a fighting chance to guess that a petunia is a kind of flower, so they may not need to look up *petunia* in a dictionary. One advantage of this approach is that students do not need to stop reading and break their train of thought in order to look a word up. Another is that students learn the word in a context, which helps them learn more about the word than its basic meaning.

The main problem with guessing as a strategy for discovering the meaning of new words is that it doesn't work very well unless the context is very clear or the student knows a lot about the topic; in other words, this strategy works best when students are reading very easy texts. (Even a few new words or unfamiliar cultural assumptions on a page may muddy the context enough that effective vocabulary guessing becomes very difficult.) Unfortunately, many students spend little time reading easy texts. Beginning- and intermediate-level students often have to study textbook passages that are intentionally packed with new vocabulary, and the inherent difficulty of English books, articles, and so forth can make guessing hard even for advanced-level students. Therefore, guessing new words often becomes most efficient as a strategy for learners at very advanced stages of English study who already have much lexical and cultural knowledge.

One way you can make guessing vocabulary words a more effective strategy is by having students memorize common English word roots and affixes. Many English words are constructed out of a finite stock of prefixes (e.g., *bi-, sub-, de-*), suffixes (e.g., *-ation, -ed, -er*), and word roots (e.g., *-scrib-, -graph-, -vis-*), and students who memorize the more common of these have a much better chance of correctly guessing meanings of new words constructed from these elements. Knowledge of these roots and affixes is particularly helpful in dealing with many of the low-frequency technical words of English—words that are otherwise hard to learn because they appear infrequently and are easily confused with each other.

TEXTS WITH GLOSSARIES

Glossaries are vocabulary lists with local language translations or explanations in English, and they are often found in textbooks after reading passages or dialogues. When such text-glossary combinations are available, there are considerable advantages to a strategy of relying heavily on them for discovering meanings of new words:

1. Learning a word from a glossary is faster than looking it up in a dictionary. The time saved on each word may seem insignificant, but when multiplied by hundreds, the time saved is substantial.

2. Getting the meaning of a word from a glossary is easier and often more accurate than guessing. This advantage is especially important for students at lower or intermediate levels, for whom guessing is often not an option.

3. When the glossary accompanies a text, each new word appears in a context that provides an example of its use.

In many cases, the textbooks you use in class will already have glossaries. However, in most countries, more than one series of English textbooks is available, so as a strategy for building receptive vocabulary, you might also encourage students to seek out and study other materials with glossaries.

Of course, the best glossaries are often those students make for themselves. Once students have taken the time to look a word up in a dictionary, it takes only a little additional investment of time to write down the new word, a gloss, and a brief example of usage in a notebook. Keeping a vocabulary notebook and studying and reviewing it is a particularly useful study method not only because it increases the chance that students will actually learn the words they look up (words looked up but not reviewed are generally soon forgotten), but also because over time the vocabulary notebook becomes a glossary tailor-made for a student's interests and needs.

VOCABULARY LISTS

Many English textbooks, especially those published in England and in the United States, contain lists of the vocabulary to be learned in each lesson. Such lists facilitate assigning vocabulary homework, but they are totally useless to a student who is trying to figure out what a word means. If you are using a text with such lists, it will be a great help to students if you write easy English explanations or appropriate local-language translations on the board or a printed page. This is extra work for you, but it will save students hours of paging through dictionaries.

Strategies for Learning Vocabulary: The Memorization Phase

Having located an explanation of what a new word means, the learners' next task is to get that meaning into their memories. Unfortunately, word meanings can be slippery little creatures. Even after several attempts to learn a new word, often the only thing you can remember about it when you run into it again is that you have looked it up before.

Research suggests that people have at least two kinds of memory: short term and long term. Short-term memory holds a limited amount of information (about seven items) for brief periods of time. After that, the information is quickly forgotten. Long-term memory can hold an apparently unlimited amount of information, but it takes more work to get information into long-term memory (for further discussion, see Gairns and Redman 1986, 87; Stevick 1988, 29–31; Stevick 1996, 27).

On TV shows, you may have seen memory experts who can quickly memorize long lists of information using powerful memory techniques such as associating words with mental images. (I still remember how to say the words *fried* and *elephant* in Russian because of a particularly vivid mental image I created associating these two words.) One elaborate scheme, popular in Europe in the 1600s, involved mentally placing words of one category (e.g., fruits) all in different positions in an imaginary room and then constructing an entire memory house or palace as a system for vocabulary recall.[3] The principles suggested in the following section do not promise anything quite so dramatic. However, students can do much to improve their vocabulary memorization approaches by paying attention to three basic factors: concentration, repetition, and meaningful manipulation.

CONCENTRATION

The most basic principle is that learners need to remain alert and pay attention as they try to memorize, and it helps if they seriously intend to remember what they are studying. This certainly is not a novel idea, but it is also a point that should not be neglected. Anyone who has spent much time studying a foreign language knows how easy it is for the eyes to keep moving over a glossary or text long after the brain has ceased to function.

One way for students to stay alert as they work is to use memorization methods that involve physical activity. The combination of mental and physical activity appears to enhance memory, and as long as students are moving, it is less likely that their minds will switch off. Some methods include shuffling flash cards, walking around while memorizing, mouthing words aloud, copying words, and moving pen and cover over a glossary.

Another way to improve concentration is by using memorization methods that involve performance or response, for example, constructing a sentence using the new word. Vocabulary-memorization strategies that call for response from learners tend to keep them focused on the activity and help prevent their minds from wandering. For example, when I study words on a

---

[3] For a fascinating discussion of this process as used by Matteo Ricci, missionary and language learner in Ming Dynasty China, see Spence (1984). For a general discussion of mnemonic techniques, see Rubin and Thompson (1994, 80–82).

vocabulary list, I find it more effective to test myself on each word rather than simply looking at it. Usually I cover the gloss and then check to see if I can get the word right. If so, I allow myself the gratification of slashing the conquered word with a highlighter; if not, I have to try again the next day. The point of this self-testing is not just that it helps check progress; equally as important, it helps me stay alert and keeps me moving.

REPETITION

Repetition does not guarantee that a word will find its way into long-term memory, but it certainly helps; a word that you see ten times is more likely to stick in your memory than a word you see only once, much in the same way that you are more likely to quickly learn the name of someone you see every day than someone you meet only rarely.

Sometimes a combination of sheer concentration and repetition is enough to allow a student to memorize words. The Name Game, described in chapter 5, is a case in point. Through concentration and frequent repetition, you can learn dozens of names in one class period—albeit at the price of some hard work—and I often use this exercise with classes to show what is possible.

However, research indicates that a more efficient route to memorization lies in introducing a word in a meaningful context or relatively memorable way and reviewing it later. (A good strategy is to first review new words soon after initial contact—within the next day or so—and then to review again some days or even weeks later.) In a well-structured curriculum, this kind of delayed vocabulary review can be built into the program. However, it can also happen more naturally through extensive reading. Students who read frequently and widely naturally review huge amounts of vocabulary—and are much more likely to come across low-frequency vocabulary again before they forget it completely. This is one reason extensive reading should be a part of vocabulary acquisition programs. The same beneficial effects for memorization can derive from repeated hearing, speaking, and writing of words.

MEANINGFUL MANIPULATION

Apparently, something about using a word in a meaningful way helps it sink into the long-term memory and stay there. Many language learners have had the experience of finding that a word really sticks in their memories for the first time once they have found an opportunity to use it. As Gairns and Redman (1986) note, "More meaningful tasks require learners to analyse and process language more deeply, which helps them to commit information to long-term memory" (p. 90). Using words in communicative ways is therefore one of the best ways to memorize them.

The implication for language study is again that communicative language practice of all kinds is a necessary part of a good vocabulary-learning strategy. Using words productively in meaningful speaking and writing may have a special power to aid memory, but using words receptively—seeing or hearing them—in the context of meaningful communication is also an effective way to facilitate memorization. Thus, vocabulary acquisition is best not undertaken as a program unto itself (hence the problems students have when they attempt to memorize dictionaries) but rather as part of programs of reading, listening, speaking, and writing (Nation 1990, 6).

Strategies for Learning Vocabulary: The Familiarization Phase

As I have mentioned, for productive command of a word, students need to know much more than just a word's meaning—knowledge of its usage, connotation, collocation, level of formality, and level of frequency is also important. Even for receptive use, knowing the denotation of a word may not be enough; understanding of the impact of a sentence may depend on knowing the connotation of a word or even its level of formality. How, then, are students to become familiar with all of these aspects of a word?

While introducing each new word fully in class is not practical, it is good to introduce at least some words more fully so that you can teach students what issues they need to consider in their own vocabulary acquisition. While you can do this in any lesson as the occasion arises, intensive reading lessons provide a natural opportunity for examining selected words in more depth. Consider, for example, the following reading passage:

> The world's coldest continent, and the most difficult to reach, is Antarctica. For centuries, people have wondered what this continent is really like, since it is covered with solid thick ice and deep snow. (People's Publishing House 1984, 267)

You might call students' attention to the issue of collocation by pointing out the phrases "thick ice" and "deep snow." From a purely semantic level, it isn't at all obvious why you couldn't use the word *deep* for both *ice* and *snow* (particularly for the Chinese students who study the textbook this passage is taken from—in Chinese, the same word is used to describe depth of both snow and ice). The fastest—and probably most accurate—explanation for why *thick* goes with *ice* and *deep* goes with *snow* is that in English this collocation is habitual.

> A TV reporter wanted to find out what people thought of a new film, so she decided to interview people as they came out of the theatre. She asked one woman what she thought of the film. "It was excellent," the woman replied. "I thought it was the best film I've seen in years." Then she stopped a young man and asked him the same question. "It was dynamite!" he said. (People's Publishing House 1984, 264)

This passage provides a good opportunity to make a point about formality. Note the switch between the proper woman respondent ("It was excellent") and the colloquial young man ("It was dynamite!"). Usage points could also be made about the words *think* (*What did you think of the film?*), and the phrase *came out* (*came out of the theatre*).

Ultimately, however, it is impossible to treat every new word in this way, so students must learn to seek this kind of information out for themselves. Another reason students need an adequate diet of extensive reading and listening is that patterns of usage, formality, and connotation emerge only if students see new words repeatedly in a variety of contexts. I remember learning a Chinese term (*jiao xun*) that my textbook translated as *teaching*. In an effort to be diligent, I tried my new word out on my teacher at the end of class with what I thought was the Chinese equivalent of *Thank you for your teaching* (*Laoshi, xiexie nide jiaoxun*), but her response was to chuckle and head off to the lounge to announce what I had just said. It was only some years later when reading a novel that I finally figured out what had gone wrong: I noticed that every time this particular word appeared, it was in the context of an elder admonishing a penitent youth. The pattern of use revealed by extensive reading showed me what the textbook had not told me.

Evaluation

Vocabulary can and should be tested as an integral part of the evaluation of all language skills. To some extent this happens naturally; when you test reading comprehension or ability to discuss an issue, you are also indirectly testing vocabulary. However, some evaluation of vocabulary acquisition per se is often desirable, the major justification for this being the positive backwash it has on students' interest in learning words (Hughes 1989, 146–47).

Learning vocabulary requires steady work over a long period. Students who cram words into their memories before a final examination often lose much of what they learn soon after the examination. According to Gairns and Redman (1986, 90), about 80 percent of what is learned is lost within the first twenty-four hours in the absence of review, so short periods of intense study followed by long slack periods do not do much for vocabulary building. A testing pattern that helps build better habits in students would consist of frequent cumulative quizzes. This would require students both to work on a regular basis and to review what they learn rather than forgetting it once the pressure is off.

The simple vocabulary quiz or test items suggested below are not ideal in terms of their backwash—better backwash results from testing listening, speaking, reading, and writing skills. Many of these items only require students to memorize a translation or explanation of the target word. However, this low-level command of new words is a good start toward receptive control, and what these quiz items lack in depth they make up for in ease, thus making it possible for you to give short but frequent quizzes.

1. **English word—definition:** Give students the words you wish to check, and have them provide definitions, synonyms, or translations into the local language. This kind of item is very straightforward conceptually and easy to explain to students. Since many words have more than one meaning, it is a good idea to provide a sample sentence with each test word.

2. **local country equivalent—target word:** For this simple quiz, write the local language equivalents of the words you wish to test. Then present these to the class, and ask students to produce the English words. This kind of item checks spelling as well as meaning.

3. **fill in the blank:** Find a reading passage that contains words you wish to test for, then delete the target words from the passage and list them at the bottom of the page. Students then choose the proper word to fill in each blank. To make this kind of quiz or test item at least somewhat communicative, you need to make sure that in most cases the context makes one of the deleted words a particularly good choice; otherwise, completing the test turns into a language puzzle.

4. **sentence with target word—response:** Write questions that contain the words you want to test, underlining them. Make sure comprehension of the words is important to understanding the question. Then have students write appropriate answers that demonstrate that they understand the test words. An alternative to this is to write true/false statements using the test words and then have students respond appropriately.

5. **matching:** Present two groups of words, and have students match them based on some kind of relationship (e.g., antonyms, synonyms, same kind of thing, same part of speech).

6. **writing sentences:** For testing productive command of vocabulary items, have students use the test word in a sentence that demonstrates that they know the meaning of the word. (Sentences like *Pragmatic is an English word* don't count.) This kind of item encourages students to memorize example sentences along with new words and is most appropriate for high-frequency words that students need in their productive vocabulary.

For Thought, Discussion, and Action

1. **your vocabulary-learning experiences:** Reflect on your previous English study, and ask yourself how you learned most of your vocabulary. (Was it taught in class? Did you memorize lists? Did you simply use the language a lot?) In order of importance, list the ways you learned vocabulary, and then compare notes with a classmate or friend.

2. **all about *contact*:** Review the different aspects of mastering a word by analyzing the word *contact* the same way the word *dog* is analyzed at the beginning of this chapter.

3. **textbooks with glossaries:** Visit a local bookstore, and look for English textbooks that have good vocabulary lists with glosses. Make a list of books you could recommend to students who want to build their vocabularies.

4. **memorization of words:** Survey several classmates or friends on what methods they have used for memorizing new words in English study and how they feel these methods worked.

5. **word memorization strategies:** Experiment with different strategies for memorizing words as follows:
    *   List two or three different memorization strategies you want to try out (e.g., word association, reviewing from a list).
    *   Locate several lists of vocabulary words that are unfamiliar to you (either words from a foreign language or even obscure English words, perhaps from a Graduate Record Exam study list).
    *   Use the first strategy for list one, the second strategy list two, and so forth. Then compare the results.

6. **vocabulary teaching:** Using one of the sample courses in appendix B, design a strategy for encouraging students to build their vocabulary as part of the course. Be sure to consider the probable level of the students and the phase of the process (discovery, memorization, or familiarization) you want to assist them with. Be ready to explain the rationale for your strategies.

Sample Language Learning Project for Vocabulary Building (A)

Goal: Build receptive vocabulary for reading comprehension.

Material: English textbook that contains both reading passages and glossaries.

Plan: Study three times a week, an hour or so per session.

Method: For each session,

1. Review vocabulary from previous lessons that I have not yet learned.
    *   Cover the gloss (definition, translation, explanation) for each word I will review. Then look at the word and see if I can remember the meaning.
    *   If I can quickly and accurately recall the meaning, highlight or cross out the word and move on to the next.
    *   If not, keep it on the list and try again during my next session.

2. Study the vocabulary from today's passage or glossary.
   - Covering the gloss, test myself on each new word. If I already know it, highlight it or cross it off the list.
   - If I don't know it, pause and try to memorize it.

3. Read the passage. As I encounter new words from today's glossary, pause briefly to review them and notice how they are used.

4. End with a quick review of the new vocabulary from today's lesson.

Criteria for measuring progress: I will have succeeded if I

- study all the texts in the book
- can correctly remember the meaning of most the new words in the book after I finish studying it

Sample Language Learning Project for Vocabulary Building (B)

Goal: Build receptive vocabulary for reading comprehension.

Material: An interesting book in English that isn't overly difficult; a notebook in which I list new vocabulary.

Plan: Study three times a week, an hour or so per session.

Method: For each session,

1. Review vocabulary in my notebook that I have not yet learned (see above).

2. Read today's chapter (or passage). As I read, mark unfamiliar words that I want to learn. (Don't mark and learn every unfamiliar word. Keep the number reasonable, and give priority to words that seem to appear more frequently or appear to be more useful.)

3. After I finish reading, look up the new words in a dictionary, write them in my notebook, and try to memorize them.

4. Reread the chapter. As I encounter the new words I studied, pause briefly to review them and notice how they are used.

5. End with a quick review of the new vocabulary from today's session.

Criteria for measuring progress: I will have succeeded if I

- finish studying an entire book using this approach
- create a notebook that is at least 30 pages long
- can understand all the vocabulary items in the notebook

Chapter 11

Grammar: Finding a Balance

- In many countries, study of grammar is emphasized to the point that it almost becomes synonymous with language study—and this is one reason many students dislike studying English. One of your tasks is to help students gain a balanced view of grammar study, recognizing the importance of accuracy in language use but restoring a focus on communication that makes language study more meaningful and enjoyable.

- Mastery of grammar involves both knowledge of grammatical forms and skill in using those forms. For building the latter, adequate practice is necessary.

- Students' grammar systems normally develop through gradual elaboration from simple to complex. As with vocabulary, there are different levels of control. Students may first gain receptive control of a structure and only later learn to produce it. In the case of low-frequency structures, students may never need to gain productive command.

Many EFL classes around the world place special emphasis on teaching English grammar, devoting large portions of limited class time to explaining grammar rules, analyzing the grammar of sentences in texts, and drilling grammar structures. One problem with this tendency to give especially high priority to grammar teaching is that it can diminish students' interest in learning English. As Stevick (1988) notes, "Difficulties with grammar cause more discouragement and drive away more students than anything else in our profession" (p. 82).[1] Another problem is that emphasizing grammar rules so much may give students inaccurate ideas about what grammar is and what its proper role in language study is. In particular, many students assume that, within the grammar rules of English, they can find all the secrets for how to analyze and produce accurate English sentences, so learning English consists mainly of mastering its grammar (and some vocabulary).

Accuracy is most certainly important in English, and an understanding of English grammar rules can help students both produce and understand English more accurately. One of your roles as an English teacher is, therefore, to help students improve their command of English grammar. However, it is at least equally important for you to make sure that the students understand what grammar is and what its appropriate role in language study is.

Grammar: Some Basic Points

WHAT IS GRAMMAR?

One source of problems in the EFL grammar classroom lies in misunderstandings about what grammar is. Some students view grammar rules as an unimportant set of conventions that are useful for passing tests but of dubious value in actual English conversation. However, the more common tendency is to go overboard in the other direction, viewing grammar rules as the language learner's version of the Ten Commandments.[2] In this view, grammar rules prescribe correct and unequivocal answers to all language problems, and each rule is an indispensable imperative that learners must obey at all costs.

A better understanding of grammar would fall somewhere between these two extremes, and such an understanding involves several important points. First, students need to understand that grammar rules are really not laws; rather, they are descriptions of patterns in the way English speakers construct sentences. Like most human behavior, language use tends to be patterned, and some of these patterns are stronger than others. For example, a great number of English nouns form their plural by adding an -s at the end, so knowing this basic rule enables students to both comprehend and accurately produce many utterances.[3] Knowledge of such common patterns is very helpful to students as they attempt to construct sentences. Other patterns are weaker, and the rules that describe them cover fewer situations. For example, no single, easy rule can enable a student to predict whether an infinitive (to + verb) or a gerund (verb + -ing) should be used following another verb, so mastery of this problem requires a lot of memorization of individual words and situations. For the student who wants a rule for everything, you could find or

---

[1] Farber (1991) gives a vivid account of how grammar-obsessed teachers in Latin courses almost destroyed his love of language learning. As he comments, "They're right in insisting on the importance of grammar, but who says you've got to have it first, as some kind of brutal initiation?" (pp. 13, 43).

[2] This analogy is only partly meant in fun. In many cultures, the written word is treated with a very high level of respect, and the grammar book often inherits some of this almost sacred authority.

[3] This rule is actually a little more complex than it seems, especially in speech. The -s ending is sometimes pronounced /-s/, sometimes /-z/, and sometimes /-ez/.

create rules to explain even the most idiomatic expressions, but the more complex the set of rules becomes and the fewer situations it covers, the more it hinders attempts to learn language rather than facilitating them.

A second point students need to understand is that, since a grammar is simply a description of language patterns, there is no single definitive grammar of English. Instead, descriptions of English use a variety of grammar systems and terminology. (The commonly used systems tend to be quite similar, but there are some differences.)[4] In other words, to argue over whether the word *eating* in the sentence *I like eating hamburgers* is a verb or a noun misses the point—once students understand what the sentence means and how it works, the proper categorization of each word is of marginal usefulness (unless students will face a test that demands such analysis).

A third important point you should teach students is that, like languages, grammar rules change over time. Even a quick look at a Shakespeare play or the King James Bible will show you examples of changes in English over the past few centuries. For example, many English speakers are familiar with the Bible's Ten Commandments in the old King James wording (*Thou shalt not kill*), which uses vocabulary and grammar that has long since disappeared in normal English usage. Changes are still in occurring, and students may hear or read English that does not conform to the rules they have memorized. For example, one change now taking place in American English involves the growing tendency to use *their* rather than *he* or *she* in sentences such as *I hope no one forgot their book*. (In this case, the change is due to a growing unwillingness to use *his* or *her* to refer to a group that includes both men and women.) Thus, occasionally when answering questions about what is grammatically right, you will have to answer that two alternatives are both correct, although for different settings.

A final point is that, in constructing English sentences, English speakers do not rely entirely on grammar rules. To a large extent, speakers build English sentences by using prefabricated blocks of language such as set phrases and sentence patterns. For example, to deny knowledge of something, English speakers often use the sentence *I have no idea what you are talking about*. Such chunks of language may be flexible to a degree (e.g., you could also say *I don't have any idea what you are talking about*), but essentially this is a fairly fixed set of words in a certain order. More to the point, speakers don't create this sentence from scratch by applying grammar rules to vocabulary items; instead, they learn and use this set of words as a whole. In a similar way, many sentences are created by using common patterns such as *If I were you, I would . . . .* While such a pattern can be analyzed grammatically, that analysis is beside the point. Speakers don't construct this sentence pattern using rules; instead, they simply learn it and apply it as a set pattern. Such prefabricated chunks of language are very common in language use, and it does learners little good to analyze such chunks grammatically—each should simply be memorized and used as a whole.[5]

The point is that students will have a better perspective on language learning if they take a more descriptive and utilitarian view of grammar. Their purpose in studying grammar should be to find out how speakers of English construct sentences, not to master a divine canon of grammar rules per se. A rule that enables a student to construct many correct sentences is worth learning; a rule that is impossible to understand or covers only one or two situations is a hindrance rather than a help. Grammar rules are helpful to students if and only if they make the mastery of English easier.

---

[4] One system you may run into that is quite different from traditional grammars is transformational grammar (TG); however, TG is intended more for linguists than for language teachers.

[5] I wish to thank Stephen Ting for making me more aware of this aspect of language use.

HOW IS GRAMMAR LEARNED?

It may be instructive to briefly consider how children learn a language. A baby learning English usually begins speaking with single-word sentences like "Cookie!" often accompanied by much waving of arms and feet. Later, she progresses to "Sally cookie!" (which probably means *Sally wants a cookie* instead of *Sally is a cookie*). She then moves on to "Sally cookies now!" and then over time slowly but surely continues experimenting and elaborating on her sentence constructions. No matter how diligently parents teach or correct, Sally is not likely to jump in a week from "Sally cookie!" to "Mother, may I please have a cookie?"

Adults may not learn language exactly the same way children do, but current wisdom in the field suggests that there are similarities. Adults also tend to start by learning simple basic rules and then gradually elaborating their system through experimentation. To use the analogy of drawing a picture, adults will naturally tend to sketch an outline first and then go back to fill in ever finer levels of detail later rather than completing one corner of the picture in full detail before moving on to another. In other words, adults are not likely to master all of the verb system before going on to nouns; they are more likely to gain a rudimentary control of both and then—through trial and error, aided by whatever input is available—to elaborate that control (Hedge 2000, 11). As Bowen, Madsen, and Hilferty (1985) describe the process, "Students usually learn their grammar one small piece at a time; they do not need (and indeed could not immediately assimilate) an entire system" (p. 166).

The first implication of this for teaching is that it is normal for students to go through an *interlanguage* period during which they have incomplete control of structures they are trying to learn—a "Give Sally cookie" stage. It is not normal for them to rapidly master the verb system of English down to a fine level of control, no matter how clearly you explain it to them. A second is that students need an opportunity to digest grammar input by trying out modifications in their interlanguage grammar system through language practice. To improve their control of grammar, listening to you explain grammar is not enough—they need to practice using it.

HOW WELL SHOULD GRAMMAR BE LEARNED?

One way in which grammar is similar to vocabulary is that it can be used in two basic ways: receptively for comprehension in reading or listening, and productively in speech and writing. This suggests that, as in the case of vocabulary, it is normal for a student to have complete productive control over some grammar rules and only receptive control of others. Of course, this is what normally happens whether you want it to or not; usually students gain receptive control over a structure before they learn to use it productively. However, you need not assume that students must ultimately master all grammar rules for productive control. Some grammatical structures in English are not used very much, and students don't need to be able to produce all such structures. Even basic verb tenses such as the past perfect (e.g., *By 8:00 he had slept for ten hours.*) or the past perfect progressive (e.g., *By 8:00 he had been sleeping for ten hours.*) are not often used and can usually be replaced with a rough equivalent that is more straightforward (e.g., *He slept ten hours before 8:00.*).

One implication is that some grammar points are more important than others, and another is that there is no need for students to gain total productive control over every structure they encounter—certainly not right away. The goal is rather for students first to learn rules that are relatively useful and easy to grasp and then to fill in the details as time and need dictate (Scarcella and Oxford 1992, 174). The teacher who insists on complete productive control of every fine point of detail runs the risk of overloading students' circuits and burning them out. Again, students and teachers need to remember that the goal is not mastery of an abstract system of theory but practical mastery of a communication skill, and the goal in learning grammar is to learn that which is of use in communicating.

Teaching Grammar

Usually when you teach grammar, you will be working with a textbook that determines what grammar structures are to be introduced and provides exercises that are intended to teach these structures. As you prepare for your class, the issue is thus usually not deciding what to teach but rather how to approach the material in your text.

The steps I suggest below for a grammar lesson follow more or less those described in Ur (1988, 7–10): (1) presenting a structure, (2) explaining it, and (3) practicing it.[6] The approach is basically inductive, that is, it allows students a chance to figure out the structure before you explain it to them. In general I favor this approach because problem solving makes students more active participants in the learning process; I also suggest it because a deductive approach (explanation first, examples and practice later) may lead you into overly long and elaborate grammar lectures. An inductive approach allows students to try a structure out before you explain it, thus giving you a chance to assess what problems they have with it and what needs to be explained. However, for reasons of culture or learning styles, some students are more comfortable with a deductive approach, so you should experiment with the ordering of steps below to find out what works best with your students.[7]

PRESENTATION

For students, the first step in mastery of a new grammar structure is simply noticing it. This point is easy to overlook when you are teaching students from a textbook that explicitly highlights grammar points in a way that forces students to attend to them whether or not the students are ready and willing to do so. However, the natural development of students' emerging grammar systems doesn't always follow the neat plan laid out in a textbook, and for their command of grammar to continue developing, they need to get into the habit of noticing new grammar structures when they read or listen to English. The idea is that "once a student becomes aware of a particular grammar point or language feature in input—whether through formal instruction, some type of focus-on-form activity, or repeated exposure to communicative use of the structure—he or she often continues to notice the structure in subsequent input, particularly if the structure is used frequently" (Fotos 2001, 272).[8]

The most basic way to present a structure in class is to use it communicatively in conversation with students. For example, if the structure for the lesson is the future verb tense, you might begin the day's lesson by asking a few students, "What are you doing this weekend?" At this first stage, the goal is to let students hear or see multiple examples of the new structure and give them an opportunity to figure out for themselves first what it means and then how it works, so you need not demand that students immediately use the structure when responding to your questions. They may well have already studied the structure in their books and have some idea how it works, but reading about a structure in a book and using it in conversation are two very different things,

---

[6] Cross (1991, 17–19) and Eisenstein (1987, 287) suggest a very similar approach.

[7] Eisenstein (1987, 286–88) suggests that an inductive approach may work less well with older students, with students who are used to grammar explanations, or in cultures where guessing—especially in public—isn't favored.

[8] This idea is known as Schmidt's noticing hypothesis. See also Larsen-Freeman (2001, 37).

so it is nice to give them a breathing space before requiring production. (Given that students may already have had some contact with the new structure, another goal of this part of the in-class lesson is to find out how much they already know about it.)

You might also focus presentation of a new structure through games or drills specifically chosen to illustrate it. For example, when introducing a new structure such as the plural ending, you might first hold up one book and say, "One book," then hold up two and say, "Two books." Here, once students seem to understand, you could encourage them to start experimenting with production, responding to what you hold up. However, as above, your main goal is receptive comprehension, so you should only involve production as students seem willing and ready.[9]

EXPLANATION

There are good reasons not to expect that lectures will have a dramatic impact on students' progress toward grammatical accuracy. One problem is that, even in the same class, students will often have different levels of grammar knowledge, so when you lecture on a grammar point, some of the students will already understand it, others will lack the foundation to comprehend your explanation, and others will probably be bored and not pay attention. Only a percentage—all too often a small one—will actually learn much from your lecture. A greater problem is that conscious knowledge of grammar rules does not guarantee the ability to produce accurate English. In fact, conscious knowledge of grammar rules is not a necessary precondition to the ability to produce English accurately, a fact demonstrated daily by most native speakers (who have little explicit knowledge of grammar rules) and by many students who do well on grammar tests but still make frequent errors in communication situations. Understanding a grammar point may be the first step toward mastering it, but it is only the first step.

Then why explain grammar structures at all? At a very practical level, one reason is that in many countries, lectures on grammar are an expected staple of the language classroom diet, and if this familiar part of the routine suddenly vanishes, students may be disoriented or dissatisfied. (Another argument for explanation of grammar is that it helps language teachers learn it better themselves!) However, beyond such practical concerns, explicit teaching of grammar points can also be of genuine use to students, particularly if—as Brown (2001) argues—it calls new grammar structures to students' attention in ways that

- are embedded in meaningful communicative contexts,

- contribute positively to communicative goals,

- promote accuracy within fluent, communicative language,

- do not overwhelm students with linguistic terminology,

- are as lively and intrinsically motivating as possible. (p. 363)

Often text materials will provide explanations of new structures and examples of their use, so by the time students reach your class, they will presumably have already encountered some explanation of new structures. Also, if you have allowed students to play with the structure during the presentation stage, you should have some idea of how well students already understand the structure. The goal of the explanation phase is thus generally to clarify major problem areas, advancing students' understanding of the structure by one or two steps. Here are a few pointers on explanations:

---

[9] Larsen-Freeman (2001, 257) suggests that if you introduce grammar using texts generated from your computer, one trick for calling students' attention to new grammar structures is highlighting them in bold text.

- Try to start explaining at the right level so that you do not waste time telling students what they already know or talking over their heads. It is more important to be to the point than to be comprehensive. In this regard, local teachers have a distinct advantage over foreign teachers because your previous English learning experience will help you better understand what points will and won't cause the students difficulty.

- Keep explanations as short and simple as possible, and limit the number of variations and details that might confuse and overload students. Avoid the temptation to prepare overly thorough explanations of grammar points in order to impress your class.

- Remember that some points are better memorized than explained. For example, little needs to be said about irregular past tense verb forms (*eat/ate, write/wrote, read/read*)—students just need to learn them.

- Examples are often much easier to understand than explanations, so be sure to include several. Given the tendency of students in many countries to read better than they listen, it is also a good idea to write examples on the board.

- Use pictures, diagrams, and graphs in communicating a point. For example, many grammar teachers explain English verb tenses with time-line drawings.

- As you feel it is appropriate, use the local language in explaining grammar points. While there are some advantages to using English in such explanations, such as sustaining an English atmosphere in class, you may also choose to use the local language more in those portions of a class period when you explain grammar structures. It is also often helpful to explicitly compare and contrast English structures with those of the local language.

PRACTICE

Obviously, understanding a grammar rule is not the same thing as being able to apply it to communication problems, so a third important step in the study of grammar is practice. Grammar practice ranges on a continuum from highly controlled practice, in which learners need to make very few choices, to free communicative practice, in which learners need to apply grammar rules to real language use situations. The challenge is greatest in productive use of grammar, and here I focus on speaking. (See chapter 9 for discussion of responding to grammar accuracy issues in written compositions.)

Highly Controlled Practice

One problem usually not faced by teachers is having to design controlled grammar exercises (e.g., fill in the blank, find and correct the error in the sentence, restate the passive sentence in the active voice)—many English textbooks have an adequate supply of these. Such exercises can be of value as the first step toward mastery of a grammar structure because they allow the learner to concentrate on applying a structure in a controlled situation in which other problems are eliminated. These exercises are also useful for checking to see if students have a basic understanding of the grammar point.

The simplicity of these exercises is, however, also their major drawback. Exercises such as choosing the right verb tense to fill in a blank or restating a passive sentence in the active voice are unlike actual language production precisely because the learner can focus on one problem to the exclusion of all others. They are very unlike real-world grammar application problems and should not constitute the major part of a student's grammar-practice diet. You certainly should not feel that your duty consists primarily of seeing that students do every exercise in the book.

Moderately Controlled Practice

An intermediate step between highly controlled exercises like those mentioned above and natural practice activities would be controlled communicative activities in which students must construct their own sentences and express their own ideas but with their attention still clearly focused on the target structure you want them to learn. For example, consider the following activity for practicing relative clauses in which students are divided into pairs and asked to practice a short conversation as follows:

> A: (pointing into a crowd) Who is that woman?
> B: Which one?
> A: The one . . . . (e.g., who is wearing a hat, who looks like an angel)
> B: Oh, that is . . . . (e.g., Angie, Kim).

This exercise is communicative in that it can involve real conversation about real people (e.g., other students in the class or people in a picture), and students have some freedom to express their own ideas. However, students still know exactly what grammar structure they need to produce and can focus their attention on it. Many textbooks contain such exercises, and they can also generally be readily adapted from dialogues in the textbook.

Free Practice

For grammar practice to be realistic, it needs to involve solving multiple language problems at the same time. To this end, the best free practice takes place in a communicative context where the students need to pay attention to what they are saying as well as getting their grammar right. You can often find topics of conversation that will naturally require the target structure to appear frequently, thus providing good practice in the use of that structure. Here are some examples:

- For the present continuous tense, have students talk about something while they watch it happen—perhaps the actions of a classmate or action on a videotape. This will elicit many sentences such as *Sally is smiling* or *The man is eating dinner.*

- For relative clauses, have students discuss what kind of friends (or movies, food, weather, etc.) they like. Of course, the different kinds can be distinguished with adjectives as well as relative clauses (e.g., *I like rich friends.*), but many other ideas virtually demand relative clauses (e.g., *I like friends who do my homework for me.*).

- To practice use of plural nouns as topics, have students discuss what kinds of animals they like or don't like and why (e.g., *I don't like dogs because they are stupid.*).

Writing is an especially good skill to combine with grammar lessons because it serves as an intermediate step between applying a grammar rule in discrete-point exercises and quickly applying it in speaking. Like speaking, the process of writing requires students to apply grammar rules while in the midst of a host of other decisions, but unlike speaking, writing allows students time to think about how to apply a grammar structure and even time to consult reference tools. Writing also makes it possible for students to go back and check the language they have produced in order to learn from their mistakes.

Evaluating Grammar

There are two issues to address in evaluation of student grammar competence. One is whether or not students know the target structure—in other words, whether or not they can manipulate it under ideal circumstances. The second question is whether or not they can apply their knowledge under the conditions of normal language use.

EVALUATING BASIC GRAMMAR KNOWLEDGE

The classic grammar test involves use of discrete-point grammar items that focus students' attention on a particular grammar problem. The main value of such items is that they allow you to determine whether or not students have a basic understanding of the target structure. Basic types include

- multiple choice, for example, *Tommy _____ the apple. (eat, eaten, eated, ate)*

- fill in the blank, for example, *Tommy _____ (eat) the apple.*

- correct the error, for example, *The apple falled on Newton's head.*

- rewriting, for example, *Rewrite the following in passive voice: Tommy ate the apple.*

As pointed out in chapter 4, creating good discrete-point test items is a complicated science, but there are two rules of thumb that will help you ensure that a discrete-point test is reasonably good. First, always have someone else check your test items to ensure that you haven't overlooked any ambiguities during test construction. Second, use a large number of test items. If your test has only a few items, a few poorly designed questions or lucky guesses by students can make a big difference in the final grade.

Discrete-point grammar tests have a number of advantages: they are easy to grade, they let you check whether or not students have studied specific grammar points, and they prepare students for other discrete-point tests (such as the Test of English as a Foreign Language [TOEFL]) that they may face in the future. On the other hand, they also have very serious disadvantages. While such tests tell you whether or not students have grasped the basic concept of a grammar structure, they do not tell you how well students can apply this knowledge. Worse, the backwash from heavy use of such test items is generally negative because they reinforce the belief that knowledge of grammar theory is more important than the ability to apply it to real-life situations. So, as much as possible, it is best to test grammar knowledge in conjunction with other skills such as speaking and writing, where grammar knowledge is actually applied to language use.

EVALUATING THE ABILITY TO APPLY GRAMMAR KNOWLEDGE

Evaluating grammar in the context of language use rather than through discrete-point tests has two major advantages. The first is that evaluating grammar in use (usually speaking or writing) allows you to assess not only how well students know grammar rules but whether or not students can apply them. The second is that the backwash from this kind of testing encourages students to learn how to apply their knowledge rather than being satisfied with an understanding of grammar theory.

The simplest way to assess grammar as a part of speaking tests is to add a grammatical accuracy component to whatever scoring system you use for interviews or other kinds of speaking tests. (See chapter 7 for discussion of assessing speaking skills.) Of course, if you want to test whether or not students have learned particular grammar structures, you will need to use speaking tasks that ensure that students produce the target structures. In other words, in your interviews, pair work, or whatever format you use for evaluation, you will need to include some tasks that are at least somewhat controlled. These might be exercises like the moderately controlled exercises mentioned above or topics that naturally elicit certain structures. (Note that in the latter case, you also need to let students know that you are looking for certain target structures.)

When you attempt to assess grammar during interviews or other kinds of speaking tests, one problem is how to note (1) whether students used the target structures and (2) how successful students were in doing so. Imagine that you want to check how well students have mastered use of the past tense in verb use, and you are using a small-group assessment approach like the one described in chapter 7. The task you have given students is to ask each other what their very first day at their university was like (e.g., were there problems? surprises?), and you have also told them you will be paying attention to how well they use past tense verbs. For such a test, scoring may be easier if you make up a simple criteria system like the following.

4:   Produced the target structure frequently and was usually correct

3:   Produced the target structure a number of times; may have hesitated or self-corrected but was ultimately correct at least half of the time

2:   Tried to produce the target structure several times but was generally slow or inaccurate

1:   Rarely produced the target structure; slow and inaccurate

0:   Never produced the target structure

Admittedly, such a simple system is rather impressionistic and does not allow you to achieve a high degree of precision in your scoring. However, it is simple enough to use quickly. More importantly, such an approach has good backwash in that it encourages students to use the target structure in a relatively natural conversational setting. (For a higher degree of precision, you can record the students' conversation and then score it more carefully at your leisure. This, however, involves a lot more work.)

Written work is the other natural context within which to assess grammar, not only because grammatical accuracy is especially important in writing, but also because it allows you to assess grammar at your leisure. In the same way that you can design practice activities to call for certain grammatical constructions, you can plan a writing task so that it naturally elicits target structures. For example, a written dialogue about favorite kinds of fruits should elicit use of plural nouns as general subjects (e.g., *I like pear**s** but I hate grape**s.***); a composition about childhood experiences should elicit past tense verbs (e.g., *I **wore** diapers for several years.*). If you wish to ensure that students produce certain target structures, list those structures and tell students to be sure to use them. Writing tasks that are explicitly designed to test grammar are, of course, less natural than normal writing tasks because they focus students' attention on grammar rather than communication, but the loss in naturalness may be made up for by the certainty that you will get the material you need for your evaluation.

Answering Grammar Questions

It seems fitting to conclude this discussion of grammar with a few comments on the art of coping with knotty grammar questions in class. It seems that almost every English class has at least one student who is obsessed with grammar and loves to ask questions like "Should I use an infinitive or a gerund after a verb?" The problem teachers often face is not only that they may not know the answer to a question like this but that they may not really understand the question itself (at least not when presented this way).

The first and most important rule for survival is that when students ask general grammar questions—especially if they use lots of abstract grammar terms—you should ask them to give an example, too. This helps make the question clearer, and it also helps you check whether or not the student asked the grammar question correctly. Over the years, I have found that a great many impressive-sounding grammar questions, once understood, turn out to be essentially gibberish. Student grammar questions often begin as specific examples that the student has recast (often incorrectly) in half-understood theoretical language. Once you make the student present the original example, it is much easier to get to the heart of the matter. A final reason to require examples is that it reminds students that the study of grammar is intended to lead to application and that application of grammar rules is often highly situational, a fact that tends to get lost when discussion of a rule remains theoretical.

When you can't answer a question, even after you understand it, you may be tempted to try to bluff your way through the situation with a long answer containing lots of obscure grammarlike terms. However, a better choice is probably to confess your ignorance and promise to find out the answer. This may be somewhat embarrassing at first (though most language teachers get used to it rather quickly), but if you actually carry through, you will demonstrate diligence and learn something at the same time.

For Thought, Discussion, and Action

1. **students' attitudes toward grammar:** Imagine that you are orienting a newly arrived foreign English teacher in your country who wants to know how students typically view grammar and grammar study. Make a list of points you would make.

2. **grammar and you (task A):** Reflect on your experience studying English grammar. Did you enjoy learning it or not? What did and didn't you like about it? How do you feel about teaching grammar? Share your thoughts and experiences with a classmate.

3. **grammar and you (task B):** Reflecting on your experience studying English, list lessons (words of wisdom) you would pass on to someone else trying to learn English grammar. What did and did not seem to work for you? What would you try if you could start over?

4. **grammar and you (task C):** Make a list of the English grammar points that were most difficult for you to learn. Then, for one or more of these, prepare an explanation for students that would help them learn the structure.

5. **ever-changing grammar:** The chapter gives two examples of how English grammar has changed over time. List examples of how the grammar of your own language has changed over the centuries.

6. **grammar terms:** See if you know the following English grammar terms and concepts and can explain them:
   - verbs (regular and irregular; transitive and intransitive)
   - nouns (singular and plural; countable and uncountable)
   - adjectives
   - adverbs
   - pronouns
   - articles (definite and indefinite)
   - determiners
   - prepositions
   - modal auxiliaries
   - verb tenses (e.g., simple present, simple past, simple future, present progressive, present perfect)
   - voice (active and passive)
   - gerunds and infinitives
   - clauses (dependent and independent)

7. **presentation of grammar points:** Think of activities you could use to present the grammar points listed in number 6 to students, especially activities that give students a chance to figure out what the structure you are introducing is used for before you explain it explicitly.

8. **explanation of grammar points:** For one or more of the grammar points in number 6, prepare a clear, simple explanation. Use examples, visual aids, or anything else that will help you explain clearly and effectively.

9. **practice of grammar points:** For one or more of the grammar points in number 6 above, prepare a moderately controlled practice activity that will help students learn to use the structure accurately and appropriately.

10. **grammar as fun:** For one or more points in number 6, create a game that will help students learn the point in a way that is effective and at least relatively entertaining.

Sample Language Learning Project for Grammar

Goal: Build ability to (quickly) use sentence patterns.

Materials: An English textbook that contains many common English sentence patterns and common sentences; note cards or small pieces of paper I can make into flash cards.

Plan: Study twice a week, an hour or so per session.

Method: For each session,

1. Review my sentence-pattern flash cards from previous lessons, testing myself to see if I can quickly produce the correct English sentence pattern and a sample sentence after looking at the clue.

2. Make note cards for the new sentence patterns in today's lesson. For each new sentence pattern,
   - write down the pattern and a sample sentence on one side of the note card
   - on the other side of the note card, write down an equivalent in my first language that I will use as a clue when I test myself

3. Study the new sentence patterns by testing myself with the note cards, looking at the clues and trying to produce the correct pattern and one or more sample sentences. Practice until I can do this quickly.

Criteria for measuring progress: I will have succeeded if I

- have made fifty sentence-pattern flash cards

- have studied and memorized the English sentence patterns on each card, and can quickly remember all the new patterns and correctly use them to produce English sentences

Chapter 12

Teaching Culture

- Study of culture and intercultural communication should be included in language courses because it can enhance students' ability to understand and interact effectively with people from other cultures and more effectively express themselves to foreign audiences. Study of culture can also make language courses more interesting.

- The culture of a group consists of members' shared ideas, particularly their shared knowledge, views, and patterns.

- Western culture, U.S. culture, British culture, and other cultures are not monolithic entities; there is also considerable cultural variety even within any nation.

- In many countries, students may have mixed feelings about Western culture. It is therefore important to present Western culture in a way that is as objective and sensitive as possible.

English has become a world language, used far beyond the confines of the United States and United Kingdom, so it can no longer be assumed that all English speakers come from Western cultural backgrounds. Many nations in which English is not indigenous, especially ex-British colonies, recognize English as one of their national languages. English has taken on a life of its own in countries such as India, Nigeria, and Singapore, which have cultural backgrounds decidedly different from those of the United States and United Kingdom.[1] In fact, in some non-Western nations that have adopted English, there is a conscious attempt to divorce the English language from British and U.S. culture so that the language will be identified more closely with its new national culture. It could thus be argued that in some situations an English teacher should avoid associating English with the teaching of British or U.S. culture.

More often, however, sensitive incorporation of Western culture into your English courses will benefit both the students and you. One obvious reason is that bringing culture into your courses may make them more appealing to students because of the natural interest many students have about other nations and cultures, especially those most closely associated with the English language. By bringing culture topics into your courses, you create opportunities for meaningful sharing of important and interesting information, and this helps raise students' interest in communication.

A second reason to address issues of culture is that many of the situations in which learners use English will involve intercultural communication. This might take the form of an African student reading magazines from Britain or a Latin American business executive chatting with a North American client. It could mean an Asian watching TV programs or films from Australia or listening to the BBC radio news. It could mean a Middle Eastern student writing an application letter to a U.S. university or a secretary in Hong Kong writing a business letter to a Canadian company. In all of these cases, the learner of English not only needs to cope with the problems of using a foreign language but also needs to understand and communicate directly or indirectly with people from a very different culture.

Obviously, there are also challenges involved in addressing culture topics in English language courses, not the least of which is that your own experience with foreign cultures may be limited, especially if you have not spent a long time living in another country. However, this does not disqualify you from being an effective teacher of culture any more than not being a native speaker of English disqualifies you from being an English teacher. Natives of a foreign culture have the advantage of an insider's perspective on their own culture, and this is a valuable perspective for students to be exposed to. However, just as native speakers of a language take the language for granted and are often not very aware of how it works or how it is learned, natives of a culture are often not consciously aware of all aspects of their own culture. In contrast, an outsider who takes the time to study and learn about a culture is often in a very good position to notice things that an insider would miss. Furthermore, your familiarity with your own culture—the culture of the students—also means that you can see how the target culture compares with the local culture, and this knowledge is beneficial in knowing how to best help students make sense of the target culture. Ultimately, your credentials as a teacher of any given culture depend more on the effort you make to learn about that culture than on whether or not you are a native of it.

---

[1] A highly readable treatment of this issue can be found in McCrum, Cran, and MacNeil's (1987) book. See also Crystal (2003).

What Is Culture?

The term *culture* is very broad, and an exhaustive listing of all that it includes would require a book in itself. In a review of various attempts to define the term, Seelye (1993) concludes, "The most widely accepted usage now regards culture as a broad concept that embraces all aspects of human life, from folktales to carved whales. What is culture? It is everything humans have learned" (p. 22; for further discussion, see Damen 1987, 73–74, 85–86). Unfortunately, such a broad definition of culture—correct as it no doubt is—does not provide much direction for teachers who are trying to set an agenda for the teaching of culture. Thus, at the risk of being less than fully comprehensive, I define culture in a way that is narrower but more helpful to the language teacher. In my view, the essence of a culture lies more in the minds of a group of people than in their physical surroundings and consists primarily of ideas that the group members share. I find it convenient to think of the ideas that make up a culture as falling into three basic categories:

1. **shared knowledge:** information known in common by members of a group

2. **shared views:** beliefs and values shared by members of a group

3. **shared patterns:** shared habits and norms in the ways members of a group organize their behavior, interaction, and communication

Granted, these three categories overlap to some degree, and most cultural phenomena can and must be analyzed in view of more than one of them. However, this system is fairly simple and manageable, yet has enough explanatory force that it is helpful in setting an agenda for the teaching of culture. I examine each of these categories briefly here.

SHARED KNOWLEDGE

Within a culture group, members all know much of the same information, and their shared knowledge is often rather different from that of outsiders. Compare, for example, the following two identification tests:

1. (1) Dec. 7, 1941; (2) home plate; (3) Benedict Arnold; (4) Bill Cosby; (5) Niagara Falls

2. (1) May 4, 1919; (2) dragon boat; (3) Yue Fei; (4) Deng Lijun; (5) Dun Huang

Americans with a high school education would no doubt come close to a perfect score on test 1, and even an American with no education would probably get several right answers. However, few Americans would get more than one answer correct on test 2. In contrast, the average Chinese schoolchild would score a clean sweep on test 2 but probably miss most of the items on test 1.[2]

These seemingly isolated bits of information are important in communication because they facilitate use of top-down comprehension strategies. Consider the following sentences, the opening lines of a (fictitious) novel: "There was a warm gentle breeze blowing on the morning of December 7, 1941. Bob let his thoughts linger on the slim figure and dark eyes of the woman

---

[2]Answer key for test 1: (1) Japanese attack on Pearl Harbor; (2) place where batter stands in baseball; (3) traitor in U.S. Revolutionary War; (4) family-oriented comedian; (5) scenic spot for honeymooners. Answer key for test 2: (1) protests against Japan that mark the beginning of the modern period in Chinese history; (2) boat used yearly in races on Dragon Boat Festival to commemorate the poet Qu Yuan; (3) ancient hero who resisted foreign invaders until betrayed by his own government; (4) pop singer; (5) site where ancient Buddhist manuscripts and cave paintings were found.

he had met the night before." By the time they finish reading these two sentences, many U.S. readers would already be able to guess a great deal about the story that is to follow. It is probably set in Pearl Harbor and revolves around the attack. Even the time of day can be guessed with considerable accuracy—it is probably early in the morning, before the attack. Of course, these are only guesses, but they enable a reader to skim forward much faster in the story, checking guesses rather than trying to piece the story together from scratch. In contrast, students of English who didn't know the significance of December 7, 1941, would find little more in these sentences than the aggregate meaning of the words and would be at a disadvantage in comprehending the story.

The other pieces of information included in test 1 could also set the scene for a story, convey an emotion, symbolically suggest values, or simply function as vocabulary. For example, in the United States, the mention of Niagara Falls conjures up images of honeymooners and people going over a waterfall in a barrel. Bill Cosby is seen by many Americans as more than a successful comedian; he also serves as a role model of the family-oriented father and the successful black professional. Finally, Benedict Arnold is synonymous with *traitor*.

Another reason attention to background information is important in language courses is that students need to learn to be aware of assumptions they make about what an audience from another culture does and does not know. Take, for example, a Chinese tour guide who begins his introduction to a temple by saying, "This fine structure was built during the Qin Dynasty." Such an introduction would help a Chinese audience place the temple in a historical context but would probably be of no use at all to a group of foreign tourists who didn't know what or when the Qin Dynasty was. If the tour guide has some idea what he can and cannot expect his audience to know, he has a better idea of what needs to be explained and what doesn't. This enables him to provide appropriate clarification when necessary and avoid boring an audience with superfluous explanation when none is needed.

Much of the material that makes up the shared knowledge of a culture is passed intentionally from one generation to the next, often through the educational system or in the home. In modern societies, another very important source of shared cultural knowledge is the electronic media (the performing media may have a similar role in more traditional societies). A final source of cultural knowledge is widely shared experiences such as Little League baseball for boys in the United States or the turmoil of the Cultural Revolution for urban Chinese old enough to have experienced it.

SHARED VIEWS

Within a culture group, people not only know many of the same things but also believe many of the same things and share many of the same views on a huge spectrum of issues. To some extent, a culture is composed of widely held opinions on such mundane questions as these: What is the best treatment for a cold? Is *ain't* an acceptable word? Who is the world's greatest soccer player? However, a culture is shaped much more by a shared worldview consisting of the beliefs and values of a culture, its shared answers to basic questions inherent in human existence such as these:

- Are there supernatural forces?

- Are humans basically good or evil?

- Who am I/who are we?

- What is my proper relationship to other people?

- How should other people treat me?

- Is my life more defined by what I am like or what I do?

- Should I look more to the future or the past?[3]

Answers to questions such as these are often found in the dominant religious or philosophical thought of a culture, but they are also embedded in its stories and its models of excellence (e.g., heroes, art, achievements). These beliefs and deeply rooted cultural orientations tend to change slowly, if at all, and play a major role in shaping a culture.

A very practical advantage of understanding the beliefs and values of a given culture is that it improves the ability to accurately interpret what people from that culture do and say. This is of major importance in intercultural communication, where misunderstandings are common and can have serious consequences. Consider the simple example of an Asian student meeting a North American tourist who is obviously floundering in her attempts to shop in an Asian city. The student—partly out of altruism and partly to get English practice—offers to translate but is surprised when the tourist firmly insists that she wants to do things for herself. Students who have some idea of the importance North Americans place on self-reliance are not so likely to be puzzled or offended by this rebuff; students who understand little of North American culture have no recourse but to interpret this refusal in terms of their own culture and may mistakenly assume that the refusal implies a lack of trust or perhaps even sheer prejudice.

A second reason that students should have some knowledge of the beliefs and values of the target culture is that it will enhance their ability to express their own ideas, especially in situations where they need to persuade. Take, for example, the problem of application letters. In many countries, students study English in part because they hope to study or work abroad, so they must write application letters for jobs, scholarships, and admission to schools. A problem that often crops up in such letters is that, when applying to Western institutions, students do not understand the Western norms for making themselves look good while not seeming boastful. In Asia, one problem I have often seen is that students make broad assertions about their merits ("I was the best student in my school.") without supporting their claims with quantifiable objective evidence. Also, it is difficult for them to gauge what kind of arguments will appeal to a Western employer or admissions officer, and they thus sometimes sound too idealistic ("I wish to devote myself to the construction of my Motherland.") or too mercenary ("I hope to get a degree in business and then become wealthy in the construction industry.").

Knowing something of the beliefs and values of a culture is especially important in helping students understand why its members act and speak as they do, a level of comprehension that goes beyond the surface meaning of words. An additional benefit of studying this level of culture is that, as students look at the assumptions underlying another culture, the contrast may enable them to clearly see for the first time the assumptions that underlie their own.

SHARED PATTERNS

Not all human activity falls into neat patterns, but a great deal of it follows at least a general pattern, and much of it is rather strictly ordered (see Damen 1987, 142–45, for discussion of this aspect of culture). More or less clear cultural patterns can be found in a huge range of things, including daily schedules, events of the year, ordering of events in a meeting, the way people date and find a mate, or even the way a story or article is organized. Sometimes these patterns are cultural habits that have no particular values attached to them, such as the U.S. tendency to

---

[3] Students of cultural anthropology will recognize the influence of Clyde and Florence Kluckhohn's cultural models in my choice of questions. For an approachable introduction to their model, see Kohls (2001, 31–38, 150–51).

shower in the morning rather than the evening or the custom of starting a fairy tale with *Once upon a time*. Often, however, these patterns are evaluative norms, deviation from which is at best odd or impolite and at worst criminal.

Of particular concern to the language learner are the patterns in how a culture deals with communication situations. While conversations don't always closely follow a preordained script, neither is each one improvised entirely anew. Many common functions of language use, such as polite refusals, responses to compliments, and introductions, are fairly conventional. For example, in mainstream U.S. culture, a polite refusal to an invitation generally involves an expression of thanks or regret followed by a specific reason that the invitation cannot be accepted (*I would love to, but I won't be in town on that day.*); a vague excuse like *I will be busy* is not as polite. When responding to compliments, Americans will often say thank you but follow it by either passing the credit on to someone or something else (*Thank you, my mother taught me how to cook this.*) or using the compliment as a springboard into a conversation topic, hence deflecting attention from the praise given (*Thank you. I bought this shirt on a business trip to Nigeria last year . . . .*).

Obviously, one reason students have a vested interest in study of these aspects of the target culture is that knowing them will help students communicate more politely and appropriately— or at least avoid unintentionally giving offense. A second and less obvious advantage of knowing these patterns is that it enhances students' ability to predict what they might hear or read. This, in turn, makes comprehension easier. For example, if students can narrow the probable range of responses to a compliment, they are more likely to be able to catch key words even when listening to somebody who talks too fast.

A second set of conventions that are especially important to language students are the genre conventions that shape so much printed and audiovisual communication. Many kinds of books, articles, TV shows, films, and other structured forms of discourse tend to follow a formula. For example, romances generally consist of a boy, a girl, and a problem that has to be overcome if the couple is to find happiness. Westerns usually have one or more good guys, a bunch of bad guys, a pretty girl, and a final shootout from which the hero generally rides away more or less intact. Even newspaper news articles are laid out in a predictable pattern, starting with location and date, followed first by the main points of the story and then by details in order of decreasing importance. The significance of these formulas for readers and viewers is that once they know which one is being followed, their ability to predict and guess—hence to comprehend—is greatly enhanced.

A final set of conventions of special importance to language students consists of those surrounding written language. Most writing, especially more formal types such as business letters and academic writing, follows rather strict rules as to how ideas are to be organized and presented. Even the layout of the components of a business letter—where to place the date and addresses— is governed by conventions.

SUMMARY

The main reason I have gone into such detail here in describing different types of culture and their roles in communication is that this information is useful to pass on to students so that they see why study of culture is an inherently important aspect of language study. I do not mean to imply that you need to burden students with a series of lectures on the importance of culture in language learning, but when you discuss any given point of culture with students, it is helpful to mention why knowing such a point may be beneficial and how it relates to communication. For example, cultural background knowledge is especially important for its ability to enhance top-down comprehension strategies, knowledge of a culture's beliefs and values improves one's ability to interpret behavior and communication more accurately, and knowledge of genre patterns enables learners to more accurately predict—hence more easily understand—as they read and view. Knowing how different kinds of culture affect communication will help students see more clearly both the connection between language and culture, and the importance of studying culture as well as language.

English—Whose Culture?

As you consider the issue of culture in English courses, you may tend to think first and foremost of U.S. and British culture, but with a little reflection it is clear that neither of these terms is fully satisfactory as a label for the kind of culture most closely associated with English. Even if you consider only those countries in which English is used as the first (and usually only) language, this category includes several large nations and quite a few smaller ones. And within any given English-speaking nation, the culture is hardly uniform; lumping the culture of an ethnic neighborhood in New York City under the same label as that of a rural community in Texas or a retirement community in Florida would be problematic at best. So considering incorporation of culture into English courses means asking exactly whose culture you are going to teach.

Perhaps the best way to approach this problem is by recognizing that culture in English-speaking nations involves at least three general levels: Western culture, national culture, and group culture.

LEVEL ONE: WESTERN CULTURE

Many important aspects of culture are shared not only by the United States, United Kingdom, and other English-speaking nations but also by other European nations and even non-European nations in which there has been substantial European influence. For example, all Western countries share a considerable portion of their philosophical and religious traditions, a similar approach to law and government, and even much of their literary heritage.

LEVEL TWO: NATIONAL CULTURE

The stratum of culture that people tend to think of most readily is the national level: U.S. culture, Canadian culture, British culture, and so forth. While one cannot assume that all Americans (or Canadians, Australians, etc.) are exactly alike, some cultural characteristics are certainly shared widely within a nation and distinguish it from others. For example, even despite the immediate geographic proximity of Canada and the United States, people of the two nations tend to have rather different views of government, Canadians assuming that it is proper for government to play a greater role in provision of medical care and other social services than Americans would expect.

LEVEL THREE: GROUP CULTURE

In casual discussion of culture, working with broad terms like *Western culture* and *U.S. culture* is easier than being more precise about exactly what stream of Western or U.S. culture you are referring to. However, the danger of overusing such terms, particularly in a teaching situation, is that you may obscure the importance of regional, class, religious, ethnic, gender, and occupational cultures. For example, no picture of U.S. culture would be fully complete if it only represented the culture of suburban, middle-class, white families. A complete picture also needs to recognize strong regional cultures (e.g., New York City, the deep South), ethnic cultures (e.g., black, Hispanic), class cultures (e.g., the urban poor, working class, the wealthy), gender cultures (e.g., male and female), religious cultures (e.g., evangelical Christian, Catholic, Jewish), and even professional and occupational cultures (e.g., the military, doctors, truck drivers).

The question of whose culture to teach is complicated even further by the issue of how much relative weight should be given to dominant cultural norms as opposed to minority cultures. In North America, controversy on this point was sparked by Hirsch's (1987) book *Cultural Literacy: What Every American Needs to Know,* in which he argues that there is a core of cultural knowledge that all U.S. schoolchildren need to know and then presents a list of names, dates, and terms that he feels represents this cultural core. Most of the controversy about the book arose from Hirsch's list, which was criticized as representing only a dominant white, educated culture and ignoring the existence and importance of a diverse range of minority traditions.[4] While this debate primarily concerns the question of what culture should be taught to students in the United States, the larger issue of how much to include regional, ethnic, or other subnational cultures has implications for culture teaching in EFL classes as well.

As you consider how to approach culture in your English classes, perhaps your first goal should be to help students see that there are different levels of culture associated with English—in short, that not every point of culture taught in an English class can be neatly labeled *U.S. culture* or *British culture.* By being careful to distinguish between aspects of culture shared all over the West, those distinct to a particular nation, and those particular only to a smaller group, you will be helping students learn an important lesson about the complexity of culture.

With regard to the question of dominant versus minority cultures, I suggest a pragmatic approach. In most countries, students will often encounter the dominant streams of U.S. and British culture through books, magazines, and the media, so it is especially important that students learn about this level of culture. However, you do not want to go so far in this direction that students get the impression of the West or any given Western country as a culturally homogeneous entity. You might even make a special point of introducing aspects of group cultures outside the Western culture mainstream with which you have had experience.

Teaching Culture

LOCAL TEACHERS AND CULTURE TEACHING

For reasons that I have discussed above, part of your task as a teacher of culture involves teaching students cultural information about the target culture(s). In fact, as often as possible in language courses, you should try to kill two birds with one stone: have students learn about culture at the same time as they develop their language skills. For example, there is no reason for students to read a story about "Harold the Lazy Badger" created by a textbook writer when they could just as well read "The Tortoise and the Hare." By reading the former, students only develop reading skills; by reading the latter, students also become familiar with a story that is known throughout the West. Similarly, a listening exercise in which you call out instructions for a series of meaningless motions is not as rich as one in which you give directions for walking through a wedding or a baseball game. Of course, on some occasions you will need to use material with little cultural content for pragmatic reasons—you can't find an appropriate cultural topic, appropriate materials are not available, and so forth—but language practice activities should be used to also teach genuine culture information whenever possible.

---

[4]For critiques of Hirsch, see Walters (1992, 6) and Seelye (1993, 27); see also Murray (1992).

A second important goal in culture teaching is to help students build a better general understanding of what culture is and what it involves. As noted above, *culture* is an extremely broad term and concept, and unless it is made more clear and specific, it doesn't provide much guidance to students who want to learn more about the culture of the target countries—or, for that matter, of any other countries. In contrast, students who have more specific and clearer notions of what culture consists of have a clearer idea of what they need to learn if their goal is to understand the culture of another country or people. To that end, teaching students a framework of what culture consists of, such as the one presented earlier in this chapter, can help them set clearer goals in their learning about any culture.

A third goal in culture teaching may be even more important—teaching students to be careful in how they generalize about the target culture based on new cultural input they receive. Here I assume that it is normal and natural for students to make generalizations based on cultural input. So, for example, in movies if they see Americans frequently drinking coffee and British people frequently drinking tea, it is reasonable for them to generalize that Americans tend to drink coffee and British tend to drink tea. If, however, students overgeneralize and draw the conclusion that all Americans always drink coffee rather than tea, they have a problem because this conclusion is inaccurate—many Americans also drink tea, at least some of the time. The point is that students need to learn to generalize carefully and avoid drawing overly broad and simplistic conclusions that often become stereotypes.

Local teachers vary considerably in terms of how much they know about the target culture(s); some have spent substantial amounts of time living in other countries and know a great deal about several cultures other than their own, while other local teachers have never had a chance to spend any significant amount of time in another country and haven't had the opportunity to study the target culture(s) in depth. However, with regard to culture teaching, several assumptions are safe to make about most local teachers. First, you probably know more about at least one target culture than the students do, perhaps quite a lot more, and teaching students what you know about the target culture(s) is one way you can contribute to their education. Second, continuing to learn more about the target culture(s) yourself would almost certainly be good, so one additional reason to teach culture is that it provides both encouragement and opportunity for you to continue your own culture learning. (This, of course, would hold true for all language teachers, not just local English teachers.) Finally, one of your most important roles is teaching students to ask the right questions about whatever cultural input they receive, questions such as

- What underlying patterns do I see in how the people in the target culture act and think? What common threads tie these various ways of thinking and acting together?

- How much can I generalize based on any particular example of the behavior of people from the target culture? Is this behavior typical? Does it represent most of the people in the target culture? Only a few? Only those from a certain social class or region?

Students who learn to ask the right questions—to be alert to both the general patterns in the target culture and the limitations to those patterns—are better prepared to be wise and effective learners of any culture they encounter.

METHODS FOR TEACHING CULTURE

Chapters 6–10 mention some of the main ways to incorporate teaching about culture into practicing language skills, but a brief reminder of these may be helpful here.

Dialogues as Models of Culture

From the earliest stages of English study, most students are exposed to dialogues in textbooks. If these dialogues are at all realistic, they should provide a model of not only speech but also normal patterns of social interaction. Thus, when studying dialogues, students should also study how members of the target culture interact. As pointed out in chapter 7, one way to use textbook dialogues as models of culture is to emphasize the functions (i.e., ways to invite, change a topic, politely disagree). When teaching the dialogue, call attention to the pattern of moves involved, and teach students not only language tools but also how these tools are normally used. You can emphasize this aspect of dialogues by giving students practice assignments that are organized around functions and moves rather than around language per se; simply by presenting dialogues in this way, you will be reminding students of the patterns of interaction underlying the language.

Culture Talks

The most direct way to approach the teaching of almost any aspect of culture is simply to talk about it. A lecture format allows you to teach students about cultural background knowledge, beliefs and values, and cultural patterns while you provide students with listening comprehension practice. The richness of lessons based on culture talks can be enhanced by having students respond by talking or writing about corresponding aspects of their culture. (See chapter 6, Talks and Lectures; see also appendix C.)[5]

Press Conferences

The press conference format allows you to teach about essentially the same aspects of culture as the talk format does. However, because it is more interactive, this format makes it easier for students to pursue topics they are interested in or puzzled about. This, in turn, increases the chances that you will be able to adequately explain views in the target culture that differ significantly from those in the local culture. (See chapter 6, Press Conferences; see also appendix C.)

Below I introduce in more detail two additional types of activities that can be used to teach culture: research projects and the study of the target culture through printed and electronic media.

Research Projects

Over the past few decades, it has become ever easier for students in many countries to find out more about other cultures and even meet people from those cultures. Library collections have improved in many countries, as has the range of offerings in bookstores, so printed information about other cultures now tends to be more readily available. More foreigners are living in many countries now than ten or twenty years ago, so there are more opportunities to talk with foreigners and learn directly from them about other cultures. Finally, and perhaps most dramatically, the expansion of the Internet gives many students access to a range of information and contact with people around the globe that would have been unthinkable not so many years ago. All of these changes create the opportunity for students in many countries to engage in their own research projects, choosing their own questions about the target culture, seeking out their own answers, and then presenting the results in the form of classroom presentations and reports. Depending on how projects are structured, they can be used to help students build their background knowledge about the target culture, their understanding of the views of people in the target culture, or both.

---

[5] One type of resource book that would be helpful to you in preparing talks would be a basic introduction to the culture and society of the country or culture you expect to teach about. Examples for U.S. culture would include Althen (1988) and Lanier (1988).

The following research project activity encourages students to actively find out more information about the target culture and share what they learn with others in their class.

CULTURE INFORMATION RESEARCH PROJECTS

The primary focus in this kind of project is on having students gather information through library or Internet resources to gain a deeper and more nuanced understanding of some aspect of the target culture. However, the project also encourages students to be more aware of what their starting point is as they attempt to learn more about the target culture so that they can also better see how their understanding of the target culture grows and develops. One suggested procedure for a culture information research project would be as follows (for specific topic ideas for culture information research projects, see appendix C):

1. Individually or in groups, have students choose a topic or question they want to investigate. Fairly specific questions (*How do U.S. university students pay for college?*) tend to result in more interesting projects than broad topics do.

2. Have students write up a simple plan (including the topic, research questions, and how they will find the answers to these questions) and turn it into you for feedback and suggestions. The plan should include the following:
   - a list of what they already know and think about the topic—a snapshot of their starting point
   - specific research questions they will try to answer (These should be based on what they don't know yet about the topic or are not sure about.)

3. Have students research their question(s) using library or Internet resources, or by interviewing people from the target culture (either in person or over the Internet).

4. Have students prepare presentations, reports, or both, focusing on what they learned—ways in which their understanding moved beyond their original snapshot.

5. As you respond to the reports, help students understand not only how accurate their information and conclusions are but also how typical and generalizable they are.

Media-Based Culture Study

You can almost take it for granted that students around the world will be exposed to Western culture, especially North American and British, through the printed and visual media. In particular, English language movies are often available, and so are English language books. Use of these resources is discussed in chapters 6 and 8, respectively, as they relate to building listening and reading skills, but such resources are also valuable in a variety of ways as a vehicle for allowing students to learn about the cultures of other nations.

Media products such as films and books can obviously provide a great deal of cultural knowledge input covering many aspects of the target culture. Particularly valuable materials include

- **materials that realistically portray contemporary daily life and typical social interactions:** Magazines and newspapers—particularly the advertisements in them—are especially rich in daily-life realia and cover a range of contemporary culture and social issues. Even when magazine and newspaper articles are too difficult to read (or it is too much trouble to get copies made), they can still be adapted for listening exercises. When available, television programs and films are also an excellent resource.

- **materials that teach basic background information about the target culture—its history, geography, government, economy, and society:** Books with this kind of information are probably available in your country. You can find additional resources on the Internet, and you might also be able to get resources from the target country's embassy or consulate in your country.

- **books or films that tell the well-known stories of the target culture:** These are often inherently interesting and usually raise a rich range of cultural issues. Additionally, they are important to know about simply because they are well known. Traditional Western stories would include the Greek and Norse myths; Bible stories; nursery rhymes; Grimm's and Andersen's fairy tales; and legends surrounding figures such as Ulysses, King Arthur, Joan of Arc, Robin Hood, and Davey Crockett. Modern characters who have moved into legend would include figures like Superman, Helen Keller, Babe Ruth, Marie Curie, Martin Luther King, and even Elvis Presley. Of course, many of these stories can be found in film as well as printed versions, and in many countries, simplified readers based on the classic works of Western literature are available.

- **material that tells the story of the target culture:** To some extent, this is the story drawn from the history of the target culture or nation, but it is not a cold, academic rendering of facts. Instead, it is a rather selective account that focuses on people and events that have special significance in defining a culture. In fact, it is often a rather simplified and patriotic version of history. Special attention is usually paid to those people, things, and events of which the culture is most proud—its heroes, victories, great achievements, great creative works, and other models of excellence. This kind of shared cultural knowledge is especially important not only because it is widely known but also because it plays a significant role in establishing the identity of a group and often offers important clues as to the values of the culture. This kind of history is often found in school textbooks.[6]

However, in addition to being an effective way to build students' knowledge of the target culture(s), study of media texts is also valuable because it provides the opportunity to practice skills of careful generalization—that is, finding patterns in the target culture but at the same time noting the limitations of those patterns. While students can learn—and will learn—much about the target culture from books, movies, and so forth, media portrayals of a culture are often not typical, complete, or entirely realistic, and students may not know how much they can generalize based on any particular portrayal of target-culture behavior. For example, when they see an American in a Hollywood film behaving in a certain way (e.g., a woman getting upset at a man who holds a door open for her), they may not know whether this particular behavior is typical of the target culture, unusual but still within the normal range, or well within the bizarre zone. So one of your main duties when dealing with media products is helping students evaluate how useful a given text is as a portrayal of culture. The following is one possible procedure for an in-class activity.

CULTURE GENERALIZATIONS EXERCISE
This activity is intended to help students not only pay attention to the cultural content in the printed and electronic media but also develop the habit of being careful in how they generalize based on that content.

---

[6] While this aspect of the target culture is important, it is also potentially sensitive. The identity of a nation is often forged in conflict with other nations, so a nation's story often has strong us-versus-them undertones and substantial elements of boosterism. While the story should be presented with empathy, it should also be presented with a degree of critical distance.

1. Select a text (from a book, magazine, or even a film or television program) that attempts to realistically portray life in the target culture (as opposed to, e.g., science fiction texts that portray imaginary worlds). It is best if, before class, you go over the text yourself to see what cultural generalizations can be drawn from it and perhaps even discuss it with someone who is from the target culture.

2. Have students read or view the text and take notes on possible lessons one could learn from the text about the target culture. These should be stated as generalizations, and students should be prepared to explain how they drew whatever generalizations they report.

3. Have students report their generalizations and how they came to them. Then, for each generalization, have students discuss how typical it might be and what limits might need to be placed on it.

4. Close by giving students as much of a reality check as you can, telling them whether their generalizations capture real patterns in the target culture and what limits might need to be placed on the generalizations. While you may not always know precisely how typical or realistic any particular example of behavior is, you can often give students some help in determining how accurate and fair their generalizations are. Also, simply by calling students' attention to this issue, you help students form the habit of asking the right questions and of not simply accepting anything they read or see in the media as the final word on how people in the target culture behave.

Teaching Intercultural Communication and Intercultural Competence

THE IMPORTANCE OF INTERCULTURAL COMMUNICATION

In today's world, the growing global role of English means that students may need to use English not only for communicating with people from English-speaking countries but also for communicating with people from many other nations and cultures. It is therefore impossible for students to adequately prepare themselves for international English use just by studying the culture of one or more English-speaking target countries; knowing a lot about the culture of the United States or United Kingdom does not help much if a student needs to communicate with someone from Jordan, Thailand, Nigeria, or Brazil. So, in addition to studying specific cultures, students should also try to develop basic skills in intercultural communication, that is, general skills and habits that enhance the effectiveness of communication between people who are not very familiar with each other's cultures. In particular, they need to learn two basic sets of skills and habits.

The first has to do with what is known as the interpretation process, in other words, the process by which people make sense of the words and actions of other people. Sometimes one might think of communication as a simple process in which person A encodes meaning in a message, and then person B takes A's original meaning out of the message, rather like one person putting an apple in a bag that is then passed to a second person, who takes exactly the same apple out of the bag. However, actual communication isn't so simple. Both in direct, face-to-face communication and in indirect communication (e.g., through letters, books, films), the receiver of a message always actively makes sense of the message, based not only on the words in the message but also on the expression on the sender's face, the tone of voice used, the setting in which the message appears, the background information that the receiver has, and so forth. For example, the sentence *Your dress is really beautiful* might mean one thing if said by an admiring boyfriend and something very different if said by a jealous rival, so the receiver of the message must interpret the meaning. Interpretation naturally occurs in all communication, even between people from the same culture, but it tends to be more of a problem in intercultural communication. People from different cultural backgrounds have less in common, so the danger of miscommunication is greater. Students therefore need to learn to interpret messages more slowly and carefully when communicating with people from other cultures.

The second set of skills and habits has to do with ethnocentrism and the ability to see things from other cultural perspectives. Human beings tend to be ethnocentric; in other words, they tend to understand and interpret the world from the perspective of their own culture. This is because people first learn about the world in childhood, from the perspective of the culture that surrounds them, and naturally tend to see that cultural perspective as being normal and right. This tendency to be ethnocentric is natural and even inevitable, and it is a habit that is not easy to break. It is also, however, a major source of problems in intercultural communication because ethnocentrism tends to make people judge things according to the standards and norms of their own culture, which tends to create a negative bias toward anything that differs from those norms. To avoid the effects of this negative bias, students need to learn the habit of trying to view things from cultural perspectives other than their own. Of course, this is easier said than done, and students can't simply will themselves to see things from other cultural perspectives. However, they can develop the habit of pausing to ask how something might appear from another cultural perspective and of using their imaginations to put themselves in other people's shoes. These are two of the most important habits of intercultural competence, and you should encourage students to develop them.

Just as local teachers' knowledge of the target culture varies, local teachers will vary a great deal in how much they know about intercultural communication and how much experience they have interacting with people from other cultures. However, it is safe to assume that most local teachers have more experience interacting with foreigners than most students do and that they are more likely to have studied intercultural communication to some degree, and this experience and knowledge is one of the resources you can draw on as you teach. However, as with knowledge of local culture, often your main role lies not so much in teaching particular concepts as it does in teaching students what questions to ask. Ultimately, whether or not students know what *interpretation* or *ethnocentrism* mean is not as important whether or not they pause to ask questions such as the following when interacting with foreigners:

- Am I sure the other person means what I think he or she means?

- Other than the explanation that seems most obvious to me, have I overlooked any possible explanations of the other person's words and actions?

- How would this situation look from the perspective of the other person?

METHODS FOR TEACHING INTERCULTURAL COMMUNICATION SKILLS

Some of the activities in appendix C can be used to teach not only information about the target culture but also basic intercultural communication skills. In particular, you can design some pair or small-group discussion activities so that students are required to imagine what the perspective of a different group of people might be like—for example, so that men are required to imagine how women would view an issue and women are required to imagine how men might view the same issue. While this kind of activity does not involve intercultural communication per se, the basic habits it encourages are similar to those involved in intercultural competence.

In the following section, I introduce three kinds of activities that can be used in English lessons for building basic intercultural communication skills. First, critical-incident exercises are useful for encouraging students to be more careful and think more broadly as they interpret the behavior of people from unfamiliar cultural backgrounds. Second, culture perspective interview projects encourage students to see issues from a different cultural perspective by requiring them to seek out the views of people from other cultures. Finally, reflexive culture research projects encourage students to gain a better understanding of what influences shape the perspectives of their own culture toward the target culture.

Critical-Incident Exercises

Critical-incident exercises (sometimes called *culture-bump stories*) consist of two basic parts: (1) a story in which people of different cultural backgrounds have a communication problem and (2) a discussion question that invites students to analyze the incident and attempt to arrive at a better understanding of why the problem occurred. These exercises are a good springboard for discussion of cultural differences, especially differences in beliefs and values. They also help students develop a number of very basic but important intercultural communication skills and habits:

- They help students become more consciously aware of the processes by which they interpret (i.e., make sense of) the behavior of foreigners.

- They encourage students to pause and think rather than jumping rapidly to conclusions.

- They help students build the habit of considering a broad variety of possible explanations of behavior that seems strange or problematic rather than stopping with obvious, knee-jerk interpretations.

One possible procedure for using critical-incident exercises in EFL classes is as follows:

1. Present students with an incident in which a person from the students' culture has a puzzling or problematic encounter someone from another culture. For example, *You are applying for an important scholarship, and your U.S. English teacher writes a nice recommendation letter for you. You finally get the scholarship and feel grateful to your teacher, so you buy her an expensive gift. On the day that you present it to her, after class, she refuses to accept it.*[7] (If you present the situation orally, you might check comprehension by quickly asking students questions covering the main points of the situation.)

2. In groups, have students come up with at least five possible reasons why the U.S. teacher is refusing the gift. Stress that the goal is not to find one right answer but rather to brainstorm and come up with a variety of possible interpretations of the U.S. teacher's behavior. (Have one person take notes.)

3. Have the groups present their theories to the class for discussion. (To allow each group to contribute, it is best to have each group offer just one suggestion while you note it on the board and then move to the next group.)

4. Once the possibilities are listed on the board, ask students to indicate which they think are most and least likely. One way to do this is to have students divide them into categories such as *likely, possible,* and *not likely but still possible.*

---

[7] Based on an activity in Levine, Baxter, and McNulty (1987); a version can be found in Snow (2004). For other critical-incident exercises for EFL classes, see Snow (2004); Amity Foundation (2003). Fictional stories from films and books, or real stories from newspaper or magazine articles, can sometimes also be fashioned into interesting critical-incident exercises.

5. After students categorize the possibilities, it is your turn to provide a reality check, commenting on how likely you think each might be and suggesting possibilities students might not have thought of. (During this phase, try to give credit to as many suggestions as possible. For theories that are way off the mark, a smile and "Good guess, but no" will usually do the trick without hurting too many feelings.)

TIPS

- Remember that the main goal of critical-incident exercises is to encourage students to think broadly and cautiously about how to interpret behavior across cultural lines. Try to avoid having the exercise turn into a game in which students try to generate nice but unrealistic explanations or simply try to guess the right answer. The focus should be on discovering as many realistic explanations of the situation (nice and not so nice) as are reasonably possible.

- This kind of exercise is somewhat challenging both conceptually and linguistically, so it is best used with students at intermediate or advanced levels.

Culture Perspective Interview Projects

These are similar to the culture information research projects introduced above, but they differ in two ways. First, they should involve actual communication with people from the target culture, whether through face-to-face interviews or over the Internet. Second, the main focus of this kind of project is on learning more about the perspectives that members of the target culture have on their own culture, not just on gathering culture data. The purpose is to expose students to views that may differ from their own and suggest new perspectives on issues. Students do not need to accept or like the views they hear, but they should attempt to understand them. A suggested procedure for this kind of project is as follows:

1. Choose one or more questions about the target culture to serve as a focus for the project (e.g., *Why do so many Americans support the idea of easy access to guns?*). For this kind of project, students should investigate aspects of the target culture that they genuinely find strange or difficult to understand (though they should also be careful not to choose topics that their informants might find offensive).

2. In groups, have students plan how to locate informants and arrange interviews with them, either face-to-face or via the Internet.

3. Have each group make a list of specific interview questions. These should focus on inviting informants to not only say what people in the target culture think but also explain why. (You may also ask students to predict and write down what they think informants will say in response to the questions, thus making the interview a kind of reality check.)

4. Have the students find and interview people from the target culture.

5. Have each group prepare and give a presentation, a report, or both focusing on what they learned from the informants, especially things that were not what they had expected.

When students interview foreigners about topics that may be somewhat sensitive, there is always the possibility that the students may have disagreements, or even arguments, with the people they interview. When summing things up after the groups report, help students draw fair and calm conclusions based on their experiences rather than jumping to overly broad negative—or even positive—conclusions based on experiences with only one or two people.

Reflexive Culture Research Projects

This kind of project encourages students to more closely examine how people in their culture view the target culture and to get a better understanding of the sources of information that shape the views of people in the local culture toward the target culture. Have students do the following:

1. Choose an issue on which they think local people have (strong) opinions about the target culture.

2. Make up a list of specific interview questions asking what the informants think about the issue and from what sources they get their information about it. (As with culture perspective interview projects, it may also be good for students to write down their predictions of what informants will say.)

3. Find several informants, and interview them.

4. Using library or Internet resources, study the issue to learn more about the issue and to check how well informed the views of informants were.

5. Prepare a presentation, a report, or both focusing especially on (1) the views informants expressed about the issue—and how accurate the students' predictions about these views were, (2) what students learned about where and how people get their information, and (3) students' assessment of the quality of information people have and the effect of this on their views.

Sensitivity in Teaching Western Culture

The main reason English has such a dominant role in so many parts of the world is that, over the past two centuries, English-speaking nations have wielded tremendous economic, political, and military power. One consequence of this fact is that the experience of many countries with the English-speaking nations has been less than entirely positive. Westerners have often been invaders, colonizers, or economic competitors rather than friends, and the desire of some people to learn English is complicated by feelings of resentment toward the power and wealth of the countries that English represents. The other side of the coin is that students of English in some cultures may have an overly rosy and uncritical admiration for Western nations and cultures. Discussion of Western culture is therefore sometimes complicated by strong feelings.

One of the most important lessons you can teach students about viewing other cultures is that they should strive for objectivity and fairness. You cannot erase the attitudes and feelings—positive or negative—that students have toward Western cultures, but it is within your power to see that your culture lessons present a model of fair objective treatment of cultural issues, a model that will help students learn to approach other cultures in the same way themselves.

One strategy that will make your discussion of culture more objective is to habitually point out that almost every major facet of a culture carries advantages and disadvantages. For example, when discussing the United States' advanced health care system, you should also point out its expense; when discussing the U.S. cultural emphasis on self-reliance, note that this contributes both to a high level of national productivity and to a willingness to tolerate poverty among those who will not or cannot work hard; when discussing the high rate of U.S. car ownership, mention both the freedom and mobility it allows and the price paid for gas, insurance, and repairs (not to mention the problem of air pollution). This habit of always presenting two sides to an issue may seem somewhat artificial, but it is beneficial because it makes your presentation of issues more objective and because it forces you to think through issues more carefully in order to find two sides. This habit is also, incidentally, good training for both you and the students because it serves as a reminder that most aspects of any culture generally have both a good and a bad side.

For Thought, Discussion, and Action

1. **attitudes toward Western culture:** Imagine that you have been asked to orient a Western teacher who is coming to your country to teach English, and she wants to know about the attitudes students are likely to have toward Western culture. What would you tell her about the following?
    *   How interested are students in studying about Western cultures or other foreign cultures? Which cultures are they most interested in?
    *   How much do students already know about Western cultures, and what kinds of things do students to tend to know and believe about them?
    *   From what sources do they get most of their information and ideas about Western culture?

2. **definition of** *culture*: The term *culture* has been defined by many different people in many different ways. Are there ways in which you would revise the definition of culture given in this chapter to provide a better guide for your culture teaching?

3. **shared culture knowledge:** This chapter gives several examples of names and dates that have cultural significance. Make a list of names and dates that have significant symbolic meaning in your own culture.

4. **basic cultural values:** Using the list of questions given in the Shared Views section of this chapter, compare and contrast your own culture and the target culture. Then discuss your analysis with a native of the target culture.

5. **genres:** Choose several genres of movies (TV programs, newspaper columns, books, etc.) in your culture, and list the basic conventions of the genre, in other words, how it is organized and what rules it follows. Then ask a native of the target culture about the conventions and rules of similar genres in his or her culture.

6. **culture talks:** Imagine that you are preparing to give a series of talks about the target culture. (1) List topics you think it would be good to talk about. (2) Check the Internet (library, local bookstore, etc.) for sources of information, making a list of information sources that you can use for future reference—and that you can exchange with other teachers.

7. **the target-culture story:** Imagine that you are preparing a one-hour talk covering the story of the target culture. (1) List the events, dates, and names that would be most important to include, and consider why each is important. (2) Ask a native of the target culture for his or her opinion on what things would be most important.

8. **culture beyond the mainstream:** Choose one or more subcultures of the target culture you will teach about and then search the Internet, the library, or bookstores for information about this subculture. If possible, also interview one or more natives of the target culture to see what they can tell you about the subculture you are interested in.

9. **the problematic points of culture:** List several aspects of the target culture students in your culture find difficult to understand or accept. Then discuss these with natives of the target culture to see what their perspective on these issues is.

10. **literature as a reflection of culture:** List several literary works (e.g., films, novels) in which the behavior of characters reflects important aspects of the target culture and that would be useful in teaching about it. Then, for each work, design a teaching strategy that would effectively exploit the cultural material.

Chapter 13

A Troubleshooter's Guide to the Classroom

This book concludes with discussion of some of the most common problems teachers in EFL settings encounter as they attempt to bring communicative language teaching (CLT) approaches into the English classroom, especially if they try to include more oral skill practice in class through pair and small-group activities. Many of the suggestions in this chapter have been mentioned in other chapters, but here they are organized around how they relate to specific problems you may encounter.

Overly Large Classes

In many countries, large class sizes (thirty to fifty students or more) are perceived as a major obstacle to the adoption of CLT or student-centered teaching approaches. For listening comprehension or reading lessons, such large classes are generally not an insurmountable obstacle; for speaking and writing lessons, however, large classes can present serious problems. In a speaking class with fifty students, you simply cannot give much individual attention to students, and writing classes of this size mean that you have to face either mountains of compositions or guilt for assigning students too little writing.

Obviously, the ideal solution to this problem would be to reduce the size of the classes. Unfortunately, this is often not possible. Large classes are generally a result of necessity (e.g., lack of funds, staff) rather than a philosophy of education; most educators the world over would agree that smaller classes are better and would reduce class sizes if they could. So generally you need to cope with the situation instead of hoping it will change. The danger for you in this situation is that you may consciously or unconsciously assume that, with such large classes, it is impossible to use CLT approaches. However, while CLT approaches can be harder to use in classes with many students, they are not necessarily impossible to use there.

In all but the smallest speaking classes, students will get most of their practice talking to each other rather than to you, so the problem presented by a class of fifty is different from that presented by a class of twenty only in degree, not kind. In both cases, speaking practice should ideally consist primarily of pair and small-group work rather than dialogue between teacher and student. The real problem in large classes is one of management, specifically of ensuring that students will actually speak English when you are out of earshot. (This issue is discussed below.)

If most of the students in a class will not speak English unless you are present, the problem becomes much more difficult because the class must be more teacher centered. In such cases, until you solve the attitude problem that keeps students from speaking English in pairs and groups, you may be forced to rely heavily on listening comprehension exercises and teacher-focused question-and-answer exercises. While less than ideal, such use of class time is by no means the end of the world. The development of listening skills contributes to the development of speaking skills, and teacher-focused dialogue can be useful even in a large class if you remember to interact with students in a random pattern so that all of them need to listen and think through responses to questions. Remember, the mental process of creating sentences is the most difficult part of the speaking process, and any practice that forces students to go through this process under time pressure is valuable for the development of speaking skills.

Overly large writing classes are somewhat more problematic in that they almost inevitably require you to work very hard just to respond to a small amount of writing per student. As suggested in chapter 9, in large writing classes it is particularly important to make sure that students edit and polish work as much as possible before you go over it, so in-class self-editing and peer editing are recommended. Putting strict length limits on assignments—as well as emphasizing the virtues of terse writing—can also help. Finally, you can stress activities in which students are the audience rather than you. (See chapter 9 for more discussion of this problem.)

Classes with Disparate Skill Levels

A particularly frequent and annoying problem is classes in which some students have much better English skills than others do. This situation is especially common in night schools and other institutions in which students come from a variety of backgrounds, but it is also found in school systems where groups of students move up the educational ladder together as a class. Because of differences in background, or simply in the diligence with which students study, some students already know most of the material you plan to cover while others have fallen completely behind in both mastery of the material and skill development. This situation makes lesson planning difficult because it is hard to meet the needs of students at one skill level without neglecting those of students at another skill level. It may also produce motivation problems in the class; students with more advanced-level skills may be bored while students with less advanced-level skills are dispirited and confused.

As with the problem of overly large classes, the ideal solution would be to redistribute students into classes of more equal skill levels, and sometimes this is possible. Schools that have little experience with CLT or proficiency-based approaches to language teaching might not yet be aware of how important it is to place students of roughly equal skill levels together. (They may tend to think of students' levels more in terms of test scores rather than actual skill levels, but sometimes test scores do not reflect actual skill levels—especially oral skills—very accurately.) So, in some situations it may be worth the effort to gradually advocate skill-based placement. However, this might involve a rather long campaign and does not provide a quick solution to your problem—especially if the school term has already started—so the immediate problem for you becomes one of how to make the best of things.

In classes with mixed skill levels, the difference between a teacher-centered class and a student-centered one becomes especially critical. The pace and difficulty of activities in a teacher-centered class will necessarily be dictated by the teacher, and this forces students to march together in lockstep. If, for example, all the students in a class must listen to the same story together, students who could understand more rapid speech have to suffer through an overly slow presentation while their weaker classmates are embarrassed to stop you and ask questions or ask for repetition. This same dynamic holds true for whole-class activities such as large-group discussions, in which students with stronger English skills usually set the pace and many of their classmates have to sit through an activity that is completely inappropriate for their skill level.

In contrast, to the extent that students work alone, in pairs, or in small groups, they are better able to work at their own pace. For example, taped listening assignments done at home allow students with better listening skills to complete the activity quickly and move on to something else; other students can stop and listen to difficult segments as many times as they need to. In small-group discussions, students with weaker speaking skills can express themselves at their own level without as much fear that they will slow down other students. Thus, one key to dealing with a class with varied skill levels is to make the class as individualized and student centered as possible.

Another way to approach the issue is by talking about it with the students. It often helps to do a little special public relations work with the students at the upper and lower ends of the class. Let students with unusually strong English skills know that you recognize their high level of ability, and then challenge them by giving them a little extra responsibility (e.g., as discussion group leaders) or some difficult but interesting extra projects. You may also suggest that they have a responsibility to help and encourage others in the class or at least give others a chance to talk. Let less advanced-level students know that you don't consider their present skill level an indication of lack of ability, but also emphasize that they need to put extra effort into catching up to the rest of the class. Students who remain below the skill level of the class average will face a constant series of activities and assignments that are not well suited to their skill level, and they will not only learn less from these activities than their classmates do but will also find the work difficult and painful. It is therefore worthwhile for them to put in the extra effort necessary to catch up.

All the pep talks in the world are not likely to be of much use in raising the morale of students with weaker skills if the talks are followed by a series of grades that tell the students they really are at the bottom of the class. Unfortunately, if all of the class assignments and exercises are graded based on of general skill level, and if assignments are all graded on the curve, less advanced-level students are unlikely to receive much encouragement from their marks. This is one reason it is good to grade based at least partly on progress rather than on absolute skill level. It is also a good argument for including a content component, such as culture, in a course. Students with advanced-level language skills do not necessarily have much more Western cultural background than their less advanced-level classmates do, so the inclusion of such an element in a course gives less advanced-level students at least one opportunity to begin from the same starting point as their classmates.

Even the most student-centered class will have at least some teacher-focused interaction, even if only when you give directions, and in these interactions you will need to decide the skill level to which you will target your communication when you speak to the class in English. My advice is that you avoid slowing your English down to the pace of the less advanced-level students. While speaking English slowly may seem to be more humane, in the end it is not. As much as I would like to believe otherwise, the problem with at least some of the weaker students in any class is that they do not put forth as much effort as their peers, and if you slow down to the level of the weakest, often the lazier students relax rather than endeavoring to catch up. Even worse, this approach discourages those students who have worked harder. My suggestion is that you tailor your English communication to a level slightly higher than that of the average student in the class, thus keeping it within the range of a majority of the students but making it challenging.

Lack of Class Response

One problem teachers in EFL settings often face when attempting to use CLT approaches is that getting the class to respond to you in English may be difficult, at least at first. The classic scenario for this problem would go like this: you ask a general question to the class at large (e.g., "What did you all do this weekend?"). However, instead of answering you, the students all look down at their books and do anything else they can to avoid being noticed by you. Finally, when you get tired of waiting for a volunteer and simply call on a student to respond, an expression of deep reluctance—or perhaps stark terror—crosses her face. She seems to have little idea what to say or how to say it, and it is only slowly and painfully that she stammers the briefest possible answer to your question and then hopes you will turn your attention to tormenting someone else.

Lack of response is particularly a problem in situations where students have had little previous experience speaking in English and simply aren't used to it; it also tends to be more of a problem in cultures where individual display is not encouraged and where face is considered very important. However, fear of speaking out in a foreign language—especially in front of the whole class—is a rather common problem in many settings and cultures because it is quite natural for students to be reluctant to make mistakes in public. Keep in mind that being forced to express their ideas in a foreign language robs students of the competence and dignity that they possess when speaking their mother tongue; to put it bluntly, it forces them to sound incompetent or even stupid. For students who are not yet confident of their ability to express ideas in English with a passable degree of fluency and accuracy, every sentence they utter is a challenge that forces them to pluck up a considerable amount of courage, and the temptation to simply avoid the challenge is often great. So, for teachers, the question is, what can you do to make it easier for your students—or at least most of them—to pluck up their courage and take the plunge?

One strategy has to do with reducing the difficulty of the challenge, thereby giving students more confidence that they can cope with it in a reasonably effective way. As pointed out in chapter 7, speaking in English is actually a rather complicated process that requires students to do many things simultaneously under time pressure. For the purposes of this chapter, these might be summarized as two kinds of challenges: the challenge of figuring out what to say and the challenge of deciding how to say it. You can make it easier for students to speak out in English by reducing the difficulty of either of these two challenges. In situations where students do not easily or rapidly respond to questions you address in English to the class, there are several specific measures you can take:

1. Make it easier for students to formulate responses by asking questions that only require a yes/no or true/false answer, or questions that allow students to respond with a body motion like shaking their heads or raising their hands (e.g., to vote). While this kind of interaction does little to build students' speaking skills, it is a useful first step toward building the habit of responding to your questions; in other words, it is better than having students hang their heads and not respond at all.

2. Allow students to prepare their responses by first discussing the question briefly in pairs or small groups or even simply thinking about the question silently for a minute and jotting down a few notes. Either of these methods allows students a little time to decide what they want to say and prepare for how they will say it; it also means that they will have something written on paper that will give them a little more confidence as they respond to you.

3. Allow students to rehearse their responses by surveying each other quickly on the question you asked. This not only gives students time to formulate answers but allows them to practice an answer one or more times in pairs before they have to present it with the whole class listening.

A second strategy involves reducing the sense of threat and making the situation feel safer. Students are more likely to take a risk and speak out if the potential rewards (praise, sense of achievement, encouragement) seem greater than the potential costs (embarrassment, criticism). One way to convince students that the chances of reward are relatively high is to make a conscious habit of rewarding effort, even if the results are not always correct. For example, when a student answers a question incorrectly (with regard either to content or accuracy of English), it is more encouraging to respond with "Good try, but . . ." than to simply say "Wrong!" In any classroom, students will quickly figure out whether the teacher rewards them more for playing safe by taking few risks (thus avoiding mistakes but also cutting down on language use) or for taking chances by speaking out even when they are not sure if they are right (thus making more mistakes but also using language more). A teacher who does not punish students too much for taking risks is more likely to get responses from students.

Teachers can also reduce the sense of threat in the classroom by establishing a warm, supportive atmosphere in the class. Teachers can contribute to such an atmosphere directly by smiling, offering praise and encouragement, and bringing humor into the classroom; they can also contribute indirectly by teaching students to encourage each other and discouraging students from criticizing each other.

In setting the tone of a class, an element of challenge and pressure can obviously be useful; in fact, motivation tends to be enhanced by tasks in which the goal is relatively challenging, though not so difficult that students perceive it as being impossible (Dörnyei 2001b, 20, 26). So what I am advocating here is not an atmosphere in which there is no discipline and any and all behavior is rewarded; rather, I am suggesting a need for balance in which the class atmosphere is warm and encouraging as well as challenging. Students need to be inspired to make an effort but are also more willing to try if they feel an honest effort will be fairly rewarded.

Reluctance to Speak English in Pair and Small-Group Activities

Another problem is that students are often not very willing to speak to each other in English during pair or small-group activities, in other words, during activities in which you cannot watch them all the time. Sometimes this lack of willingness is due to the awkwardness of talking to their friends in a foreign language, or even to sheer laziness. However, it is also sometimes encouraged by a belief that the only useful kind of speaking practice is conversation with an English teacher who will correct all their errors—in short, they expect to do their practicing with you. Students who believe this may be reluctant to practice with their peers because they doubt the usefulness of such practice or because they fear making uncorrected errors, building bad habits, and incurring a vague host of other evil consequences.

Faced with students who resist practicing spoken English with each other, you probably need to resort to a combination of persuasion and persistent pressure. For your campaign of persuasion, you might begin by suggesting that the main problem in speaking is one of quickly forming thoughts into English sentences and that this kind of practice does not require a teacher as listener. (In fact, it doesn't require any listener at all, and I quite heartily advocate that students talk to themselves in English if they don't mind occasional curious looks from passersby.) A culturally relevant analogy may also help; for example, you might have students ask themselves who will learn guitar (violin, kung fu, basketball, etc.) more rapidly—a student who practices two hours every day or one who only practices during a weekly half-hour lesson with the teacher?

It may also help to point out that students should not be worried that their errors will be reinforced if they spend too much time talking to classmates. As Brown (2001) notes, "There is now enough research on errors and error correction to tell us that (1) levels of accuracy maintained in unsupervised groups are as high as those in teacher-monitored whole-class work, and that (2) as much as you would like not to believe it, teachers' overt attempts to correct speech errors in the classroom have a negligible effect on students' subsequent performance" (p. 181).

To encourage students to speak English in class, I personally prefer a prescription of light-toned nagging ("Kim, that doesn't sound like English") and occasional pep talks on the importance of practice.[1] It is also important to be realistic about how far from supervision you can reasonably expect the students to actually practice English. A good rule of thumb is this: break students into the smallest groups in which most of them will speak English a significant percentage of the time.

---

[1] Some teachers have students monitor each other, levying a minimal fine on students who speak something other than English in class (the proceeds eventually to go to a class party). I am personally uncomfortable with demanding money from students and even less comfortable making the speaking of their native tongue a misdemeanor, but it seems to work for some. Ur (1981, 20) suggests that placing a tape recorder near an offending group may increase their amount of English practice.

Students Who Participate Too Little

There is yet a third problem related to reluctance to speak English—the problem of individual students who rarely or never volunteer to participate by speaking English in class, at least in whole-class discussions. Here, however, the question is whether this is really a problem or not.

Teachers often assume that participation means answering questions or offering opinions during all-class activities, and it is generally assumed that this kind of participation is an important part of the learning process. On reflection, however, it should be clear that the few moments a semester students spend speaking in front of the whole class are not a significant part of their total speaking practice time, and students who never volunteer in a large-group setting do not necessarily get much less practice than their classmates. In fact, the only unique benefit of speaking out in front of the whole class is that it trains students to pluck up their courage for speaking in front of large audiences. So I would suggest that the failure of a few reluctant students to speak up in large-group settings should not be considered a serious problem.

In fact, pressuring quiet students to participate unwillingly in whole-class settings may be counterproductive. They may be less than entirely confident of their English skills and already somewhat intimidated in English class. Knowing that they could be called on to publicly perform in front of a large audience increases the level of anxiety, and fear may well become more salient in their minds than interest in learning. If you single out such students by calling on them, the result is tension and wasted class time; the reluctant student often sits in embarrassed panic, unable or unwilling to answer, while classmates become either more nervous or bored. The only thing that such an exercise accomplishes is putting enough fear into students' hearts that they are more likely to do their homework; it achieves little in terms of in-class learning.

The saddest aspect of trial by questioning in class is that it may torment students who are in fact participating, in other words, students who pay attention in class, actively think through responses to questions, and participate actively in pair or small-group activities. These are the most important forms of participation because it is through them that students will get the bulk of their English practice. Only a very few highly vocal students will get significant amounts of practice in an all-class forum.

I have mentioned strategies you can use to make it easier for students to respond to you in class, and use of such strategies may help some of your quieter students find the courage to speak out. Ultimately, however, there is a point at which you have done what you can to provide opportunities and encouragement, and then it is up to students to take advantage of those opportunities. One element of treating students with respect is allowing them the freedom to make choices, and beyond a certain point further intervention on your part may do more harm than good by creating fear and tension or simply by wasting time that could have been better spent on other students who are more willing to respond. Make sure that opportunities and channels of communication remain open, but don't feel guilty about every student who chooses not to speak up in class.

Students Who Participate Too Much

You are probably familiar with the kind of student who tends to dominate, always being the first to answer a question or offer an opinion. The problem is that such behavior limits the other students' opportunities to participate and may also discourage their willingness to try. For you, the problem is how to control the behavior without discouraging the student; the student who participates frequently is, after all, doing what teachers wish most students would do.

One approach is to simply ignore the eager student's hand when it goes up and to direct activity to other members of the class. This approach, however, often makes the eager student more vigorous in efforts to be noticed. Students who talk a great deal tend not be shy or overly sensitive types, so more direct approaches may be necessary. One is to speak to these students individually, praising their willingness to participate but asking them to give others a chance. During class, when the hand pops up again, you might even say, "I see your hand, but let's see if we can't get someone else to respond first."

Try not to become visibly annoyed with such students. They may already be viewed as teacher's pets who have popularity problems in class (though they may also be class leaders), and your disapproval can encourage other students to be more critical of them. They may also, quite understandably, feel there is no good reason to let speaking opportunities go to waste if others won't take advantage of them, a view that you should encourage rather than discourage. Your ultimate goal is to encourage other students to participate more rather than to make overly talkative students participate less, and you may make more progress toward this goal by showing appreciation of eager students' efforts than by becoming irritated at them.

Getting Students Interested

In EFL settings, the greatest challenge English teachers face is often one of getting students interested in English study, and this is especially true if teachers try to make greater use of CLT approaches. Of course, student interest and motivation is important even when teachers use traditional teacher-centered approaches, but when using a traditional lecture approach, the teacher finds it is somewhat easier to keep class going simply by continuing to lecture; students don't actually have to respond much in order for a class period to keep right on moving along. However, when teachers try to employ methods more typical of a CLT approach, such as pair and small-group work, the level of student interest has a greater impact on how well a class goes because if students are not interested in what they are doing, there are many long uncomfortable silences and much wasted class time.

Of course, the underlying problem is that students in EFL settings often have relatively little inherent interest in studying English, which often seems quite distant and unrelated to their lives. To be more precise, students are often interested for a while at the beginning of English study because the subject is novel and perhaps even a little exotic; they may also have heard from teachers or other people that learning English may in various ways be good for their future prospects. In addition, study of English tends to be somewhat simpler and easier at the beginning, and progress is relatively more visible because there is such an obvious difference between knowing absolutely no English and knowing some.

However, as time goes on and students move further into English study, their interest often begins to diminish. The novelty of learning a foreign language wears off, and students begin to tire of hard work that seems to have no end in sight. There are also generally few opportunities in EFL settings for students to make genuine use of beginning- or intermediate-level English skills, so the ratio of reward to effort tends to be rather low. Additionally, it becomes harder for students to see what—if any—progress they are making, especially in the intermediate stages of English study when they study low-frequency vocabulary items and grammar structures that may not reappear for months or years after students first learn them. Finally, the ultimate goal—a good command of English—may still seem quite distant and unreal. In EFL settings, this intermediate phase of English study is something like a wide desert that students need to cross on their journey toward English proficiency. In this phase, many students lose interest in building genuine proficiency in English—or lose hope that they will ever be able to attain such proficiency—and begin to settle for the less ambitious goal of simply doing what is necessary to pass tests whether or not this actually helps them build genuine skills. In fact, the most important question in language teaching may be: How do you help build and sustain students' interest through the long middle stages of language study until they reach a breakthrough point where the reward/effort ratio begins to improve and sustaining continued language study becomes easier?

There is no single easy solution to this problem, but there are a number of strategies that will increase the number of students who are interested in English study in general—or your classes in particular—and the number who will sustain their motivation long enough to reach the green meadows at the other side of the desert. These strategies have been mentioned elsewhere in this book, but a review of them seems an appropriate way to close this chapter.

INTERESTING CONTENT

It is not always within your power to determine what kinds of topics and issues are addressed in the study materials that students use. However, to the extent that you have a say in what students read about, listen to, talk about, and write about, their motivation will generally be better sustained if the topics themselves are at least somewhat interesting. Of course, the problem lies in figuring out what will be interesting, and there is unfortunately no single magic indicator that will tell you what topics will and won't catch the interest of any group of students.

Two rough guidelines may be of help, however. First, topics tend to have more appeal to students if they are intellectually as well as linguistically challenging. Especially for beginning- and intermediate-level students, an incomplete command of English will place limits on how well students can express ideas, but this does not necessarily mean that they can deal only with simplistic topics, and students will generally be more willing to make an effort to express ideas if the content seems worthy of talking about. Second, when assessing how interesting a topic is likely to be to students, ask yourself what your own level of interest in the topic is. You will often discover that topics that are genuinely interesting to you are more likely to be interesting to the students, if only because your interest can be contagious. (The other side of this coin is that topics you find boring are also more likely to be boring to students.)

GENUINE COMMUNICATION

As I have suggested repeatedly in this book, people tend to be interested in sharing their ideas, opinions, and feelings with other people, and the more opportunities students have to do this in English courses, the more likely they are to keep investing effort in learning how to express their ideas. Including as much genuine communication as possible in English courses not only tends to make them more interesting but also helps remind students of the ultimate goal of English study: to build skill proficiency that allows them to communicate and share ideas with people from other countries and cultures, whether face-to-face or indirectly through books, magazines, films, and other media.

A SENSE OF PROGRESS AND ACHIEVEMENT

As suggested in this chapter, one of the main challenges in the intermediate stages of language study is that it becomes difficult for students to see and feel the progress that they are making, and this difficulty is often a major factor in causing them to give up on English study. Often the problem is not that they are making no progress; rather, the problem is that the progress has become harder to quantify and see. This idea can be illustrated by the analogy of a person rowing a boat in the ocean, out of sight of land. As the person rows, the boat moves forward, but because the water around the boat tends to always look the same, there is little visible evidence to convince the boat rower that the boat is actually making any progress. So, to see progress, the rower can occasionally drop little floating things in the water, buoys or perhaps even little bits of wood. As the boat moves away from the buoy, the rower is then able to see and measure progress. This, in turn, helps the rower sustain a feeling of progress and motivation.

The kinds of buoys that are effective in helping students see their progress in English will depend on what skills students are working on and at what level; specific ideas have been introduced in the Criteria for Measuring Progress sections of the sample language learning projects at the ends of chapters 6–11. The point here is that one of the most valuable steps you can take as an English teacher is to find ways to help students see and feel their progress—both by dropping buoys in the water for them and, better yet, by teaching them to drop buoys in the water for themselves.

CONTROL AND EMPOWERMENT

One common danger in many EFL settings is that much of students' motivation for English study is driven by external forces such as school requirements, examinations, and demands of teachers and parents. This would not necessarily be a problem if the outside pressure were sustained long enough that students were forced to develop a functional level of proficiency in English—in other words (referring to the analogy above), if the teacher stayed with students long enough to force them at gunpoint to march all of the way through the desert. The problem is that, in many countries, the external pressure of required courses and examinations takes students only part of the way to functional English proficiency; in effect, the teacher disappears when the students are only halfway through the desert. Of course, the hope is that students will continue on the journey on their own, but the likelihood of this is smaller if students have never chosen any part of the journey themselves (especially if they have grown to dislike it precisely because it is forced on them).

As an English teacher, you are probably not in a position to change your country's educational system; however, you have the opportunity to encourage students to begin making some choices about their English study themselves. Having the opportunity to set at least some of their own goals in English study allows students to experience a degree of control over their own learning that helps enhance their motivation (Dörnyei 2001b, 128); likewise, choosing their own materials, methods, and other aspects of English study helps students increase their sense of ownership in the learning process. All of this tends to help make students willing participants in English learning rather than reluctant prisoners. It also increases the chances that they will keep moving toward the goal of English proficiency even when outside pressures such as course requirements, teachers, and examinations disappear.

STRATEGIZING

In the desert journey analogy above, the goal is to cross the desert and reach lush, green meadows on the other side; once the meadows are reached, it becomes easier to continue the journey. Let me suggest here that how close the first patch of green meadow is to the traveler depends on the route of the journey, and some routes will allow the traveler to reach the green meadows sooner than others. Obviously, a traveler who plans the journey well by choosing a shorter route is more likely to complete the journey than a traveler who takes a longer and more difficult route.

Likewise, how long students need to study English before they reach a breakthrough point where they can begin to use their English skills for rewarding purposes will depend on how they strategize their language learning campaign. If they design it so that it is as easy to sustain as possible and that it as soon as possible allows them begin using skills for personally rewarding or interesting purposes, they are more likely to eventually develop a functional command of English. In contrast, if they never reach a breakthrough point in any skill, once their formal English courses end, it is more likely that they will stop using their English and that their skills will begin to deteriorate.

You are not in a position to personally design English learning campaigns for each of your students. However, you can help students learn to strategize about their English study so that it is as sustainable as possible and so that they reach breakthrough points as soon as possible. Once students reach a point where they can actually begin using English skills for purposes that they find rewarding—in other words, once the effort/reward ratio balance tips in favor of the rewards—it will be much easier for both you and them to sustain their continued interest in English study.

INSPIRATION

In motivation, one key factor is the expectation that one can reasonably hope to succeed in a task; in other words, people who think they have a chance of success in a task are more likely to continue investing effort in it than those who think that they have no hope of success (Dörnyei 2001b, 20). With regard to language study, the idea is that students who believe that their efforts to learn English may eventually lead to success are more likely to keep trying than those who believe there is no hope for them.

From a theoretical perspective, this idea suggests that you need to convince students that there is a realistic possibility for them to learn English—and perhaps other foreign languages as well. While it might seem that this idea should be obvious to students, it often is not; in fact, many students believe that the ability to learn a foreign language is more dependent on some kind of gift for languages than on sustained, strategic effort. While aptitude seems to affect success in language study, there is little evidence that it is the determining factor; to the contrary, there is a great deal of evidence that most students will continue to make progress toward proficiency in English if they continue investing effort in reasonably well-thought-out ways.

One implication of this for you is that, as you encourage students in their English studies, you should remind them that ultimately the road to success lies mainly in sustained effort. However, this idea is more convincing to students when they see concrete evidence of it, and this is where one of your most important contributions as an English teacher lies. Unlike native speakers of English, you learned English through a sustained effort over a considerable period of time, so your achievements in English show students in a very concrete way what is possible for them as well. In this sense, the fact that you learned English as a second language is not a weakness; it is one of your greatest strengths.

For Thought, Discussion, and Action

1. **dealing with large class sizes:** If you will need to teach classes with many students, talk with one or more experienced local teachers about how they deal with the problems involved in teaching large classes.

2. **using the local language:** In classes where the skill levels of students (especially listening skills) vary considerably, one choice you will have to make is how much to use the local

language—rather than English—when speaking to the class. Make a list of informal guidelines as to when you should use the local language and when you should use English in classroom communication.

3. **grouping students with disparate skill levels:** When breaking students into small groups for language practice, one question you need to consider is whether it is better to group students of the same skill level together or to try to ensure that each group has both stronger and weaker students. (1) List the advantages and disadvantages of these two approaches. (2) Decide whether this issue is important enough that you should consider it when breaking students into groups.

4. **getting students to talk:** Interview an experienced local teacher to find out what strategies he or she uses to encourage students to respond to questions in English in class.

5. **dealing with students who don't speak up in class:** This chapter suggests that it is OK not to force each and every student to speak up in front of the whole class. Naturally, however, such an approach has disadvantages as well as advantages. First list the advantages and disadvantages of the suggested approach, and then decide what approach you think would be best.

6. **dealing with students who talk too much:** Talk to experienced local teachers to find out what they suggest about dealing with the problem of students who tend to talk too much and dominate in class.

7. **getting students interested:** Interview an experienced local teacher to find out what kinds of problems he or she encounters in keeping students interested and motivated, and what strategies he or she uses to interest and motivate students in their English studies.

Afterword: On Continued Professional Development

For a number of reasons, English teaching can be an unusually rewarding profession. English teaching allows you to make an important contribution not only to students' personal development and career opportunities but also to your nation's interaction with the rest of the world. Also, the raw material of the language teaching profession—language, culture, and communication—is inherently interesting. As an English teacher, you have the opportunity not only to teach this material but also to learn it firsthand through interaction with people of other cultures.

Many of you are probably already engaged in studying for a degree in language teaching or have already obtained such a degree. If, however, you do not have formal credentials in English teaching, the next step toward a career in English teaching would be to study for a certificate or a graduate degree in this field. In many countries around the world a variety of programs and courses are available, and you should investigate local programs that are readily accessible to you and well suited to your professional needs. To get an idea of what programs are available abroad, you might begin by checking the Web sites of the major international English teacher organizations (see appendix E). One non-Internet resource that deserves special mention is the *Directory of Teacher Education Programs in TESOL in the United States and Canada, 2005–2007* (Christopher 2005), which gives detailed descriptions of almost 400 programs in North America.

Obtaining a professional degree in an ESL/EFL-related field certainly does not exhaust the possibilities for professional training. A second highly beneficial way to prepare for a career in language teaching is through your own continued study of English and other foreign languages. As argued in chapter 1, experience as a language learner helps you grow in your understanding of language learning strategies, of the affective side of language learning, and of language in general and English in particular. EFL professionals should make language study a part of preparation for teaching, and—much like coaches or piano teachers—should continue to stay in shape by regularly practicing the skill of language learning. If you learn one language and then rest on your laurels, it is easy to grow stale and forget what it is like to be on the other side of the teacher's desk. It is thus necessary to continue to study, both deepening skills in languages you already know and occasionally going back to the beginning by learning a new language.

A third important area of study and experience that benefits EFL teachers is intercultural communication and adaptation. As argued in chapter 12, many if not most of the situations in which the students use English will involve intercultural communication of some kind, so an understanding of the special problems of communicating across cultural lines is very beneficial to a teacher. Also, you may find yourself in situations where you need to teach students about the process of adapting to life in a new culture, so your ability to understand and explain this process will be of great value to you as an EFL teacher.

All of this may seem a rather tall order to handle, and it does in fact take years of dedicated work to become prepared in all of the ways mentioned above. The good news, however, is that even in your first year of teaching, you will make considerable progress toward learning the skills that will serve as the foundation for your professional career. The road to becoming a truly professional EFL teacher is long, but it is also a rewarding journey that can enrich your life as much as it does those of the students you teach.

The Goals Menu: A Starter Kit for Course Planning

When planning a course, especially one that you have not taught before, you will almost inevitably need to make at least some decisions about the goals of the course. This is most obviously true when you are asked to teach a course for which the stated goals are either very vague or nonexistent (e.g., an evening class for adults for which the only stated goal is to "improve their English"). However, even when teaching courses that have preestablished goals, you will often need to prioritize the goals and make them more specific so that they give you—and the students—clearer guidance in deciding how to make best use of class time, how to allocate study time outside of class, and so forth.

The following menu is intended to suggest ideas for goals you might select for English courses.[1] By necessity it is general, and it is intended as a starting point rather than a final plan. A few reminders from chapter 3:

- It is good to have both short-term and long-term goals for a course. The former are limited goals that can be accomplished during the course; the latter are ultimate goals toward which students will have to work over a long time.

- You should have both content and proficiency goals for most courses. In other words, students should improve both in what they know and in what they can do.

I. General Goals for All Levels and Kinds of Courses

A. Encourage students' interest in English study

B. Help students begin to take a more active approach to language study, setting their own goals and choosing their own study approaches

C. Help students develop discipline in language study

D. Build students toward a good balance of English skills. What makes up a good balance depends greatly on the situation, but for many learners it would look something like this:

   1. Stronger in listening than speaking

   2. Stronger in reading than writing

   3. Larger receptive vocabulary than productive vocabulary

   4. Stronger knowledge of vocabulary than of grammar

II. Speaking Goals

A. General (all levels): help students improve in

   1. Ability to express meaning

   2. Flexibility and creativity in dealing with communication problems (e.g., finding another way to say something when you don't know the right word)

   3. Vocabulary

   4. Grammatical accuracy

   5. Fluency

   6. Accuracy in pronunciation

   7. Interpretation (English to local language or vice versa)

   8. Ability to interact in culturally appropriate ways

---

[1] In drawing up this menu, I am indebted to the *ACTFL Proficiency Guidelines* (American Council on the Teaching of Foreign Languages 1999; see the footnote in chapter 4). While the ACTFL guidelines are not goals in themselves, they provide a helpful basis for considering instructional goals.

B. Beginning level: help students learn to

1. Deal with predictable classroom communication

2. Handle simple courtesies

3. Ask and answer basic information questions

4. Use vocabulary to talk about themselves, family, school, environment, and daily routine and activities

5. Use basic grammar structures (e.g., *wh-* questions, basic verb tenses, plurals)

6. Construct short simple sentences with a fair degree of accuracy

7. Achieve intelligible pronunciation

C. Intermediate level: help students learn to

1. Deal creatively with daily communication situations (going beyond use of memorized material)

2. Sustain a conversation

3. Tell stories, express an opinion, explain something

4. Cope with communication problems through clarification or circumlocution

5. Use vocabulary for discussion of
    *   daily-life needs (e.g., shopping, health, transport)
    *   personal information (e.g., history, plans)
    *   their home, town, city, region, country
    *   their profession, topics of personal interest

6. Use vocabulary accurately and appropriately

7. Accurately construct short or simple sentences

8. Construct more complicated sentences that are intelligible (though perhaps not always entirely accurate)

9. Develop sufficient fluency to sustain rhythm of daily conversation

10. Develop clear (though probably accented) pronunciation

11. Handle common social interactions in linguistically and culturally appropriate ways

D. Advanced level: help students learn to

1. Handle most normal communication situations fluently

2. Explain, persuade, and negotiate proficiently

3. Produce sustained (paragraph-length) discourse

4. Resolve misunderstandings or communication problems through clarification or circumlocution

5. Handle unexpected situations, especially problematic intercultural situations

6. Use vocabulary for discussion of
   - current affairs, news, and social issues
   - professional topics
   - their own culture and Western culture

7. Use vocabulary properly (in level of formality, connotation, grammar)

8. Make few grammar errors that impede comprehension

9. Achieve clear (though probably still accented) pronunciation

10. Handle a broad range of situations in culturally appropriate ways

11. Find opportunities to practice speaking outside class

III. Listening Goals

A. General (all levels): help students improve in

1. Comprehension of oral English

2. Ability to guess

3. Ability to determine meaning from language clues (bottom-up) and from context and background knowledge (top-down)

4. Comprehension of fast or unclear speech

5. Interpretation (English to local language or vice versa)

6. Vocabulary (receptive)

7. Ability to hear and derive meaning from grammatical structure

8. Cultural background knowledge

B. Beginning level: help students learn to

1. Follow classroom instructions

2. Understand measured, clear speech

3. Comprehend aurally material learned visually from the textbook

4. Comprehend simple information questions (*wh-* questions, yes/no questions)

5. Use vocabulary for understanding
   - classroom language
   - social pleasantries
   - discussion of themselves and daily routine

6. Hear (notice) and understand basic grammar structures (e.g., past tense endings, plural endings)

7. Use knowledge of common cultural patterns to understand and deal with common social interactions (e.g., classroom activities, greetings, leave-takings)

C.   Intermediate level: help students learn to

1.   Understand clear speech at normal speeds in face-to-face communication

2.   Aurally comprehend material learned first visually from textbooks

3.   Develop skills for clarifying in conversation when they don't understand

4.   Use vocabulary for understanding
     • daily social interactions (e.g., shopping, transport)
     • questions about themselves
     • discussion of their own culture and the target culture
     • discussion of their profession and personal interests

5.   Hear (notice) and understand basic grammar structures

6.   Use context clues to guess (top-down strategies), particularly when listening to more difficult language

7.   Use knowledge of common cultural patterns to understand and deal with a wide range of social interactions

D.   Advanced level: help students learn to

1.   Understand native speech at normal speeds

2.   Understand nonstandard speech (e.g., accents, unclear pronunciation, reduced forms)

3.   Understand discussion not directed to themselves (e.g., overheard conversation)

4.   Understand radio programs, TV, and films in English

5.   Understand and take notes on lectures

6.   Use vocabulary for comprehension of a broad range of topics, including current events and their own profession

7.   Develop cultural background knowledge assumed by media news (e.g., place names, names of famous people, historical knowledge)

8.   Understand nuances and implied meanings in conversation (e.g., sarcasm, hints)

9.   Understand cultural patterns—hence expectations—for common types of discourse (e.g., lectures, stories, news programs, various film and TV genres)

10. Find enjoyable opportunities to listen in English (e.g., radio programs, TV, films)

IV. Reading Goals

A.   General (all levels): help students improve in

1.   Intensive reading, that is, carefully extracting maximum meaning from a text

2.   Extensive reading, that is, quickly getting the gist of a text

3.   Skill in using top-down strategies to increase depth of comprehension, including implied meanings, bias, and tone

4. Translation (English to local language or vice versa)

5. Vocabulary (receptive)

6. Grammar comprehension

7. Reading speed

8. Ability to guess vocabulary from context

9. Ability to guess around unfamiliar vocabulary (so they can continue reading without stopping to look words up in a dictionary)

10. Knowledge of cultural background information

B. Beginning level: help students learn to

1. Recognize letters of the alphabet

2. Recognize spelling-sound correspondences

3. Read short, simplified texts (often from a textbook) slowly (using bottom-up strategies)

4. Make preliminary guesses as to what a text may be about (using top-down strategies)

5. Recognize and use vocabulary as found in the textbook

6. Comprehend and use grammar for reading classroom materials and other simple texts

7. Use a dictionary

C. Intermediate level: help students learn to

1. Read relatively simple material quickly while still understanding and retaining main ideas

2. Slowly decode more difficult texts

3. Start building a large receptive reading vocabulary

4. Attend to vocabulary use (e.g., level of formality, connotation, grammar) when reading intensively

5. Decode grammatically complex sentences

6. Predict and guess using knowledge of the world and knowledge of discourse structures (using top-down strategies)

7. Skim

8. Effectively use dictionaries

9. Guess around unfamiliar vocabulary using context clues

10. Develop basic knowledge of Western literary culture (e.g., myths, Bible stories, other well-known stories)

11. Develop basic factual knowledge about Western history, society, and culture

12. Find and read Web sites

D. Advanced level: help students learn to

   1. Read a broad range of material (e.g., magazines, novels, general interest books, books related to their profession) with little or no dictionary use

   2. Read relatively unimportant or easy material quickly, skimming where desirable

   3. Extract main ideas, flow of thought, and logical organization from a text

   4. Build a large receptive vocabulary

   5. Attend to vocabulary use when reading intensively

   6. Decode grammatically complex sentences

   7. Read actively—predicting before and while reading, guessing from context, and skimming over unimportant material

   8. Understand Western literary culture

   9. Understand Western history, society, and culture

   10. Research topics using library resources and the Internet

   11. Enjoy and develop the habit of reading material in which they are interested

V. Writing Goals

A. General (all levels): help students improve in

   1. Ability to communicate in writing

   2. Range of vocabulary

   3. Accurate usage of vocabulary

   4. Grammatical accuracy

   5. Translation (English to local language or vice versa)

   6. Ability to edit and revise

   7. Ability to write quickly

   8. Knowledge of proper forms for written communication

   9. Knowledge of cultural information, beliefs, and assumptions of Western audiences

B. Beginning level: help students learn to

   1. Write down spoken language—dialogues, messages, personal letters, lists (material that requires little formal organization)

   2. Do dictation exercises

   3. Use proper conventions of writing (capitalization, spelling, punctuation)

   4. Fill in forms

5. Develop adequate vocabulary for writing about themselves and their immediate environment

6. Check word usage and spelling in a dictionary

7. Understand and use basic grammar

C. Intermediate level: help students learn to

1. Use proper forms for letters—personal and business

2. Write journal entries

3. Write personal narratives

4. Write creatively

5. Organize expository paragraphs and short compositions

6. Take notes

7. Use vocabulary for the above

8. Check word usage, spelling in a dictionary

9. Accurately use most common grammar structures

10. Proofread for errors

11. Revise compositions to improve organization and general effectiveness of communication

12. Write with sufficient speed and fluency to produce multiparagraph texts in a relatively short time

13. Use word-processing programs and tools for writing and revising

D. Advanced level: help students learn to

1. Use expository writing skills for academic and business purposes

2. Write for professional purposes

3. Write narratives

4. Write creatively

5. Write longer (multipage) compositions

6. Develop and use vocabulary for the above

7. Organize texts clearly, develop points effectively, write in ways that are coherent

8. Find and correct most grammar errors

9. Adjust explanation or persuasion to take into account knowledge and beliefs of target audience (Western or other)

10. Find opportunities to practice writing in English outside class (e.g., correspondence with friends by mail or Internet chat rooms, writing for publication)

Sample Course Plans: Putting It All Together

Below are several typical teaching situations found in EFL settings with general course plans and sample lesson plans for each. These plans are intended to give you an idea of how to integrate the material in this book (especially chapters 3–5) to produce a plan for a course.

Course One: Beginning-Level General English

SITUATION

This secondary school English course is for a class of fifty students who have had little previous English study. The students have already studied a few basic grammar structures and some vocabulary and can say a few common phrases, but they understand very little English—including most classroom directions. This required course is part of the regular curriculum, so students expect to do some homework most evenings. The textbook for the course contains simple dialogues, short readings, vocabulary, and grammar notes. Your school expects you to teach the material in the book.

GOALS

Because this course is part of a larger program, you need to teach certain material so that students are ready for the following course next year. To a large degree, then, the textbook will determine what material you teach and which skills you emphasize. You can certainly set some of your own goals, however. For example, one goal could consist of building students' listening skills so that they can follow directions in class. Another might be to teach classroom survival questions (e.g., *What does . . . mean?*) so they can get the information they need in class by using English. A third, rather different, goal might be to help students see that English is a tool for communication, not just a subject for classroom study.

METHODS

As much as possible, have students study new vocabulary and grammar structures as homework; they can also study short readings at home. This leaves much class time free for practice.

- Use in-class listening exercises to review vocabulary and build listening skills, especially the ability to understand classroom directions in English.

- Read the textbook dialogues aloud, and have the class repeat after you. This may be a good way to work on intonation and pronunciation and to ease students into more challenging speaking tasks.

- Have the students practice the dialogues in pairs—first as memorized set pieces and then as freer conversations. In this way, the students will get some practice in speaking and using new grammar structures and vocabulary.

- For the readings, encourage students to practice asking information questions. Also, use material from the readings to create simple reading exercises; for example, you could write statements on the board to which students are required to respond with *true* or *false*.

- Combine listening and elementary writing by asking students to write down short sentences as you say them (dictation). You could also ask students to write short dialogues.

EVALUATION

You should try to integrate your testing and evaluation methods with those of the rest of the program, finding out what methods other teachers use and following suit. However, you also need to see that your evaluation process encourages the kinds of practice you want. If your school generally only uses midterm and final examinations, you might also want to give occasional quizzes to encourage students not to put all of their study off until the night before the exam. If the testing methods already used in your school do not create positive backwash for communicative language use, add some evaluation measures that do encourage communicative language use.

TYPICAL LESSON PLAN

1. **warm-up:** For example, give students practice in understanding classroom directions by giving directions in English (e.g., *Open your books. Find a partner.*) and having students do what you ask.

2. **review of homework vocabulary:** For example, embed new vocabulary in simple sentences that are factually either true or false. Then say the sentences (or write them on the board), and have students respond with *true* or *false.*

3. **review of homework reading passage:** For example, first encourage students to ask questions about the reading; your responses then serve as listening practice. Then check comprehension by dictating simple questions—students first write down the questions and then answer them.

4. **choral dialogue reading:** Read the dialogues chorally, then have students practice the dialogues in pairs.

5. **preview of next lesson:** Introduce one or two points (sentence structures, grammar points, words, or phrases) from the next lesson by using the material in informal question-and-answer with students; see if the students can figure the new material out for themselves by guessing from context.

Course Two: Intermediate-Level Oral English

SITUATION

This intermediate-level conversation course is for a large class of university students (not English majors). The students have already studied English for several years (mostly vocabulary, grammar, and reading) but have weak speaking and listening skills. They come from a variety of different majors, so it is not clear how they might use English after graduation. They seem enthusiastic, but this is not a core course, so they will probably not have much time to do English homework. (The course was recently added to the curriculum to encourage the students to build strong oral English skills, but it is not integrated into the rest of the program and meets only once a week for two hours.) There is no textbook or tape for the course, and there is no readily available photocopy machine. You have a fairly free hand with the course because there is no standardized test or follow-up course to consider.

GOALS

The goal set by the school is to improve students' spoken English, but you should probably also set some goals that are narrower and at least a little more specific. Obviously, the main goal should be to give students opportunity to practice conversation using the English they have already studied. You may also wish to teach some new vocabulary, phrases, or grammar to facilitate classroom exercises, but as a secondary priority. A content element in the course could be based on a series of common social situations (e.g., making conversation with a new acquaintance, politely refusing an invitation) and the cultural and language knowledge necessary for dealing with these situations. Another goal might be to get students in the habit of practicing English with each other outside class—two hours a week of in-class practice won't result in much improvement in their speaking skills.

MATERIALS

Because there is no textbook, you may want to create your own. Make a list of situations that you wish to cover in class. If you don't have a book with a ready-made list, look through other English textbooks for ideas. (See also appendix C.) For each situation, write a short model dialogue containing vocabulary, phrases, or structures relevant to the situation. The dialogue should also be a good model of appropriate cultural interaction. Pertinent cultural information (e.g., what constitutes an acceptable excuse for refusing an invitation) might be presented as a brief talk or embedded in the model dialogues.

METHODS

- In class, use dictation or dictocomp (see chapter 6) to give the students listening practice and as a way to dictate your "textbook" to them, lesson by lesson.

- Spend class time on speaking practice based on the situations (e.g., practice dialogues, role plays).

- If possible, have students practice speaking in pairs or groups outside class. Alternatively, if you can make and reproduce tapes and students have access to tape players, listening homework would be a good use of their time.

EVALUATION

For this kind of course, you will probably have to give a final grade, but it may not count for very much and hence may not be a very potent motivator for students. The best approach to such situations is often to do enough testing to show that you take the course seriously but to be rather generous with your grades. In short, this situation calls for the carrot more than the stick.

If possible, do beginning and final interviews—either with individuals or groups—to encourage students to practice communicative conversation during the course. Participation grades based on in-class pair and group practice would also reinforce the message that the main goal of the course is to practice and build skills. Quizzes or tests that require students to write dialogues dealing with the kinds of situations discussed in class would be another way to assess mastery of language and culture points.

TYPICAL LESSON PLAN

This plan is for a lesson on how to politely borrow something.

1. **warm-up:** For example, ask to borrow things from several students, using the language you want to introduce. If the class likes to joke around, ask to borrow some more absurd items or offer to return things after ridiculously long periods of time. This tests their listening and introduces the idea that there are cultural rules as to what can be borrowed from whom for how long.

2. **dictation of model dialogue:** Dictate a model dialogue (which you have written) that contains the language and culture points you wish to introduce (e.g., *Could I borrow . . . ? Would you lend me . . . ? I need this because . . . . Would it be all right if I gave this back tomorrow?*).

3. **pair practice:** Using the material in the model dialogue, have students politely borrow things from each other. As they get the hang of this, you might introduce ways to politely refuse to lend something.

4. **practice activity:** Have students try to borrow as many things as possible from as many other students as possible. Insist that in order to borrow, they need to come up with good reasons—and the same for refusing to lend.

5. **discussion/talk:** Have a discussion with students about the "rules" in the target country for borrowing money (books, notes, etc.)—whom can you borrow from, how much can you borrow, and for how long?

6. **homework:** Have students meet in pairs or small groups to practice the material from the dialogue. For the next class, they should be ready to report what happened.

Course Three: Intermediate-Level English for the Test

SITUATION

This general university English course prepares students for a standardized examination. The students are non-English majors who have studied English for several years. They can understand classroom directions and simplified talks as long as you speak slowly and clearly, and they can express themselves in basic spoken English; their reading skills are stronger, although they tend to read slowly and use their dictionaries often. The required textbook consists mainly of reading passages, vocabulary lists, and grammar notes and exercises. At the end of the year, the students have to take a standardized examination that has reading, vocabulary, grammar, and listening sections. Student interest in the course does not appear very strong, although students are willing to do some homework because they want passing scores on the standardized examination.

GOALS

Obviously, the main goal of the course should be to prepare students for the examination. An important secondary goal should be to get students to see English as a tool for communication—not just a test subject. If students do not become interested in English, they may abandon it as soon as the test is over.

METHODS

Because of the pressure of the examination, students will probably be willing to study grammar and vocabulary and do listening and reading practice as homework. Use in-class time for relatively communicative forms of language practice.

- In class, review and practice grammar and vocabulary through speaking exercises.

- Focus in-class reading practice on skimming and reading for main ideas. (These skills are useful for both test situations and real-life reading.)

- For listening practice, give talks based on topics from the reading texts, using vocabulary introduced in the texts.

EVALUATION

Aspects of the course not directly related to student examination performances are probably best not included in the grading process—you will need to sell these to students on their inherent interest and value. Tests modeled on the standardized examination would help students prepare for it.

TYPICAL LESSON PLAN

This plan is for a one-hour lesson introducing conditional sentences and containing a story on a girl who finds a lot of money.

1. **warm-up:** For example, ask students, "What would you do if somebody gave you $100?" Follow up with pair practice.

2. **discussion of the reading text:** Have students ask any questions they have about the homework reading text. Then check comprehension by orally asking a few questions and having students write short answers.

3. **practice activity/survey:** Have students practice using conditional sentences by surveying each other, asking what they would do if somebody gave them a million dollars.

4. **talk:** Give a short talk related to the reading text and using vocabulary from it. Have students take notes. Follow up with comprehension questions.

5. **preview of next lesson:** Prepare for the next reading text by quickly skimming it in class.

Course Four: Preparing for Study Abroad

SITUATION

This special, one-semester preparation course is for people who are going abroad to study for graduate degrees in an English-speaking Western country. The students can read a broad range of materials in English, although they tend to read slowly, carefully, and with much dictionary use. They can understand much of what you say on general topics as long as you speak slowly and clearly, but they have trouble with natural or quick speech, and there are many words they can read but don't understand when spoken. The students are well motivated, but most also have jobs and sometimes cannot come to class or do homework. The course textbook consists mainly of articles about life abroad, and there is an accompanying tape on which the articles are read aloud.

GOALS

Building reading skills should be a major goal of this course because academic work in the West will require students to cope with long reading assignments quickly. They will also need to be able to follow lectures, even those that contain unfamiliar vocabulary and are not delivered in standard English. (Faculty may be from a variety of countries.) Students will need to be able to discuss readings, express their own opinions, and critically evaluate readings. If time permits, it would also be desirable to introduce the basics of writing an academic paper.

METHODS

- In class, build students' listening skills by playing recorded talks or giving your own talks on subjects such as culture, study skills, and university life. Have students practice taking notes. The talks should challenge students' listening skills and force them to guess.

- In class, have students practice skimming articles to get the gist as quickly as possible. Focus the discussion of readings on analysis of the author's main ideas, bias, and assumptions.

- For practice of basic academic writing skills, have students write critiques of the readings.

- Have students work independently at home as much as possible. In particular, encourage them to read as much as possible outside class, using whatever materials are available but limiting dictionary use.

- Because the students' reading skills are stronger than their listening skills, a good approach to listening homework might be to have the students first listen to the tape, taking as many notes as possible, and then check their comprehension by reading.

EVALUATION

Students in such a class will probably already be quite motivated to improve as much as they can before departure, so formal evaluation might not even be necessary except to help students pinpoint weaknesses. To encourage students to work as much outside class as possible, you could offer to go over any work they do independently. For example, encourage students to tell you about any extra reading they do. If they want to practice writing, you might suggest that they write and submit short reviews of books they read.

TYPICAL LESSON PLAN

1. **warm-up:** For example, give anyone who independently read a book or article the chance to do a quick review and recommendation for the class.

2. **small-group discussion of readings:** Have students in groups quickly discuss the homework reading, answering questions like these: *What were the main ideas of the text? Was the author objective? Was this a good article?* Stress that students need to explain and back up their opinions.

3. **large-group discussion:** Have the groups report their decisions and then discuss them. During the discussion, answer questions about the reading.

4. **talk:** Give a talk (or play a recorded talk) on a topic related to the reading, using some of the new vocabulary introduced in the reading. Have students practice taking notes.

5. **preview/reading practice:** Have students skim the next article under time pressure.

Course Five: TOEFL Preparation

SITUATION

This private night-school course is for advanced-level students, many of whom are preparing to take the Test of English as a Foreign Language (TOEFL) in the hope of studying abroad. The class meets two evenings a week. The school has provided a textbook that has dialogues and readings about life in the West. You have also been able to obtain a book with sample TOEFL materials, but the students don't have a copy. This course is not a TOEFL course per se, but you know that in advertisements for the course the school claims it helps people prepare for the TOEFL, and this is the reason approximately half of the students are in your class. The others are interested in improving their English for a variety of reasons.

GOALS

In this course, helping students prepare for the TOEFL is clearly important, but you also need to provide a general English course that will benefit students who will not take the test. A good strategy would be to strengthen students' skills in areas that will both enhance their test performance yet also improve their ability to use English for other purposes.

METHODS

- It is probably safe to assume that those students who want to take the TOEFL will be willing to invest extra time doing TOEFL-related homework, so you might organize them at the beginning of the course to copy parts of your TOEFL book for their homework. This will give them a chance to practice TOEFL-specific skills without requiring the whole class to spend a lot of time doing multiple-choice grammar or vocabulary items. Other students in the class can do homework from the course text.

- Reading exercises that stress rapidly getting the gist of a text would benefit both the test takers and the non–test takers. You can add a speaking component to these exercises by having students read a passage, then trying to answer comprehension questions on their own, and finally discussing their answers in small groups.

- Listening exercises modeled roughly on TOEFL items would be of use to anyone in the class.

- A useful approach to writing practice would be to find out what kind of writing is required by the current TOEFL and use it as a vehicle for teaching more general writing skills.

EVALUATION

In a private school, grades are likely to be unimportant or not given at all. Since students have presumably paid for the course, they are also likely to be self-motivated. Feedback on performance would thus be more useful than emphasis on scores. For students who are interested, you might also organize a practice TOEFL that simulates the general format, rules, and time pressure of the examination.

TYPICAL LESSON PLAN

1. **warm-up:** For example, start with a short listening comprehension exercise based on and using vocabulary from the homework reading. The format might be modeled on one kind of TOEFL test item.

2. **question and answer:** Answer any questions students have about language points in the homework reading.

3. **small-group discussion:** Have students in small groups discuss comprehension questions about the reading, covering both content and reading-between-the-lines issues such as main idea and author bias. Close with large-group discussion.

4. **writing:** Have students write a short in-class essay following a TOEFL-type format. Follow up with class discussion of ways to organize an essay on this topic.

5. **preview of next lesson:** If time permits, quickly skim the next reading assignment.

Course Six: The English Club

SITUATION

This informal evening class, which is open to anyone, meets once a week for English conversation practice. The students who come have a huge range of skill levels. There is little consistency in who shows up or how large the group is. Some students are very interested in improving their English, and others are mainly interested in having fun and meeting new friends. There is no textbook, and no examination is expected. The sponsors' only stated goal is that participants improve their English, but an important implicit goal is that participants enjoy the class.

GOALS

With such a wide range of skill levels and no consistency in attendance, you should not expect to carry out an organized program of study. More realistic goals would be to give students a chance to practice their speaking and listening in a communicative setting and let them have as much fun as possible in the process.

METHODS

*   Use games for warm-ups, conversation practice, and opportunities for people to meet each other.

*   Use many pair and small-group activities because these allow students to work at their own level much more than large-group activities do. Interviews and opinion surveys are especially good because they are conceptually simple—hence can be done even by beginning-level students—yet can also result in in-depth conversations. (For ideas, see appendix C.)

*   Give simple talks introducing Western culture so students have a chance to improve their listening and learn something interesting.

EVALUATION

Probably none.

TYPICAL LESSON PLAN

This plan is for a lesson on occupations.

1. **warm-up:** For example, start with a game, especially one that gives students a chance to meet and chat briefly with others in the class they don't know (e.g., *Find the person in the class whose birthday is closest to yours, and be prepared to introduce him or her.*). Close with introductions of anyone you haven't seen before.

2. **survey:** Briefly introduce the topic and a few key language items. Based on the topic, give students one or more questions, and then ask them to conduct a quick survey of their classmates (e.g., *What are the most difficult kinds of jobs?*). Close with survey results from a few volunteers.

3. **talk:** Give a short talk on the general topic, introducing Western culture and comparing it with the local culture.

4. **small-group discussion task:** Allow students to divide themselves into groups (so that they work with others they are comfortable with), and give them a discussion question (e.g., *Which occupations are more suitable for women, and which are more suitable for men?*). Close the exercise with reports from a few groups and general class discussion.

Course Seven: The Last English Course

SITUATION

This general English course is for students who will finish a degree program at the end of the semester and begin working as secondary school English teachers. A reading text is available for your course, but the school has given you considerable freedom to decide what you will teach and what materials you will use. The students have a fair command of basic grammar and vocabulary, can understand clear English, and can read newspaper and magazine articles—although only with difficulty and the help of a dictionary. After graduation, these students will work in places where there are few naturally occurring opportunities to use English outside their classrooms, and, when teaching, they will only need to use very basic English. (Their future colleagues may not use English in class at all.) Under these circumstances, it is not unusual for the skills of graduates to gradually deteriorate. While there are few local opportunities for students to use English, there is a locally published weekly newspaper in English, and English language radio broadcasts can be received almost everywhere in the country.

GOALS AND MATERIALS

For students in this last semester, becoming more independent and self-motivated as language learners, and learning how to design and carry out language learning projects (LLPs), is probably more important than studying one more textbook. Given the availability of the English newspaper and radio broadcasts, these resources would seem to be a reasonable focus for your course in the hope that greater familiarity will increase the likelihood that students continue to take advantage of these after graduation.

METHODS

- Set up a program of reading the English language newspaper, especially skimming through and picking out interesting material rather than slowly working through all of each issue.

- Set up a program of listening to radio news. Have students choose the types of stories they will focus on according to their interests.

EVALUATION

Since the goal is to encourage students to be self-motivating, you should minimize evaluation in favor of encouragement. If possible, dispense with testing altogether, and instead have students self-report how much they read and listen. If they don't begin evaluating their own progress now, they will be less ready to do it after they graduate. If you need to give a grade for the course, you might either give relatively easy quizzes and tests or have students write reports on what they read and listen to.

TYPICAL LESSON PLAN

1. **warm-up—bulletins of the day:** Have students report what they heard on the previous night's news. You are available to answer questions about vocabulary, names, or anything students ask about.

2. **small-group discussion:** Have one or two students take responsibility for organizing a small-group discussion of one of the articles from this week's newspaper. The discussion leaders assign discussion questions and manage the time. Circulate among the groups to answer questions or join in the discussion until the leaders call a halt. Then, as the groups report, be available to answer questions and make comments.

3. **closure:** Close, for example, by asking for predictions related to a number of ongoing stories in the news. Students can then check their guesses when listening to the news that night. (See chapter 6 for more discussion of courses based on radio news.)

Culture-Topic Activity Ideas for Oral Skills Classes

This appendix containing discussion activities based on culture topics has been included in this book for three main reasons. First, in recent years, English programs in many countries have begun to emphasize oral English proficiency more and more. While there has also been an increase in the amount of teaching materials available for oral skills, this is still generally an area in which teachers feel a need for more resources.[1]

Second, students need speaking activities that allow and encourage them to talk about aspects of their own culture in English. Many English textbooks, especially those published in the West, tend to assume that students need practice talking about topics similar to those native speakers of English would talk about. However, when students in EFL settings need to talk about cultural issues in English, the purpose is often to explain aspects of their own culture to someone from a foreign cultural background (perhaps foreign tourists, business executives from abroad, or classmates from other countries). The activities here attempt to cover much of the range of topics students might need to discuss in English.

Finally, to a large extent, the improvement of students' speaking ability is a process of expanding the range of topics they can talk about in English. Improvement in speaking skills is often seen as a question of fluency, but fluency is determined by topic as much as it is by a student's general skill level in oral English; students can normally discuss some topics much more fluently than they can discuss others. Improvement in oral skills is thus largely an issue of how broad a range of topics students can talk about fluently in English. Such improvement is like a widening circle in which students first become comfortable talking about themselves and their immediate environment; then learn to talk about life issues with which they and those around them have direct experience; and finally learn to talk about broader, more abstract social issues that may be further removed from their daily experience. The topics covered by the activities in this appendix are organized so that you can help students expand the range of culture-related topics they have experience talking about.

Using This Appendix

The activity ideas in this appendix are organized into modules corresponding to broad areas of culture. In turn, each module is divided into units organized around specific topics. Finally, each unit consists of in-class activity ideas. Within each unit, the first three activities are presented in some detail, including suggested goals, detailed procedure notes, and suggested language points the activity might be used to teach or rehearse. (General suggestions for how to close the activities are also included, but these are intended mainly as a reminder to end the activity with some kind of closure. The actual closing you use will be shaped by the goals you set and by what happens during the activity.) The remaining activities in each unit are presented only as bare-bones ideas that you will need to flesh out by setting goals for the activity, preparing any necessary materials, planning the steps of the activity, and choosing an appropriate closing for the activity.

While the activities in each unit do not need to be used in the order listed, I have tried to sequence the first three activities in a logical progression.

All modules and units contain activities of varying levels of difficulty, but, on the whole, the earlier modules (Daily Life, The Cycle of Life, and Relationships) are somewhat closer to students' daily lives and therefore somewhat easier to handle conceptually. I assume that you will modify activities as necessary so that they are appropriate to the students' skills levels.

---

[1] While the activities in this appendix are geared toward oral skills courses, they can also be adapted for use as writing assignments or for other language skill areas.

This appendix can be used as a grab bag to provide supplementary material for your courses. However, the modules can also serve as the core outline for all or part of a course. If you choose the latter option, you can give the course more coherence and validity in students' eyes by providing students with a syllabus or course plan that lets them know in advance the range of topics they will practice talking about. Without such a syllabus or plan, the course may seem like a random series of disconnected activities; with such a plan, students can more clearly see that they are developing skills in discussing a defined and coherent set of topic areas.

GOALS

For all of the activities in this appendix, I assume that there are three general underlying goals:

1. building students' speaking and listening skills in general

2. building students' ability to talk about and understand conversation about the specific topic areas covered

3. enhancing students' knowledge about the target culture and their general awareness of the various aspects of culture

In addition to those general goals, it is often desirable to set more specific goals for each activity, for example, building vocabulary related to a certain topic, practicing sentence patterns used for giving advice, and so forth. Students should be told the specific goals of activities and be frequently reminded of the general underlying goals. (For those activities that are described in detail, one or more specific goals are suggested at the beginning of the activity under Specific Goal Ideas.)

While the primary goal of these activities need not be to learn about the target culture per se, it is obviously helpful if you can take advantage of these activities to teach some information about the target culture. In cases where you are not very familiar with the aspect of the target culture the activity focuses on, you may need to prepare by searching on the Internet, asking a native of the target culture, or doing other kinds of research. While this requires additional effort on your part, it is also a good way for you to continue building your own knowledge of the target culture.

ACTIVITY TYPES

For each activity, I have suggested one or more specific activity types (e.g., survey, dictocomp) by which you can turn culture topics into activities that are useful in a foreign language class. These activity types are all discussed in more detail in chapters 6, 7, and 12. For many topics, activity types other than those suggested might work just as well. For example,

- Pair and small-group tasks may also work as debates, and vice versa.

- Survey, interview, and cocktail-party activity types are often interchangeable.

- Talks can often be redesigned as press conferences, focused listening, or even dictocomp or dictation activities.

In choosing which format to suggest for each activity, I have considered where the main information gap lies. In activities that may involve a significant information gap between students as well as between students and teacher, I have suggested activities that emphasize discussion between students; where the main gap would seem to be between students and teacher, I have suggested activities that highlight conversation between students and teacher.

TARGET CULTURE

In these activities, I use the term *target culture or country* to refer to the culture or country you are teaching students about. Presumably, the target culture will often be that of the largest English-speaking countries, the United States and the United Kingdom, but you may at times wish to teach about other cultures or countries in order to remind students that the English-speaking world is not confined to these two nations.

A word of caution: Some of the topics may be quite sensitive in some cultures, so consider this issue before embarking on an activity.

Module 1: Daily Life

GETTING TO KNOW YOU

Getting to Know Me (Press Conference, Chapter 6)

Specific goal ideas: Allow students to get to know you; find out how well students work in groups and how willing they are to speak in class; provide practice in actively asking questions as a strategy for learning about another culture; provide practice asking *wh-* questions (*who, what, where, when, how,* and *why*).

1. Tell the students that you want to introduce yourself to them but would like to respond to questions rather than just talking.

2. Divide the students into groups of three or four, and have each group list questions they want to ask you—ones they are really interested in. As students list questions, help them with proper question form; also put sample question structures on the board as necessary.

3. Conduct the interview following the procedure in Press Conferences (chapter 6).

4. Closure suggestion: Check comprehension by asking the students what your answers to their questions were.

Getting to Know Each Other (Interview, Chapter 7)

Specific goal ideas: Help students get to know each other better; have students practice asking and answering questions; provide practice asking *wh-* questions.

1. Tell the students that you want them to interview a classmate they don't know well and find out one or more interesting things about that person. They should also practice using correct question forms. (This activity could also be conducted in cocktail-party format.)

2. Have the students choose and interview a partner—in English.

3. Closure suggestion: Have each student briefly report an interesting fact they learned about the person they interviewed.

Advice on Learning English (Pair or Small-Group Task, Chapter 7)

Specific goal ideas: Learn about the students' ideas on language learning; have students practice giving advice (*You should . . . . Always . . . . Never. . . .*); teach vocabulary related to language study.

1. Ask the students in groups to list five important bits of advice they would give someone on how to learn English effectively. They should be as specific as possible. For example, *Practice listening* is not as helpful as saying *Listen to tapes every night before you go to bed.*

2. If a group finishes early, have them prioritize their list, deciding which advice is most important and so on.

3. Have each group report one piece of advice; then allow everyone to chime in with other tips that have not been mentioned. Write these on the board as they are reported, using the proper form for advice. Then have the students discuss which tip is most important and why.

4. Closure suggestion: Have the students vote on which tip is best.

Other Activity Ideas

- Pictures (show and tell): Bring some pictures of your life to class, and talk a little about them.

- Life Story (interview): Have the students interview a partner about his or her life story. Closure suggestion: Ask a few students to tell about the most interesting thing they discovered about their partner.

- Childhood Memories (survey): Have the students survey several classmates on some of their earliest childhood memories.

- My Life (press conference): Tell the students they are newspaper reporters who need to interview you about your life in order to write a story for the local newspaper; then have them prepare questions and interview you. (If some questions would be too personal, tell the students before the interview.)

- Special Memories (cocktail party): Ask the students to think of the most exciting (or dangerous or wonderful) thing that ever happened to them. Then have everyone get up, find a partner, and ask about his or her story. Closure suggestion: Ask a few volunteers to report on a good story they heard.

DAILY SCHEDULES

My Ideal Schedule (Survey, Chapter 7)

Specific goal ideas: Warm up; have students practice asking hypothetical questions (*What would your ideal schedule be?*); teach schedule-related phrases (*I would get up at . . .*).

1. Have the students quickly consider what their own ideal schedule would be, for example, when they would get up and go to bed.

2. Have the students survey each other on what their ideal schedule would be.

3. Closure suggestion: Have several students report the most interesting ideal schedule they heard.

Typical Target-Culture Daily Schedules (Dictocomp, Chapter 6)

Specific goal ideas: Teach terms for making generalizations (e.g., *usually, in general, generally*); teach terms for making approximations (e.g., *around, approximately*).

1. Write out a passage in which you describe a typical daily schedule for people in the target culture. (You may need to be specific about what kind of people you are talking about.) Include terms and sentence patterns for making generalizations and approximations.

2. Present the passage to the students using the dictocomp procedure.

3. Review language points you want to call attention to by asking the students to describe typical schedules in their culture.

4. Closure suggestion: Ask the students to point out differences between typical schedules in their culture and in the target culture.

Late and Early (Pair or Small-Group Task, Chapter 7)

Specific goal ideas: Have students practice specifying situations (*For dates . . . , For business meetings . . .*); provide practice explaining rules for being on time (*You should never be more than . . . late or more than . . . early*).

1. Find out what the rules are in the target culture for what is considered too late and too early. (In virtually all cultures, it is acceptable to arrive at an appointment either before or after the exact time specified—the question is how much flexibility is allowed in each direction.)

2. Explain to the students that one difference between cultures lies in their rules for how early is too early and how late is too late.

3. Have the students prepare to explain the rules for being on time in their culture. For each of the following engagements, have them decide how early is too early and how late is too late: a business appointment, a dinner, a date, other.

4. Closure suggestion: Comment on any differences you are aware of between the local culture and the target culture in the rules for being early and late.

Other Activity Ideas

- Our Typical Schedule (pair or small-group task): Explain that one aspect of any culture consists of the patterns—schedules—into which its members organize their days (e.g., normal times for eating, sleeping, and working). Have the students imagine that they need to introduce the typical schedules for different kinds of people in their culture (e.g., students, farmers, office workers) to a foreign visitor. Have them draw up typical schedules and be prepared to explain them.

- Early to Bed and Early to Rise (pair or small-group task): Introduce the saying *Early to bed and early to rise makes a man healthy, wealthy, and wise.* (Or introduce the saying *Time is money.*) Then, in small groups, quickly have the students decide whether they think this is true or not, and be ready to explain why they think so.

- What's Nice about Our Schedule? (pair or small-group task): Have the students list three good things about the average schedule in their culture (or in the target culture) and three things that are not so ideal.

- Should Students Have Class on Saturday? (debate): Have the students debate the merits of requiring students to have classes on Saturdays.

- When Is the Best Time to Study? (survey): Have the students survey several classmates on the best time of day for studying.

FOOD

Typical Western Meal Contest (Pair or Small-Group Task, Chapter 7)

Specific goal ideas: Have the students practice making generalizations; provide practice using plural forms for countable nouns when discussing things in general (e.g., *eggs, potatoes*); teach food-related vocabulary.

1. Find out what a typical breakfast (or lunch, or dinner) would consist of in the target country.

2. Have the students list what foods they guess a typical breakfast (or lunch, or dinner) would consist of in the target country. Foods should be listed so they fit grammatically into this pattern: *Forians[2] eat . . . for breakfast.*

3. Have each group write its list, being careful to use proper grammatical form.

4. Go over the lists, providing a reality check and correcting any problems.

5. Closure suggestion: Lead a round of applause for the group(s) whose guesses were closest.

Restaurant (Activity)

Specific goal ideas: Have students practice ordering meals; teach names for types of Western restaurants and names of foods; teach phrases for ordering meals (e.g., *I'll have . . . . Do you have any . . . ?*).

1. On the board, list typical types of restaurants found in the target culture (e.g., steak-houses, hamburger joints, Chinese restaurants) and common phrases used for ordering meals. Introduce these to the students as necessary.

2. Have groups of students choose a type of restaurant and—as best they can—create an English language menu appropriate to that type of restaurant. As the students work on this, go from group to group and assist as necessary.

3. Choose half of the groups to display their menu and open their restaurants. Give fake money to the other students, and set them loose to read the menus, choose a restaurant, and order a fine meal using the phrases listed on the board.

4. Have everyone switch roles and repeat.

5. Closure suggestion: Review newly introduced words and phrases. Then have the students vote on which was the best menu or restaurant.

---

[2] I use *Foria* as my generic term for the target nation or culture and *Forians* for the people and language.

Banquet Etiquette (Pair or Small-Group Task, Chapter 7)

Specific goal ideas: Have students practice stating contingencies and responses (*If . . . , you should . . . .*); provide practice explaining etiquette and customs; teach vocabulary related to dining.

1. Tell the students they have been asked to give a foreign visitor advice on how to behave properly if invited to a banquet in their country.

2. Have them first list problems a foreigner might encounter and then suggestions for what the foreign visitor should do (e.g., *If you don't know whether the water in the little bowl is for washing your hands or drinking, you should ask the host.*).

3. As each potential problem and solution is reported, check with other students to see if they agree with the advice.

4. Closure suggestion: Comment on which of the tips you think would be valuable to a foreign visitor.

Other Activity Ideas

- What Do You Eat? (classroom chat): Ask the students what they like best for breakfast, lunch, or supper. If the students cannot name the food item in English, have them practice explaining in English what it is.

- Food Contest (game): Have the students in groups list as many fruits (or meats, vegetables, or other foods) in English as possible within three to five minutes, without using dictionaries. When you call time, have each group count up the items on the list. Ask which group has the most, and then have that group read the list so that everyone can check. Write the words on the board. A group wins only if all (or most) entries are right. Closure suggestion: Lead a round of applause for the winning group.

- My Favorite Foods (show and tell): Bring in pictures of a few of your favorite foods, and describe how to make them.

- A Memorable Meal (talk, dictocomp): Tell a story about a memorable meal you had while traveling somewhere.

- What Is Your Favorite Food? (survey): Have the students survey each other on their most (or least) favorite foods.

- What Foreign Foods Have You Had? (survey): Have the students survey several classmates on what, if any, foreign foods they have had and what they think of them.

- What Would You Feed a Foreigner? (pair or small-group task): Have the students in groups decide what (local) dishes they would prepare for a banquet for a foreign guest. If necessary, they should be prepared to explain what these dishes are.

- If Yan Can Cook . . . ![3] (pair or small-group task): Have the students describe step-by-step how to make some wonderful dish that is unique to their home area. As each group reports, allow other groups to comment (and critique).

---

[3] This is a phrase from a popular U.S. TV show on Chinese cooking. The host, Martin Yan, always closes the show by saying, "If Yan can cook, so can you!"

- Fast Food (survey): Have the students survey each other on this question: *What do you think of Western fast food?*

- You Want Me to Eat That? (pair or small-group task): Have the students prepare to explain several culturally appropriate strategies to foreign guests for how to politely avoid eating something they don't want to eat.

- The Dinner No-No (pair or small-group task): Have the students list five things they would tell a foreign visitor never to do at a meal in their culture, and be ready to explain why.

- Toasting 101 (pair or small-group task): Have the students prepare to explain to a foreigner the local rules for toasting.

- Should There Be a Drinking Age? (debate): Have the students debate whether there should be a set drinking age below which it is illegal to buy or drink alcoholic beverages.

CLOTHING

What Do You Like? (Survey, Chapter 7)

Specific goal ideas: Have students practice explaining preferences; have students practice describing clothing; teach vocabulary related to clothing styles, materials, items, colors, and patterns.

1. Have the students interview several classmates, asking them what they like most in current local fashion and why (e.g., *I love leather jackets because . . .*) and what they hate most and why (e.g., *I hate pink shoes because . . .*).

2. Have the students report an opinion on fashion they heard that they especially agreed with. They need to clearly explain what fashion trend they are talking about, what the opinion about it was, and why they agree with that opinion.

3. Closure suggestion: Share some of your own apparel preferences. Also review any new vocabulary that came up.

Fashion Show (Pair or Small-Group Task, Chapter 7)

Specific goal ideas: Have students practice describing clothing; have students practice making complimentary comments about clothing (and have some fun in the process); teach clothing-related vocabulary describing styles, materials, clothing items, colors, and patterns; teach complimentary adjectives related to clothing (e.g., *stylish, gorgeous, chic, glamorous*).

1. Pair the students, and have them decide which will be the model and which will be the announcer. Then have them prepare a fashion-show-style presentation in which the announcer describes—in flattering terms—what the model is wearing while the model calls attention to whatever is being announced. Ideally, students should actually stand up and rehearse a bit before the show.

2. Have the fashion show. (Music, applause, gasps of admiration, and so forth would add to the atmosphere.)

3. Closure suggestion: Give awards for the best models and announcers, decided by the class as a whole, a panel of judges, or you.

What Should I Wear (or Not Wear)? (Pair or Small-Group Task, Chapter 7)

Specific goal ideas: Have students practice giving advice on how to dress; teach phrases for giving advice (e.g., *You should . . . ; Never . . .*); provide practice specifying situations (e.g., *For a date . . .*); teach clothing-related vocabulary.

1. Tell the students they have been asked to give a visiting foreign teacher tips on what to wear for a busy schedule of events, including a formal banquet, a job interview, a class she will teach, a walk in the park with a local friend, and a visit to the house of an official for dinner. For each event, she wants to dress as appropriately as possible according to local custom and doesn't want to seem too foreign.

2. Have the students list tips on how she should dress for each of the occasions listed above (or others you choose). Tips should be quite specific, and each should be stated as a piece of advice (e.g., *For a job interview, you shouldn't wear tennis shoes.*). The students should also be prepared to explain why dressing in a certain way is more or less appropriate.

3. Have the students report one situation at a time, and have several groups offer their advice on how to dress for each occasion. Discuss as appropriate.

4. Closure suggestion: Praise the group you think offered the best advice. Also, if you are aware of ways in which appropriate dress in the target culture would differ significantly from that in the local culture, point these out.

Other Activity Ideas

- Changes in Fashion (classroom chat): Ask the students to describe—in English—changes in local fashions during the last few decades. As they attempt to describe, put relevant clothing and fashion vocabulary on the board.

- Dressing for Winter (pair or small-group task): Tell the students they will be tour guides for a group of tourists from the target culture. Since the local climate may be colder (hotter, wetter, etc.) than the tourists are used to, the students should make a list of tips for them on how dress to be warm in winter (cool in summer, etc.), especially tips that are not so obvious. Then have the students list suggestions, stating each as a piece of advice (e.g., *Be sure to wear a hat when you sleep at night.*). If necessary, first introduce sentence patterns for giving advice.

- What Should a . . . Wear? (pair or small-group task): Have the students describe the proper dress for different kinds of people (e.g., teachers, business people, officials).

- Can You Judge a Book by Its Cover? (classroom chat): Ask the students to describe—in English—how they can guess about the backgrounds (e.g., profession, social class, region, income level) of people in their country based on what the people wear.

HOMES, BUILDINGS, AND SPACE

My Dream House (Interview, Chapter 7)

Specific goal ideas: Have students practice describing dwelling layouts; have students practice describing space relations (e.g., *in front of, to the left, in the rear*); teach house and apartment-related vocabulary (e.g., *living room, bedroom, kitchen*).

1. In pairs, have the students interview each other on this question: *If you could build your dream house (apartment), what would the layout be like?* The students can draw pictures of the layout but also need to practice describing the layout in English. As the students talk, wander and assist with vocabulary, putting new words on the board.

2. Before having the students report, go over any new words on the board.

3. Have one or more students describe the layout of their partner's dream house as you draw the layout on the board, following the description. Ask why the students would lay the house out as they did.

4. Closure suggestion: Lead into Blueprint.

Blueprint (Pair or Small-Group Task, Chapter 7)

Specific goal ideas: Have students practice describing dwelling layouts; have students practice describing space relations (e.g., *in front of, to the left, in the rear*); teach house and apartment-related vocabulary (e.g., *living room, bedroom, kitchen*).

1. In pairs or groups, have the students prepare to describe to a foreign visitor the most typical layout of a house or apartment in their country.

2. When the students are ready, ask one group what the general outline of the apartment (exterior walls) would be like and then where the kitchen would be. As the students describe, you draw the blueprint on the board—literally following the description the students give you. (Force them to explain clearly.)

3. Then ask a different group to tell you where the next room is, and so on. (Going from group to group like this will almost certainly generate good-natured confusion—no two groups will have drawn exactly the same layout. This will force them to practice clarifying instructions and repairing miscommunications.)

4. Closure suggestion: Give a prize to the group that gave the clearest instructions.

Buying a House (Culture Information Research Project, Chapter 12)

Specific goal ideas: Have students practice interviewing foreigners; have students learn vocabulary and phrases related to home purchasing and financing (e.g., *realtor, classified ads, mortgage*).

1. Assign the students a project in which, working in groups, each group locates one or more foreigners and interviews them about the typical process of finding and buying a new dwelling in the foreigners' home country. The students should ask about issues such as how to find available homes, what factors to consider in choosing the right one, and how to finance the purchase.

2. After their interviews, the groups should each prepare a brief oral report presenting the most important or interesting things they learned. (Rather than having each group give a full report, you might have each group report only one interesting point and then move on to the next group. After each group has reported one point, you could allow groups to report additional interesting discoveries they made.)

3. Closure suggestion: Review new vocabulary that came up during the reports.

Other Activity Ideas

- Renting an Apartment (pair or small-group task): Have the students imagine that they work for a company and that they have been assigned to help a new foreign colleague who will soon arrive their country. The colleague will need to rent an apartment (or buy a house, etc.), so the students need to prepare a step-by-step explanation of how to go about doing this. Things to include would be how to find the apartment, how to choose a good one, and how to handle paying for it.

- Moving House (pair or small-group task): In pairs or groups, have the students prepare to describe to a foreigner, step by step, how to arrange moving one's belongings to a new home in their country. (Tip: Rather than having each group describe the whole process, ask the groups what their first step would be, establish a consensus, and write it on the board. Then move to the second step, and so on.)

- My Office (survey): Have the students survey each other on the following question: *If you had your own office and could arrange it any way you wanted to, how would you arrange the furniture, and why?* (Variation: Have the students ask how they would arrange a living room, bedroom, or kitchen.)

- Receiving Guests (classroom chat): For receiving guests in a living room (meeting room, etc.), what is the best way to arrange chairs?

HEALTH AND HYGIENE

Health Proverbs (Pair or Small-Group Task, Chapter 7)

Specific goal ideas: Have the students practice translating; teach proverbs; teach health-related vocabulary.

1. Write several English proverbs and sayings about health on the board (e.g., *An apple a day keeps the doctor away. An ounce of prevention is better than a pound of cure. Early to bed, early to rise makes a man healthy, wealthy, and wise.*).

2. Then have the students try to guess each proverb's meaning and say whether they agree with the wisdom contained in the proverb or not.

3. In pairs or groups, have the students think of similar health sayings in the local language and translate these into English.

4. Have groups report. Different groups will probably have translated the same sayings, so you can compare the translations.

5. Closure suggestion: Choose the translations that seem closest to idiomatic English.

The Latest Way to Stay Healthy (Culture Information Research Project, Chapter 12)

Specific goal ideas: Have the students practice finding culture information on the Internet; teach vocabulary related to health.

1. Have the students in groups research current ideas in the target culture about how to stay healthy. Either assign each group a topic, or have each group pick its own. (Sample topics would include dieting, aerobic exercise, controlling cholesterol, vegetarianism, health food, and vitamins and other diet supplements). After conducting their research, the groups should each prepare a brief report—and should prepare to teach several new vocabulary items they learned.

2. Have each group report in class and teach the vocabulary items.

3. After the reports, have the students evaluate how effective they think any of the approaches mentioned might be and why.

4. Closure suggestion: Review new vocabulary with the students.

Eating for Health (Pair or Small-Group Task, Chapter 7)

Specific goal ideas: Have students practice giving and explaining advice; have students practice considering what might or might not need to be explained to a foreigner.

1. Have the students list five bits of advice for a foreigner on what to (or not to) eat and drink in order to develop and maintain good health in their country. In particular, they should try to think of tips that a foreigner might already not know and might benefit from knowing.

2. As each tip is reported, give feedback on whether foreigners might know what is suggested already and whether they would be able to understand the tip.

3. Closure suggestion: Give special praise to tips that would be genuinely useful to a foreigner—and are stated clearly enough to be readily understandable.

Other Activity Ideas

- A Healthy Diet (talk, dictocomp): Research the issue of what people in the target culture think makes up a healthy diet. Then give a short talk on the topic, allowing time for questions. Closure suggestion: Have the students tell you which points in your talk most people in their country would agree with and which many might disagree with.

- Cold Remedies (pair or small-group task): Have the students list what people should eat and drink if they have a cold.

- Living a Long Life (pair or small-group task): Have the students in groups list the five most important things people can do to ensure that they remain healthy and live a long life.

- A Healthy Menu (pair or small-group task): Have the students design a healthy weeklong meal plan, using locally available food. (Alternatively, have them design an exercise plan.)

- Teach Your Children (pair or small-group task): Have the students list—in order of importance—the five most important things parents should teach children about hygiene.

- Night or Morn? (debate): Is it better to bathe (shower) in the morning or evening?

WORK

Occupations (Game)

Specific goal ideas: Teach vocabulary for names of occupations; have the students practice pronunciation for names of occupations; teach that in English the norm is to use the same parts of speech for all items in a list.

1. In small groups, give the students exactly three minutes to list the names of all the occupations they can think of in English (e.g., driver, farmer, teacher.) All occupations must be stated in the same part of speech.

265

2. Call time, and ask each group to count the occupations on their list.

3. Have the group with the longest list read it aloud as you write it on the board. If the group makes a mistake, move on to the next group.

4. Closure suggestion: Read over the list with the class for pronunciation.

Part-Time Jobs (Debate, Chapter 7)

Specific goal ideas: Practice explaining and justifying opinions; teach vocabulary related to part-time jobs.

1. Have the students in groups decide whether or not they think students should be allowed to take part-time jobs (or whether it is a good thing for students to take part-time jobs). Then have each group prepare to explain and justify its viewpoint.

2. Debate the issue using the debate procedure in chapter 7.

3. Closure suggestion: Mention and praise some of the best points made by the students during the debate.

The Best and Worst Occupations (Pair or Small-Group Task, Chapter 7)

Specific goal ideas: Have students practice explaining advantages and disadvantages; teach vocabulary—especially adjectives—related to the virtues and disadvantages of different occupations (e.g., *rewarding, lucrative, boring, dangerous*).

1. Have the students list—in order—the three best occupations and the three worst, and be ready to explain why these occupations are good or bad. (The definition of *best* and *worst* is intentionally left vague here—the students will need to decide what criteria they use to decide whether a job is good or bad.)

2. For student reports, have different groups each nominate their choice for best and worst, and explain their reasons. This can open into discussion and debate.

3. As the students report, note appropriate adjectives on the board.

4. Closure suggestion: Review any new vocabulary.

Other Activity Ideas

*   What Is Most Important in a Job? (survey): First, have the class as a whole list the rewards a job can potentially have (e.g., status, salary, satisfaction, challenge, opportunity to learn). Then have the students survey several other classmates on this question: *What is most important in a job?* (Alternative: Have the students in small groups try to reach consensus on which rewards are most important and to agree on a prioritized list.)

*   My Working Life (talk, dictocomp): Give a talk about different jobs you have had in your life, including any part-time jobs you have had.

*   And What Do You Do? (cocktail party): Using fictional identities and professions, have the students meet, greet, and interview each other about their work.

*   Starting a Business (survey): Have the students survey each other on this question: *If you were going to start a business, what kind would it be?*

- How Do You Like Your Job? (interview, survey): Have the students interview or survey each other on their feelings about present and future jobs.

- Finding a Job (pair or small-group task): For a foreign visitor, have the students describe the steps in finding and getting hired in a new job. (Alternative: Have the students decide on the three best ways to get a job.)

- When They Grow Up . . . (survey): Have the students survey each other on this question: *What are the top three jobs you would want your child to have?*

- To Be in Business? (pair or small-group task): Have the students list the advantages (or disadvantages) of business as a career.

- To Start a Business (pair or small-group task): Have the students discuss how one goes about starting a business.

- Big Firm or Small? (pair or small-group task): Have the students discuss the relative advantages of working in a big versus a small company.

- Getting Ahead (pair or small-group task): As a series of tips, have the students list the rules for success in business.

- Life on the Farm? (pair or small-group task): Have the students list the advantages and disadvantages of life as a farmer.

RECREATION AND ENTERTAINMENT

What Do You Do for Fun? (Survey, Chapter 7)

Specific goal ideas: Have students practice asking and answering questions about likes and dislikes; have students practice stating activities as gerunds (e.g., *hiking, swimming, listening to music*).

1. Ask a few students what they like to do when they have free time. Put answers on the board as infinitives (*I like to sleep*), gerunds (*I like sleeping*), or both.

2. Have the students survey each other on what they normally like to do if and when they have free time.

3. Have the students report some of the more interesting answers they heard from classmates. Make sure the answers are correctly formed.

4. Closure suggestion: Encourage the students to ask you about what you like to do.

Entertainment (Culture Information Research Project, Chapter 12)

Specific goal ideas: Have students practice interviewing foreigners; teach vocabulary related to entertainment.

1. In groups, assign the students to locate foreigners and interview them about their favorite form of entertainment and the reasons they like it. The students should take note of any new vocabulary their interviewee uses and prepare to teach it to their classmates.

2. In class, have the groups each report briefly and teach one or more of the new vocabulary items they learned.

3. Closure suggestion: Review the new vocabulary.

A Hobby for the Teacher (Pair or Small-Group Task, Chapter 7)

Specific goal ideas: Have students practice explaining and justifying opinions; teach vocabulary for names of hobbies; teach vocabulary for describing virtues of hobbies (e.g., *healthy, educational*).

1. Tell the students you would like to learn a hobby or pastime but don't know what to choose.

2. Have the students decide in pairs or groups which hobby or pastime to recommend to you and why it would be good for you.

3. Closure suggestion: Tell the students which of the hobbies they recommended sounds most appealing to you and why.

Other Activity Ideas

- My Hobby (show and tell): Take something to class that is related to a hobby of yours. Show the object, and chat a little about your hobby. Encourage questions. (Variation: Tell the students they need to write an article about you and your hobby for the local newspaper, and then have them interview you.)

- How to . . . (talk): Teach the students how to do some aspect of one of your hobbies.

- Hobbies Galore! (pair or small-group task): Have the students list as many hobbies as they can think of in three to five minutes.

- The Best Hobby (pair or small-group task): Have the students decide which hobbies are the three best (or most fun, most useful, strangest, most dangerous).

- The Most Popular Hobby (survey): Have the students survey their classmates to find out which is the most popular hobby and why.

- Target-Culture Hobbies (culture information research project): Have the students conduct Internet research to find out what kinds of hobbies are most popular in the target culture.

- Enough Holidays? (pair or small-group task): Have the students decide how many holidays (i.e., days off from work) a country should ideally have each year and be ready to explain their decision. (Alternative: Have the students decide whether their country needs more or fewer holidays.)

- Fun Galore! (pair or small-group task): Have the students list (mainly using gerunds such as *playing basketball, drinking tea*) the most popular leisure activities in their country.

- Party Types (pair or small-group task): Have the students list the most common kinds of parties (or social gatherings, or activities) in their country and be ready to describe to a foreigner what happens at each.

- Work or Play? (debate): Have the students debate this question: *Is it better to work a lot and have more income, or to work less and have more vacation?*

- Top Tourist Attractions (pair or small-group task): For foreign tourists, have the students list their county's top tourist attractions and the virtues of each.

- Weekend Fun (survey): Have the students survey each other on the best way to spend a weekend.

- Pets? (survey): Have the students ask each other whether keeping pets is a good hobby.

- Gardening for Fun? (survey): Have the students survey each other on whether they think gardening sounds like an appealing hobby or not.

- Can a Green Thumb Be Taught? (pair or small-group task): Have the students list five rules for raising healthy plants.

SPORTS AND GAMES

What Is Your Favorite Sport? (Survey, Chapter 7)

Specific goal ideas: Have students practice explaining; teach vocabulary for names of sports.

1. Have each student interview several classmates on this question: *What are your three favorite sports, and why are they your favorites?*

2. Have the students call out the names of sports their informants mentioned; write these on the board.

3. After the sports are listed, ask the students to report why the informants said these were favorites.

4. Closure suggestion: Mention a few sports that are missing from the list, and ask the students about these.

A Foreign Sport (Culture Information Research Project, Chapter 12)

Specific goal ideas: Teach about popular sports in English-speaking countries; teach sports-related vocabulary, especially words and phrases that are often used outside their original sports context (e.g., in U.S. baseball, *strike out, throw someone a curve*).

1. In groups, assign the students to research sports that play a major role in the life of the target countries, such as baseball and (U.S.) football for the United States, and rugby and cricket for the United Kingdom. They should investigate questions such as how the sport is played, how the sport is organized, how important the sport is in the culture and life of the nation, and what vocabulary and phrases from the sport are widely used in society.

2. Have each group make a brief report. (You may want to set a time limit and encourage the students to report only the most interesting things they discovered.)

3. Closure suggestion: Review new vocabulary that was introduced, or introduce other English terms you are aware of that originated in sports.

Teaching a Local Sport (Pair or Small-Group Task, Chapter 7)

Specific goal ideas: Have students practice giving directions; teach vocabulary related to sports.

1. Have the students pick an interesting local game or sport—one that would not be very familiar to foreigners—and draw up simple directions in English explaining how to play it.

2. Have the students explain their game or sport to you. (This is more fun if you try to walk through the motions as the group explains, following their instructions very literally.)

3. Closure suggestion: Praise the group that explained most clearly.

Other Activity Ideas

- Popular Sports (pair or small-group task): Have the students choose the five most popular sports in their country and then, for each, prepare an explanation of what makes it so popular.

- If Our Country Were a Sport . . . (pair or small-group task): Have the students decide what sport best symbolizes their country and be ready to explain to a foreigner why.

- Children's Games (total physical response): Learn a children's game that is popular in the target culture, and teach it to the students, giving directions and having the students follow.

- Party Games (classroom chat): Have the students pick a popular local party game and prepare to teach it, step by step, to a foreigner.

SHOPPING

Teaching the Teacher to Bargain (Pair or Small-Group Task, Chapter 7)

Specific goal ideas: Have students practice explaining strategies; have students practice describing steps in a process (e.g., *first, next, finally*); teach vocabulary related to bargaining (e.g., *offer, counteroffer*).

1. Tell the students you want them to teach you the most effective strategy for bargaining in a local market.

2. Have the students in groups list the steps you should follow. Help the students by putting new vocabulary they need on the board.

3. Have groups report their strategies. As groups suggest strategies, do a market role play with a willing student, literally following the student's advice. (If your role-play partner has any gumption at all, the advice won't work as smoothly as promised—to everyone's amusement—which gives you an excuse to ask advice from the next group.)

4. Closure suggestion: Praise the best strategy, or offer one of your own.

Foreign Stores (Culture Information Research Project, Chapter 12)

Specific goal ideas: Have students practice researching foreign cultures on the Internet; teach vocabulary for different kinds of stores.

1. Assign each group of students to do Internet research on one common kind of store in the target culture and be ready to report on issues such as what kinds of goods it sells, whether it allows self-service, whether bargaining is allowed, how people usually pay for goods there, and whether it allows returns. The students should also make note of any new vocabulary items they learn related to that kind of store and to shopping there.

2. Have the groups each give a brief report, sharing their most interesting discoveries and teaching new terms they learned.

3. Closure suggestion: Have the students summarize differences they noticed between shopping in the target culture and in their own.

Selling Bikes (Pair or Small-Group Task, Chapter 7)

Specific goal ideas: Have students practice persuasion; teach vocabulary related to products.

1. Have the students create and prepare to present a short advertisement in English—about one minute long—for one brand of bicycle (computer, etc.). As new vocabulary emerges, put it on the board.

2. Have each group perform their ad for the class while one student keeps time. Threaten to charge for extra airtime if a group's ad goes over one minute.

3. Closure suggestion: Ask the class to vote for which ad was best. Also review new vocabulary.

Other Activity Ideas

- What Did It Cost? (game): Bring to class a few inexpensive items for which students may not easily guess the price. Then show the students an item and allow them to ask yes/no questions to get clues for the item's price. (They have to form the question correctly to get an answer.) After you have answered several questions, make everyone announce their guess. To close, have a round of applause for the winner.

- Which Bike Is Best? (debate): Have the students in groups debate which local brand of bicycle is best and why. (Variation: Ask about motorcycles, computers, stereos, etc.)

- Language in Advertising (pair or small-group task): Tell the students that they work in a packaging company in the sales department, and they must decide which language to use on the packaging of many goods. Have the students list products under three categories: (1) those which should only have the local language on them, (2) those which should have mostly or all English, and (3) those which should have about half and half. They should be ready to explain why.

- Buying and Selling in a Store (activity): Assign half of the students to be sellers and half to be customers. Set the sellers up as a certain type of store (e.g., shoe store, fast-food restaurant), and show them normal procedure in that kind of store. Then turn customers loose. Variation: Set up a shopping mall (with many kinds of stores).

- Buying and Selling in a Market (activity): Set up a market to practice bargaining, and assign some students to be sellers and some to be customers. Give each seller an object (or picture of something) to sell, and each buyer a limited amount of fake money. See which sellers can earn the most for their products and which buyers can get the most for their money.

- Get Rich! (pair or small-group task): Have each group make a plan for getting rich in business. They should decide what would they sell, to whom, where, and so on.

- I Want My Money Back! (activity): Divide the students into two groups: merchants and customers. Each customer needs an item that he or she will try to return to the merchant for a refund, and should prepare to explain why he or she should be allowed to return it; the merchant explains why not to give a refund. (Either have the students bring in items, or you prepare some.) If time permits, switch roles or partners. Closure suggestion: Ask volunteers to share the best explanations (excuses) they heard.

- Returns (debate): Have the students debate whether stores should allow customers to return items they are not satisfied with.

- Store Genres (pair or small-group task): Have the students make a list for a foreign visitor describing the different kinds of stores in their country and what one would buy there.

TRANSPORT AND TRAFFIC

Road Safety (Pair or Small-Group Task, Chapter 7)

Specific goal ideas: Have students practice trying to think from the perspective of an outsider; have students practice giving advice; teach vocabulary and phrases related to traffic (e.g., *stay in your own lane, look before you pass*).

1. Tell the students that a foreigner wants their advice on how to stay safe when biking (driving, etc.) on crowded streets in their country.

2. Have the students list the five most important safety tips they think a foreigner would need.

3. As students report, as appropriate ask them to explain why each tip is important.

4. Closure suggestion: Let the students know which of the tips you think would be most useful for a foreigner.

Improving Transport (Pair or Small-Group Task, Chapter 7)

Specific goal ideas: Have students practice making a case and stating a rationale; teach vocabulary for kinds of transport (e.g., *subway system, bus system*).

1. Have the students call out possible forms of (urban) transport as you write them on the board.

2. Tell the students the local government has recently been given a significant loan for the purpose of improving local transport.

3. Have the students decide which kind of transport they think should be promoted the most and make a proposal for how to use the loan money to promote that form of transport. Each pair or group should be prepared to explain why its proposal is the best one.

4. Have the students present their proposals and rationales. As each pair or group reports, the others should take notes.

5. Discuss or debate the proposals.

6. Closure suggestion: Have everyone vote on which is the best proposal.

Should More People Have Cars? (Survey, Chapter 7)

Specific goal ideas: Have students practice justifying opinions; teach vocabulary related to car ownership (e.g., *maintenance, insurance, convenience*).

1. Start by having the students survey each other on this question: *Would it be a good thing if most people could have their own car? Why or why not?*

2. Have the students report the results of their surveys.

3. Lead into a debate on the merits of promoting car ownership.

4. Closure suggestion: Point out any advantages and disadvantages of car ownership you can think of that the students haven't mentioned.

Other Activity Ideas

- Which Rules Are Really Important? (pair or small-group task): Tell the students they have been asked to give their city recommendations for the revision of its traffic rules. Ask the students to place the rules in the following categories: (1) rules police should strictly enforce, (2) rules that should be revoked, and (3) rules that should be kept on the books but not strictly enforced.

- Transport in the Target Culture (culture information research project): Using the Internet, have the students research and report on the transportation systems in different cities in the target country. Close with discussion of which city seems to have the best transport system.

SOCIAL LIFE

Gifts (Pair or Small-Group Task, Chapter 7)
Specific goal ideas: Have students practice explaining local customs to a foreigner; teach vocabulary related to gift giving and to gift-giving occasions.

1. Have the students prepare to explain to a foreign visitor (1) on what occasions in the local culture are gifts normally given and (2) what kinds of gifts are typically given for each occasion.

2. Have the students list the occasions as you write them on the board. Then, going through the occasions one by one, have the students explain what gifts would be appropriate and why. Ask for clarification as necessary.

3. Closure suggestion: Ask the students how much they think a foreign visitor would be bound by the local rules for gift giving.

Gift Giving in the Target Culture (Dictocomp, Chapter 6; Talk, Chapter 6)
Specific goal ideas: Help students become more comfortable with guessing; have students practice clarification questions (e.g., *What does . . . mean? How do you spell . . . ?*).

1. Prepare a dictocomp passage on gift giving in the target country, including what occasions call for giving gifts and what gifts are appropriate for each occasion. Make sure to include a few words you think the students won't know.

2. Present the passage following the dictocomp procedure.

3. After the students have tried to recreate the passage, allow them to ask about any unfamiliar words.

4. Closure suggestion: Review the clarification questions that were used in the lesson.

Refusing an Invitation (Pair or Small-Group Task, Chapter 7)

Specific goal ideas: Have students practice explaining strategies for turning down invitations; have students practice stating excuses (*I would love to come, but . . . .*).

1. Tell the students that a foreigner has been invited to a banquet or some other social occasion that he or she doesn't want to attend, so the foreigner has come to them for advice on how to politely turn down the invitation.

2. Ask the students to prepare several culturally appropriate (and effective) excuses for turning down (or not accepting) invitations.

3. Have the students report the excuses and the advantages of each.

4. Closure suggestion: Have the class decide which suggested excuses were best. Also introduce some commonly used excuses in the target culture, and comment on how they are used.

Other Activity Ideas

- What Should We Talk About? (culture information research project): Have the students investigate the most common topics people in the target culture chat (or gossip) about when making small talk.

- How Do I . . . ? (culture information research project) Have the students investigate how to do each of the following according to the rules of the target culture:
  — How do you introduce people?
  — How do you make an invitation? How can you politely refuse an invitation?
  — How do you strike up conversations with strangers? When is it appropriate and not appropriate to strike up a conversation with a stranger?
  — How and when do you apologize?
  — How and when do you compliment? How does one respond politely to a compliment?
  — When is it necessary to say something like *Excuse me*?
  — How does one disagree politely?
  — How do you give advice? In what kinds of situation do people often give advice?
  — How do you interrupt someone? When is it acceptable and not acceptable to interrupt?
  — How do you refuse a gift politely? When should you say no to a gift?

Module 2: The Cycle of Life

BABIES AND CHILDREN

Should Children Be Given Chores? (Survey, Chapter 7)

Specific goal ideas: Have students practice expressing and explaining opinions; have students practice using gerunds to describe chores.

1. Briefly explain what chores are, and list names of typical chores on the board. These are usually stated as gerund phrases (e.g., *cleaning your room, washing the dishes*).

2. Have the students survey each other on this question: *Should children be given household chores? Why or why not? If yes, what chores would be appropriate?*

3. Have the students report.

4. Closure suggestion: Contrast the students' ideas with what you know about chores typically given to children in the target country.

Lessons I Learned as a Child (Interview, Chapter 7)

Specific goal ideas: Have students practice preparing interview questions; have students practice talking about the past using past tense verbs.

1. Tell the students you are interested in what kinds of lessons their parents (grandparents, etc.) taught them as children and how these lessons were taught.

2. Have each student prepare to interview a classmate by making a list of interview questions (e.g., *What are some of the lessons you remember being taught as a child? Who taught these lessons? How?*).

3. Pair the students, preferably with classmates they don't know very well, and have them interview each other.

4. Have a few volunteers report on interesting lessons and teaching methods they were told about (but first have them ask the permission of the person whose memories are being publicly shared).

5. Closure suggestion: Share a few memories of your own.

What Is a Mother (or Father) to Do? (Pair or Small-Group Task, Chapter 7)

Specific goal ideas: Have students practice stating and justifying strategies.

1. Have the students in groups list the best strategies for dealing with a child who is misbehaving and be ready to explain why these strategies are best.

2. Have groups report their strategies and rationales.

3. Closure suggestion: Share your perspective on the suggested strategies.

Other Activity Ideas

- Childbirth in the Target Culture (culture information research project): Have the students research practices and customs in the target culture surrounding childbirth.

- Childbirth in Our Culture (pair or small-group task): Have the students list and be ready to explain to a foreigner the local customs surrounding birth.

- Taking Care of Babies (pair or small-group task): Have the students prepare to describe to a foreigner how babies are fed and taken care of in the local culture.

- Childhood Memories (interview): Tell the students they are going to interview a classmate about his or her childhood memories. Ask them to prepare several questions. (Some suggested questions are *What are your earliest childhood memories? What are you fondest childhood memories? Can you remember doing anything that got you in trouble?*) Pair the students with other students they don't know well, and have them interview each other. Then have a few volunteers report on interesting memories they were told about (but first have them ask the permission of the person whose memories are being publicly shared). Closure suggestion: Share a few memories of your own.

- Spare the Rod? (debate): Is it better to err on the side of strictness or leniency with children?

- Who Should Take Care of the Kids? (pair or small-group task): Have the students decide who should be primarily responsible for taking care of children: The wife? The husband? Grandparents? Relatives? Day-care centers?

- Teach Your Children Well (pair or small-group task): Have the students decide on the five most important lessons parents should teach young children at home.

- The Best Years? (pair or small-group task): Have the students decide whether or not they think childhood is the best time of life, and be ready to defend their decision.

- How Tight Should the Apron Strings Be? (pair or small-group task): Have the students decide whether, on the whole, children should be trained to be more obedient or more independent.

ADOLESCENCE

The Difficult Years (Culture Information Research Project, Chapter 12)

Specific goal ideas: Have students learn about adolescence in the target culture; teach vocabulary related to adolescence (e.g., *maturing, dating, puberty, growth spurts*).

1. Have the students in groups research why Westerners consider the early years of adolescence, especially junior high school age, the difficult years. They should prepare to report their findings and any new vocabulary learned.

2. Have the groups each briefly report one interesting thing they learned and one new word they learned.

3. Closure suggestion: Have the students consider how similar the pressures of adolescence in the target culture are to those in the local culture.

Independence? (Pair or Small-Group Task, Chapter 7)

Specific goal ideas: Have students practice stating and justifying opinions.

1. Have the students prepare to answer questions about how much independence they think adolescents should be allowed (e.g., *How much should adolescents have to tell their parents about what they do and where they go? How late should they be allowed to stay out at night? How much say should parents have in who their adolescent children are friends with?*) They should be ready to explain and justify their opinions.

2. Have the students report.

3. Closure suggestion: Comment on any differences you are aware of between the local culture and the target culture.

To Date or Not to Date (Pair or Small-Group Task, Chapter 7)
Specific goal ideas: Have students practice stating and justifying opinions.

1. Have the students decide at what age they think it is appropriate for young people in their country to start dating or having a boyfriend or girlfriend and be ready to explain their position.

2. Have the students report.

3. Closure suggestion: Comment on the various views held on this topic in the target country.

Other Activity Ideas

- Western Adolescents (talk): Research and give a talk on the question of how much freedom parents allow young people in the West. Closure suggestion: Ask the students which facts they found most different from what someone in their culture would give.

- Generation Gap (classroom chat): Ask the students whether they think there is a generation gap in their country. If so, what are some of the differences between the generations?

DATING AND CHOOSING A MATE

Dating in the Target Culture (Culture Information Research Project, Chapter 12)
Specific goal ideas: Have students learn about dating in the target culture; teach vocabulary related to dating.

1. Have the students in groups do Internet research on dating in the target culture. The groups should each prepare to report five interesting facts that they discover and one or more new words they learned.

2. Have the groups report.

3. Closure suggestion: Share with the students what you know about dating in the target culture.

The Advantages and Disadvantages of Matchmaking (Pair or Small-Group Task, Chapter 7)
Specific goal ideas: Have students practice stating advantages and disadvantages.

1. Tell the students that in virtually every culture some people seem to like matchmaking.

2. Have the students list the advantages and disadvantages of matchmaking as a way to help single people find mates.

3. Have the students report.

4. Closure suggestion: Share what you know about how people matchmake in the target culture.

Advice Columns (Problem-Solving Situation, Chapter 6)
Specific goal ideas: Have students practice focused listening; have students practice giving advice.

1. Find (or write) a short letter from a personal advice column in a magazine or newspaper (e.g., Dear Abby, Dear Clare Rayner).

2. Read the letter to the students, and have them take notes on the situation described so that they can respond to it.

3. Have the students play the role of advice columnist in groups and jointly write a response.

4. Have each group read its response to the class.

5. Closure suggestion: Present the advice actually given by the source from which you got the original letter, and see how it matches any of the students' suggestions. You might also collect the students' written responses and give feedback on the language and content.

Other Activity Ideas

- Meeting Your Mate (pair or small-group task): Have the students prepare to explain to a curious foreign visitor ways couples usually first meet in their country. Closure suggestion: Comment on differences between the local culture and the target culture.

- What Is *Love*? (pair or small-group task): Ask the students to explain what they think love really means (in their context). Give them a few minutes to think and jot down notes. Then have the students share their ideas and try to come to agreement. Each group should be ready to present an explanation that group members (more or less) agree on.

- The Ideal Boyfriend or Girlfriend (pair or small-group task): Divide the class into small groups composed of either all women or all men. Have the women list the characteristics of the ideal boyfriend; have the men do the same for the ideal girlfriend. Then have the women report their top five characteristics, have the men report their top five, and ask how each group feels about the expectations of the other.

- Cupid Tricks (pair or small-group task): Have the students list clever ways to introduce two people who would make a good couple.

- How Much Say Should They Have? (pair or small-group task): Have the students decide how much influence parents should have in deciding whom their children marry.

- Who Makes the First Move? (pair or small-group task): Ask the students to decide whether it should be acceptable for women in their culture to invite men out.

- Blind Dates? (pair or small-group task): Explain what a blind date is, and then have the students list advantages and disadvantages of blind dates.

- Right? (pair or small-group task): How do you know which person is Mr. Right or Miss Right? Have the students list the most important signs.

MARRIAGE

Wedding Pictures (Culture Information Research Project, Chapter 12)

Specific goal ideas: Have students learn about wedding customs in the target culture; teach wedding-related vocabulary (e.g., *bride, groom, bouquet*).

1. Have the students in groups research the steps in a typical wedding in the target culture. They should be ready to report the typical steps and also new vocabulary they encountered.

2. In class, have one group report and briefly explain the first step as you write it on the board. Then have another group report the next step, and so on.

3. Have groups report and teach new vocabulary they learned.

4. Closure suggestion: Lead into Mock Wedding below.

Mock Wedding (Total Physical Response, Chapter 6)

Specific goal ideas: Teach wedding-related vocabulary and phrases (e.g., *If anyone has any objections, let them speak now or forever hold their peace. Do you take this man/woman . . . ?*).

1. Tell the students you want to teach wedding-related vocabulary and phrases by walking them through a typical wedding ceremony in the target culture.

2. Assign roles to everyone in the class (or have them draw roles from a hat), and explain everyone's duties. Put key phrases and vocabulary on the board. (You might even dictate some of the key phrases.)

3. Arrange the furniture in the room as best you can, and walk everyone through the rehearsal—you give directions, and the students respond by following instructions.

4. Close by having the wedding—maybe even take pictures.

Tips on a Happy Marriage (Pair or Small-Group Task, Chapter 7)

Specific goal ideas: Have students practice viewing issues from another's perspective.

1. In same-sex groupings, have the students list tips on what wives and husbands should or should not do in order to have a happy marriage. Men list tips they think women would suggest; women list tips they think men would suggest. You might want to have the students use sentence completion (e.g., *Men would say that wives should always . . . .*).

2. After women suggest a tip they think men would suggest, have the men comment on whether the tip is one they would actually give, in other words, how well the women understood their perspective. Then do the reverse. On the board, list tips on which consensus is reached.

3. Closure suggestion: Praise the group that seemed best able to see things from the other's viewpoint.

Other Activity Ideas

• Please Can I Marry Him or Her? (pair or small-group task): What do you do if you want your parents' approval to marry someone they don't like? Have the students list strategies.

• To Marry or Not? (pair or small-group task): Divide the class into A and B teams. (If the class is large, divide A and B into smaller teams.) Have the A team list the advantages of being single and the disadvantages of being married; have the B team list the opposite. Then discuss or debate.

• The Ideal Mate (pair or small-group task): Have the students list the most important characteristics of the ideal wife or husband.

• Should Cutting the Knot Be Easy? (pair or small-group task): Have the students decide whether it should be easy (with regard to law and procedure) to get a divorce, and have them list reasons for their position.

ADULTHOOD AND CAREERS

Getting a Promotion (Pair or Small-Group Task, Chapter 7)

Specific goal ideas: Have students practice explaining strategies and their relative advantages; teach vocabulary and phrases related to career advancement (e.g., *promotion, good relations*).

1. Begin with a quick survey, having the students ask each other what kind of job they want after graduation (or already have). As they report, ascertain the kind of job that most students seem interested in.

2. Using a job that many students seem interested in, have them list strategies that are commonly used in their country for getting a promotion. (Alternative: List strategies for getting a raise.) Each needs to be clearly explained.

3. Have the students report.

4. Closure suggestion: Have the students discuss the relative advantages and disadvantages of the strategies suggested.

Saving for the Future (Pair or Small-Group Task, Chapter 7)

Specific goal ideas: Teach vocabulary related to savings (e.g., *bank account, investments*).

1. Ask the students what advice they would give to a couple—married, about thirty-five years old, with one child—about how much of their income they should be saving. What percentage of their income should the couple try to save, and what they should do with that money (e.g., invest it? put it in a bank?).

2. Have the students come up with a plan, stated as advice to the couple (e.g., *They should try to save . . . each month.*).

3. As the students report, have them discuss the relative merits of their plans.

4. Closure suggestion: Give the students advice on saving.

Success (Pair or Small-Group Task, Chapter 7)

Specific goal ideas: Have students practice discussing and justifying priorities; have students practice stating criteria (factors) as nouns.

1. Have the students list factors that might be used as criteria for deciding whether one is successful or not (e.g., wealth, health).

2. Have the students in groups decide—in order of priority—which three criteria are most important and give their rationale for each choice.

3. Have each group report the criteria ranked as most important, and discuss them.

4. Closure suggestion: Share your own ideas on what factors are most important in defining whether someone is a success or on which factors people in the target country would tend to rank highest.

Other Activity Ideas

- The Best Age for Having Children (pair or small-group task): Have the students decide what the best age is for couples to have a child. They should be ready to explain the advantages of that age.

- Saving for Retirement (culture information research project): Have the students research how people in the target culture typically plan and save for retirement.

- To Have Kids or Not? (debate): Have the students debate the relative advantages of having versus not having children. (Only use this topic if it is culturally appropriate.)

- Career or Home? (debate): Which is more important: career or home life?

- Life Insurance, Anybody? (pair or small-group task): Have the students decide whether or not it is good for married couples (or people in general) to buy life insurance.

RETIREMENT

What Do You Look Forward to Doing When You Retire? (Survey, Chapter 7)

Specific goal ideas: Have students practice the *look forward to + gerund* pattern; teach vocabulary for retirement activities.

1. Ask a few students: *What do you look forward to doing when you retire?* Put their responses on the board as gerunds (e.g., *watching lots of TV, sleeping in*).

2. Have the students survey each other on the same question.

3. Have the students report as you list responses on the board—as gerund phrases if possible.

4. Closure suggestion: Share a few of your own retirement dreams.

Retirement (Culture Information Research Project, Chapter 12)

Specific goal ideas: Have students learn about retirement in the target culture; teach retirement-related vocabulary (e.g., *pension, investments, retirement community*).

1. Tell the students they are reporters writing a story on postretirement life in the target country, especially what living arrangement options are typical and where retirement income comes from.

2. In groups, have the students research these questions on the Internet. They should be ready to report both their findings and any new vocabulary they learned.

3. Have groups report their most interesting findings and teach new vocabulary.

4. Closure suggestion: Give special praise to the groups that came up with the most interesting findings.

Should Retired Parents Live with Their Grown Children? (Pair or Small-Group Task, Chapter 7)

Specific goal ideas: Have students practice stating advantages and disadvantages.

1. Have the students list the advantages and disadvantages of retired parents living in the same home with their grown children and decide whether or not the advantages outweigh the disadvantages.

2. For reports, divide the board into two columns, Advantages and Disadvantages. Have each group report one advantage or disadvantage.

3. Closure suggestion: Comment on the question from your perspective.

Other Activity Ideas

- When You Retire . . . (survey): Have the students survey several other classmates on this question: *After you retire, what do you expect from your children? (What should they give you or do for you?)* Give everyone a minute to think about the question before the survey starts. Closure suggestion: Have a few students report results.

- Should Granny Teach the Kids? (pair or small-group task): Have the students discuss advantages and disadvantages of having retired parents take care of and teach their grandchildren.

- Should There Be a Set Retirement Age? (pair or small-group task): Have the students discuss the advantages and disadvantages of having a set age at which people (in a given profession) are required to retire. If there is a set retirement age, what should it be?

- How about a Retirement Home? (survey): Have the students survey each other on whether they would be willing to live in a retirement home when they get old.

PASSING THE TORCH[4]

Looking Back (Survey, Chapter 7)

Specific goal ideas: Have students practice using the future perfect tense.

1. Ask a few students: *When you are eighty years old looking back on your life, what will you most want to see? (What would you want to have accomplished or become?)* Help them state the response correctly using the future perfect verb tense, and put a few examples on the board (e.g., *I hope I will have had a successful career. I hope I will have been a good parent*).

2. Have the students survey each other using this question.

3. Have the students report the most interesting answers they heard—being sure to use the proper verb tense.

4. Closure suggestion: Tell the students your hopes.

Euphemisms (Dictocomp, Chapter 6)

Specific goal ideas: Introduce the concept of euphemisms; teach vocabulary and phrases related to death.

1. Prepare a passage introducing and explaining some of the euphemisms for *to die* used in English. Include both more genteel and sensitive terms (*pass away, gone*) and others that are more colloquial, informal, and even a bit humorous (*kick the bucket, croak, six feet under pushing up daisies*) and make it easier to talk about an awkward topic.

2. Explain that people in the West, like people in most cultures, are somewhat uncomfortable talking about the end of life, so often use indirect euphemistic terms.

3. Conduct the dictocomp exercise.

4. Closure suggestion: Ask students to mention similar euphemisms in the local language.

---

[4] Death can be a sensitive topic, so only use these activities if they are culturally acceptable.

Funerals (Culture Information Research Project, Chapter 12)

Specific goal ideas: Teach vocabulary related to funerals.

1. Have the students in groups research procedures and customs for funerals in the target country. They should be ready to report on questions such as where funerals are held, how they are arranged, what costs are involved, and what typical funeral ceremonies are like. Also have them make note of new vocabulary.

2. Have each group report one or more interesting discoveries and teach one or more new words.

3. Closure suggestion: Ask the students to comment on what similarities and differences they noticed between customs in the target culture and those in their culture.

Other Activity Ideas

- Remembering Those Who Have Gone Before (talk): Research and give a talk on how the departed are remembered in the target culture, especially any holidays or special occasions devoted to that purpose.

- Wills (talk, culture information research project): Research and give a talk on wills and inheritance procedures and laws in the target culture.

- Causes of Death (talk, culture information research project): Research and give a talk listing and explaining the leading causes of death in the target culture.

Module 3: Relationships

FAMILIES AND RELATIVES

Family Tree (Game)

Specific goal ideas: Have the students practice asking yes/no questions; teach vocabulary for relatives.

1. Research the family tree of some famous person from the target culture (e.g., the U.S. president, a British rock star), and draw up a family tree for that person.

2. In class, draw the start of the family tree on the board—just the famous person and his or her parents.

3. Have the students ask you yes/no questions to find out about other relatives the famous person has (e.g., *Does she have any cousins?*). If the question is asked correctly, you answer it, and draw any new information into the family tree. If the question is incorrectly formed—or if it is not a yes/no question—have the student correct it before you answer.

4. Closure suggestion: Review the vocabulary for kinds of relatives.

Family Members (Interview, Chapter 7)

Specific goal ideas: Teach vocabulary for relatives.

1. Ask the students each to find a partner they don't know well. Partner A should interview partner B about his or her family and then draw B's family tree.

2. When the students are finished, ask them what relatives they normally view as being part of their family. Is the pattern similar to that in the target culture? Is the range of relatives with whom they interact larger than in the target culture? Or is it more restricted?

3. Closure suggestion: Review terms for relatives.

Extended Family? (Debate, Chapter 7)

Specific goal ideas: Have students practice stating and justifying views; teach vocabulary for different types of family patterns (e.g., *nuclear family, extended family*).

1. Following the procedure for debates, have the students debate the issue: *Is it better to live in nuclear families (just parents and children) or extended families?*

2. Closure suggestion: Note especially good points made during the debate, and explain why you thought they were good.

Other Activity Ideas

- My Family Tree (press conference): On the board, draw the start of a family tree—your parents and you (but not the entire tree). Note names and occupations. As necessary, also write a few of the question patterns students might use in asking about your family (e.g., *Do you have any . . .* [e.g., *brothers, sisters, cousins*]*? What does . . . do? Is/are your* [e.g., *grandmother, grandfather, parents*] *. . . still alive?*). Then have the students interview you about your family (tree). As you answer questions, fill out the family tree on the board.

- My Aunt Minnie (talk): Give a talk introducing one of the more interesting members of your family and that person's career—the more entertaining, the better.

- My Family (show and tell): Bring pictures of family members to class. Show the pictures, and talk about the people. Having the students come up and circle around your desk makes it easier for them to see; this also creates a warmer atmosphere.

- The Ideal Family (pair or small-group task): Ask the students in groups to decide what the ideal family household would consist of (e.g., two parents and one child? two parents, one child, and grandparents?).

- Who Does What? (classroom chat): Have the students prepare to explain to a foreign visitor what tasks various family members (e.g., father, mother, grandparents, children) are usually responsible for in a countryside or urban family.

- Terms for Relatives (classroom chat): Have the students call out for you local language terms for relatives as you list these terms on the board. Then ask the students to produce the corresponding English terms, or explain—in English—what the term means.

- Was Your Grandfather Really a Pirate? (interview): Have the students interview a classmate they don't know well, asking the classmate to tell them about an ancestor they are especially proud of or one who is interesting (or notorious, or unusual). They should be sure to find out why the ancestor was notable. As they listen, they should take notes and be ready to introduce that ancestor to the class. After the interviews, ask a few eager students to tell about an interesting ancestor they heard about. Closure suggestion: Talk about an interesting ancestor of yours.

- Passing on the Story (survey): Have the students survey each other on this question: *How are memories of ancestors passed on in your family?*

- Where Are They From? (culture information research project): Have the students locate foreigners from English-speaking countries that have been populated to a large extent through immigration (e.g., the United States, Canada, Australia, and New Zealand) and ask them about where their ancestors came from.

FRIENDS

The Perfect Friend (Survey, Chapter 7)

Specific goal ideas: Have students practice using adjectives to describe the characteristics of people (e.g., *honest, kind, entertaining*); teach vocabulary related to virtues of friends.

1. Ask one or more students: *What are the characteristics of the perfect friend?* Write the answers on the board in the correct part of speech. The answers will probably be something like *The perfect friend is + adjective* (e.g., *faithful, entertaining*).

2. When the students have the idea, have them survey each other on what the characteristics of the perfect friend are. The students should take notes and be ready to report.

3. As students report, list the characteristics on the board in the correct form to fit the pattern *The perfect friend is . . . .*

4. Closure suggestion: Mention a few more characteristics that you think are important but have not yet been mentioned, and teach the necessary words.

Making Friends in the Target Culture (Culture Information Research Project, Chapter 12)

Specific goal ideas: Have students learn more about the target culture; teach vocabulary for places where people meet others (e.g., *school, workplace, clubs, churches, synagogues, mosques, bars*).

1. Have the students in groups do Internet research (or interview foreigners) to find out where and how people in the target culture normally find and make their friends.

2. In class, have each group report and explain one of its most interesting discoveries.

3. Closure suggestion: Lead into How to Make Friends below.

How to Make Friends (Pair or Small-Group Task, Chapter 7)

Specific goal ideas: Have students practice explaining aspects of the local culture.

1. Have the students in groups list tips for a foreign visitor on how to go about making friends with people in the local culture.

2. As each group reports its tips, respond with follow-up questions until the idea is fully explained.

3. Closure suggestion: Have the students summarize the main differences they noticed between the target culture and their own culture with regard to where and how people normally make friends.

Other Activity Ideas

- What Is a Friend? (pair or small-group task): Have the students prepare to explain to a foreigner what the concept of friend entails in their culture and what different categories of friends there are.

- A Friend in Need . . . (pair or small-group task): Have the students list the kinds of help you should always be able to expect of a friend and the kinds of help you cannot necessarily expect of friends.

- Where's the Line? (pair or small-group task): Have the students discuss how much they think it is appropriate for friends to help each other with school homework. Where is the line between what is appropriate and what is not?

MEN AND WOMEN

Housework according to Gender (Pair or Small-Group Task, Chapter 7)

Specific goal ideas: Have students practice explaining opinions; teach vocabulary for household chores.

1. Have the students call out the various housework tasks that need to be done in a typical home in their country. Write these on the board.

2. Have the students divide the tasks into three categories—those more appropriate for women, those more appropriate for men, and those equally appropriate for both. They should be ready to explain their choices.

3. Have groups report and explain. Ask follow-up questions, and encourage discussion.

4. Closure suggestion: After the students report and discuss, comment on the list from the perspective of the target culture. Also review the chore-related vocabulary.

Gender and Jobs (Pair or Small-Group Task, Chapter 7)

Specific goal ideas: Have students practice trying to see things from someone else's perspective; teach vocabulary for names of occupations.

1. Divide the students into all-male and all-female groups.

2. Have the groups make two lists—one of occupations that are more suited for women and one of those more suited for men.

3. Then ask the groups to make a second pair of lists. Men should now list the jobs they think the women said are more suited for men and for women; women should list the jobs they think men listed for men and women. In other words, the men try to guess what the women wrote, and the women try to guess what the men wrote.

4. Have the men share their guesses on what the women wrote and vice versa. Encourage discussion.

5. Closure suggestion: Reward the side that most accurately guessed the perspective of the other.

Do Women and Men Think Differently? (Survey, Chapter 7)

Specific goal ideas: Teach vocabulary related to ways of thinking (e.g., *logical, sensitive*).

1. Have the students survey each other on whether they think there is a difference in the way men and women think.

2. Have the students report what they were told and then discuss.

Other Activity Ideas

- Should Both Men and Women Work Outside? (pair or small-group task): Have the students discuss the relative advantages and disadvantages of having both members of a couple work outside the home. Is it better to have one person stay at home?

- How Well Can Men Understand Women? (pair or small-group task): Have the students decide: *Is it more difficult for men to communicate with women—and vice versa—than with other men?*

HOSTS AND GUESTS

The Perfect Guest (Survey, Chapter 7; Pair or Small-Group Task, Chapter 7)

Specific goal ideas: Have students practice discussion skills for working toward consensus; have students practice explaining and justifying priorities; teach vocabulary related to the virtues of guests.

1. Have the students survey each other on the characteristics of the ideal guest. These could be stated as sentence completions (e.g., *The ideal guest is . . . .*).

2. As the students report, list the characteristics on the board—as adjectives, if possible.

3. Introduce basic discussion skills for working toward consensus (e.g., make sure each person expresses an opinion, ask clarifying questions if you don't understand, try to find points you agree on).

4. In pairs or groups, have the students discuss which five characteristics are most important and in what order. They should try to work toward consensus.

5. Have groups report and explain their choices.

6. Closure suggestion: Ask groups whether or not it was difficult to come to consensus and why or why not.

The Perfect Host (Pair or Small-Group Task, Chapter 7)

Specific goal ideas: Have students practice discussion skills for working toward consensus; have students practice explaining and justifying priorities; teach verb phrases to describe duties of hosts (e.g., *bring tea, make conversation, suggest interesting conversation topics*).

1. Have the students list (in order of importance) the three main duties of the ideal host in their culture. These could be stated as sentence completions (e.g., *The ideal host should . . . .*). Have each student take notes on what the group decides.

2. After each pair or group has a list, redivide the class so that each student is now with different partners. Each student should explain what his or her previous group decided and why; the new groups should then try to come to consensus.

3. Have groups report.

4. Closure suggestion: Ask the students whether it was difficult for the (new) groups to come to consensus and why or why not.

Hosting a House Guest (Culture Information Research Project, Chapter 12)

Specific goal ideas: Have students practice checking guesses; have students practice actively asking questions as a strategy for learning about another culture.

1. Tell the students that a friend of theirs is planning to go to the target culture for several weeks on an exchange program and will be living with a Western host family. He doesn't know what this will be like so has come to them for advice.

2. Have the students in groups research this question on the Internet (or by interviewing foreigners) and prepare a list of things a target-culture host generally expects—and doesn't expect—to do for a house guest and of things a target-culture host will generally expect of a house guest.

3. In class, have groups report.

4. Closure suggestion: Ask the students which of the discoveries they made was most unexpected and why it was so.

Other Activity Ideas

- Who Would You Invite to the Party? (problem-solving situation): Tell the students you are having a party. There are five acquaintances you would consider inviting, but you only have enough room to invite three guests. Introduce each of the five acquaintances, and give reasons you do and don't want to invite each. Then have the students discuss the problem, give you recommendations, and explain them.

STRANGERS

Stranger in a Strange Land (Interview, Chapter 7)

Specific goal ideas: Encourage students to imagine what feelings might affect someone in a foreign culture; teach vocabulary for kinds of feelings (e.g., *isolated, confused, excited*).

1. Ask the students to think of an experience they had where they were a stranger in an unfamiliar place.

2. Have them interview one or more classmates about the experience of being a stranger, especially how they felt.

3. After the interviews, ask volunteers to report some of the feelings they heard others mention. As you put these on the board, make one list for adjectives (e.g., *lonely, fascinated*) and another for other phrases (e.g., *It seemed very new and strange.*).

4. Closure suggestion: Share any experiences you have had being a stranger in a new place (or a foreigner in a new culture), including both the good and the bad aspects. Also, go over the words for the feelings mentioned, and make sure the students can use them properly in sentences. (They may tend to confuse the nouns and adjectives.)

To Help or Not? (Pair or Small-Group Task, Chapter 7)

Specific goal ideas: Have students consider how value-based choices are made and what factors affect such decisions; have students practice stating conditions and criteria (*I would . . . if . . . .*).

1. Start by telling the students: "We have all had the experience of passing strangers on the street who seem to need help. Sometimes we decide to offer help; other times we pass on by. The question is: How do you decide whether or not to stop and offer help?"

2. Have the students list—in order of importance—the criteria that would influence their decision about whether or not to help. You might have them do this as a sentence completion, such as *I would stop if . . .* (e.g., *the stranger seemed to be in serious difficulty, I wasn't in a big hurry*).

3. Have the students report their criteria and discuss.

4. Closure suggestion: Share your own thoughts.

You Should Never Trust a Stranger (Debate, Chapter 7)

Specific goal ideas: Encourage students to be more aware of decisions about whether or not to trust strangers and the factors that affect these decisions; have students practice stating conditions or criteria (*I would . . . if . . . .*).

1. Following the procedure for debates, have the students debate the proposition *You should never trust a stranger.*

2. Closure suggestion: Ask the students to discuss how they would decide whether or not to give a stranger the benefit of the doubt.

Other Activity Ideas

- The Stranger on the Train (classroom chat): Tell the students that in the West it is not unusual for people on planes (trains, long-distance buses, etc.) to get into conversations with strangers in which they wind up talking about personal problems or issues, perhaps telling the stranger things they wouldn't tell their friends or family. Ask the students to list reasons why this might happen.

- Interesting Encounters (cocktail party): Have the students share stories of interesting encounters they have had with strangers.

- To Trust or Not? (pair or small-group task): Have the students list criteria they would use in deciding whether or not to trust a stranger.

- Never Talk to Strangers? (pair or small-group task): Have the students decide: *Should we teach children not to talk to strangers?* List the advantages and disadvantages.

- Lonely or Alone? (survey): Have the students survey each other on this question: *Do you enjoy being a stranger in a place where no one knows you?*

- Obligation (debate): Have the students debate whether or not people should have as much obligation to help strangers as they have to help people they know.

- Being Polite in the Target Culture (pair or small-group task): First, do some research on the most important golden rules for being polite in the target culture. Then have the students make a list of tips on politeness they would give to a friend who was going to travel to the target culture. Finally, after the students share ideas from their lists, provide a reality check based on what you know about politeness in the target culture.

- Local Golden Rules (pair or small-group task): Have the students list five golden rules for foreigners on being polite in the local culture.

BOSSES AND EMPLOYEES

The Ideal Boss (Survey, Chapter 7)

Specific goal ideas: Have students practice stating characteristics as verb phrases; teach vocabulary related to qualities of bosses (e.g., *fair, friendly, well organized*).

1. Have the students survey each other on the characteristics of the ideal boss.

2. As students report, have them state the responses they heard as completions for the sentence *The ideal boss* . . . . (e.g., *treats employees nicely, is easy to talk to*).

3. Closure suggestion: Share your own list.

Motivating the Staff (Pair or Small-Group Task, Chapter 7)

Specific goal ideas: Encourage students to think about how motivation relates to their language study; have students practice discussing motivation.

1. Tell the students that a friend of theirs has just been made manager of a shoe company. The friend has never been a manager and comes to them for advice on how to motivate the company's employees.

2. Have the students list ways the new manager can motivate employees to work hard and enthusiastically.

3. Have students report.

4. Closure suggestion: Ask the students to what extent similar strategies would work for motivating students to learn English.

If I Had My Own Company . . . (Cocktail Party, Chapter 7)

Specific goal ideas: Have students practice explaining motivations; teach vocabulary for kinds of companies.

1. Introduce the procedure for cocktail parties.

2. Have the students do a cocktail-party activity using the following question: *If you could be the boss of any kind of organization (e.g., company, institution, agency) in the world, what would you want to be boss of and why?*

3. Have volunteers report on what kinds of companies they heard others mention. List these on the board. Also ask the students what people's motivations were.

4. Closure suggestion: Have the students list some of the headaches they might wind up with if their wishes were granted.

Other Activity Ideas

- Bosses and Employees in the Target Culture (talk): Research and give a talk on what management-employee relations are normally like in companies in the target culture. (Alternative: Have the students research this and report.)

- My Best Boss (talk): Give a talk on the best (or worst) boss you ever had.

- How Should a Boss Boss? (pair or small-group task): Have the students discuss and decide: *What is the best way for bosses to make decisions? Consult? Put issues to a vote? Decide by themselves?*

- One Rule to Rule Them All? (pair or small-group task): Have the students discuss: *Should leaders and bosses always be bound by the same rules as employees?*

- If I Were the Boss . . . (survey): Have the students survey each other on this question: *If you were the leader of your organization (school, company, agency, etc.), what changes would you make?*

- One of the Gang? (pair or small-group task): Have the students list the advantages and disadvantages of an office situation where the boss tries to treat everyone as equals.

HUSBANDS AND WIVES

The Ideal Spouse (Pair or Small-Group Task, Chapter 7)

Specific goal ideas: Have students practice seeing an issue from someone else's perspective; have students practice stating characteristics as adjectives, verb phrases, or both.

1. Divide the students into all-men and all-women groups. Then ask each group to make two lists, one of the characteristics of the ideal husband and one of the ideal wife. These can be set up as sentence completions; for example, *The ideal husband . . .* (e.g., *always comes home on time, is handsome*). (Alternative: Have groups make lists of what they think the other group will list as the characteristics of the ideal wife or husband.)

2. When it is time for groups to report, first have the men present their list of characteristics of the ideal husband, and then have the women compare what the men said with their list. Then reverse the process. Encourage good-natured disagreement and debate.

3. Closure suggestion: Comment on some of the characteristics people in the target culture would agree with and some on which the general view in the target culture would be quite different.

Who Should Wear the Pants? (Debate, Chapter 7)

Specific goal ideas: Have students practice explaining and justifying arguments.

1. Start by explaining the expression *wear the pants in the family.*

2. Divide the students into groups, some to argue that women should wear the pants, and some to argue that men should.

3. Conduct the debate following the procedure in chapter 7.

4. Closure suggestion: After the debate, comment on which of the arguments presented you found most compelling.

Separate Vacations? (Pair or Small-Group Task, Chapter 7)

Specific goal ideas: Have students practice seeing two sides of a (possibly strange) aspect of a foreign culture; have students practice stating advantages and disadvantages.

1. Tell the students that some Westerners feel that husbands and wives should take separate vacations so that they get a little break from each other.

2. Have the students list the advantages and disadvantages of such a custom.

3. Have the students report.

4. Closure suggestion: Point out that while some Westerners do this, this is not necessarily typical (i.e., not all couples do this). Then share what you know about other modes of vacationing typical in the target culture.

Other Activity Ideas

- Keeping the Flame Burning (survey): Have the students survey several classmates on this question: *What should husbands and wives do to keep romance alive in their marriage?* Closure suggestion: Have the students vote on the most efficacious or cleverest strategy.

- Who Should Hold the Power of the Purse? (debate): Have the students debate: *Who should manage family finances?*

- Shall We Overcommunicate? (pair or small-group task): Tell the students that some Westerners feel it is best if wives and husbands overcommunicate with each other, in other words, make an effort to communicate in words as much as possible of what they think and feel. Have them list the advantages and disadvantages of such an approach. (Alternative: Have the students decide approximately how much time husbands and wives should spend talking to each other alone each day.)

- Raising the Kids (pair or small-group task): Have the students decide which roles husbands and wives should each play in raising the children.

- He's Always . . . ! (pair or small-group task): Have groups of men list the most common complaints they think women in their culture have about husbands, and have the women list the complaints they think men most often have about wives. Then have groups share their lists—to be critiqued by groups of the other gender.

PARENTS AND CHILDREN

Child Raising in the Target Culture (Culture Information Research Project, Chapter 12)

Specific goal ideas: Have students learn about the target culture; teach vocabulary related to child raising.

1. Have the students in groups do Internet research to discover and list common ideas and beliefs about child raising in the target country (e.g., *Children should be given the chance to learn from their own experiences.*).

2. In class, have each group report and explain one interesting belief they discovered.

3. Closure suggestion: Have the students discuss what they think of these beliefs—which would they agree with, and which not?

Golden Rules for Raising Children (Pair or Small-Group Task, Chapter 7)

Specific goal ideas: Have students practice making and qualifying generalizations (e.g., *Most people think that . . . . People usually believe . . . .*); have students practice explaining and justifying opinions; teach vocabulary related to child raising.

1. Have the students list five tips on what parents should and should not do to raise children well (e.g., *Parents should always . . . . Parents should never . . . .*).

2. When the students report, have each group report one rule; as rules are reported, ask the other students whether or not they agree.

3. Closure suggestion: Share your own views.

Allowances (Pair or Small-Group Task, Chapter 7)

Specific goal ideas: Have students practice looking for two sides of a (possibly strange) cultural custom; teach vocabulary related to chores and allowances.

1. Tell the students that in Western countries, children are often paid for doing chores like mowing the lawn, babysitting, and even cleaning their rooms. They may either be paid for each chore, often at some set rate, or be given a regular allowance that is contingent on performance of set chores (a kind of contract).

2. Have the students discuss and list the advantages and disadvantages of this custom.

3. Have the students first report the advantages and disadvantages. Then open the floor to discussion of whether this system is—overall—a good idea or not.

4. Closure suggestion: Comment on how this custom fits into the overall cultural values of the target culture.

Other Activity Ideas

- Were Your Parents Strict or Lenient? (classroom chat): Ask the students if their parents were strict or lenient. Ask for examples of behavior that illustrate their opinions. Closure suggestion: Use this as lead-in to the activity Strict or Lenient? below.

- Strict or Lenient? (survey): Have the students survey several classmates on whether it is worse for parents to be too strict or too indulgent toward children.

- My Childhood (show and tell): Bring some pictures of your own childhood (or your children, nieces and nephews, etc.) to class.

- Adoption (survey): Have the students survey each other on whether they think adoption is a good thing.

SIBLINGS

The Joys of Siblings (Pair or Small-Group Task, Chapter 7)

Specific goal ideas: Have students practice stating advantages and disadvantages as noun phrases.

1. Have the students list the advantages and disadvantages of having siblings and of being an only child. This could be done as a sentence completion, such as *One advantage of having siblings is . . .* (e.g., *you have someone to borrow money from*).

2. Have the students report.

3. Closure suggestion: Share your own thoughts.

Duty toward Siblings (Pair or Small-Group Task, Chapter 7)

Specific goal ideas: Have students practice explaining aspects of culture; have students practice stating duties as verb phrases.

1. Have pairs or groups of students prepare to explain to a foreign visitor the duties that people in their culture expect siblings to have toward each other. This could be done as a list of sentence completions, such as *Siblings should always . . .* (e.g., *financially support brothers and sisters who are in school*).

2. Have the students report.

3. Closure suggestion: Comment any differences you are aware of as to which duties people in the target culture would also expect from siblings.

Keeping the Family Together (Debate, Chapter 7)

Specific goal ideas: Have students practice explaining and justifying opinions.

1. Have the students debate whether it is more important for family members (or relatives) to live near each other (even at the cost of giving up job or career opportunities) or to move to where job opportunities are best.

2. Closure suggestion: Summarize—and praise—the best points made on each side.

Other Activity Ideas

- To Be an Only Child? (survey): Have the students survey several classmates on this question: *Do you think it is better to have siblings or to be an only child?* Closure suggestion: Use this activity as a lead-in to The Joys of Siblings above.

- Better by the Dozen? (pair or small-group task): Have the students list the advantages and disadvantages of having a family with many children.

- Sibling Rivalry (classroom chat): Explain what the term *sibling rivalry* means, and note that Westerners tend to believe that this is quite common. Provide any examples you can think of, and introduce any necessary vocabulary that arises. Ask the students how they would respond to a foreigner who asked about sibling rivalry in their culture.

Module 4: Our Nation

VISITING OUR COUNTRY

Five Top Attractions (Pair or Small-Group Task, Chapter 7)

Specific goal ideas: Have students practice explaining local tourist attractions in English; teach vocabulary for virtues of tourist locations.

1. Have the students list the five best places in their country for a foreign visitor to travel to and the reasons these are the best ones. (Variation: Have groups of students decide which city or other place in their country would be best for a foreigner to work in and why.)

2. Have the students report and explain their choices.

3. Have the students discuss the suggested options and try to agree on a top-five list.

4. Closure suggestion: Suggest a few other places you think foreign visitors might be interested in, and tell the students why.

Welcome to Our Country! (Pair or Small-Group Task, Chapter 7)

Specific goal ideas: Have students practice introducing their country; teach vocabulary related to popular destinations.

1. Tell the students they will be tour guides for a group of foreign tourists, and have groups of students prepare a brief introduction to a local tourist destination. As they prepare, they should consider what the tourists would probably already know about the spot (so as not to bore them) and what would need to be explained (so as not to confuse them). They should also prepare to introduce any unfamiliar (English) vocabulary they will need to use.

2. Have each group first teach necessary new vocabulary; then have each group present its introduction.

3. Closure suggestion: Give the students feedback on what parts of their presentations might have been inadequately explained or overly simple for a foreign audience—and give special praise to especially interesting points they made.

You Absolutely Must Visit . . . (Culture Information Research Project, Chapter 12)

Specific goal ideas: Have students practice focused listening for reasons and explanations; teach vocabulary for names of famous places.

1. In groups, assign the students to research the main tourist attractions in a location (e.g., city, state, province) in the target country. They should then prepare a short talk introducing the chosen sites, the reasons people like to go there, and the significance the sites have for the target country's history or culture.

2. Have the groups give their reports. (Encourage them to use pictures, Microsoft PowerPoint slides, or other visual aids.) While each group presents, other students should listen and take notes.

3. Closure suggestion: Ask the students which of the sites introduced they would most like to visit and why.

Other Activity Ideas

- If You Could Go Anywhere in Our Country . . . (survey): Have the students survey their classmates on this question: *If you could visit anywhere in our country for one day, where would you go and why?*

- The Trip of a Lifetime (pair or small-group task): Tell the students they have an unlimited supply of money for three weeks of travel. Have them plan where they will go and what they will do.

- What Kinds of Places Do You Like? (survey): Have the students ask each other what kinds of places they like to visit (e.g., temples? rivers?).

- Tour Planner (pair or small-group task): Have groups plan a ten-day trip for a foreign visitor in their country. The plan should be as detailed as possible, including information on mode of travel, accommodations, and so forth.

GEOGRAPHY

Our Nation's Geography (Classroom Chat, Chapter 7)

Specific goal ideas: Teach geographic and spatial terms; teach vocabulary related to geography and topography.

1. Draw a rough outline map of your country on the board, or have a student do it for you. Do not include details; just sketch an outline of the outer boundary.

2. Have the students explain to you in English where major geographic features of the country (e.g., rivers, mountains, cities) are. You draw them on the map, following the students' instructions literally.

3. As the students give you directions for where to draw, have them use either geographic terms (e.g., *in northern . . .*, *west of . . .*) or spatial terms (e.g., *a little to the left, further down*). Teach these terms, and write them on the board as necessary.

4. Closure suggestion: Lead into The Target Country's Geography (below).

The Target Country's Geography (Pair or Small-Group Task, Chapter 7)

Specific goal ideas: Teach vocabulary for geographic features; teach target-country place names.

1. Draw an outline map of the target country on the board.

2. Have the students prepare to tell you where to draw the major geographic features of the target country (as they did for their own country in Our Nation's Geography above).

3. As the students tell you what features to mark and where, put them on the outline map.

4. Closure suggestion: Make any necessary corrections to the picture the students provided, and add important features they missed.

Regions of the Target Country (Culture Information Research Project, Chapter 12)

Specific goal ideas: Encourage students to be more aware of the diversity in the target country; teach vocabulary related to features of various regions.

1. Have the students in groups research and prepare a brief talk on the main regions of the target country and ways they differ from each other. They should consider things such as topography, climate, history, economy, special features, and special problems. They should also prepare to introduce any necessary new vocabulary they learn.

2. Before they give their talks, the groups should each quickly introduce necessary vocabulary. Then have the groups give their talks, using visual aids if possible. While each group presents, other students should listen and take notes.

3. Closure suggestion: Check everyone's comprehension by giving a quick quiz covering some of the points made in the presentations.

Other Activity Ideas

- The Map (talk): Bring a big map of the target country (and something to hang it with) to class, and give a talk pointing out major features, important cities, and so on.

- My Province or State (small-group task): Place students from the same area in groups. Then have them prepare to introduce the geography and topography of their area to the rest of the class in English.

- Geography and Me (pair or small-group task): Have the students list ways in which the geography of their province (region, etc.) affects life there.

- Economic Regions (pair or small-group task): Have the students prepare to describe the different economic regions of their country to foreign visitors.

- Famous Peaks (pair or small-group task): Have the students prepare to describe the most famous land features (e.g., mountains, rivers, deserts) in their country to foreign visitors.

- By Land or by Sea? (pair or small-group task): Have the students list the advantages, the disadvantages, or both of living near the seacoast or in the mountains.

THE CLIMATE

Packing List (Pair or Small-Group Task, Chapter 7)

Specific goal ideas: Have students practice describing local climate and weather in English; teach vocabulary related to climate, weather, and clothing.

1. Tell the students that they have been asked to write an e-mail message to a foreign tour group that will visit their country advising the group on what the local weather will be like and what kind of suitable clothing group members should bring.

2. Divide the students into groups, and assign each group one season of the local year. Then have them write their e-mail message.

3. Have each group read their e-mail message aloud, teaching any necessary new vocabulary.

4. Closure suggestion: Comment on what tips would probably be very useful to the foreign group—and what points might be a little too obvious or unclear.

Staying Cool (Pair or Small-Group Task, Chapter 7)

Specific goal ideas: Have students practice giving advice; teach vocabulary related to climate and weather.

1. Have the students in groups list five tips to suggest to foreign visitors for staying cool in the summer (or staying warm in winter, coping with high humidity, coping with very dry climates, or staying safe in a typhoon or blizzard).

2. Have each group offer its best tip, put each on the board, and then vote on which is best.

3. Closure suggestion: Review newly introduced vocabulary.

Extreme Weather (Focused Listening, Chapter 6)

Specific goal ideas: Have students practice focused listening; teach vocabulary relating to kinds of storms.

1. Prepare a talk in which you introduce the types of storms and extreme weather experienced in the target country.

2. On the board, list the names of different types of storms you will discuss. Ask the students to take notes as they listen and be prepared to explain what these different kinds of storms are and how they differ from one another.

3. Give the talk.

4. Closure suggestion: Ask the students to tell you the difference between the different kinds of storms, using the pattern *The difference between . . . and . . . is that . . . .*

Other Activity Ideas

- The Rain in Spain (culture information research project): Have the students research the climate in different parts of the target country and prepare a presentation. They should make special note of unusual or extreme climates.

- The Perfect Storm (survey): First, have the students list as many kinds of storms and natural disasters as they can think of. Then have the students survey each other on which of these natural disasters they think is most frightening and why. Closure suggestion: Tell the students which of these you would least—or most—like to experience.

- The Perfect Climate (survey): Have the students survey each other on what they think the perfect climate would be. (Alternatives: *What is the best season of the year? What is the most perfect possible kind of weather? The worst?*)

- Weather Porn (pair or small-group task): Mention that in many countries, documentaries about extreme weather and other natural disasters are a common and popular form of TV programming. Have them discuss why this might be so and list possible reasons.

- It's All in the Climate (pair or small-group task): Have the students prepare to explain to a foreigner the ways the climate of their country influences its culture.

ANIMALS AND PLANTS

Useful Creatures (Survey, Chapter 7)

Specific goal ideas: Have students practice using the plural form of countable nouns when discussing something in general; teach vocabulary for animal names.

1. Ask one or more students to tell you what kinds of animals are most useful (dangerous, interesting, friendly, etc.). Note that the correct response should generally be in the plural (dogs, cats, tigers, etc.).

2. Have the students survey each other on this question: *What kinds of animals are most useful? Most dangerous? Nicest?* As they respond, they should use the plural form when the animal name is a countable noun.

3. Have the students report some of the more interesting responses they heard.

4. Closure suggestion: As necessary, go over the names of animals for pronunciation and plural form.

Dirty as a Pig (Talk, Chapter 6; Pair or Small-Group Task, Chapter 7)

Specific goal ideas: Have students practice explaining aspects of the local culture in English; have students practice stating qualities as adjectives; teach vocabulary for qualities and animal names.

1. Research and give a brief talk on what qualities are associated with different animals in the target culture (e.g., in the West, pigs = dirty; lions = brave; foxes = crafty).

2. Have the students list animals and the qualities that their culture associates with them so that they could explain these to a foreign visitor. (Remind them that when speaking of animals in general, the plural form of countable nouns is used, e.g., *lions, foxes.*)

3. Have the students report. Ask the students to explain any associations that would not be immediately obvious to a foreigner.

4. Closure suggestion: Review vocabulary related to qualities that arose during the activity. Make sure the students know the proper part of speech for each quality. (For this situation, this would normally be the adjective form.)

Flora and Fauna (Pair or Small-Group Task, Chapter 7)

Specific goal ideas: Have students practice explaining local plants and animals in English; teach vocabulary related to plants and animals.

1. Prepare to take the students through a short nature hike in the target country using pictures (photographs, Microsoft PowerPoint slides, etc.).

2. Have the students in pairs or groups imagine they are going to lead a group of foreign tourists on a nature hike to introduce the main plants and animals that are important in their country. (This hike could be set in a city park, the local countryside, or a national park.) They should be prepared to name and introduce these plants and animals in English.

3. Have each pair or group report by naming a plant or animal, describing it, and saying something about why it is interesting (important, dangerous, etc.).

4. Closure suggestion: Take the students through your target-country nature hike.

Other Activity Ideas

- As Tough as Hickory (culture information research project): Research and give a talk on the main plants (trees, flowers, etc.) in the target country and what they symbolize.

- Local Plant Life 101 (pair or small-group task): Have the students list five plants (trees, flowers, etc.) that everyone in their country would recognize and that every visitor to their country should recognize. Have them be ready to describe the plants and why it is important to recognize them.

HOLIDAYS

My Favorite Holiday (Survey, Chapter 7)

Specific goal ideas: Introduce the topic of holidays; teach English names of local holidays.

1. Have the students survey each other on this question: *Which is your favorite holiday and why? Which is your least favorite holiday and why?*

2. As the students report, list the names of holidays on the board in their best known English translation.

3. Closure suggestion: Tell about your own favorite holiday and why you like it.

Listing Holidays (Pair or Small-Group Task, Chapter 7)

Specific goal ideas: Teach holiday names and holiday-related vocabulary.

1. Make sure you know the major target country holidays, when and how they are celebrated, and what their origins are.

2. Put a table on the board with columns for the following: *Holiday Name, Date, How Celebrated, Origin.*

3. Have the students in groups list as many of the holidays of the target country as they can think of and fill in the graph as best they can.

4. Tell groups they get one point for every box in the graph they have filled in. Have them count up their scores and report.

5. Starting with the group that reports the highest score, choose one holiday (preferably a relatively obscure one), and have the students report what they put in each box they claimed points for. If they get anything wrong, praise their courage, disqualify them, and move on to the next group. If a group gets everything right, that group wins.

6. Ask the students which holidays they knew least about, and then hold a question-and-answer session about them.

7. Closure suggestion: Review holiday names.

A New Holiday (Pair or Small-Group Task, Chapter 7)

Specific goal ideas: Have students practice explaining and justifying opinions; teach holiday-related vocabulary.

1. Have the students in groups invent a new holiday for their country and plan how to celebrate it.

2. Have each group introduce its proposal.

3. Closure suggestion: Have the class choose the best (the most creative, the most fun, etc.) new holiday.

Other Activity Ideas

- The Top Ten Holidays (pair or small-group task): Have the students in groups list their culture's ten most important holidays in order of importance. As groups report, have them justify the rankings they gave.

- What Do You Know About . . . ? (culture information research project): In groups, assign the students a target country holiday, preferably one they don't know much about, and have them research it for a presentation.

- Christmas in the Target Culture (press conference): Research one holiday of the target culture in some detail, and then have the students interview you about it.

- Why a Christmas Tree? (pair or small-group task): Introduce a custom of a target-culture holiday that the students won't know the origin of (e.g., Christmas trees, trick-or-treating). Have groups of students discuss the issue, make one guess as to the origin, and present the guess. Award one prize (e.g., a piece of candy per group member) for the closest guess, one for the most original, and so on. To close, explain the origin.

HISTORY

History Talk (Pair or Small-Group Task, Chapter 7)

Specific goal ideas: Have students practice explaining local history in English.

1. Tell the students they have been asked to give a short talk on their country's history to a visiting group of foreign guests.

2. Have the students in groups choose three important events they would focus on and prepare talking points for an interesting explanation of each. (They should keep in mind that it is important not to bore or confuse their audience.)

3. Have the groups each report on one event and list their talking points.

4. After each group reports, move into discussion of the relative importance of each talking point.

5. Closure suggestion: Comment on which points you think a foreign audience would find especially interesting.

History Time Line (Pair or Small-Group Task, Chapter 7)

Specific goal ideas: Have students practice talking about the target culture's history; teach vocabulary related to the target culture's history.

1. Have the students in groups list as many major events in the history of the target country as they can think of in approximate chronological order. (Exact dates are not necessary.) As the groups work on this, assist them with vocabulary as needed.

2. Draw a long horizontal line on the board, possibly marked with year dates (e.g., 1500, 1600, 1700, 1800, 1850, 1900, 1950). Then have groups contribute events one at a time as you write them in on the time line.

3. Mention a few other important events that you have prepared to say a little about.

4. Closure suggestion: Have the students choose the five events that they think people in the target country would probably list as being the five most important in their history. Comment on their choices.

History as the Target Culture Sees It (Culture Information Research Project, Chapter 12)

Specific goal ideas: Have students gain a better understanding of how people in the target country view their own history; teach vocabulary related to the target country's history.

1. Have the students in groups locate a person from the target country and interview him or her on the history of the target country as the average person in the target country sees it.

2. Based on what they learned in their interview, have the groups each prepare to introduce one or more pieces of information that they found especially interesting and one or more new vocabulary words.

3. Have the groups report.

4. Closure suggestion: Comment on which pieces of information in the reports you found especially interesting.

Other Activity Ideas

- Proudest Moments (pair or small-group task): Have the students list the achievements in their history that people are proudest of and be ready to explain these to a foreign visitor. (Alternative: Have them list their country's achievements of the past ten years.)

- Back to the Future? (debate): Have the students debate this question: *Does a country's past determine its future?*

- Those Who Do Not Study the Past . . . (survey): Have the students survey each other on these questions: *Is it important to study your own country's history? Why or why not? How about the history of other countries? Why or why not?*

- Ten Years from Now (pair or small-group task): Have the students decide what their country might be like ten years from now.

- Local History (pair or small-group task): Have the students decide what points they would include if they were asked to give a short talk on local (i.e., regional or city) history.

CONTACT WITH OTHER COUNTRIES

Borrowing from the Neighbors (Pair or Small-Group Task, Chapter 7)

Specific goal ideas: Have students practice explaining aspects of the local culture in English; teach vocabulary related to (borrowed) aspects of culture.

1. Have the students list elements (e.g., customs, artifacts, institutions, technology) other cultures have borrowed from their culture and also elements their culture has borrowed from other countries.

2. First, have the students report the things other countries or cultures have borrowed from theirs, explaining what was borrowed, who borrowed it, and how. Then have the students report on what their culture borrowed from others.

3. Have the students discuss what kinds of elements they think should and should not be borrowed from other cultures.

4. Closure suggestion: Make the point that as long as there is interaction between cultures, cultural borrowing is natural and virtually inevitable.

Who Shaped Us? (Culture Information Research Project, Chapter 12)

Specific goal ideas: Encourage students to see the target culture in part as the product of cultural borrowing; teach vocabulary related to the influence of other cultures on the target culture.

1. In groups, assign the students to do Internet research on what influence various nations have had on the target country. (You may wish to assign each group one nation's influence.) Have the groups each prepare to report a few interesting points they discover and any relevant vocabulary.

2. Have the groups each introduce any new vocabulary and then give their report.

3. Closure suggestion: Comment favorably on any points that were new to you.

Neither a Borrower nor a Lender Be? (Pair or Small-Group Task, Chapter 7)

Specific goal ideas: Have students practice explaining and justifying opinions.

1. Start by giving some examples of English words that were borrowed from other languages. (e.g., *lariat*—Spanish; *beef*—French; *quorum*—Latin; *vodka*—Russian). Ask what other examples students can think of.

2. Ask the students to give you examples of words in the local language that are borrowed from English.

3. Have the students discuss and decide: *When borrowing new words from English, is it better to borrow words directly in their original form (transliteration)? Or should new vocabulary always be translated into the local language?*

4. Have the students explain and support their conclusions.

5. Closure suggestion: Summarize the advantages and disadvantages of each approach that the students mentioned, and add any others that you can think of.

Other Activity Ideas

- The World Out There (pair or small-group task): Have the students list the ways in which people in their country learn about foreigners.

- The People in the Target Country (culture information research project): Have the students research and give a short talk on different ethnic (social, etc.) groups in the target culture. (Alternatives: Have them research different social classes or regional differences in the people.)

- What Makes One a Utopan?[5] (pair or small-group task): Have the students list the features that make them distinctive and different from the people of other countries. Have them do this as a set of sentence completions: *A Utopan is someone who . . .* (e.g., *likes Utopan food*).

FAMOUS PEOPLE

How Many Famous People Can You Think of? (Pair or Small-Group Task, Chapter 7)

Specific goal ideas: Teach names of famous people.

1. Have the students in groups quickly list—in English—the names of as many famous people from the target country as they can think of. Tell them this is a race and they will only have two minutes.

2. When time is up, have groups count the number of names on their lists and announce how many they have. Then pick one group—probably the one that claims to have the most—and have members call out the names on the list one by one as you write them on the board. As each name is called out, ask the rest of the class to say whether the name is right or not (whether the group member pronounced it properly and whether the person is actually from the target country). Then decide if this group should festively be declared the winner or if another group should be given a chance.

---

[5] I have created *Utopa* as a generic term for the students' nation and *Utopan* for the local people and language.

3. Closure suggestion: Go over the list on the board, and see if everyone knows who these people are and why they are famous. Explain as necessary.

Famous but Unknown (Culture Information Research Project, Chapter 12)

Specific goal ideas: Have students practice explaining; teach vocabulary related to the person being introduced.

1. Have the students in groups choose one important target-country person they think most other people in the class would not be familiar with and prepare a brief presentation on why this person is important—and interesting. The report should be short—no more than three minutes—and as interesting as possible.

2. Have the groups each quickly introduce any necessary new vocabulary and then give their reports. As they report, everyone else should take notes and prepare an interesting follow-up question.

3. After each report, allow a few students to ask their questions.

4. Closure suggestion: Praise the best points of each report—and the best follow-up questions.

Utopa's Most Famous (Pair or Small-Group Task, Chapter 7)

Specific goal ideas: Have students practice explaining the local country's history in English.

1. Ask the students in groups to list—in order of importance—the ten people from their country they think foreigners should know about and be ready to explain why each of these people is important in their history.

2. Have the groups report. Each group adds one person to the list and introduces that person. Keep going from group to group until the students run out of candidates. (This should result in a list of more than ten on the board.)

3. Have the class discuss which people should be on the top-ten (or top-five) list and try to come to consensus.

4. Closure suggestion: Tell the students what people from the target country would typically already know or not know about these famous people and what would need to be explained.

Other Activity Ideas

- The Most Famous (talk, dictocomp): Research and give a talk on one of the target country's most famous people (e.g., leaders, thinkers). Tell the story of this person's life, why he or she is famous, and what impact he or she had on the target country.

- Beyond the Spotlight (talk): Give a talk about a lesser known but interesting person from the target country you think students should know about.

- Fame? (survey): Have the students survey each other on this question: *Would you want to be famous? If so, for what?*

- Famous Women (pair or small-group activity): Have the students list the most famous women (e.g., leaders, scientists, soldiers) in their country's history and prepare to introduce them to a foreign visitor.

- Listing the Leaders (pair or small-group task): Have the students list as many of the target country's leaders (e.g., presidents, prime ministers, kings) as they can.

HEROES AND VILLAINS

Heroes (Pair or Small-Group Task, Chapter 7)

Specific goal ideas: Have students practice justifying opinions; teach vocabulary for virtues.

1. Suggest that a hero is someone admired for being courageous physically and morally and for bravely persisting in the face of difficulties and obstacles.

2. Have the students in groups list—in order—the top ten heroes (not just famous people) of their country and be ready to explain why each is considered a hero. (You can make the task more challenging by restricting the list, e.g., to people who are still alive or those who lived before modern times.)

3. When groups are ready to report, have each group contribute one or more names to the list and explain why this person should be on the list.

4. Once a list of candidates is compiled, have the students discuss and decide what the rank ordering of these people should be.

5. Closure suggestion: Have the students analyze what virtues the suggested people embody, and have them discuss what the list suggests about the virtues their culture especially values.

Heroes of the Target Country (Culture Information Research Project, Chapter 12)

Specific goal ideas: Have students investigate how people from the target culture view their own history.

1. In class, have the students make a list of who they think people in the target country would consider their greatest heroes (or villains).

2. Have the students in groups check their guesses through Internet research and prepare to report any discrepancies they discover between whom they thought people in the target country would consider their greatest heroes and what the research results seem to suggest.

3. Have each group report.

4. Closure suggestion: Mention one or more target-country heroes (or villains) that the students didn't mention.

My Hero (Focused Listening, Chapter 6)

Specific goal ideas: Have students practice focused listening; teach vocabulary for virtues.

1. Prepare a talk introducing the life of one or more of your favorite heroes and explaining what qualities made this person a hero.

2. Introduce any necessary vocabulary (but not words for the virtues you will speak about). Tell the students you want them to listen for the qualities for which this person is considered a hero. Then give the talk.

3. Closure suggestion: Check comprehension by having students list the qualities that made this person a hero.

Other Activity Ideas

- A Hero (talk): Give a talk on one or more interesting heroes or villains of the target country and why they are considered heroes or villains. Be sure to explain the qualities of these heroes or villains that people in the target country find particularly admirable or detestable.

- Makers of History (pair or small-group task): First, have each of the students write down, according to their own opinion, (1) the name of the greatest person who ever lived, (2) the most important event in the last century, and (3) the most important invention. Then have the students in groups compare their lists. Have the students explain and justify their answers to other members of the group and try to reach consensus. After the students report, if time permits, discuss what criteria may be used to make a choice within each of the categories.

- A Scene from History (activity): Have small groups prepare and perform a brief skit involving a hero in a famous scene from history or folklore. Allow them to prepare props as well.

NATIONAL SYMBOLS

The Flag (Classroom Chat, Chapter 7)

Specific goal ideas: Have students practice explaining aspects of the local culture in English.

1. Find a picture of the target country's flag that you can show in class, and find out what the various parts symbolize.

2. In class, show the picture, and ask the students to tell you what they know about the symbolism of the flag.

3. After the students have shared all they know, fill in any points they missed.

4. Closure suggestion: Make sure the students can explain the symbolism of their own country's flag in English.

Our National Anthem (Pair or Small-Group Task, Chapter 7)

Specific goal ideas: Have students practice translating into English.

1. Have the students in groups translate their national anthem (or perhaps only the first verse) into English.

2. Have one group dictate a line to you as you put it on the board; then work on it as a class. Repeat the process with the remaining lines.

3. Closure suggestion: If possible, compare the students' versions with an official English language translation.

The Target Country's National Anthem (Talk, Chapter 6; Dictocomp, Chapter 6)

Specific goal ideas: Teach vocabulary from the anthem.

1. Prepare a talk telling how the target country's national anthem was written and why it was chosen for its national role.

2. First, introduce any necessary vocabulary. Then dictate the anthem (or its first verse) to the students using the dictation or dictocomp procedure.

3. After the students have an understanding of the lyrics, give a talk about the background of the anthem.

4. Closure suggestion: Play the anthem for students.

Other Activity Ideas

- The Flag (talk, dictocomp): Give a talk on the story of the target nation's flag.

- Symbolic Animals (culture information research project): Have the students investigate what—if any—animals serve as symbols of cities, states, or provinces in the target country and be ready to explain what they symbolize.

- The National Flower (survey): Have the students survey each other on what flower or plant they think would best symbolize their country and why.

Module 5: Society

CITY AND COUNTRYSIDE

Urban or Rural Life? (Survey, Chapter 7)

Specific goal ideas: Have students practice explaining advantages; teach vocabulary related to urban and rural life.

1. Have the students survey each other on which location they think is best to live in and why: village, small town, or city.

2. Have the students report on which setting most of their classmates preferred, perhaps even keeping a tally on the board.

3. As students report why their classmates preferred a given setting, note the main advantages of each setting on the board.

4. Closure suggestion: Go over useful vocabulary and phrases that emerged during the activity.

Advising the Mayor (Pair or Small-Group Task, Chapter 7)

Specific goal ideas: Have students practice explaining local social issues; teach vocabulary related to urban issues.

1. Tell the students that the mayor of the city is preparing to apply for funding from the central government for programs to deal with social problems in the city.

2. Tell the students they are a committee that has been appointed to give the mayor advice on what problems to address and how. In groups, have them list the three most important issues that need to be addressed and be ready to present a simple proposal for how to address each. As groups prepare, assist them with new vocabulary.

3. Have groups present their proposals and then discuss these in an expanded council meeting (i.e., a whole-class discussion).

4. Closure suggestion: Review new vocabulary. Also comment on how similar the issues they mention are to those facing cities in the target country.

Trouble on the Farm (Culture Information Research Project, Chapter 12)

Specific goal ideas: Have students learn about the target country; have students practice explaining local social issues; teach vocabulary related to rural issues.

1. Have the students in groups research the main issues and problems facing rural areas in the target country. They should also prepare to introduce at least one new vocabulary item they learn in their research.

2. Have the groups each introduce their new vocabulary item(s) and then briefly describe one interesting thing they learned in their research.

3. Closure suggestion: Review new vocabulary. Also ask the students to comment on how similar and different the issues facing rural areas in the target country appear to be from those facing rural areas in their country.

Other Activity Ideas

- Town versus Country (pair or small-group task): Have the students the list advantages and disadvantages of living in a town (city) as opposed to the countryside (village, small town).

- Town and Country (talk, dictocomp): Research and give a talk in which you compare countryside and city life in the target country, noting the relative virtues of each.

- The Place to Be (survey): Have the students ask each other which city in their country they think is best to live in.

- Our Most Important Cities (pair or small-group task): Have the students prepare to introduce the most important cities in their country—and the characteristics of each—to a foreign visitor.

- The Biggest City Is . . . ? (pair or small-group task): Have the students list (in order of size) the cities they are familiar with in the target country and what they know about them. Follow up by giving a talk introducing the main target-country cities.

- Trouble in the City (pair or small-group task): Have the students list the major social problems facing cities in their country and prepare to explain these to a foreign visitor. (Alternative: Do the same for rural life.)

GOVERNMENT AND POLITICAL LIFE

How the Target Country Government Works (Pair or Small-Group Task, Chapter 7; Talk, Chapter 6)

Specific goal ideas: Have students practice explaining government structures; teach vocabulary related to government.

1. Prepare to introduce the government system of the target country.

2. Have the students in groups quickly write down as much as they know about the structure of the target country government—what its main parts are and what each does.

3. Have groups report.

4. Tell the students to listen for information that fills in holes in their picture of the target country's government system, and introduce any necessary new vocabulary. Then give a talk introducing the main government bodies, what each does, and how the system works. Focus especially on areas students didn't know about or were confused about.

5. Closure suggestion: Review new vocabulary.

How Our Government Works (Pair or Small-Group Task, Chapter 7)

Specific goal ideas: Have students practice explaining their home country's government structure in English; teach vocabulary related to government.

1. Tell the students they are tour guides who need to introduce the government system—clearly and in an interesting way—to foreign tourists.

2. Have the students in groups prepare a brief introduction to their government's system in English. They should introduce the main government bodies and what each does.

3. When students report, have each group introduce and explain one body. Ask for further clarification and explanation as necessary.

4. Closure suggestion: Comment how well each group did in terms of being clear and interesting.

Taxing Matters (Culture Information Research Project, Chapter 12)

Specific goal ideas: Have students learn about the target country; teach vocabulary related to taxes.

1. Have the students research taxes in the target country, investigating questions such as these: *What kinds of taxes are there? Who needs to pay? How is the amount determined? How are taxes collected?* Then have the groups each prepare to introduce several interesting discoveries they made, along with any relevant new vocabulary.

2. Have each group share one discovery it made (that hasn't yet been mentioned by another group), and also teach relevant new vocabulary.

3. Closure suggestion: Move into A Better Tax? below.

Other Activity Ideas

- Wanna be Mayor? (survey): Have the students survey each other on this question: *Would you want to be a mayor (president, general secretary, etc.)? Why or why not?*

- The Pains of Power (pair or small-group task): Have the students list the joys and headaches of being a mayor (president, prime minister, etc.).

- Political Parties (culture information research project): Have the students research the main political parties in the target country and the differences between them.

- A Better Tax? (pair or small-group task): Have the students design the ideal tax system. (Alternatives: Have the students discuss and decide these questions: *What is the best way to tax? How much—what percentage of income—is it fair to tax? Should the tax system be used to redistribute wealth?*)

- Elections (culture information research project): Have the students research elections in the target country and how they work.

ECONOMIC LIFE AND DEVELOPMENT

Bringing in New Industry (Survey, Chapter 7)

Specific goal ideas: Have students practice stating names of industries as nouns (e.g., *tourism, mining, shipbuilding*); teach vocabulary for names of industries.

1. Have the students survey each other on this question: *If you could establish a new industry in your area, what kind would it be, and why?*

2. As students report, write names of industries on the board (generally as nouns).

3. Closure suggestion: Go over the industry names, and add others to the list.

Reeling in the Clients (Pair or Small-Group Task, Chapter 7)

Specific goal ideas: Have students practice making and justifying recommendations; teach vocabulary related to industry.

1. Tell the students that they have been asked to advise their local government on how to attract outside companies to set up enterprises locally, creating more jobs and helping the local economy.

2. Have the students in groups come up with recommendations for what kind of industry the local government should try to attract and how to go about it. (Each recommendation could be stated as a sentence completion, e.g., *Our first recommendation is that* . . . .)

3. Have the groups present and justify their recommendations; then have the students discuss the relative merits of the recommendations.

4. Closure suggestion: Have the students vote on the best recommendation.

What Keeps the Economy Afloat? (Culture Information Research Project, Chapter 12)

Specific goal ideas: Have students practice (carefully and mindfully) drawing lessons from the experience of other countries; teach vocabulary related to economic life.

1. Have the students in groups research the economic life of the target country (or region), investigating the main products, services, industries, and sources of employment. They should analyze both strengths and weaknesses of the country's economy and be prepared to comment on what—if any—relevant positive or negative lessons they can draw about their own economy from the experience of the target country.

2. Have the groups each present one or more interesting discoveries they made.

3. Closure suggestion: Comment on some of the insights you thought were particularly interesting.

Other Activity Ideas

- Do We Want to Reel the Clients In? (pair or small-group task): Tell the students they have been asked to advise their local government on whether it is a good idea to attract foreign companies to set up operations locally in order to create jobs and help the local economy. Have them list advantages and disadvantages, and come up with a recommendation.

- Our Industries (pair or small-group task): Have the students list and be prepared to introduce the most important national or local industries.

- A Development Strategy (pair or small-group task): Have the students create an economic development strategy for their province (county, etc.).

- On the Farm (pair or small-group task): Have the students prepare to explain the following in English: (1) the main agricultural products produced in their area, (2) the normal schedule of the farming year, and (3) the steps for planting and harvesting the main local crop.

- Opportunity Knocks (classroom chat): Ask the students: *If a business person from another country asked you what investment opportunities there were in your home area, what would you say?*

- Creating Jobs (survey): Have the students survey each other on this question: *What is the best way to create jobs for the local economy?*

- Controlling Inflation (survey): Have the students survey each other on this question: *What is the best way to control inflation?*

- Made in Utopa (pair or small-group task): Have the students prepare to introduce their country's exports to a foreign visitor.

- WTO or No? (debate): Have the students debate whether or not membership of their country in the World Trade Organization (WTO) is a good thing for their country.

- How Good an Idea Is Industrialization? (pair or small-group task): Have the students list the advantages and disadvantages of industrialization and be ready to explain whether they think their country should industrialize further.

MONEY AND BANKING

Spare Change (Survey, Chapter 7)

Specific goal ideas: Have students practice explaining local investment opportunities in English; teach vocabulary related to investment.

1. Have the students survey each other on this question: *If you were unexpectedly given an extra sum of money and wanted to invest it for the future, what would be the best thing to do with it?*

2. Have the students report their findings. As new vocabulary is needed, list words and phrases on the board and explain them.

3. Closure suggestion: Have the students discuss the relative merits of the different options.

Investment Tips (Culture Information Research Project, Chapter 12)

Specific goal ideas: Teach vocabulary related to investment.

1. In groups, have the students do Internet research on investment in the target country and find several kinds of investment opportunities that seem to be promising. They should also learn and be ready to teach one or more useful new vocabulary items they encounter.

2. Have each group introduce and explain one opportunity (that has not been introduced by other groups), as well as relevant new vocabulary.

3. Closure suggestion: Have the students vote on which of the options presented seems most promising.

Credit Cards (Debate, Chapter 7)

Specific goal ideas: Practice explaining the advantages and disadvantages of credit card use.

1. Have the students in groups decide whether wide use of credit cards is a good or bad thing for a society and then prepare a case to support their position.

2. Conduct the debate.

3. Closure suggestion: Comment on especially good points made by each side.

Other Activity Ideas

- Target-Country Money (culture information research project): Have the students find out what denominations of coins and bills the target country uses and learn the relevant vocabulary.

- Investment Tips (pair or small-group task): Have the students prepare a presentation for foreign investors on investment opportunities in their country—what the options are and the advantages and disadvantages of each.

- Borrowing Money (culture information research project): Have the students research how one normally goes about borrowing money in the target country and for what purposes people are most likely to borrow money.

- Financing a Home (talk): Research and give a talk on how one normally goes about financing a home in the target country. (Alternative: Talk about financing a child's university education.)

MEDICAL CARE

Health Problems (Focused Listening, Chapter 6)

Specific goal ideas: Teach vocabulary related to health problems.

1. Prepare a talk on common health problems in the target country.

2. Before the talk, introduce necessary vocabulary. Also put a list of questions on the board that will guide students' listening during the talk.

3. Give the talk.

4. Check comprehension.

5. Closure suggestion: Review new vocabulary.

Improving the System (Pair or Small-Group Task, Chapter 7)

Specific goal ideas: Have students practice explaining health care issues; teach vocabulary related to health care.

1. Tell the students to imagine that they have been appointed to a blue-ribbon panel of experts asked to make recommendations for improving the health care system in their country. (Some funding is available to implement the recommendations, but the funding is limited, so not all recommendations can be funded.)

2. Have the students decide what recommendations they will make. They should be ready to explain both the recommendations and why they made them.

3. Before the reports, tell the students that they will eventually be asked to vote on which recommendations should be funded (and they cannot vote for their own).

4. As students report, encourage other groups to ask follow-up questions; you may also want to ask follow-up questions on anything you think needs further explanation.

5. Closure suggestion: Vote on which proposals should be funded.

Health Care in the Target Country (Culture Information Research Project, Chapter 12)

Specific goal ideas: Have students practice explaining health care issues; teach vocabulary related to health care.

1. Have the students first generate several interesting questions about health care in the target country. Then have them conduct Internet research to try and find the answers to their questions.

2. In class, have the groups each report one or more questions, what they found out, and what new vocabulary they learned.

3. Closure suggestion: Have everyone vote on which were the most interesting questions.

Other Activity Ideas

- Seeing a Doctor (pair or small-group task): Have the students prepare an explanation for foreign visitors of the steps involved in seeing a doctor at a local clinic or hospital.

- Health Care (culture information research project): Have the students research the health system in the target country—how health care is paid for, what common health problems there are, advantages and disadvantages of the current system, and so forth.

- Home Remedies (classroom chat): Ask the students about home remedies their parents and grandparents use to cure various ailments. Have the students explain the remedies in English.

- To Tell the Truth (debate): Have the students debate this question: *Is it better to tell dying patients who have incurable diseases the truth about their condition or to encourage them to believe that they might recover?*

- Cure for the Common Cold (survey): Have the students survey each other on the best steps to take if you have a cold, fever, or stomachache.

- No Smoking? (debate): Have the students debate the question: *Should smoking be restricted? If so, how?* (Variation: Have the students debate whether access to alcohol should be restricted and, if so, how.)

LAW AND ORDER

Crime and Punishment (Classroom Chat, Chapter 7)

Specific goal ideas: Teach vocabulary for names of crimes and punishments.

1. Prepare a list of crime names in noun form.

2. Ask students to call out as many names of crimes as they can think of. List these on the board (using the noun form). Add names for other common crimes that students don't know.

313

3. Do the same for names of punishments.

4. Teach the new words on the board.

5. Closure suggestion: Erase the board, and give the students a short, informal quiz to see how many of the new words they remember.

Improving Public Order (Pair or Small-Group Task, Chapter 7)

Specific goal ideas: Have students practice explaining crime control measures; have students practice making recommendations.

1. Tell the students that they are law enforcement experts who have been asked by local government to come up with a plan for reducing crime in the area.

2. Have the students in groups make plans that include (1) an assessment of what the most serious local crime problem is and (2) several recommendations for what should be done about it.

3. When students report, first ask the groups what they think the most serious problem is. Try to reach consensus as to the order of importance. Then, starting with the most important, elicit recommendations, and have the class discuss the merits of each.

4. Closure suggestion: Share what you know about crime control in the target country.

Crime in the Target Country (Culture Information Research Project, Chapter 12)

Specific goal ideas: Teach vocabulary related to crimes.

1. Have the students in groups research what kinds of crimes are most common—and which present the most serious problems—in the target country. They should prepare to share several interesting findings and relevant new vocabulary.

2. Have groups report their findings and teach the vocabulary.

3. Closure suggestion: Review new vocabulary and phrases.

Other Activity Ideas

- Crime and Punishment (pair or small-group task): Have the students prepare an information sheet for foreign tourists, warning them about what kinds of crimes they should watch out for and what precautions they should take.

- Keeping the Peace (culture information research project): Have the students research the various law enforcement agencies in the target country and what they do.

- Order in the Court! (talk): Research and give a talk explaining the main steps of a typical trial in the target country, including key terms and phrases used in trial procedure (e.g., *I object, innocent until proven guilty, defendant, prosecutor*). Closure suggestion: Have the students role-play a trial, following the steps you outlined.

- The Death Penalty A (pair or small-group task): Have the students list advantages and disadvantages to society of having capital punishment.

- The Death Penalty B (debate): Have the students debate whether it is good for a society to have capital punishment.

- Behind Bars (culture information research project): Have the students research prisons in the target country.

- A Lawyer-to-Be? (pair or small-group task): Have the students list the advantages (disadvantages) of a career as a lawyer (policeman, judge, etc.).

- Behind Bars? (pair or small-group task): First, have the students list alternatives to prison as approaches to dealing with criminals. Then have them list the advantages and disadvantages of each approach.

SCIENCE AND TECHNOLOGY

A Better Mousetrap (Survey, Chapter 7)

Specific goal ideas: Practice explaining unfamiliar (imaginary) things.

1. Have the students survey each other on this question: *If you could invent one new thing, what would it be?*

2. When students report the results of their surveys, help them as necessary as they try to explain any strange new inventions.

3. Closure suggestion: Ask the class to come up with creative new names for any promising new inventions that don't already have one.

The Down Side of Technology? (Pair or Small-Group Task, Chapter 7)

Specific goal ideas: Have students practice explaining benefits and unfortunate effects of technological developments.

1. As a whole class, list several important examples of technological development that have affected the country (or the whole world) in recent years.

2. In groups, have the students list both the benefits and disadvantages of these technological developments.

3. Have the groups report.

4. Closure suggestion: Discuss whether societies should try to control the implementation of technological advances in some way.

Should Ideas Be Patented? (Debate, Chapter 7)

Specific goal ideas: Have students practice arguing points.

1. Introduce the concept of intellectual property rights, and point out that opinions differ on the degree to which intellectual property rights should be protected through means such as copyrights and patents.

2. Organize the students into teams, and have them prepare to argue either that intellectual property rights should be protected as much as possible or that people should have as much freedom as possible to borrow and use the ideas of others.

3. Follow the procedure for a debate.

4. Closure suggestion: Rather than choosing a winner, have everyone list and review the advantages and disadvantages for their society of promoting protection of intellectual property rights.

Other Activity Ideas

- If You Were a Scientist . . . (survey): Have the students survey each other on this question: *What kind of scientist would it be most interesting (dangerous, boring, profitable, etc.) to be?*

- A Famous Scientist (talk): Research and give a talk about a famous scientist (inventor, etc.) from the target country.

- Cultivating Scientists (pair or small-group task): Tell the students that their local government is exploring ways to promote technological innovation in order to boost the local economy and wants advice on how to train young people so that more of them will become good scientists, inventors, and technicians. Then have the students come up with a set of recommendations for their local government. Closure suggestion: Have the class decide which are the three best recommendations.

- Training Scientists (culture information research project): Have the students research how scientists and technicians are trained in the target country.

- Research (pair or small-group task): For foreign visitors, have the students prepare to explain how and in what kinds of institutions scientific research is carried out in their country; they should also introduce the most famous centers of scientific research and learning.

- A Scientist-to-Be? (pair or small-group task): Have the students list the advantages (or disadvantages) of a career as a scientist.

- Famous Scientists (pair or small-group task): First, have the students list several of the most famous and important scientists in their country—past and present. Then ask them to prepare to explain to foreign visitors who these scientists are and why they are important.

- The Down Side of Science? (pair or small-group task): First, have the students list unfortunate effects of scientific advancement, and then have them decide whether the benefits outweigh the costs.

- Cell Phones (debate): Have the students debate whether the increasing use of mobile phones is more advantageous or more disadvantageous for society.

- The Magic Bullet? (survey): Have the students survey each other on this question: *Can technology solve most of society's problems?*

- Off into Space? (pair or small-group task): Start by noting that more and more countries are developing space programs. Then have groups list the advantages and disadvantages for a country of having a space program. Finally, have them decide whether the costs are greater than the benefits.

COMPUTERS AND THE WEB

Bill Gates II (Survey, Chapter 7)

Specific goal ideas: Have students practice explaining types of software; teach vocabulary related to software.

1. Have the students survey each other on this question: *If you wanted to get rich by designing computer software, what kind would you design?*

2. Have the students report and explain the best ideas they heard. Introduce new vocabulary, and put it on the board as appropriate.

3. Closure suggestion: Have the students vote on which idea is most likely to make money.

Computers and Wealth (Pair or Small-Group Task, Chapter 7)

Specific goal ideas: Have students practice explaining and justifying opinions.

1. Have the students decide whether they think the increasing use and availability of computers will tend to increase or lessen the gap between the rich and the poor. Ask them to try to reach consensus and be ready to explain their position.

2. Have the students report and justify their positions.

3. Closure suggestion: Ask for suggestions on what could be done to minimize wealth-gap problems that might be created by increasing reliance on computers.

Shareware (Debate, Chapter 7)

Specific goal ideas: Practice talking about computer software in English.

1. Have the students in groups decide whether computer software should be freely available to the public (shareware) or whether people should be required to pay for it. Once the groups have each chosen a position, they should prepare to argue it.

2. Have the debate.

3. Closure suggestion: Summarize the best points made by either side, and then declare a winner (or have the class vote).

Other Activity Ideas

- Giving Computer Directions (pair or small-group task): Have the students prepare to explain to you in English—from turning the computer on—how to write and send an e-mail message (visit a Web site, etc.). As they prepare, help them with computer-related vocabulary. When the first volunteer group reports step-by-step, stand in front of the class and do exactly what the group tells you to do. If you have a computer that can serve as a visual aid, fine. If not, pretend. As new computer-related words come up, write them on the board and explain how they are used. Closure suggestion: Review the new words, and have the students use them in sentences.

- A Bad Computer Day (talk): Tell a story about an amusing or disastrous experience you have had with computers. Closure suggestion: Review computer-related vocabulary from the story.

- Computers—Blessing or Bane? (pair or small-group task): Have the students list the advantages and disadvantages for society of increasing computer availability and use. (Alternative: Discuss the advantages and disadvantages of the growing use of the Internet.)

- The World of Local Web Sites (classroom chat): Have the students explain in English for a foreign visitor what kinds of Web sites are available in the local language. As they explain, introduce necessary vocabulary, and put it on the board.

- Computers in Kindergarten? (pair or small-group task): Have the students decide whether schools should teach children to use computers and, if so, starting at what age.

NEWS AND INFORMATION

A Typical TV News Broadcast (Pair or Small-Group Task, Chapter 7)

Specific goal ideas: Encourage students to view culture as patterned behavior; teach vocabulary for types of TV news items.

1. Point out to the students that TV news broadcasts tend to follow a formula—there is usually a fairly clear pattern for what kinds of stories are presented in what order.

2. Have the students prepare to describe—in order—the normal elements of a typical TV news broadcast in their country. As they prepare, assist with necessary vocabulary.

3. Have groups report.

4. Closure suggestion: Go over any new vocabulary introduced for kinds of news items.

What's in a Newspaper? (Culture Information Research Project, Chapter 12)

Specific goal ideas: Encourage students to view culture as patterned behavior; teach vocabulary related to types of newspaper articles, pages, and columns.

1. Have the students research the typical organization of a popular newspaper in the target country. They should investigate the kinds of pages (e.g., news page, sports page) found in the newspaper and the kinds of items normally found on each. Then they should prepare to report several differences they find between target-country newspapers and those in their own country.

2. As the students work, assist them with necessary vocabulary.

3. When the students report, have the class come to consensus first on what the main kinds of pages are and then on the kinds of articles, columns, and items usually found on each. Finally, have them report differences they notice.

4. Closure suggestion: Mention any additional differences you are aware of.

Traffic Accidents in the News (Pair or Small-Group Task, Chapter 7)

Specific goal ideas: Have students practice explaining and justifying opinions.

1. Start by noting that, in many Western countries, reports on local car accidents, crimes, and other kinds of unfortunate occurrences are a staple of local TV news.

2. Have groups of students list the advantages and disadvantages of giving such stories prominent coverage in the news.

3. Have the students report and explain.

4. In follow-up discussion, have the class try to generate guidelines for a local TV news station producer on how to handle such news items. Questions to consider would include where they should be placed in the broadcast, how long the stories should be, and what the video should and should not show.

5. Closure suggestion: Compare the students' suggestions with what local TV stations in the target country actually tend to do.

Other Activity Ideas

- How Do You Stay in Touch? (survey): Have the students survey each other on how they normally get their news (e.g., TV, newspapers, word of mouth).

- All the News That's Fit to Print? (pair or small-group task): Have the students list—in order of priority—the five most important kinds of information that should be printed in newspapers and five kinds of information that should not be printed.

- The Daily News (culture information research project): Have the students research the news industry in the target country. What are the main outlets for news? What kind of news does each tend to focus on?

RELIGION AND PHILOSOPHY

Great Thinkers (Classroom Chat, Chapter 7)

Specific goal ideas: Have students practice explaining traditional philosophical ideas in English; teach English names of local philosophical figures.

1. Have the students choose the top five major thinkers (e.g., philosophers, religious figures) in their country's history and list them in order of importance. Then have them prepare to introduce each figure to a foreign visitor and explain why each was great and what his or her main ideas were.

2. For each person listed, have the students explain one philosophical idea that the thinker is famous for. Help with vocabulary as necessary.

3. Closure suggestion: Review any new vocabulary.

Religions and Values (Pair or Small-Group Task, Chapter 7)

Specific goal ideas: Teach vocabulary for values (e.g., *patience, hospitality*).

1. Assign each pair or group one of the local culture's traditional religions (or schools of thought). Have them prepare to explain to a foreign visitor several ways in which it influences the values of their culture. As students prepare, help them with relevant vocabulary.

2. As the students report, list values (in noun form) as they are mentioned.

3. Closure suggestion: Review the list of values in their noun forms, and then have the students generate the adjective forms.

Religion in My Country (Culture Information Research Project, Chapter 12)

Specific goal ideas: Teach vocabulary related to religion in the target culture.

1. Have the students research religious life in the target country, investigating questions such as these: *What religions are represented? What are the basic beliefs and practices of each? What role do they play in society?*

2. Have the students report the findings that they found most surprising and introduce any new vocabulary they learned.

3. Closure suggestion: Of the findings they reported, tell the students which you found most interesting or surprising.

Other Activity Ideas

- The Sage's Influence Today (pair or small-group task): Have the students discuss how much impact one or more of the important thinkers of their country's past have on their culture today.

- Utopan Religions 101 (pair or small-group task): Have the students prepare to explain to a foreigner the main religions in their country and the main beliefs of each.

- A Traditional Religion (pair or small-group task): Have the students prepare to introduce in detail one of their country's main traditional schools of thought to a foreigner.

LANGUAGES AND DIALECTS

Your Next Language (Survey, Chapter 7)

Specific goal ideas: Teach names of languages; encourage additional language learning.

1. Have the students survey each other on this question: *If you were to learn another language, what would it be, and why?*

2. As the students report, list the (English) names of the languages on the board.

3. Follow up by asking students whether they have any plans to actually learn additional languages and, if so, how. Also share any desires or plans you have for your own continued foreign language study.

4. Closure suggestion: Review the names of languages, perhaps adding other important ones that were not mentioned.

Our Languages and Dialects (Pair or Small-Group Task, Chapter 7)

Specific goal ideas: Have students practice explaining the language situation in their country.

1. On the board, have a student draw an outline map of the students' country.

2. Have the students in groups prepare to explain to a foreign visitor what different languages (dialects) are spoken in their country and where they are spoken. The students need to be ready to explain—in English—where on the map these language or dialect areas are, say something interesting about each of them, and say how similar and different they are from each other.

3. As the students report, fill in the map on the board according to what they tell you. Ask follow-up questions as necessary to clarify the explanations.

4. Closure suggestion: Review new words that emerged during the course of the discussion.

Languages in the Target Country (Culture Information Research Project, Chapter 12)

Specific goal ideas: Have students learn more about the target country; teach vocabulary related to languages.

1. Have the students research the target country, investigating questions such as these: *What languages are spoken, where, and by whom? How much difference is there between one part of the target country and another in terms of accent, vocabulary, and other aspects? How much can one tell about people from their speech?*

2. Have the groups each report one or more interesting findings and teach any relevant new vocabulary they encountered.

3. Closure suggestion: Review new language-related vocabulary.

Other Activity Ideas

- English Only? (talk): Research and give a talk about a current language-related issue in the target country (e.g., bilingual education, English-only versus multilingualism).

- High School French (culture information research project): Have the students research which foreign languages students in the target country most often learn and why.

- A Social Language Map (pair or small-group task): (in multilingual countries) Have the students prepare to describe to a foreign visitor the situations in which people would normally speak the country's standard or national language and the situations in which they would normally speak some other language or dialect. (To describe a setting, have the students consider who is speaking to whom, where, under what circumstances, and what the topic is.)

SOCIAL PROBLEMS

A Litany of Social Ills (Survey, Chapter 7)
Specific goal ideas: Teach vocabulary relating to social problems (using noun forms, e.g., *poverty, unemployment*).

1. Have the students survey each other on which social problem is their country's most serious one.

2. As students report, write the names of the social problems on the board, all in noun form.

3. List some of the main social problems facing the target country (also in noun form).

4. Closure suggestion: Move into Whatever Shall We Do? below.

Whatever Shall We Do? (Pair or Small-Group Task, Chapter 7)
Specific goal ideas: Have students practice asking follow-up questions; have students practice explaining social issues.

1. Put a list of social problems on the board (or use the one students came up with in A Litany of Social Ills above).

2. Assign each of the pairs or groups one problem, and have them produce a plan for dealing with it. They should also be ready to state the main advantage of their plan and its main drawback or problem.

3. As each group reports its plan, have the other groups listen and come up with a follow-up question that helps clarify the plan or its advantages and disadvantages.

4. Follow up with general discussion of the merits of the plans.

5. Closure suggestion: Praise especially good (well-explained) plans and especially insightful follow-up questions.

321

A Social Problem (Culture Information Research Project, Chapter 12)

Specific goal ideas: Practice explaining social problems in English.

1. Have the students in groups choose and research one of the main social problems facing the target country (e.g., drugs, poverty, crime, unemployment). They should be ready to explain the causes of the problem and the efforts being made to deal with it.

2. Have groups report some of their findings. As each group reports, other students should listen and prepare to ask good follow-up questions.

3. Have the students ask their follow-up questions.

4. Closure suggestion: Say which follow-up questions you thought were best and why.

Other Activity Ideas

- The Best Way to . . . (survey): Have students survey each other on one or more of the following questions:
    — What is the best way to combat drug use and addiction?
    — What is the best way to deal with juvenile crime?
    — What is the best way to combat illiteracy?
    — What is the best way to alleviate poverty?
    — What is the best way to prevent children from dropping out of school?
    — What is the best way to deal with unemployment?

ENVIRONMENT AND ECOLOGY

Who Should Pay? (Pair or Small-Group Task, Chapter 7)

Specific goal ideas: Have students practice analyzing advantages and disadvantages; have students practice explaining pollution-related issues, especially with regard to costs.

1. Point out that everyone is in favor of eliminating pollution—the problem is that stopping pollution and cleaning it up is usually expensive, at least in the short run.

2. Have the students decide who should bear the main costs of cleaning up pollution— national government, local government, or the producers of the pollution. They should be ready to explain (1) who should pay, (2) why, and (3) what the main disadvantages of their choice are.

3. Have groups of students report and explain their positions.

4. Review the disadvantages of each choice, and then move to the advantages.

5. Closure suggestion: Praise especially good points students made as they analyzed the problem.

The Spotted Grubil (Problem-Solving Situation, Chapter 6)

Specific goal ideas: Have students practice analyzing and explaining costs and benefits; teach vocabulary related to ecology and development.

1. Prepare (flesh out) a problem situation along the following lines: The local government of Sylvania (a mythical country) wants to build a dam on a river in a poor, mountainous region of the country as a way to generate clean, inexpensive electric power that may help the region develop economically. However, within the region, there is currently no

immediate need for the extra power the dam will generate, and it is not clear whether cheap power alone will attract industry to the region. Also, the resulting lake that grows behind the dam will destroy the habitat of the spotted grubil, a rare (mythical) rodent, and will almost certainly result in the extinction of this endangered—and largely unstudied—animal.

2. Present the problem to the students orally, and have them take notes.

3. Have the students first analyze and list the potential costs and benefits of building the dam, and then decide whether or not the dam should be built. They should be ready to explain and justify their position.

4. Have groups present their cases and discuss.

5. Closure suggestion: Praise any especially insightful comments students made as they analyzed the possible costs and benefits of the proposed dam.

Pollution (Culture Information Research Project, Chapter 12)

Specific goal ideas: Have students practice explaining pollution problems; teach vocabulary for types of pollution.

1. Have the students research pollution in the target country, investigating what kinds of pollution there are, what measures have already been taken, and what challenges and problems still await solution.

2. Have the students report their more interesting findings. As others listen, they should generate at least one follow-up question for each report.

3. Have the students ask their follow-up questions.

4. Closure suggestion: Review the names of pollution types and any other new vocabulary.

Other Activity Ideas

- To Dam or Not? (pair or small-group task): Have students list advantages and disadvantages of building dams on major rivers.

- Don't Be a Litterbug (pair or small-group task): Have the students come up with a plan for an antilitter campaign.

- Global Warming (pair or small-group task): Have the students decide whether or not they think global warming is really a serious problem and why.

- The Last of the Tigers? (pair or small-group task): Have the students decide whether it is really important to protect endangered species and why.

- Development or Environment? (debate): Have the students debate which is more important—economic development or environmental protection. Closure suggestion: Discuss the following questions: *Is there is necessarily a trade-off between economic development and environmental protection? Can a society have both? Or can environmental protection only be made a priority after a society becomes fairly wealthy?*

- Jobs or Clean Air? (debate): Have the students debate this question: *Should polluting industries that will bring in jobs be encouraged?*

Module 6: Arts, Entertainment, and Media

MOVIES

Local Movies (Pair or Small-Group Task, Chapter 7)

Specific goal ideas: Have students practice translating film titles.

1. Have the students tell you (the original) names of popular local films. List them on the board, with the titles in the original language.

2. Have the students in groups translate the titles into English.

3. For each film, have each group offer its English translation of the title while other class members reward its efforts with applause, booing, or whatever is appropriate.

4. Closure suggestion: Give a round of applause to the group that did best.

Kinds of Movies (Pair or Small-Group Task, Chapter 7)

Specific goal ideas: Teach vocabulary for kinds (genres) of movies.

1. Have the students imagine that a foreign visitor is asking them what kinds of local films are made in their country.

2. In groups, have them list the different genres (kinds) of movies that are made locally (e.g., love stories, war films, mysteries). They should also come up with one or more examples of films that fall into each genre. As they work, assist them in coming up with good English terms for the genres they describe.

3. Have the students report the genre names they came up with as you write them on the board. Try to generate good names for any genres that do not already have widely used English terms.

4. Closure suggestion: Comment on which genres are the same in the target culture—and which might not be found there.

Movie Formulas (Culture Information Research Project, Chapter 12)

Specific goal ideas: Encourage students to look for similarities and differences in the patterns by which different cultures organize things; have students practice explaining genre conventions.

1. Point out that, in a culture, a given kind of film often follows a rough formula (genre conventions). Using a popular kind of local film, give an example.

2. Have the students describe the formula for a popular film genre in their culture. Then have them find and watch a target-culture movie of a similar genre and make notes on how the formula seems to be the same or different.

3. Have the students report interesting differences or similarities they noticed

4. Closure suggestion: Praise some especially good insights.

Other Activity Ideas

- Your Favorite Movie (survey): Have each student ask several others what their favorite movies are. (If they only know the film title in their first language, they should try to translate it into English.) Closure suggestion: Have a few volunteers report, and as films are mentioned, have the rest of the class rate them with a quick voice vote. (Alternative: Have the students interview you about your favorite films.)

- Movie Stars (pair or small-group task): Have the students list their country's top movie stars and be prepared to explain to a foreign visitor why each is popular.

- My Idol (talk): Give a talk about one or more movie stars you really like and why.

MUSIC

Your Favorite Kind of Music (Survey, Chapter 7)

Specific goal ideas: Teach vocabulary for kinds of music.

1. Have the students ask each other what their favorite kinds of music are.

2. As students report, list the kinds of music on the board. If the students don't know how to say a certain kind of music in English, ask them to do their best to explain it, and you can then help with necessary vocabulary.

3. Review and clarify the terms for kinds of music.

4. Closure suggestion: Have the students rate how much they like each kind of music with a quick voice vote.

Is Music a Necessary Part of Education? (Pair or Small-Group Task, Chapter 7)

Specific goal ideas: Have students practice explaining the impact of music.

1. Start by telling the students that, in Western education, music is sometimes viewed as less important than other kinds of courses. (When funds are short, music programs are often among the first to be cut.) This raises the question of how important it really is to teach music in public education programs.

2. Have the students decide whether not primary and secondary schools in their country should require training in music and what kind of music training should be provided. They should be ready to explain and justify their positions.

3. Have the students report, explain, and justify their decisions. Follow up with general class discussion.

4. Closure suggestion: Share your own views.

What Would You Like to Learn to Play? (Survey, Chapter 7)

Specific goal ideas: Teach names of musical instruments.

1. Have the students call out the English names of as many musical instruments as they can think of; you fill in with others. Don't forget to include local instruments (which may or may not have English names).

2. Have the students survey each other on this question: *If you could magically learn to play one instrument brilliantly, what instrument would you pick and why?*

3. Have the students report what they found out.

4. Closure suggestion: Explain what instrument you would want to learn to play and why.

Other Activity Ideas

- Music Education (pair or small-group task): Have the students design a curriculum for music in elementary (or middle) schools. They should decide things such as what kind of musical training students should be given (e.g., singing, instrumental music, music appreciation), whether musical training should be required or optional, where and how music would be taught in the curriculum (e.g., outside class, in a special music class), and how much time a week should be devoted to music.

- Local Musical Instruments (classroom chat): Ask the students to practice introducing the traditional folk instruments of their culture, explaining each in English.

- Music Lessons (talk): Give a talk describing experiences you—or someone you know—had learning to play a musical instrument.

- Funding for the Arts? (debate): Have the students debate the following question: *Should classical (or traditional) music be financially supported by the government?*

- A Folk Song (pair or small-group task): Have the students prepare to teach a local folk song in English. They will need to translate the song—or perhaps the first verse—into English. Closure suggestion: Have the class decide which group's translation is best.

- Should Pop Rule the Roost? (debate): Have the students debate the following question: *Is the growth of an international modern pop style of music a good thing?*

TELEVISION

Local TV Shows (Survey, Chapter 7)

Specific goal ideas: Teach names of genres of TV programs.

1. Have the students survey each other on what kinds of television shows they like most and least.

2. As students report their findings, if a genre clearly corresponds to one that has a widely used English term, put the term on the board. If the genre does not seem to have a corresponding English term, work with the students to come up with one.

3. Follow up by introducing the genres common in the target country.

4. Closure suggestion: Review the terms for TV program genres.

The Latest Hit TV Show (Pair or Small-Group Task, Chapter 7)

Specific goal ideas: Have students practice explaining ideas for television shows.

1. Tell the students that the local television station has come to them asking for an idea for a new hit TV show.

2. Have the students come up with an idea for a kind of show they think would be successful and be prepared to explain it to the class.

3. Have each group report its idea. Follow up with class discussion of the relative merits of the proposals.

4. Closure suggestion: Have the students vote on which idea they would be most willing to invest money in.

TV—the Boob Tube? (Debate, Chapter 7)

Specific goal ideas: Have students practice explaining and justifying views; teach vocabulary related to the impact of television.

1. Point out that the advent of television has had a major impact on societies and cultures all around the world and that—as is often the case with major technological innovations—the impact has been both positive and negative.

2. Have the students list positive and negative impacts of increased television viewing in their country. These should be stated as sentences (e.g., *It has reduced the amount of time children spend playing with their friends.*).

3. As the students report, make sure each idea is explained adequately—in other words, that it is clear why the impact is positive or negative.

4. Divide the class into teams, and have them debate whether the overall impact of television on their society has been more positive or more negative.

5. Closure suggestion: Comment on especially good points made during the debate.

Other Activity Ideas

- Target-Culture TV Shows (culture information research project): Have the students investigate what kinds of television programs are found in the target country.

- What's Your Favorite Television Program? (survey): Have the students survey each other on what their favorite television programs are—using only English. When saying the name of their favorite programs, they have to translate the name into English and have their classmates guess which show it is.

- TV Show Formulas (pair or small-group task): Have the students prepare to describe the formula of a popular type of TV show.

- TV Viewership (culture information research project): Have the students investigate how much television most people in the target country watch and what they usually watch.

- Lock on the Box? (debate): Have the students debate whether parents should limit the amount of time per day children watch television. (Alternative: Discuss whether parents should put limits on the kinds of shows children are allowed to watch.)

ADVERTISING

An Effective Ad (Survey, Chapter 7)

Specific goal ideas: Teach vocabulary for qualities (as adjectives); teach vocabulary related to advertisements.

1. Start by asking a few students what qualities they think make an advertisement effective. Write the responses on the board (probably as adjectives that would fit into the sentence *A good advertisement should be . . .*).

2. Have the students survey each other on this question: *What are the key qualities of an effective advertisement?*

3. As the students report, list the qualities mentioned on the board.

4. Closure suggestion: Review any new vocabulary.

New and Improved! (Pair or Small-Group Task, Chapter 7)

Specific goal ideas: Have students practice trying to think from the target-culture perspective; have students practice persuasion.

1. Tell the students that a newly opened local soap factory has asked them to design an ad campaign for a new brand of soap in the target-country market.

2. Have the students design and prepare to perform a one-minute advertisement. Encourage them to be creative and entertaining.

3. Have the students perform their ads.

4. Closure suggestion: Comment on how effective you think the various strategies students tried are likely to be in the target culture.

Ads on TV (Pair or Small-Group Task, Chapter 7)

Specific goal ideas: Have students practice explaining and justifying opinions; teach vocabulary related to broadcasting.

1. Point out that, in some countries, television broadcasting is paid for by the state; in others, it is supported mainly by advertising.

2. Have the students decide which approach they think is better and be ready to explain why.

3. After each group reports, have students in other groups ask follow-up questions to clarify (and perhaps call into question) the position of the reporting group.

4. Closure suggestion: Praise groups that ask especially good questions or respond especially effectively to questions, and explain why you thought these questions or answers were especially good.

Other Activity Ideas

- Your Favorite Ad (survey): Have the students survey each other on this question: *What are your favorite advertisements? What ads do you like least?*

- Ad Genres? (pair or small-group task): First have the students list the most common types (genres) of advertisements in their country. Then have them choose one, analyze it, and be ready to explain how it works.

- Can You Trust an Ad? (debate): Have the students debate this question: *Are advertisements totally untrustworthy?*

SPORTS

Sports Galore (Pair or Small-Group Task, Chapter 7)

Specific goal ideas: Teach names of target country sports.

1. Prepare a list of sports names in English, and be ready to pronounce all of them.

2. Give groups of students five minutes to correctly list the English names of as many popular sports in the target country as they can think of.

3. For reporting, let each group add one sport to the list. In order for the group to get a point, the sport must be spelled and pronounced (more or less) correctly. Keep going from group to group until all the sports are on the board. Then see which group has the most points.

4. Briefly introduce any sports that students did not think of.

5. Closure suggestion: Go over the list to make sure that the students have some idea of what each sport is—and know how to pronounce it.

Curling (Talk, Chapter 6)[6]

Specific goal ideas: Teach sport-related vocabulary.

1. Prepare a talk on a sport from the target country that is not widely known in the students' country (e.g., curling). Discuss things such as who plays it, where and when it is played, what the rules are, and what its history is.

2. Introduce any necessary vocabulary; then give the talk.

3. Check comprehension.

4. Closure suggestion: Check to see whether the students think this sport has the potential to be successful in their country.

The Winning Team (Pair or Small-Group Task, Chapter 7)

Specific goal ideas: Have students practice persuasion; have students practice explaining how the art of persuasion works in the local culture.

1. Tell the students that they are famous sports coaches who have been approached by the national government for advice on how to train the national football (soccer) team for the next Olympics.

2. Have the students in groups come up with a plan for creating a winning team. The more creative it is, the better.

3. Have each of the groups present their plan and its virtues.

4. Closure suggestion: Have the students vote on which plan they think is best.

Other Activity Ideas

- Your Favorite Sport (survey): Have the students survey classmates to find out which sports they enjoy playing—or watching—the most.

- Popular Sports (talk): Give a talk on what sports are popular in the target country.

- World Cup (culture information research project): Have the students research a famous sporting event in the target country and be prepared to explain both how the competition itself is organized and its role in society.

- A Good Spectator Sport (pair or small-group task): Have pairs or groups of students decide—in order of importance—what the key elements of a good spectator sport are.

---

[6] *Curling* is a shuffleboard-like winter sport played with brooms on the ice in the northern climes of North America.

- Phys. Ed. or Just Playing Around? (pair or small-group task): Have the students decide whether or not it is important for schools to stress sports—especially during school time.

- Pay for Play? (debate): Have the students debate whether the government should financially support sports teams for the Olympics or whether teams should find private funding.

THEATER

Theater and Language (Dictocomp, Chapter 6)

Specific goal ideas: Teach theater-related expressions; have students practice guessing the meaning of unfamiliar phrases.

1. Prepare a short dictocomp passage containing expressions in English that derive from theatre, such as *the show must go on, break a leg, the final curtain, in the limelight,* and *stage fright.*

2. Do the dictocomp, and then check for comprehension.

3. After the students have checked their dictocomps, have them work in groups to try to guess what the expressions mean.

4. Closure suggestion: Have groups share their guesses. Then reveal the correct answers.

Traditional Opera (Pair or Small-Group Task, Chapter 7)

Specific goal ideas: Have students practice explaining local performing art forms.

1. Ask the students in groups to choose a local traditional performing art that would probably be unfamiliar to foreigners and then prepare a brief and interesting explanation of what the art form is. They should also explain why it was traditionally popular, mentioning as many reasons as they can think of.

2. As groups present their introductions, ask follow-up questions for clarification.

3. Closure suggestion: Ask the students how they themselves now feel about the performing art in question.

School Plays (Pair or Small-Group Task, Chapter 7)

Specific goal ideas: Have students practice explaining and justifying opinions.

1. Tell the students that schools in the West, especially secondary schools, often sponsor school plays as part of their programs.

2. Have the students decide whether or not schools should put on plays involving students as part of students' education and be ready to explain why or why not.

3. Have the students present their positions and rationales. Follow up with discussion of the merits of the positions suggested.

4. Closure suggestion: Share your views.

Other Activity Ideas

- Plays or Films? (survey): Have the students survey classmates on whether and why they prefer to watch movies or plays.

- Famous Plays (pair or small-group task): Have the students prepare to introduce their culture's most famous plays to a visiting foreigner.

- Theater in My Country (culture information research project): Have the students research and prepare to report on theater in the target country.

- An Actor's Life (survey): Have the students survey each other on these questions: *Would you want to be a professional actor? Why or why not? Would you want your child to become an actor?*

- Plays or Films? (survey): Have the students survey each other on this question: *If you were an actor, would you rather do plays or films?*

DANCE

The Best Kind of Dance (Pair or Small-Group Task, Chapter 7)

Specific goal ideas: Have students practice explaining and justifying opinions; teach names of dance types.

1. Have the students call out all the different kinds of dances they can think of in English (e.g., ballet, square dancing) while you list these on the board.

2. Have the students in groups rank these kinds of dances according to beauty and be ready to explain their rankings.

3. Have each group state the kind of dance members think is most beautiful and their reasons. After each group reports, let other students respond using applause (loud or soft) to indicate how much they agree or disagree.

4. Have each group state the kind of dance members ranked as least beautiful and why. Allow others to respond as above.

5. Closure suggestion: Share your own opinions, and see how much applause they get.

Learning to Dance (Total Physical Response, Chapter 6)

Specific goal ideas: Teach vocabulary related to dance movements.

1. Prepare to teach a dance (perhaps a simple folk dance from the target country) in class using verbal explanation. (This may take some preparation, as the normal inclination is to show rather than explain verbally.)

2. Teach the students the dance as a total physical response activity: give verbal instructions, and have the students respond by doing what you tell them to. Try as much as possible to explain what the students should do rather than showing them.

3. If time allows, follow up by having the students prepare in groups to teach a dance they know—preferably one that not all the other students know—using the same approach.

4. Closure suggestion: Review new vocabulary that emerged during the activity.

Why Would Anyone Want to Dance? (Pair or Small-Group Task, Chapter 7)

Specific goal ideas: Have students practice explaining and justifying opinions.

1. Point out that, in some ways, dancing could be considered a rather strange kind of activity—after all, it involves movements that are quite unusual and different from one's daily movements. Yet, all around the world, virtually every human culture has developed dances.

2. Have the students in groups discuss the question *Why do people dance?* Have the students list possible reasons and be ready to explain them.

3. Have groups offer their explanations.

4. Closure suggestion: Comment on any explanations you thought were especially ingenious or insightful.

Other Activity Ideas

*   Do You Like to Dance? (survey): Have the students survey each other on these questions: *Do you like to dance? If so, what kind of dancing do you like?*

*   Dancing in the Target Country (talk): Research and give a talk on the different kinds of dancing that are popular in the target country.

*   Shall They Dance? (pair or small-group task): Have the students try to reach a consensus on whether children should be taught to dance in school.

READING AND LITERATURE

Utopa's Greatest Literary Hits (Pair or Small-Group Task, Chapter 7)

Specific goal ideas: Have students practice translating book titles; have students practice explaining their country's literary culture.

1. Have the students in groups list—in order of greatness—their country's greatest works of literature and prepare to introduce these to a foreigner. They should find out what the English title of the work is—or translate the title into English—and be ready to explain what makes the work great.

2. After groups report, have the class try to agree on a prioritized list; then move on to the question of what makes these works great.

3. Follow up by asking the students to explain what values are promoted, upheld, or reflected in these works and what the popularity of these works says about the culture.

4. Closure suggestion: Ask the students to tell you titles of famous literary works in English they are familiar with (perhaps as you list them on the board). Then comment on which of these—plus any others—you consider to be the greatest.

Books for the Countryside (Pair or Small-Group Task, Chapter 7)

Specific goal ideas: Have students practice explaining and justifying a proposal.

1. Point out that in most countries, people in cities have much better access to reading material than people in rural areas do, especially because libraries are usually found in cities. So a problem governments face is how to make reading material and information available to people in remote areas.

2. Have the students design the most practical and cost-effective plan possible for making books and other reading material more available in rural areas of their country, especially small, remote villages. They should be ready to explain and justify their plan.

3. Have the students present their plans and their rationales. Follow up with discussion of the relative merits of the plans.

4. Closure suggestion: Share any other solutions you can think of to this problem.

That Special Book (Interview, Chapter 7)

Specific goal ideas: Encourage students to read, both in English and in general.

1. Have the students interview each other about which book they have read has had the most influence on their life and why it had so much influence.

2. Have a few students report on books they wish to recommend to others in the class. (These can be books they have read themselves, not necessarily books their interview partner has read.)

3. Closure suggestion: Recommend books in English you think the students might be interested in reading.

Other Activity Ideas

- What Do You Like to Read? (survey): Have the students survey others about what they like to read and why.

- Where Can I Get a Magazine? (classroom chat): Ask the students to prepare to explain to a foreign visitor the different places where people in their country buy books, magazines, newspapers, and other reading matter, and what kind of reading matter each place sells. They should also explain where reading matter in English can be found.

- What Makes Great Great? (pair or small-group task): Have the students list, in order of priority, the criteria that determine whether a work of literature is great.

- Traditional Story Characters (pair or small-group task): Have the students prepare to introduce their country's most popular traditional stories and the characters in those stories.

- The Funniest Book (survey): Have the students survey each other on what the funniest (most boring, etc.) book they have ever read is.

- You've Got to Read This (pair or small-group task): Have the students decide on an answer to this question: *If you could recommend one book to a foreigner who wants to learn about your country, what would it be and why?*

- Famous Story (talk): Tell—or read aloud from—a famous story from the target culture. (Alternative: Tell about famous characters from novels.)

- Formula for Success (pair or small-group task): Have the students describe the formula for a popular genre of book (e.g., detective stories, romances).

ART

Types of Art (Survey, Chapter 7)

Specific goal ideas: Teach names of art forms (e.g., *sculpture, painting*).

1. Have the students quickly call out—in English—as many kinds of (visual) art forms as they can think of (e.g., painting, sculpture) while you list these on the board using noun or gerund forms. (Use a very broad definition of art form.)

2. If necessary, discuss which items on the board should be considered art. (There may be considerable room for discussion on this point.)

3. Have each student survey several classmates on what their favorite form of art is and why.

4. Have volunteers report their findings.

5. Closure suggestions: Tell the students about your own preferences. Also comment on what people in the target country would normally include—and not include—in the category of art forms.

Our Most Famous Artists (Pair or Small-Group Task, Chapter 7)

Specific goal ideas: Have students practice explaining aspects of local culture.

1. Have the students in groups decide who their country's three most important (or famous) artists are and prepare to introduce these people to a foreign visitor, saying a little about the artists and why they are considered great.

2. For reports, have each group introduce one artist who hasn't yet been mentioned by another group.

3. Follow up with discussion of who should be on the top three list and why.

4. Closure suggestion: Tell the students which of the artists you think is greatest and why.

Is Art Just in the Eye of the Beholder? (Pair or Small-Group Task, Chapter 7)

Specific goal ideas: Have students practice explaining and justifying criteria.

1. Note that people often argue about whether or not there are objective criteria for judging whether a work or art is great or not. Is it just a question of personal opinion? Is greatness established by community approval and popularity?

2. Have the students list the three most important criteria they think should be used in determining whether a work of art is great or not. (The criteria might be stated as completions of the sentence *A great work of art is one that . . . .*) Each pair or group should try to reach consensus. They should be ready to clearly explain the criteria they chose and to justify their choices.

3. Have the students report and justify their criteria. Move into general discussion and try to work toward a class consensus on the issue.

4. Closure suggestion: Share your own opinion and prevailing views in the target country.

Other Activity Ideas

- Art for Art's Sake? (debate): Have the students debate this question: *Should the value of art be determined primarily based on (1) its social impact (art for the sake of serving society) or (2) its artistic merits (art for art's sake)?* Closure suggestions: Share your own opinion.

- Great Artists in the Target Country (culture information research project): Have the students research who the target country's greatest artists were and why they are considered great. Have some groups investigate painters, some sculptors, and so forth.

- The Making of an Artist (culture information research project): Have the students research how artists are trained in the target country.

- To Make an Artist (pair or small-group task): Have groups discuss what the best way to train artists is and come up with a plan.

Module 7: Teaching and Education

GETTING AN OVERVIEW

The School System in My Country (Culture Information Research Project, Chapter 12)

Specific goal ideas: Teach vocabulary related to education.

1. Tell the students they have been asked to explain the education system in their country to a group of foreign visitors.

2. Before preparing their explanations, have the groups do Internet research to find major areas of difference between the education systems in their country and the target country. Then they should prepare an introduction that points out areas of similarity and difference and provides a little extra explanation on points where the two systems differ. They should also introduce new vocabulary they encounter.

3. In class, have each group report on one point they would address. As new vocabulary emerges, put it on the board.

4. Closure suggestion: After the talk, summarize differences, similarities, or both between education in the target country and the home country.

Problems in Education (Pair or Small-Group Task, Chapter 7)

Specific goal ideas: Have students practice explaining educational issues.

1. Have the students list, in order, which three major problems or challenges faced by schools in their country are most serious. They should be ready to explain their rankings.

2. As the students report, first have the groups explain which problem they think is most serious and why, and then try to reach consensus. Then do the same with the second most serious, and so on.

3. Closure suggestion: Lead into Solutions below.

Solutions (Pair or Small-Group Task, Chapter 7)

Specific goal ideas: Have students practice explaining educational issues.

1. Have the students come up with suggested solutions to the major problems or challenges faced by schools in their country. They should be ready to explain why they think their solutions are best.

2. As the students report, first pick one problem, and have each group explain what solution they propose. Then try to reach consensus through discussion. Repeat for the second most serious problem, and so on.

3. Closure suggestion: Comment on which proposed solutions seem promising to you.

Other Activity Ideas

- Utopa's School System (pair or small-group task): Have the students prepare to introduce the school system in their country to a foreign guest, starting with kindergarten (or the equivalent) and then moving on up. You might chart the system and put up new vocabulary on the board.

- The School System in the Target Country (talk): Research and give a talk on education and schools in the target country.

- Problems in Education (culture information research project): Have the students research the main problems facing education in the target country.

- Paying the Bills (pair or small-group task): Have the students decide whether they think education should be run—and paid for—mainly by local government or by national government.

- Private Education (pair or small-group task): Have the students list the advantages and disadvantages of a country's having private education alongside public (state-funded and state-managed) education.

STUDENTS

The Golden Years? (Survey, Chapter 7)

Specific goal ideas: Have students practice explaining advantages and disadvantages of student life.

1. Have the students survey each other on whether or not they think one's student years are the best years of life and why.

2. Have the students report both what they heard and what rationales were given.

3. Closure suggestion: Tell the students about some of the advantages of life after the student years.

How Much Is Their Life Like Ours? (Culture Information Research Project, Chapter 12)

Specific goal ideas: Have students practice talking about student life.

1. Have groups of students research student life in the target country, finding and listing interesting ways in which student life in the target culture is similar to or different from that in the students' home culture. They should then prepare a brief report summarizing their most interesting findings.

2. Have each group report on one or more of their interesting findings.

3. Closure suggestion: Ask the students whether they felt that, on the whole, their lives were mainly different from those of students in the target country or basically similar.

Through Other's Eyes (Culture Information Research Project, Chapter 12)

Specific goal ideas: Give students a chance to look at their own country from an outsider's perspective.

1. Have the students in groups prepare a list of interview questions to ask foreign students studying in their country, focusing on what it has been like to be a student in a foreign country.

2. Have each group locate and interview a foreign student.

3. In class, have the group each report one or more interesting things they learned through their interview.

4. Closure suggestion: Note which questions and findings you thought were especially interesting.

Other Activity Ideas

- Survival Tips (pair or small-group task): Have the students list the five most important survival tips for life as a student.

- Word to the Wise (pair or small-group task): Have the students prepare lists of tips they would give to foreign students coming to study in their country.

- Gripes (culture information research project): Have the students find out what are the most common complaints that students in the target country have about student life.

- Student Life in the Target Country (culture information research project): Have the students in groups choose one aspect of student life in the target country and research it.

TEACHERS

A Teacher-to-Be? (Survey, Chapter 7)

Specific goal ideas: Have students practice stating advantages and disadvantages related to life as a teacher.

1. Have the students survey each other on whether or not they would consider teaching as a career and why or why not.

2. Have the students report their findings and the rationales given.

3. Closure suggestion: From your perspective as a teacher, comment on the assumptions students made about the advantages and disadvantages of life as a teacher.

Teaching in the Target Culture (Culture Information Research Project, Chapter 12)

Specific goal ideas: Teach vocabulary related to the teaching profession.

1. Have groups of students research the main challenges that face teachers in the target country.

2. In class, have the groups each report one challenge they discovered. Then, after all groups report, discuss which challenges seem to be most widespread or serious.

3. Closure suggestion: Compare the students' findings about the target country with the teaching profession in the home country.

My Best Teacher (Survey, Chapter 7)

Specific goal ideas: Have students practice stating qualities.

1. Tell the students about one of the best teachers you ever had and why you thought he or she was a great teacher. Then ask the students to summarize the good qualities your teacher had. (These will probably be stated as adjectives—e.g., *friendly, encouraging.*)

2. Have the students survey each other about the best teachers they ever had. What made those teachers good? What did they learn from them? As the students listen to each other, they should note down qualities that they hear.

3. Have the students report the qualities that they heard about as you write these on the board as adjectives (if possible).

4. Closure suggestion: Have the students generate the antonyms of each of the positive qualities listed on the board.

Other Activity Ideas

- A Good Teacher (pair or small-group task): Have the students list—in order—the most important characteristics of a good teacher.

- My Teacher (talk): Give a talk about one of the best teachers you ever had and what you think was so good about him or her.

- Should I Take the Job? (pair or small-group task): Tell the students that a foreign teacher is considering taking a job as a teacher in their country but first wants their advice. Then have the students analyze and list the advantages and disadvantages of being a foreign teacher in their country.

- Getting Ahead (culture information research project): Have the students investigate what things a university (secondary school) teacher in the target country needs to do in order to get promoted.

- The Big Class (pair or small-group task): Ask the students to imagine they are giving advice to a Western English teacher who has never taught a large class (fifty to eighty students) before. In groups, they should prepare a list of advice, each given as a sentence completion: *You should . . . , You should not. . . . .* Have them be ready to present their advice and explain why it is important.

- To Be Strict or Lenient? (pair or small-group task): Have groups of students list the advantages and disadvantages of teachers being strict and of being lenient. Then have each group decide whether it is better to err on the side of being too strict or too lenient.

PRIMARY SCHOOL AND BEFORE

What's the Point of Preschool? (Pair or Small-Group Task, Chapter 7)

Specific goal ideas: Have students practice stating goals.

1. Have the students list what they think the main goals of preschool education should be. These might be done as sentence completions, for example, *The main goal of preschool education should be to . . .* (e.g., *get kids used to being in school*).

2. Have the students report and explain their ideas on goals.

3. Try to reach class consensus on which goals are most important.

4. Closure suggestion: Move into Preschool below.

Preschool (Culture Information Research Project, Chapter 12)

Specific goal ideas: Teach vocabulary related to preschool education.

1. Have groups of students research preschool education options in the target country and be ready to describe the differences between the different kinds of options and what the primary goals of each seem to be. They should also prepare to introduce useful new vocabulary items they encounter.

2. Have each group report on one option. As new vocabulary is introduced, put it on the board.

3. Closure suggestion: Review new vocabulary.

How Much Homework? (Debate, Chapter 7)

Specific goal ideas: Have students practice explaining and justifying positions.

1. Divide the students into teams, and have them prepare to argue one of the two following positions: A: Primary schoolchildren should be given very little or no homework. B: It is all right to give primary schoolchildren homework.

2. Conduct the debate.

3. Closure suggestion: Note especially good points made during the debate and the reasons you thought they were good. Also, comment on the issue of homework for primary school students in the target country.

Other Activity Ideas

- Parents' Choice? (pair or small-group task): Have groups of students discuss the following question: *Should all children just go to the closest school? Or should parents have some choice as to what school their child goes to?* The groups should try to reach consensus and then be ready to explain their view to the class.

- English in Primary School? (pair or small-group task): Have the students decide whether they think children in their country should start learning English in primary school.

SECONDARY SCHOOL

A Student's Day (Culture Information Research Project, Chapter 12)

Specific goal ideas: Have students learn about student life in the target country; have the students practice stating and checking guesses.

1. On the board, list a number of questions about the typical day of a high school student in the target country. These might include *What time do students go to school? How many class periods do they have? What extracurricular activities are available, and how popular are they? When do classes end? How much homework do students usually have?*

2. Have the students write down educated guesses about the questions.

3. Then, have the students in groups do research on the Internet to find information and check the answers they gave to these questions.

4. In class, question by question, have the students present their guesses and the answers they found through their research.

5. Closure suggestion: Comment on any unexpected findings that are particularly interesting.

Should Schools All Use the Same Books? (Debate, Chapter 7)

Specific goal ideas: Have the students practice stating and supporting arguments.

1. Have the students prepare to argue either for or against the proposition: *All schools throughout a given country should use the same textbooks for the same courses.*

2. Conduct the debate.

3. Closure suggestion: Comment on how books and other teaching materials are selected and distributed in the target country.

Getting into University in the Target Country (Culture Information Research Project, Chapter 12)

Specific goal ideas: Have students practice talking about university admission processes; teach vocabulary related to university application.

1. Have the students in groups conduct Internet research to learn about the process of university application in the target country. Each group should try to come up with several interesting discoveries to share and one or more useful vocabulary terms to teach their classmates.

2. In class, have the groups each teach one or more new terms and report one interesting discovery they made. After each group reports, have the class piece together the general overall process of university application in the target country.

3. Closure suggestion: Share any stories you know of students from the home country applying to university in the target country.

Other Activity Ideas

- A Student's Day (talk): Research and give a talk describing the typical day of a high school student in the target country. Organize your talk chronologically. As you give the talk, suggest that the students take notes in the form of a rough schedule.

- Guide to Getting into College (pair or small-group task): Have the students prepare to describe to a foreign visitor, step by step, the process for choosing and getting into a college or university in their country.

- Getting into University (pair or small-group task): In pairs or small groups, have the students list, in order of importance, the things that a teacher in the last year of secondary school should do to prepare students for university entrance. When groups report, ask one group to suggest what it thinks is most important. Then ask if other groups agree, and discuss as necessary. Once there seems to be adequate agreement on something, write it on the board as number 1 and move on to the next group and suggestion.

- Secondary School My Way (culture information research project): Have the students research what courses are typically offered in secondary schools in the target country. Issues to investigate would include how much choice students have in the courses they take, whether they can choose majors, and what the requirements of a typical course are.

- Courses (pair or small-group task): Have the students list for a foreign visitor the courses usually offered in a secondary school curriculum in their country as well as explain which are considered most important and why.

- How Much Homework Is Reasonable? (pair or small-group task): Have the students decide how much homework per night they think is reasonable for secondary school students.

- The Exams (Pair or Small-Group Task): Have the students prepare to explain to a visiting foreign teacher what kinds of standardized examinations and other kinds of tests students in the home country face.

- Heading Off Failure (pair or small-group task): Have the students discuss: *What should a teacher do if a student is headed toward failing a course?*

- School Fees (culture information research project): Have the students research costs involved in secondary school education in the target country.

- After Secondary School? (culture information research project): Have the students investigate what educational options there are for students in the target country at the end of secondary school other than traditional university programs.

UNIVERSITY

A University Course (Talk, Chapter 6)

Specific goal ideas: Teach vocabulary related to university courses.

1. Prepare a talk on what a typical university course (preferably a course in a major that would be relevant to the students) in the target country is like. Possible questions to address would include these: *What people do in class (e.g., lecture, discussion)? What kinds of homework assignments are given (e.g., papers, projects, reading for tests)? What materials are used (e.g., the number and kind of textbooks, library readings)? How is the course evaluated (e.g., tests, papers, presentations)?*

2. In class, warm up by having the students list the names of all the university majors they can think of as you list them on the board. Also introduce any other necessary vocabulary.

3. Give the talk, and then check comprehension.

4. Closure suggestion: Review new vocabulary.

Advance Warning (Press Conference, Chapter 6)

Specific goal ideas: Have students practice imagining what challenges life in the target country might pose; teach vocabulary related to university teaching.

1. Tell the students they have been asked to go teach their language at a university in the target country for two years. Before they go, they need to interview you to get more information on how they should teach courses in a Western university. (You will need to anticipate what questions students may ask, and prepare.)

2. Have the students list questions. (You might suggest some examples to get them started, e.g., *What is the grade curve in the target country like? How much homework should I give? How should I evaluate students' performance? What should I do if students cheat or don't do their homework?*)

3. Have the students interview you.

4. Closure suggestion: Comment on what you have heard from foreign teachers in your country about the challenges and joys they encounter there.

How Much Choice Should Students Have? (Pair or Small-Group Task, Chapter 7)

Specific goal ideas: Have students practice stating and supporting arguments.

1. Point out that universities need to decide how much, if any, choice to allow students in the courses they take. Should the department decide all the courses? Or should students be free to take whatever courses they want? Should the policy fall somewhere in between? If so, where?

2. Ask the students to list the advantages and disadvantages of university departments deciding most or all of students' courses for them and then do the same for students being allowed to choose many of their own courses. The students should also decide which they think is preferable and be ready to explain why.

3. Have the students present the advantages and disadvantages of each approach. Follow up with discussion.

4. Closure suggestion: Ask the students whether they think university faculty would hold the same views they do, and why or why not.

Other Activity Ideas

- College Football? (pair or small-group task): Have the students decide what role they think sports should play in university life. Should there be college teams for intercollegiate competition? Should there be only intramural sports? Or should colleges sponsor no sports at all?

- Are Tests the Best? (pair or small-group task): Have the students decide which methods university teachers should use to evaluate students. Are tests the best way?

- Getting into Grad School (culture information research project): Have the students research the process for getting into graduate school in the target country.

- Paying for College (culture information research project): Have the students research the costs involved in university or graduate school education in the target country and how students generally pay for these costs.

- Liberal Arts (culture information research project): Have the students research the concept of liberal arts education and how it differs from other approaches to higher education.

LANGUAGE LEARNING[7]

How Do You Like Language Learning? (Survey, Chapter 7)

Specific goal ideas: Encourage students to consider issues of motivation in language study.

1. Have the students survey each other on this question: *What do you like most (least) about language study, and why?*

2. Have the students report.

3. Move into discussion of what would motivate students more in language learning.

4. Closure suggestion: Make the point that motivation is one of the most important factors determining how well students learn languages, so the students should be at least as concerned about motivation as they are about study methods.

The Right Method? (Pair or Small-Group Task, Chapter 7)

Specific goal ideas: Encourage students to analyze language skills and consider how effectively various kinds of practice build these skills.

1. Have groups of students analyze one of the major language skills (e.g., listening, speaking, reading). They should list the steps involved in using the skill and any other subskills or knowledge that are important in its use. (These are described in the relevant chapters of this book.)

2. As groups report, list the aspects of the skill on the board.

3. Have the students choose a practice method they might use to build this skill, and have them decide which aspects of the target skill the practice method helps build, what the practice method would be most effective for, and what it would not be very useful for.

4. Have groups report.

5. Closure suggestion: Tell the students that the ability to analyze a target skill and the strengths and weaknesses of practice methods is a useful skill for language learners because it helps them choose practice and study methods wisely.

---

[7] Some activities and ideas from the For Thought, Discussion, and Action sections at the ends of the chapters in this book could be adapted for use in discussion lessons addressing issues of language learning.

Foreign Language Study in the Target Culture (Culture Information Research Project, Chapter 12)

Specific goal ideas: Help students get a better understanding of the role of foreign language study in the target country.

1. Have the students research the role of foreign language study in the target country, investigating questions such as these: *Is foreign language study optional or required? What languages are usually studied? How many years of foreign language study do most students have? At what age does foreign language study usually start? How are foreign languages usually taught? What kinds of foreign language tests do students have to take? How do scores on foreign language examinations affect students?*

2. Have the students report some of their more interesting findings.

3. Closure suggestion: Ask the students which findings were most surprising to them.

Other Activity Ideas

- Is There a Best Way to Learn a Language? (survey): Have the students survey each other on whether they think there is a best (and realistic) way to learn a foreign language and, if so, what it might be.

- Memorization Tricks (survey): Have the students survey each other on what good methods or tricks they know for vocabulary memorization.

- Increasing Reading Speed (pair or small-group task): Have the students decide what they think the best strategy would be for building reading speed. They should write it up as an language learning project and be prepared to explain its virtues to their classmates.

- Improving My Grammar (pair or small-group task): Have the students decide what they would do if they were teaching a writing course and wanted to build the grammatical accuracy of their students' writing. They should design an approach and be prepared to explain its virtues to their classmates.

- Cramming for the Test (survey): Have the students survey each other on what good methods or tricks they know for preparing for examinations.

- Lost in Translation? (pair or small-group task): Have the students discuss whether or not they think translation practice is a good way to study a foreign language. Move into discussion of what kinds of knowledge and skills translation does and does not teach.

Books for Further Reading

This brief appendix lists Western books that you might find useful or interesting as you further explore issues of language and culture teaching. By and large, these books are accessible to the general reader and appropriate to EFL settings.

Azar, B. 1998. *Understanding and using English grammar.* 3rd ed. Englewood Cliffs, NJ: Prentice Hall Regents. Azar's grammar books contain straightforward explanations of grammar structures, accompanied by charts, examples, and a multitude of exercises (some of which are set up so that they can be done orally).

Brown, H. D. 2001. *Teaching by principles: An interactive approach to language pedagogy.* 2nd ed. New York: Longman. Brown's book is an effective and readable introduction to how theory relates to language teaching.

Crystal, D. 2003. *English as a global language.* 2nd ed. Cambridge: Cambridge University Press. Crystal gives an overview of the rise of English to its current position as the world's most widely used international language.

Davis, L. 2001. *Doing culture: Cross-cultural communication in action.* Beijing, China: Foreign Language Teaching and Research Press. This is an accessible introduction to the practice of intercultural communication, written within the Chinese context.

Fantini, A., ed. 1997. *New ways in teaching culture.* Alexandria, VA: TESOL. Other books in TESOL's New Ways series list suggestions and activities covering a broad range of English teaching issues.

Harmer, J. 2001. *The practice of English language teaching.* Harlow, England: Pearson ESL. Harmer offers an accessible yet comprehensive introduction to English teaching.

Klippel, F. 1984. *Keep talking: Communicative fluency activities for language teaching.* Cambridge: Cambridge University Press. This is an excellent collection of speaking activities.

Lightbown, P., and N. Spada. 1999. *How languages are learned.* 2nd ed. Oxford: Oxford University Press. This book is a reader-friendly introduction to second language acquisition.

Rubin, J., and I. Thompson. 1994. *How to be a more successful language learner.* 2nd ed. Boston: Heinle and Heinle. This book is a good, brief introduction to language learning strategies and the nature of language.

Scovel, T. 2001. *Learning new languages: A guide to second language acquisition.* Boston: Heinle and Heinle. Scovel offers an entertaining yet scholarly overview of second language acquisition.

Scrivener, J. 1994. *Learning teaching: A guidebook for English language teachers.* New York: Macmillan Education. This is a brief, accessible, and very practical introduction to language teaching.

Snow, D. 2004. *Encounters with Westerners: Improving skills in English and intercultural communication.* Student text and teacher version. Shanghai, China: Shanghai Foreign Language Education Press. This book contains critical-incident exercises for teaching intercultural communication skills in English courses.

Stewart, E., and M. Bennett. 1991. *American cultural patterns: A cross-cultural perspective.* Rev. ed. Yarmouth, ME: Intercultural Press. While slightly technical, this short volume is a good introduction to the values and assumptions of U.S. culture and is very helpful in thinking through the issue of what a culture is.

Ur, P. 1981. *Discussions that work: Task centered fluency practice.* Cambridge: Cambridge University Press. This introduction to conducting discussions includes many good activity ideas.

———. 1988. *Grammar practice activities: A practical guide for teachers.* Cambridge: Cambridge University Press. This is a conveniently referenced collection of activities for grammar practice. Many of the activities are communicative ones that could serve as useful supplements in speaking and listening classes.

Appendix E

Internet Resources

There is a virtually limitless—and ever-growing—body of material on the Internet for both English teachers and English students. Given the fluid nature of the medium, by the time this book reaches your hands some of the information in the following list (current as of mid-2006) will no doubt be out of date, but presumably many of these sites will be up and running for some years to come, so this list should help get you started.

English Teaching

The Amity Foundation (Teachers Project). http://www.amityfoundation.org/. Teaching resources available under Teachers Program.

Boggle's World. http://www.bogglesworld.com/. Loads of activities; a job search site.

Capital Community College Foundation. *Guide to grammar and writing.* http://grammar.ccc.commnet.edu /grammar/. Grammar and writing resource.

Dave's ESL Café. http://www.eslcafe.com/. Teaching ideas and information on job opportunities.

EFL/ESL Games. http://teflgames.com/. Word games.

EFL Tasks. http://efltasks.net/. Activities for beginning-level students.

E. L. Easton. http://eleaston.com/. Aids for teaching English and other languages.

EnglishClub.com. http://www.englishclub.com. Lesson plans, jobs, discussion forums, and other resources.

English Language Teachers' Forum. http://www.eltforum.com/. A range of materials on English teaching.

ESL Lounge. http://www.esl-lounge.com/. Lesson plans, teaching aids, flash cards, role-play cards, book reviews, and more.

ESLnotes: The English Learner Movie Guides. http://www.ESLnotes.com/. Plot summaries, vocabulary, and discussion questions for a long list of films.

everythingESL. http://www.everythingESL.net/. Lesson plans, activities, and other resources; more ESL than EFL focused.

Gateway to Educational Materials. http://www.thegateway.org/. Search engine for lesson plans in many areas, including EFL.

John's ESL Community. http://www.johnsesl.com/. Worksheets, activities, and other teaching resources.

Karin's ESL Partyland. http://www.eslpartyland.com/. Lesson plans, materials, chat rooms, job information, and other resources.

Longman English Language Teaching. http://www.longman.com/. Resources for teachers and students, but also advertisements for Longman publications.

One Stop English. http://www.onestopenglish.com/. A wide range of resources by Macmillan, from lesson plans to culture information.

The OWL Family of Sites. http://owl.english.purdue.edu/. An abundance of resources from Purdue University, especially handouts for different aspects of writing and links to other sites.

Rubistar. http://rubistar.4teachers.org/. Aids for creating grading templates (rubrics) for oral and written assignments.

Sites for Teachers. http://www.sitesforteachers.com/. Links to many Web sites for teachers.

Sounds of English. http://www.soundsofenglish.org/. Information, activities, exercises, links, and other resources dedicated to the pronunciation of American English.

Teaching English. http://www.teachingenglish.org.uk/. Teaching ideas, downloads, and other resources from the BBC and British Council.

Teachingfish.com. http://www.teachingfish.com/. Games, activities, EFL/ESL resources, and job-search links.

TEFL China Teahouse. http://teflchina.org/. Support for English teachers in China; articles, lesson plans, and informal tips and discussion by Chinese and other teachers.

TEFL Net. http://tefl.net/. Resources, discussion forums, links, jobs, and other resources.

TEFL Professional Network. http://www.tefl.com/. Listing of English teaching job opportunities worldwide.

Wordskills.com: Services in Education and Training. http://wordskills.com/. A variety of resources, including book recommendations, level tests, and mini–grammar lessons.

Journals and Magazines

Asian EFL Journal. http://www.asian-efl-journal.com/. Academic articles on English teaching in Asia; information on conferences in the region.

Asian Journal of English Language Teaching. http://www.cuhk.edu.hk/ajelt/. Research-oriented journal on topics relevant to teaching in Asia; published by the Chinese University of Hong Kong.

English for Specific Purposes World. http://www.esp-world.info/. Web-based journal with academic articles from around the world on teaching English for specific purposes.

English Teaching Forum Online. http://exchanges.state.gov/forum/. Quarterly journal on EFL teaching published by the United States Information Agency; articles by teachers around the world.

English Teaching Professional. http://www.etprofessional.com/. Selected articles from the print magazine.

ELT Asia. http://www.eltasia.com/. Online journals and discussion lists for English teaching in Asia.

ESL Magazine. http://www.eslmag.com/. Bimonthly magazine serving ESL/EFL professionals worldwide.

Essential Teacher. http://www.tesol.org/. Quarterly magazine of the TESOL association, including columns, articles, and reviews.

Humanising Language Teaching. http://www.hltmag.co.uk/. Interesting variety of articles and features for language teaching.

IATEFL Newsletter. http://www.iatefl.org/, under Newsletter. Newsletter of the International Association of Teachers of English as a Foreign Language, an organization based in the United Kingdom.

The Internet TESL Journal. http://iteslj.org/. Monthly Web journal started in 1995; includes articles, research papers, lesson plans, teaching techniques, book reviews, links, and more than 500 quizzes students can take to test their knowledge of grammar, vocabulary, and idioms.

Journal of the Imagination in Language Teaching and Learning. http://www.njcu.edu/cill/journal-index.html. Pretty much what the title says.

The Language Teacher. http://jalt-publications.org/tlt/. Monthly publication of the Japan Association for Language Teaching; readable and practical articles. See also *JALT Journal*, linked from this site.

The Reading Matrix. http://www.readingmatrix.com/. Journal focusing on reading issues; other reading-related resources.

SEAMEO Regional Language Centre. http://www.relc.org.sg/. Under Publications, articles on language teaching in *RELC Journal.*

TEFL Web Journal. http://www.teflweb-j.org/. Quarterly magazine for teachers.

TESL-EJ: Teaching English as a Second or Foreign Language. http://www-writing.berkeley.edu/TESL-EJ/. Quarterly journal offering articles on a wide range of teaching topics.

TESL—Hong Kong. http://www.tesl-hk.org.hk/. Journal, based at City University of Hong Kong, publishing articles on English teaching in Hong Kong.

Professional Organizations

Asian Association of Teachers of English as a Foreign Language. http://www.asiatefl.org/. Based in Asia.

British Council. http://www.britishcouncil.org/. Based in the United Kingdom.

International Association of Teachers of English as a Foreign Language (IATEFL). http://www.iatefl.org/. Based in the United Kingdom.

International Society for Language Studies (ISLS). http://www.isls-inc.org/. International association with a focus on critical studies.

Teachers of English to Speakers of Other Languages (TESOL). http://www.tesol.org/. Based in the United States.

Text and Other Reference Collections

Absolutely All Free Clipart. http://www.allfree-clipart.com/. Clip art and graphics; links to other clip art and graphics sites.

Alex Catalogue of Electronic Texts. http://www.infomotions.com/alex/. Collection of public domain electronic books.

Bartleby.com: Great Books Online. http://www.bartleby.com/. Free access to a large range of great literary works, dictionaries, encyclopedias, and almost anything else you would expect to find in the reference collection of a Western library.

BookBrowse. http://www.bookbrowse.com/. Excerpts from and reviews of books.

CoolCLIPS.com. http://www.coolclips.com/. Clip art.

Drew's Script-o-rama. http://www.script-o-rama.com/. A large collection of movie scripts.

FreeFoto.com. http://www.freefoto.com/. A wide variety of photographs.

Google Images. http://images.google.com/. Search engine for pictures.

Internet Public Library. http://www.ipl.org/. Collection of links organized like a library.

JoBlo's Movie Scripts. http://www.joblo.com/moviescripts.php. Links to sites with movie scripts.

Library of Congress. http://www.loc.gov/. Web site of the U.S. Library of Congress.

Picsearch. http://www.picsearch.com/. Search engine for photographs.

Project Gutenberg. http://www.gutenberg.net/. Collection of 13,000 free electronic books, mostly older books in the public domain.

Wikipedia: The Free Encyclopedia. http://en.wikipedia.org/. Online, multilingual encyclopedia with entries on about everything you could ask for.

yourDictionary. http://yourdictionary.com/. Online dictionary and grammar resource; a variety of other language-related resources, including a section on endangered languages.

Sites for English Language Learners

1-language.com. http://www.1-language.com/. English study resources and chat rooms.

Aardvark's English Forum. http://englishforum.com/. Many resources.

Activities for ESL Students. http://a4esl.org/. Quizzes and activities.

Advanced Composition for Non-Native Speakers of English. http://eslbee.com/. Resources for learning and teaching advanced-level composition writing.

AskOxford. http://www.askoxford.com/. Dictionary resource from Oxford University Press.

Centre for Independent Language Learning, Hong Kong Polytechnic University. http://elc.polyu.edu.hk /cill/. Wide range of resources.

Churchill House School of English Language. http://www.churchillhouse.com/english/. Quizzes, games, and advice on grammar.

Dave's ESL Café. http://eslcafe.com/. Language information, quizzes, and other resources.

EnglishClub.com. http://www.englishclub.com/. Games, quizzes, chat rooms, and other resources.

EnglishLearner.com. http://englishlearner.com/. Lessons, quizzes, pen-friends, and links.

English Listening Lounge. http://www.Englishlistening.com/. Listening practice; Chinese language version available.

ESL Resource Center. http://www.eslus.com/eslcenter.htm. Lessons for students.

Interesting Things for ESL Students. http://www.manythings.org/. Games, puzzles.

John's ESL Community. http://www.johnsesl.com/. Exercises, quizzes, games, and other resources.

Karin's ESL Partyland. http://www.eslpartyland.com/. Quizzes, discussion forums, and other resources.

Learn English. http://www.tolearnenglish.com/. Placement tests, lessons, exercises, and other resources.

Listening on the Net. http://AD.Walker.org/listening.htm. Student guide to listening to English (e.g., radio programs) on the Internet; links included.

Randall's ESL Cyber Listening Lab. http://www.esl-lab.com/. Listening exercises and quizzes.

Repeat after Us. http://repeatafterus.com/. Listening and pronunciation practice.

Sounds of English. http://www.soundsofenglish.org/. Activities and exercises for English pronunciation.

Topics: An Online Magazine for Learners of English. http://www.topics-mag.com/. Features written by and for learners of English.

World News Review. http://webs.wichita.edu/ielc-lab/wnr/. News stories to listen to and read in English.

References

Althen, G. 1988. *American ways: A guide for foreigners in the United States.* Yarmouth, ME: Intercultural Press.

American Council on the Teaching of Foreign Languages. 1999. *ACTFL proficiency guidelines—speaking.* http://www.actfl.org/files/public/Guidelinesspeak.pdf.

Amity Foundation. 2003. *Amity teachers toolkit 2003.* http://www.amityfoundation.org/page.php?page=247.

Bachman, L. 1990. *Fundamental considerations in language testing.* Oxford: Oxford University Press.

Bachman, L., and A. Palmer. 1996. *Language testing in practice.* Oxford: Oxford University Press.

Bailey, K. 1998. *Learning about language assessment: Dilemmas, decisions, and directions.* Boston: Heinle and Heinle.

Bailey, K., B. Bergthold, B. Braunstein, N. J. Fleischman, M. Holbrook, J. Tuman, X. Waissbluth, and L. Zambo. 1996. The language learner's autobiography: Examining the "apprenticeship of observation." In *Teacher learning in language education,* ed. D. Freeman and J. Richards, 11–29. Cambridge: Cambridge University Press.

Bailey, K., A. Curtis, and D. Nunan. 2001. *Pursuing professional development: The self as source.* Boston: Heinle and Heinle.

Bowen, J. D., H. Madsen, and A. Hilferty. 1985. *TESOL: Techniques and procedures.* 2nd ed. Rowley, MA: Newbury House.

Braine, G., ed. 1999. *Non-native educators in English language teaching.* Mahwah, NJ: Lawrence Erlbaum.

Brown, H. D. 1991. *Breaking the language barrier.* Yarmouth, ME: Intercultural Press.

———. 2001. *Teaching by principles: An interactive approach to language pedagogy.* 2nd ed. Reading, MA: Addison Wesley Longman.

Byrd, D., and I. Clemente-Cabetas. 2001. *React interact.* 3rd ed. Harlow, England: Pearson Education.

Carrell, P., and J. Eisterhold. 1987. Schema theory and ESL reading pedagogy. In *Methodology in TESOL: A book of readings,* ed. M. Long and J. C. Richards, 218–32. Rowley, MA: Newbury House.

Carruthers, R. 1987. Teaching pronunciation. In *Methodology in TESOL: A book of readings,* ed. M. Long and J. C. Richards, 191–200. Rowley, MA: Newbury House.

Christopher, V., ed. 2005. *Directory of teacher education programs in TESOL in the United States and Canada, 2005–2007.* Alexandria, VA: TESOL.

Cross, D. 1991. *A practical handbook of language teaching.* London: Cassell.

Crystal, D. 2003. *English as a global language.* 2nd ed. Cambridge: Cambridge University Press.

Damen, L. 1987. *Culture learning: The fifth dimension in the language classroom.* New York: Addison-Wesley.

DeCarrico, J. 2001. Vocabulary learning and teaching. In *Teaching English as a second or foreign language,* 3rd ed., ed. M. Celce-Murcia, 285–99. Boston: Heinle and Heinle.

Dörnyei, Z. 2001a. *Motivational strategies in the language classroom.* Cambridge: Cambridge University Press

———. 2001b. *Teaching and researching motivation.* Harlow, England: Pearson Education.

Eisenstein, M. 1987. Grammatical explanations in ESL: Teach the student, not the method. In *Methodology in TESOL: A book of readings,* ed. M. Long and J. C. Richards, 282–92. Rowley, MA: Newbury House.

Farber, B. 1991. *How to learn any language.* New York: Citadel Press.

Fotos, S. 2001. Cognitive approaches to grammar instruction. In *Teaching English as a second or foreign language,* 3rd ed., ed. M. Celce-Murcia, 267–84. Boston: Heinle and Heinle.

Fox, L. 1987. On acquiring an adequate second language vocabulary. In *Methodology in TESOL: A book of readings,* ed. M. Long and J. C. Richards, 307–11. Rowley, MA: Newbury House.

Gairns, R., and S. Redman. 1986. *Working with words: A guide to teaching and learning vocabulary.* Cambridge: Cambridge University Press.

Goodwin, J. 2001. Teaching pronunciation. In *Teaching English as a second or foreign language,* 3rd ed., ed. M. Celce-Murcia, 117–38. Boston: Heinle and Heinle.

Gower, R., and S. Walters. 1983. *Teaching practice handbook: A reference book for EFL teachers in training.* Portsmouth, NH: Heinemann.

Guangdong Bureau of Higher Education. 1991. *A guide to the revision of college English, vol. 2.* Guangzhou, China: Guangdong Bureau of Higher Education.

Harmer, J. 2001. *The practice of English language teaching.* Harlow, England: Pearson Education.

Hedge, T. 2000. *Teaching and learning in the language classroom.* Oxford University Press.

Hendrickson, J. 1987. Error correction in foreign language teaching: Recent theory, research, and practice. In *Methodology in TESOL: A book of readings,* ed. M. Long and J. C. Richards, 355–72. Rowley, MA: Newbury House.

Hirsch, E. D. 1987. *Cultural literacy: What every American needs to know.* New York: Vintage Books.

Hughes, A. 1989. *Testing for language teachers.* Cambridge: Cambridge University Press.

Kachru, B. 1992. Teaching World Englishes. In *The other tongue: English across cultures,* 2nd ed., ed. B. Kachru, 354–65. Urbana: University of Illinois Press.

Kohls, R. 2001. *Survival kit for overseas living.* 4th ed. Yarmouth, ME: Intercultural Press.

Lanier, A. 1988. *Living in the USA.* 4th ed. Yarmouth, ME: Intercultural Press.

Larsen-Freeman, D. 2001. Grammar. In *The Cambridge guide to teaching English to speakers of other languages,* ed. R. Carter and D. Nunan, 34–41. Cambridge: Cambridge University Press.

Lee, I. 2004. Preparing nonnative English speakers for EFL teaching in Hong Kong. In *Learning and teaching from experience: Perspectives on non-native English-speaking professionals,* ed. L. D. Kamhi-Stein, 230–49. Ann Arbor: University of Michigan Press.

Levine, D., J. Baxter, and P. McNulty. 1987. *The culture puzzle: Cross-cultural communication for English as a second language.* Englewood Cliffs, NJ: Prentice Hall.

Lewis, M. 1993. *The lexical approach: The state of ELT and a way forward.* Hove, England: Language Teaching Publications.

Lightbown, P., and N. Spada. 1999. *How languages are learned.* 2nd ed. Oxford: Oxford University Press.

Littlewood, W. 1984. *Foreign and second language learning: Language acquisition research and its implications for the classroom.* Cambridge: Cambridge University Press.

Liu, D. 1999. Training non-native TESOL students: Challenges for TESOL teachers. In *Non-native educators in English language teaching,* ed. G. Braine, 197–210. Mahwah, NJ: Lawrence Erlbaum.

Madsen, H. 1983. *Techniques in testing.* Oxford: Oxford University Press.

Mahboob, A. 2004. Native or non-native: What do students enrolled in an intensive English Program think? In *Learning and teaching from experience: Perspectives on non-native English-speaking professionals,* ed. L. D. Kamhi-Stein, 121–47. Ann Arbor: University of Michigan Press.

Marshall, T. 1989. *The whole world guide to language learning.* Yarmouth, ME: Intercultural Press.

McCrum, R., W. Cran, and R. MacNeil. 1987. *The story of English.* London: Faber and Faber.

McKay, S. 1987. *Teaching grammar: Form, function, and technique.* Englewood Cliffs, NJ: Prentice Hall International.

———. 2002. *Teaching English as an international language.* Oxford: Oxford University Press.

McLaughlin, B. 1987. *Theories of second language learning.* London: Edward Arnold.

Medgyes, P. 1999. *The non-native teacher.* 2nd ed. Ismaning, Germany: Hueber.

———, P. 2001. When the teacher is a non-native speaker. In *Teaching English as a second or foreign language,* 3rd ed., ed. M. Celce-Murcia, 429–42. Boston: Heinle and Heinle.

Morley, J. 2001. Aural comprehension instruction: Principles and practices. In *Teaching English as a second or foreign language,* 3rd ed., ed. M. Celce-Murcia, 285–99. Boston: Heinle and Heinle.

Murray, D., ed. 1992. *Diversity as resource: Redefining cultural literacy.* Alexandria, VA: TESOL.

Nation, P. 1990. *Teaching and learning vocabulary.* Boston: Heinle and Heinle.

Nunan, D. 1989. *Designing tasks for the communicative classroom.* Cambridge: Cambridge University Press.

———. 1997. Designing and adapting materials to encourage learner autonomy. In *Autonomy and independence in language learning,* ed. P. Benson and P. Voller, 192–203. New York: Longman.

Omaggio Hadley, A. 2001. *Teaching language in context.* 3rd ed. Boston: Heinle and Heinle.

Oxford, R. 1990. *Language learning strategies: What every teacher should know.* New York: Newbury House.

———. 2001. Language learning styles and strategies. In *Teaching English as a second or foreign language,* 3rd ed., ed. M. Celce-Murcia, 359–66. Boston: Heinle and Heinle.

People's Publishing House. 1984. *English: Senior I.* Beijing, China: People's Publishing House.

Raimes, A. 1983. *Techniques in teaching writing.* Oxford: Oxford University Press.

Richards, J. 1990. *The language teaching matrix.* Cambridge: Cambridge University Press.

Rubin, J., and I. Thompson. 1994. *How to be a more successful language learner.* 2nd ed. Boston: Heinle and Heinle.

Scarcella, R., and R. Oxford. 1992. *The tapestry of language learning: The individual in the communicative classroom.* Boston: Heinle and Heinle.

Scovel, T. 2001. *Learning new languages: A guide to second language acquisition.* Boston: Heinle and Heinle.

Seelye, N. 1993. *Teaching culture: Strategies for intercultural communication.* 3rd ed. Lincolnwood, IL: National Textbook.

Shanghai Foreign Language Education Press. 1997. *College English, intensive reading book.* Shanghai, China: Shanghai Foreign Language Education Press.

Snow, D. 2004. *Encounters with Westerners: Improving skills in English and intercultural communication.* Shanghai, China: Shanghai Foreign Language Education Press.

———. 2006. *More than a native speaker: An introduction to teaching English abroad* (Rev. ed.). Alexandria, VA: TESOL.

Spence, J. 1984. *The memory palace of Matteo Ricci.* New York: Viking.

Stevick, E. 1988. *Teaching and learning languages.* Cambridge: Cambridge University Press.

———. 1996. *Memory, meaning, and method.* Boston: Heinle and Heinle.

Taylor, B. 1987. Incorporating a communicative, student-centered component. In *Methodology in TESOL: A book of readings,* ed. M. Long and J. C. Richards, 45–60. Rowley, MA: Newbury House.

Underhill, N. 1987. *Testing spoken language.* Cambridge: Cambridge University Press.

Ur, P. 1981. *Discussions that work: Task-centred fluency practice.* Cambridge: Cambridge University Press.

———. 1984. *Teaching listening comprehension.* Cambridge: Cambridge University Press.

———. 1988. *Grammar practice activities: A practical guide for teachers.* Cambridge: Cambridge University Press.

———. 1996. *A course in language teaching: Practice and theory.* Cambridge: Cambridge University Press.

Walters, K. 1992. Whose culture, whose literacy? In *Diversity as resource: Redefining cultural literacy,* ed. D. Murray, 3–25. Alexandria, VA: TESOL.

About the Author

Don Snow holds an MA in ESL from Michigan State University and a PhD in East Asian language and culture from Indiana University. He has taught language, culture, and linguistics for over two decades in various parts of China as well as in the United States. Currently, he teaches in the English Department of Nanjing University, in China, and he is the author of a number of books on languages, language teaching, and language learning, including *Encounters with Westerners: Improving Skills in English and Intercultural Communication* (Shanghai Foreign Language Education Press).